studysync®

TEACHER'S EDITION

Epic Heroes

GRADE 12 | UNIT 1

⠿studysync®

studysync.com

Send all inquiries to:
BookheadEd Learning, LLC
610 Daniel Young Drive
Sonoma, CA 95476

2 3 4 5 6 7 QVS 23 22 21 20 19

2016 G12U1

studysync®

GRADE 12 UNITS

Epic Heroes
UNIT 1

Overview • Pacing Guide • Instructional Path
Extended Writing Project • Research • Full-Text Study

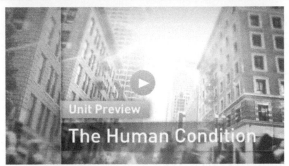

The Human Condition
UNIT 2

Overview • Pacing Guide • Instructional Path
Extended Writing Project • Research • Full-Text Study

An Exchange of Ideas
UNIT 3

Overview • Pacing Guide • Instructional Path
Extended Writing Project • Research • Full-Text Study

Emotional Currents
UNIT 4

Overview • Pacing Guide • Instructional Path
Extended Writing Project • Research • Full-Text Study

Welcome to StudySync

StudySync's comprehensive English Language Arts program for Grades 6-12 is a hybrid print and digital ELA solution. The program leverages cutting edge technology to create an engaging, relevant student and teacher experience. StudySync's multimedia content is available 24/7 from any desktop, tablet, or mobile device. In addition, the program's print resources allow for flexible, blended implementation models that fit the needs of every classroom.

StudySync's Core ELA curriculum was built from the ground up to fully align with the Common Core State Standards for English Language Arts. StudySync provides standards-based instruction that teachers can easily customize, scaffold, and differentiate to ensure all students are ready for college, career, and civic life in the 21st century.

STUDYSYNC TEACHER'S EDITION

The StudySync Teacher's Edition is designed to help you understand, pace, plan, and deliver the StudySync Core ELA curriculum to your students. In this **Teacher's Edition** you will find:

1 A list of StudySync Materials available in both your digital teacher account and this print Teacher's Edition.

2 A guide to StudySync's Core ELA Curriculum and additional content.

3 An overview of StudySync Teacher Tools and ideas and inspirations to help you get started today.

4 Resources for each Core ELA Unit in your grade:

Unit Overviews A big picture look at the key texts and skills.

Pacing Guides A day-to-day plan for integrating all Unit content from the Instructional Path, Extended Writing Project, Research, and Full-text Study with hints for reteaching and shortcuts.

Instructional Path Detailed Lesson Plans for each First Read, Skill, Close Read, and Blast.

Extended Writing Project Detailed Lesson Plans for each Extended Writing Project.

Research A teacher's guide to delivering the Research Project.

Full-text Study A Full-text Reading Guide with key passage explications, vocabulary, discussion and close reading questions.

Copyright © BookheadEd Learning, LLC

  Teacher's Edition

DESIGNED FOR TODAY'S CLASSROOMS

StudySync combines the best of print and digital resources to meet you where you are and take you where you want to be—allowing low-tech and high-tech classrooms to take full advantage of StudySync's **rigor, relevance, and flexibility.**

RIGOR AND RELEVANCE

StudySync engages students with a learning experience that reflects the ways they experience the world by providing multiple opportunities for collaboration, social interaction, and exposure to rich media and thousands of classic and contemporary texts.

In addition, StudySync challenges students and helps them meet rigorous academic expectations with:

- Access to diverse characters and points of view with an expansive digital library, searchable by grade level and Lexile®-level.
- Close reading instruction with various levels of text complexity.
- In-depth studies of canonical and contemporary texts, representing all genres including literary and informational.
- Multiple opportunities for developing foundational language and literacy skills, all while building content knowledge and helping students make meaning.
- Practice and application of analytical writing to sources, with prompts and rubrics tied to the CCSS.

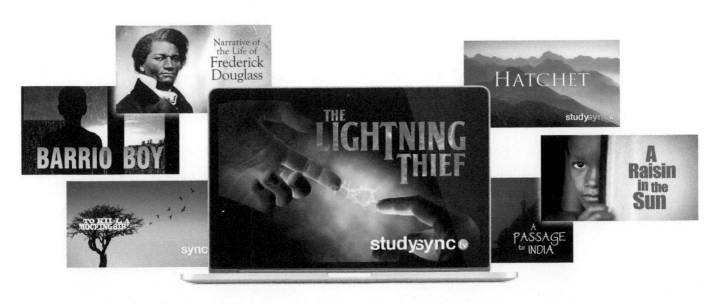

FLEXIBILITY

PRINT AND DIGITAL OPTIONS

Whichever format is right for your classroom—digital, print, or a combination of both, StudySync provides a successful learning experience for all students.

In addition to this Teacher's Edition, a *Student Reading and Writing Companion* is also available to allow students to complete assignments on or off line. This consumable handbook for students gives students printed access to all readings in a Core ELA Unit's instructional path, including First Reads, text-dependent Think questions, Skills lessons, Close Reads and writing prompts. The purpose of the student print support is to provide students with close reading opportunities so they may continue through the course successfully even without daily access to digital. *Please see page xi for a full overview of all StudySync materials available in both print and digital.*

Teacher's Edition

MULTIPLE IMPLEMENTATION MODELS

Whether you are using blended instruction, a flipped classroom, or a traditional format, StudySync provides the flexibility to meet your instructional needs. For example, you can:

- Use print options in conjunction with a projector to engage students in a whole-class discussion regarding a text, an assignment, or a StudySync® TV video.

- Have students work in pairs, small groups, or individually to read, annotate, and answer think questions. Students can work on a single computer or shared devices; alternatively they can annotate directly in their student workbooks.

- Schedule time in computer labs for students to bring their Reading & Writing Companions and submit writing online and complete peer reviews.

Specific examples of using StudySync for whole-group, small-group, and individual instruction are provided on page *xxx* of this guide.

TIPS TO DIFFERENTIATE

Classrooms have a mix of interests, learning styles, and skill levels. Integrating technology makes it easier for teachers to better differentiate and personalize instruction without substantially adding to their workload.

StudySync allows teachers to customize their lessons and to:

- Scaffold assignments based on students' interests and reading abilities
- Make assignments and choose texts based on Lexile®-levels
- Access an extensive library of 6–12 content, texts, and excerpts
- Target specific learning objectives, skills, and Common Core Standards
- Tailor instruction to whole-class, small group, or individual needs
- Offer access support—including audio support, closed captioning, and vocabulary support

CUSTOMIZING YOUR CURRICULUM

With StudySync, you can build the kind of program you've always wanted to teach.
You have the ability to:

- Assign a Library text with the existing prompt or write your own
- Modify assignments for differentiated learning levels
- Access Skills Lessons separately from the Units and assign as stand-alone lessons, or pair with another text of your choosing
- Customize assessments by creating your own rubrics and peer review prompts

Leverage StudySync's online platform and peer review system with **your own content** by:

- Creating your own writing assignments
- Adding your own Library items to your account, including images and videos

COLLABORATION AMONG TEACHERS

StudySync facilitates collaboration by allowing you to share teacher-created content, rubrics, modified assignments, and new library items with other educators in your subscription. Have a rubric used specifically by your district? Have an assignment that every English teacher in your department will be utilizing? These only need to be created once, helping teachers save time and focus on working together.

SUCCESS FOR ALL LEARNERS

StudySync supports students every step of the way. Students experience a seamless online experience for reading and writing, submitting assignments, and writing and receiving reviews with tools that encourage close reading and critical thinking. Students access their assignments and then can view completed work and reviews received in their own online "binder."

Support for All Levels of Learners

- Grade and Lexile®-leveled filters for Digital Library of texts
- Access Path for EL support
- Differentiated learning tools including customizable groups, prompts, and rubrics
- Print materials for work offline

Online Learning Tools

- Collaborative learning platform with online student binders and social learning network
- Online teacher and anonymous peer review platform
- Online test practice similar to PARCC, Smarter Balanced, and other high-stakes test formats

Audio/Visual Resources

- Audio narration of text
- Audio text highlight option
- Online annotation tool
- Closed Captioning of video resources
- Engaging StudySync® TV & SkillsTV videos

PROFESSIONAL DEVELOPMENT

StudySync's Professional Development is on target and ongoing. Our Professional Development Platform in ConnectED and the Teacher Homepage tab within StudySync provide online learning resources that support classroom implementation and instruction and connect explicitly to the standards. All audiovisual, multimedia, and technology resources include suggestions for appropriate implementation and use.

The **Professional Development course** provides an extensive overview of StudySync as well as support for implementing key instructional strategies in the English Language Arts classroom. The **Teacher Homepage** provides access to digital resources and up-to-date articles on "What's New" with StudySync features and content, plus "Ideas and Inspirations," with tips from featured StudySync users and the StudySync Curriculum team.

Review the Professional Development guides and videos within the StudySync Professional Development Implementation course in your ConnectED account and the content on your Teacher Homepage. Then turn to StudySync's Getting Started Guide to begin!

Teacher's Edition

STUDYSYNC MATERIALS

	Digital Teacher Account	Print Teacher's Edition	Digital Student Account	Student Reading & Writing Companion
Scope and Sequences	●			
Grade Level Overviews	●			
Core ELA Unit Overviews	●	●		
Core ELA Unit Pacing Guides	●	●		
Complete Lesson Plans	●	●		
Core Handouts	●			
Access Handouts	●			
Text Selections and Lessons	●		●	●
Reading Skill Lessons	●		●	
Blast Lessons	●		●	
Extended Writing Project Lessons	●		●	●
Writing Skill Lessons	●		●	●
Research Project Guide	●	●		
Full-text Reading Guide	●	●		
End-of-Unit & End-of-Course Digital Assessments	●		●	
Printable Assessments	●			

CORE ELA UNITS

StudySync's Core ELA curriculum consists of 4 **Core ELA Units** per grade. Each unit covers 45 days of instruction for a total of 180 days of instruction at each grade. A complete **Scope and Sequence** outlines standards coverage for each grade, and **Grade Level Overviews** provide teachers a more in-depth look at the reading and writing instruction in each unit. **Pacing Guides** offer detailed 45-day plans for delivering each unit's content.

Each Core ELA Unit is organized around a unique theme and essential question that challenges students to examine texts through an engaging, challenging lens. Each unit contains five key components:

1. Overview

2. Instructional Path

3. Extended Writing Project

4. Research

5. Full-text Study

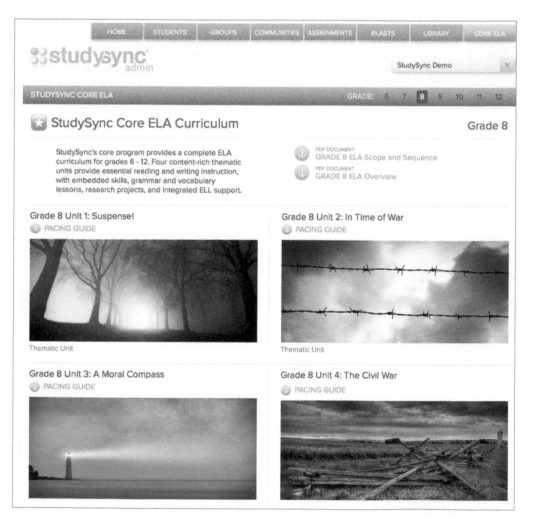

Teacher's Edition

OVERVIEW

The Overview of each Core ELA Unit provides a video preview and an introduction to the unit. The Overview also contains lists of readings, key Skills, standards, and other important general information about the unit.

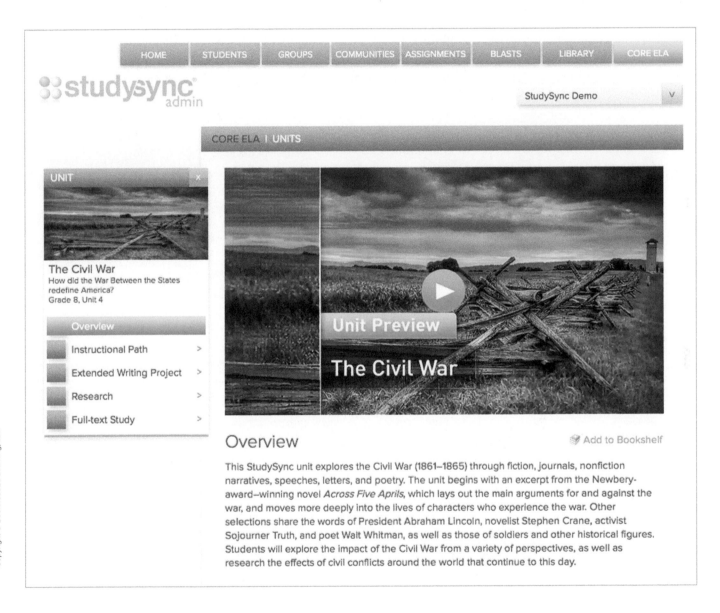

PACING GUIDE

Pacing Guides provide a 45-day plan with day-to-day guidance for implementing each Core ELA Unit. They outline when and how to incorporate instruction from the Instructional Path, Extended Writing Project, Research Project, and Full-text Study. An additional Pacing Guide column helps teachers draw connections between the Full-text Study and the shorter text selections in the Instructional Path.

Pacing Guides also offer ideas for substituting lessons, revisiting difficult concepts, creating multidisciplinary strands of instruction, and designing independent reading programs. These guides show teachers how to bring StudySync's wealth of resources together to create dynamic, engaging learning environments for their students.

DAY	INSTRUCTIONAL PATH	EXTENDED WRITING PROJECT	RESEARCH PROJECT	FULL-TEXT STUDY	CONNECTING FULL-TEXT STUDY TO THEMATIC UNIT INSTRUCTIONAL PATH LESSONS
23	**SKILL** Media			Harriet Tubman: Conductor on the Underground Railroad Chapter 5 "Flight" **COMPARE** to *Old Plantation Days*	
24	**CLOSE READ** *Harriet Tubman: Conductor on the Underground Railroad*	**EXTENDED WRITING PROJECT** Literary Analysis		Harriet Tubman: Conductor on the Underground Railroad Chapter 6 "The Underground Road"	
25	**FIRST READ:** *The People Could Fly: American Black Folktales*			Harriet Tubman: Conductor on the Underground Railroad Chapter 7 "'Shuck this Corn'"	**LINK** to *Harriet Tubman: Conductor on the Underground Railroad* – Ask students to consider the premise of the folktale and discuss why the ability to fly like a bird would be so attractive to African American slaves. In what way does Harriet Tubman help slaves to "fly"?
26	**SKILL** Compare and Contrast	**EXTENDED WRITING PROJECT** Prewrite		Harriet Tubman: Conductor on the Underground Railroad Chapter 8 "Mint A Becomes Harriet"	
27	**CLOSE READ** *The People Could Fly: American Black Folktales*	**SKILL** Thesis Statement		Harriet Tubman: Conductor on the Underground Railroad Chapter 9 "The Patchwork Quilt"	**LINK** to *Harriet Tubman: Conductor on the Underground Railroad* – How does Harriet Tubman's marriage to John Tubman keep her a "caged bird"? How is this ironic given John's status?

INSTRUCTIONAL PATH

The Instructional Path of each Core ELA Unit contains ten to twelve texts and/or text excerpts from a variety of genres and text types. Program authors, Douglas Fisher, Ph.D. and Timothy Shanahan, Ph.D., developed the instructional routines around these texts to support best practices in reading instruction.

Instruction around texts begins with a First Read lesson. First Read Lesson Plans include think alouds to help teachers model key vocabulary and comprehension skills for students before they read. Students read and annotate texts using either their digital accounts or their print Student Reading and Writing Companions, and First Read lessons conclude with a series of text-dependent Think questions that challenge students to provide textual evidence to support their understanding of the text.

At least three First Reads in every unit also include a StudySync® TV episode, one of the hallmarks of the program. Lessons with StudySync® TV contain additional metacognitive questions in which students reexamine short clips from the video to analyze how students in the model discussion construct meaning and express themselves effectively using academic vocabulary and discussion skills.

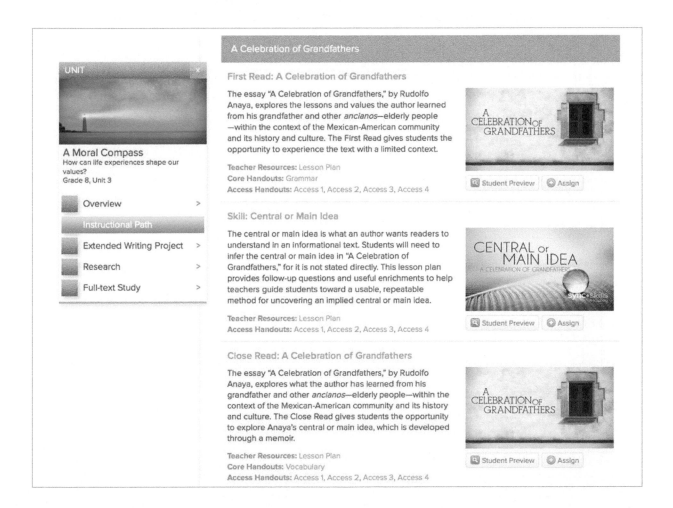

Reading Skill lessons follow First Reads, and apply the Gradual Release of Responsibility Model to deliver explicit instruction that helps students master key skills and reading strategies. Over the course of a unit, students will complete two to three of these lessons each week, offering teachers many opportunities to formatively assess student mastery and growth.

Close Read lessons culminate the instructional reading routine. Close Read lessons begin with an emphasis on vocabulary instruction as students refine or confirm their analyses of vocabulary from the First Read. Close Read lessons then challenge students to apply skills and reading strategies as they reread and annotate the text in preparation for writing their own short-constructed responses.

StudySync Blasts, the fourth lesson type found in the Instructional Path, typify the program's commitment to creating an engaging, twenty-first century context for learning. Each Blast is a short reading and writing lesson with its own research topic and driving question to which students respond in 140 characters or less.

Every assignment in the Instructional Path includes an in-depth Lesson Plan, available to teachers in their digital teacher account and this print Teacher's Edition, with both a Core Path and an Access Path of instruction. The Core Path contains the regular instructional routines that guide students toward mastery. Many lessons also contain Core Handouts—Grammar mini-lessons, Graphic Organizers, Vocabulary quizzes, or Student Writing Models.

The Access Path of each Lesson Plan contains guidance for using the Access Handouts to scaffold and differentiate instruction to insure equity and access for all students. Access Handouts provide a range of important scaffolds for English Learners and Approaching grade-level readers.

Beginner EL	→ Access 1 Handout
Intermediate EL	→ Access 2 Handout
Advanced EL	→ Access 3 Handout
Approaching grade-level	→ Access 4 Handout

EXTENDED WRITING PROJECT

Writing is an integral part of StudySync's Core ELA curriculum. The curriculum features comprehensive instruction in narrative, informative/explanatory, and argumentative writing forms, and in a wide variety of modes, including full-length essays and narratives, short constructed responses, peer reviews, Blasts, and the digital annotations of texts.

Each unit contains an Extended Writing Project (EWP) that focuses on one of the three primary writing forms and is woven into the instructional fabric of the unit. By the end of the year, each student generates a full-length narrative, informative/explanatory essay, literary analysis (in argumentative form), and an argumentative essay.

Numerous writing Skill lessons in each EWP provide instruction on skills essential to every form. EWP lessons contain Lesson Plans, Core Handouts, and Access Handouts that follow the same conventions as lessons in the Instructional Path.

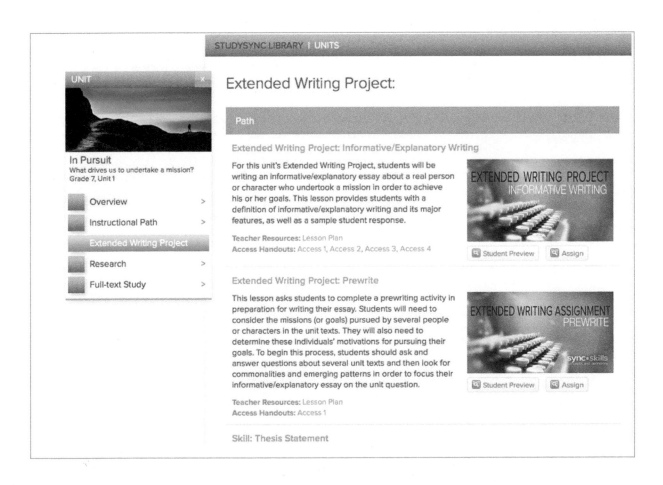

RESEARCH

In addition to the short research students complete in Blast assignments, each Core ELA Unit also contains an in-depth research project in which students explore a new angle of the unit's theme and essential question. This research project is fully integrated into the Pacing Guide, and builds on and complements the unit's key skills. Research projects deepen content knowledge, allow students to read more widely, and offer students the opportunity to present their claims and findings in a variety of formats that address key speaking and listening standards.

CORE ELA | UNITS

UNIT   x

In Time of War
What does our response to conflict say about us?
Grade 8, Unit 2

Overview	>
Instructional Path	>
Extended Writing Project	>
Research	
Full-text Study	>

Research

OBJECTIVES

1. Complete topic-specific group research projects connected to the unit theme and essential question.
2. Participate effectively in a range of conversations and collaborations to express ideas and build upon the ideas of others.
3. Practice and apply research strategies to produce a narrative presentation with multimedia features.
4. Practice, apply, and reinforce the following Grade 8 ELA Common Core Standards for reading literature and informational texts, writing explanatory pieces, conducting research projects, and speaking and listening:

> **Reading: Literature** - RL.8.1, RL.8.2, RL.8.3, RL.8.4, RL.8.6, RL.8.7, RL.8.10
> **Reading Informational Text** - RI.8.1, RI.8.2, RI.8.3, RI.8.4, RI.8.5, RI.8.6, RI.8.7, RI.8.8, RI.8.9, RI.8.10
> **Writing** - W.8.1.A, W.8.1.B, W.8.1.C, W.8.1.D, W.8.1.E, W.8.3.A, W.8.3.B, W.8.3.C, W.8.3.D, W.8.3.E, W.8.4, W.8.5, W.8.6, W.8.7, W.8.8, W.8.9, W.8.10
> **Speaking and Listening** - SL.8.1, SL.8.2, SL.8.4, SL.8.5, SL.8.6
> **Language** - L.8.1, L.8.2, L.8.3, L.8.4, L.8.5, L.8.6

TIME
140 minutes (research and presentations)

MATERIALS
Library, online resources, links to topics
StudySync Speaking & Listening Handbook

OVERVIEW
In order to better understand human responses to conflict, students will research a particular person or group of people affected by World War II. Students will explore various mediums, including diaries, letters, speeches, interviews, informational videos, historic articles, contemporary analyses, reference book entries, and images, in order to gather information about the experience of their chosen person or group.

FULL-TEXT STUDY

Each Core ELA Unit contains an anchor text. An excerpt of this anchor text is included alongside other literature and informational texts in the Instructional Path. This anchor text is the recommended Full-text Study for the unit and the Pacing Guide for each unit provides teachers a recommended schedule for reading this text alongside the excerpts in the Instructional Path. The Pacing Guide also contains helpful hints to help teachers make direct connections between sections of the anchor text and lessons from the Core ELA Unit.

The Full-text Study Reading Guide supports the close reading of the complete anchor text. Reading guide lessons preview key vocabulary words and include close reading questions. Each Full-text Study Reading Guide section identifies a key passage that will help teachers guide students through an exploration of the essential ideas, events, and character development in the anchor text. This passage will also serve as the jumping off point from which students will engage in their own StudySync® TV-style group discussion.

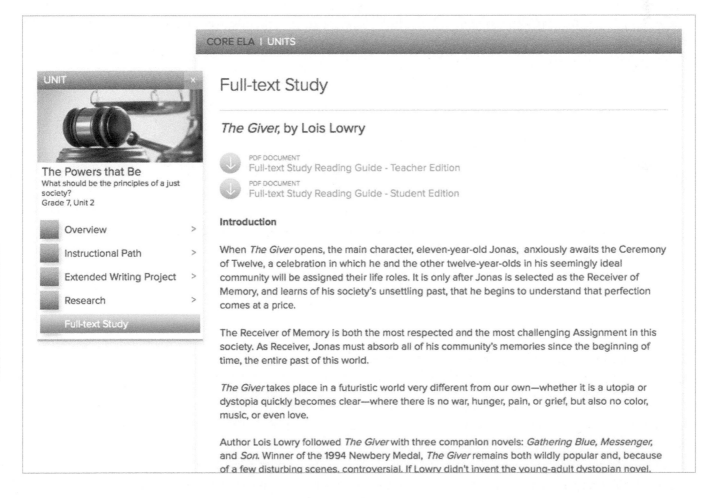

CORE ELA | UNITS

UNIT ×

The Powers that Be
What should be the principles of a just society?
Grade 7, Unit 2

Overview >
Instructional Path >
Extended Writing Project >
Research >
Full-text Study

Full-text Study

The Giver, by Lois Lowry

PDF DOCUMENT
Full-text Study Reading Guide - Teacher Edition

PDF DOCUMENT
Full-text Study Reading Guide - Student Edition

Introduction

When *The Giver* opens, the main character, eleven-year-old Jonas, anxiously awaits the Ceremony of Twelve, a celebration in which he and the other twelve-year-olds in his seemingly ideal community will be assigned their life roles. It is only after Jonas is selected as the Receiver of Memory, and learns of his society's unsettling past, that he begins to understand that perfection comes at a price.

The Receiver of Memory is both the most respected and the most challenging Assignment in this society. As Receiver, Jonas must absorb all of his community's memories since the beginning of time, the entire past of this world.

The Giver takes place in a futuristic world very different from our own—whether it is a utopia or dystopia quickly becomes clear—where there is no war, hunger, pain, or grief, but also no color, music, or even love.

Author Lois Lowry followed *The Giver* with three companion novels: *Gathering Blue, Messenger,* and *Son.* Winner of the 1994 Newbery Medal, *The Giver* remains both wildly popular and, because of a few disturbing scenes, controversial. If Lowry didn't invent the young-adult dystopian novel,

ASSESSMENT

FORMATIVE ASSESSMENT

StudySync supports all forms of assessment. Teachers provide feedback on student writing, using either the ready-made Common Core-aligned rubrics in the program or their own customized rubrics created in StudySync. Lesson plans point teachers toward minute-to-minute formative assessment opportunities. Students self-assess and peer review regularly. First Reads, Skills, Close Reads, and Extended Writing Project process steps offer medium cycle formative assessment opportunities for students and teachers to chart progress toward key learning outcomes.

ANONYMOUS PEER REVIEW

Teachers can use peer review to initiate a cycle of analyzing, writing, and revising that turns students into skilled writers and critical thinkers.

Students learn to:

- Respond frequently and meaningfully to the texts they are reading.
- Engage in multiple forms of writing, including expository, narrative, and persuasive.
- Provide timely, anonymous critiques of other students' writing.
- Thoughtfully analyze and revise their work.
- Write to an authentic audience they know will be reading their work immediately.

StudySync capitalizes on the collective intelligence in a classroom by leveraging the valuable voices of students in the learning process. The anonymous peer review feedback helps students take an active role in supporting each other in the development of their skill sets. Peer review is not anonymous for teachers. They have a window into all student work in order to mediate the process and provide appropriate direction and support.

SUMMATIVE ASSESSMENT

In addition to the formative assessment opportunities embedded throughout StudySync, each Core ELA Unit includes an end-of-unit summative assessment and each grade level includes an end-of-course assessment. These unit and end-of-course tests are located in the Online Assessment tool in the ConnectED account. They can be delivered digitally or in print. They offer robust reporting options, including tracking student proficiency with the Common Core State Standards. This assessment format provides important practice for online standardized tests for students.

Teacher's Edition

ADDITIONAL CONTENT

To go along with the Core ELA curriculum, StudySync continually provides new and additional content that allows teachers to easily customize and differentiate curriculum. The Library, Blasts, Skills, Full-text and other units, and other additional resources provide teachers thousands of extra lessons to go along with the Core ELA curriculum and make StudySync a dynamic, twenty-first century content solution in their classrooms.

LIBRARY

The extensive StudySync digital library consists of more than 1,000 texts and excerpts with supporting digital tools and lesson materials for close reading and critical writing assignments.

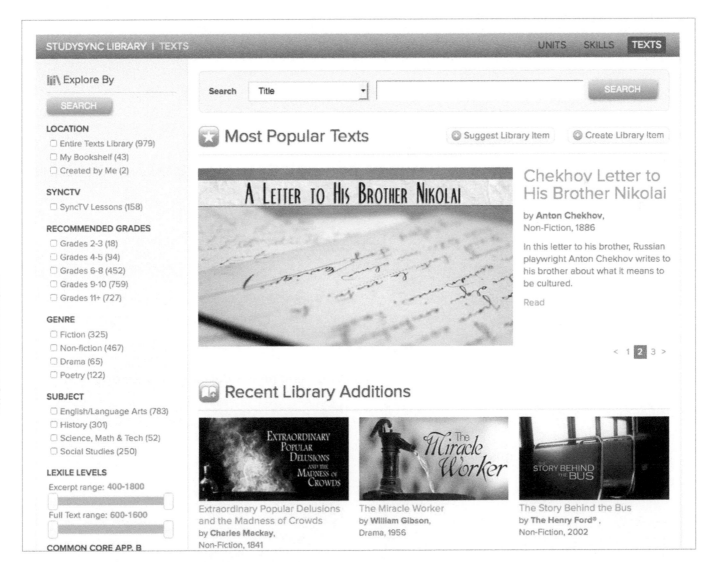

The StudySync Library is an ever-expanding resource that grows to fit the needs of all teachers. Looking for a passage of Twain's non-fiction to teach alongside *The Adventures of Huckleberry Finn*? Want to provide your students background on the political turmoil of 1960s America? Need a place to send students as a jumping off point for their own literary explorations? The StudySync Library is your answer.

To facilitate easy searching, in addition to title, author, keyword, topic, and genre searches, all texts in the Library can also be sorted by:

- Lexile®-level
- Genre
- Common Core Appendix B exemplars
- StudySync® TV Library items
- Publication date

Every Library selection includes:

- Professional audio recordings to support readers of all levels and develop speaking and listening skills
- Online annotation and highlighting
- Common Core-aligned writing prompts

Every Core ELA Library selection includes:

- An Audio Text Highlight tool that breaks texts into grammatical and syntactical chunks as students follow along with the authentic audio
- Auto-graded quizzes to formatively assess student reading comprehension
- Key vocabulary supports
- Text-dependent Think questions

As the StudySync Library continues to grow, these features will expand to selections beyond those included in the Core ELA program to provide teachers even greater flexibility and options for designing their own curriculum.

Texts with StudySync® TV lessons include additional, engaging multimedia lesson supports like:

- Movie trailer-like Previews
- StudySync® TV episodes
- Short-answer Think questions

Teacher's Edition

BLASTS

In addition to the Blasts embedded in the Core ELA Units, StudySync digital teacher accounts house an ever-growing index with hundreds of Blasts that explore contemporary issues and other high-interest topics. StudySync releases new Blasts every school day, staying on top of all the latest news and providing fresh content to help teachers create engaging, relevant classrooms.

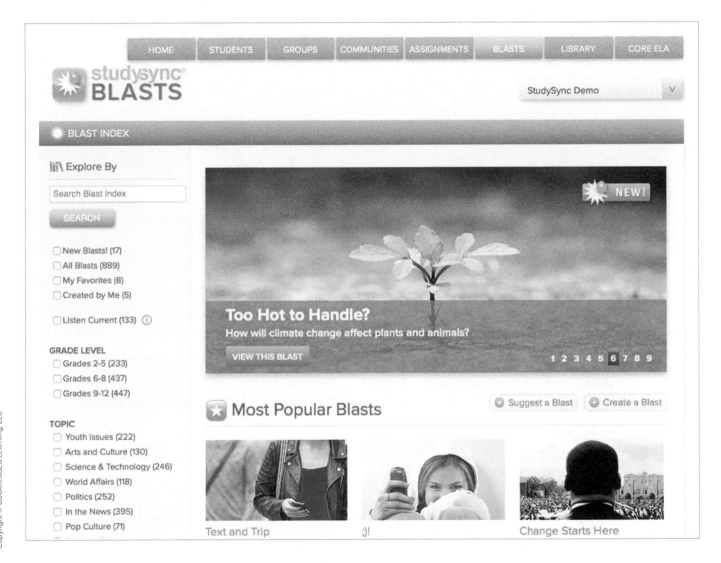

Students respond to the short informational texts and driving questions with 140-character or less Blast responses that allow them to practice clear, concise writing. The peer review platform allows students to read and respond to one another's Blasts, creating a social learning environment that teachers can easily mediate and monitor. Teachers may even elect to join the StudySync National Blast Community which enables students to read and respond to the Blasts of students from all over the United States.

Teachers can easily differentiate weekly Blasts by choosing to target any of the three Lexile® versions to students. Teachers even have the option to use the StudySync platform to create their own Blasts.

Teachers may also choose to select **Listen Current** Blasts. These weekly Blasts feature a background-building radio story to capture students' attention and help build key listening skills.

SKILLS

StudySync Skill lessons instruct students on the key reading, writing, and language skills and strategies necessary for mastery of the Common Core State Standards. The Skills index in every StudySync digital teacher account allows teachers to search for Skills lessons by grade level, topic, or keyword.

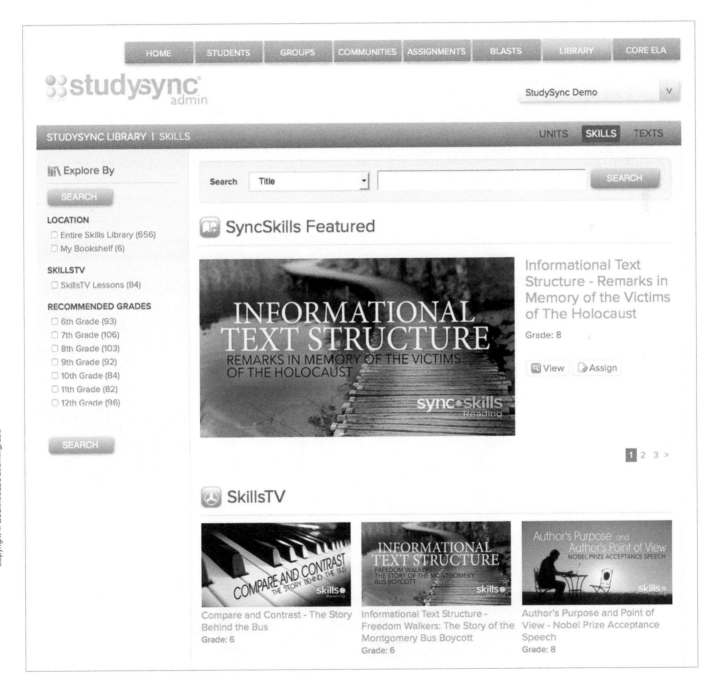

Skill lessons apply the Gradual Release of Responsibility Model. First, students learn the definition of the skill or strategy they'll be applying and watch a Concept Definition video in which students define and break down the key components of a skill or strategy. Next, teachers guide students through a "we do" portion of the lesson, facilitating discussion with follow-up questions from the lesson plan. Many Skills lessons contain SkillsTV videos in which students dramatize the application of a particular skill or strategy.

Lastly, students apply their new knowledge to short questions that ask students to both demonstrate mastery of a standard and provide textual evidence to support their understanding. Teachers receive immediate feedback on these short, formative assessments.

FULL-TEXT UNITS

Each text selected for a Full-text Study in the Core ELA Units also contains a corresponding Full-text Unit. This Full-text Unit provides readings to pair with specific passages of the anchor text and writing lessons that challenge students to compare anchor texts to additional selections.

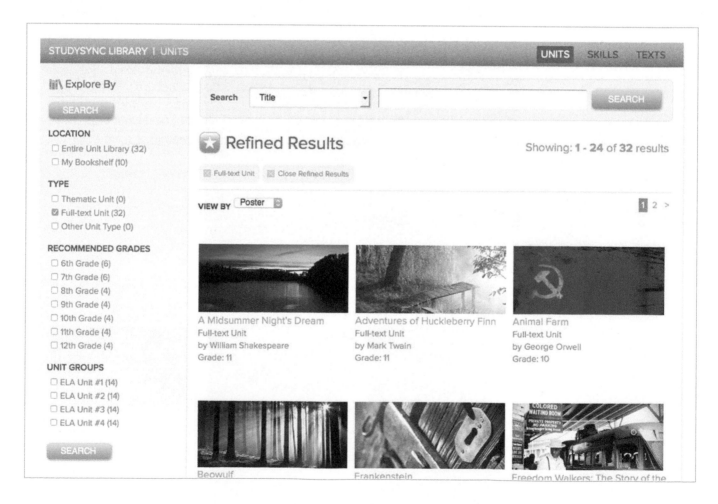

These Full-text Units are not a part of a grade level's 180 days of instruction, however teachers may wish to draw from them to incorporate materials from other disciplines or develop an alternative, novel-based approach to instruction.

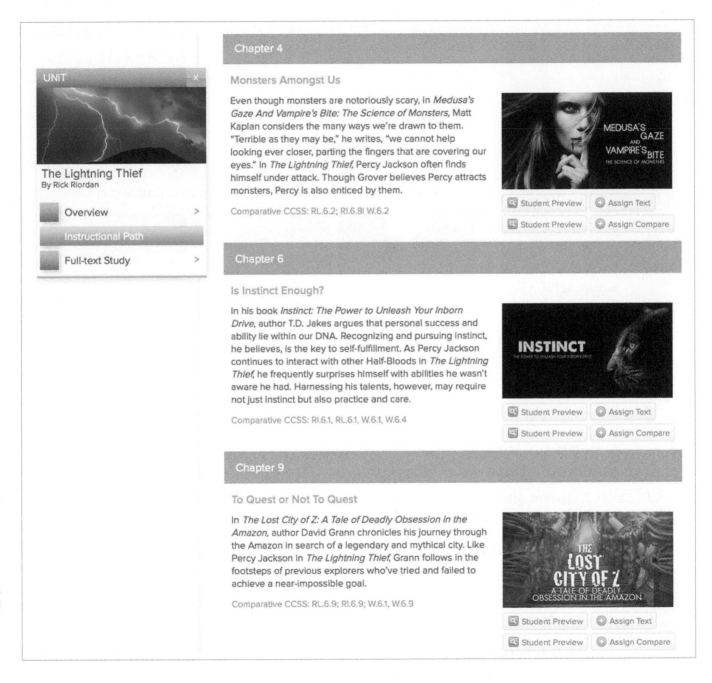

UNIT ✕

The Lightning Thief
By Rick Riordan

Overview >

Instructional Path

Full-text Study >

Chapter 4

Monsters Amongst Us

Even though monsters are notoriously scary, in *Medusa's Gaze And Vampire's Bite: The Science of Monsters*, Matt Kaplan considers the many ways we're drawn to them. "Terrible as they may be," he writes, "we cannot help looking ever closer, parting the fingers that are covering our eyes." In *The Lightning Thief*, Percy Jackson often finds himself under attack. Though Grover believes Percy attracts monsters, Percy is also enticed by them.

Comparative CCSS: RL.6.2; RI.6.8l W.6.2

MEDUSA'S GAZE AND VAMPIRE'S BITE
THE SCIENCE OF MONSTERS

🔍 Student Preview   ⊕ Assign Text
🔍 Student Preview   ⊕ Assign Compare

Chapter 6

Is Instinct Enough?

In his book *Instinct: The Power to Unleash Your Inborn Drive*, author T.D. Jakes argues that personal success and ability lie within our DNA. Recognizing and pursuing instinct, he believes, is the key to self-fulfillment. As Percy Jackson continues to interact with other Half-Bloods in *The Lightning Thief*, he frequently surprises himself with abilities he wasn't aware he had. Harnessing his talents, however, may require not just instinct but also practice and care.

Comparative CCSS: RI.6.1, RL.6.1, W.6.1, W.6.4

INSTINCT
THE POWER TO UNLEASH YOUR INBORN DRIVE

🔍 Student Preview   ⊕ Assign Text
🔍 Student Preview   ⊕ Assign Compare

Chapter 9

To Quest or Not To Quest

In *The Lost City of Z: A Tale of Deadly Obsession in the Amazon*, author David Grann chronicles his journey through the Amazon in search of a legendary and mythical city. Like Percy Jackson in *The Lightning Thief*, Grann follows in the footsteps of previous explorers who've tried and failed to achieve a near-impossible goal.

Comparative CCSS: RL.6.9; RI.6.9; W.6.1, W.6.9

THE LOST CITY OF Z
A TALE OF DEADLY OBSESSION IN THE AMAZON

🔍 Student Preview   ⊕ Assign Text
🔍 Student Preview   ⊕ Assign Compare

OTHER UNITS

In addition to Core ELA and Full-text Units, StudySync offers teachers a wide range of English Learner, Literature, and Composition Units from which to choose. In the ever-growing Units sections of the Library, teachers will find instructional content that allows them to further customize and differentiate curriculum to suit the unique needs of their students.

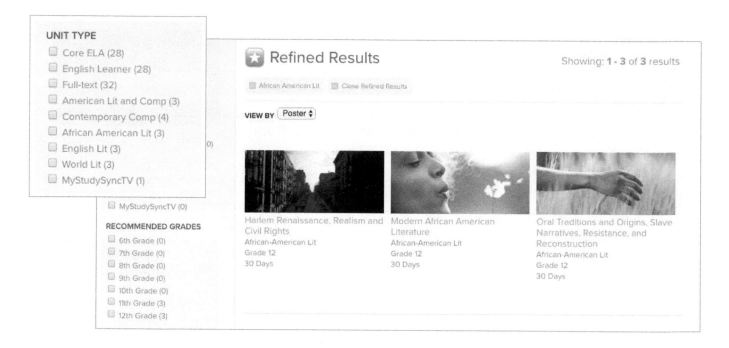

ADDITIONAL RESOURCES

- **Grade Level Assessments** documents contain printable versions of end-of-unit and end-of-course assessments for each grade.

- **Placement and Diagnostic Assessments** aid initial evaluation of student skills to decide on an appropriate instructional level for the student.

- **Foundational Skills** covers phonics, decoding, word recognition, and fluency to help build the skills that lead to students reading independently.

- **Speaking and Listening Handbook** addresses every Common Core ELA standard for speaking and listening and offers usable, repeatable methods and tools for helping students develop and master essential speaking and listening skills.

- **Grammar, Language and Composition Guide** provides additional instruction and practice that can be used for reteaching or preteaching.

- **Vocabulary Workbook** offers students additional opportunities to build and expand their vocabulary.

- **Spelling Workbook** teaches spelling patterns and concepts that apply to various word lists.

- **Standard English Learners Handbook** offers in-depth background information about different instructional routines that can be used with SELs to help them develop their Standard English and understand when it is appropriate to use it.

- **Language Transfers Handbook** provides cross linguistic transfer analysis to help teachers understand the language of students in their classroom.

- **Research-based Alignments** provides a summary of key research findings and recommendations for best practices of instruction in English Language Arts, focused on Reading, Writing, Speaking and Listening, Language, and Media and Technology. Following each section, alignment of the recommendations of the research to specific instruction within StudySync is provided.

- **The Glossary** offers basic summary of essential ELA terminology for each grade level.

Additional Resources

 PDF DOCUMENT
Placement and Diagnostic Assessment

 PDF DOCUMENT
Foundational Skills

 PDF DOCUMENT
Speaking & Listening Handbook

 PDF DOCUMENT
Grammar, Language, and Composition Guide

PDF DOCUMENT
Vocabulary Workbook

 PDF DOCUMENT
Spelling Workbook

 PDF DOCUMENT
Standard English Learners Handbook

 PDF DOCUMENT
Language Transfers Handbook

 PDF DOCUMENT
Research-base Alignments

 PDF DOCUMENT
Student Glossary

PDF DOCUMENT
Teacher Glossary

DESIGN YOUR INSTRUCTION

As outlined above, StudySync provides a rich resource of materials for all ELA students and teachers. Our dynamic, ever-growing curriculum allows for teachers to customize instruction to meet their needs. Whether in a low-tech or high-tech environment, StudySync provides multiple opportunities for whole group, small group and individual instruction. Below are some specific examples of how teachers can integrate StudySync's key features into a variety of classroom contexts.

StudySync Content	Whole group	Small group or pairs	Individuals
Preview and/or Introduction	Project the multimedia Preview and view as a class. Read the Introduction as a class. Follow with a quick discussion about the images and information in the Preview and Introduction.	Have students turn and talk after watching the Preview and reading the Introduction. What images and information stood out? How did their interpretations differ?	Based on the Preview and Introduction, have students jot down predictions, questions, and/or inferences about the text.
First Read	Project a text on the screen. Model specific skills including using context clues to determine difficult vocabulary words, and using reading comprehension strategies to parse difficult passages.	Allow students to read and/or listen to the audio reading of the text in pairs or small groups, stopping to discuss thoughts and new vocabulary words as they annotate.	Students read and annotate the text, utilizing the audio or Audio Text Highlight feature as necessary. Alternatively, students can annotate in their print Companion.
StudySync® TV	Project the episode and view as a class. See the corresponding lesson plan for discussion prompts for specific sections of the episode.	Using prompts from the lesson plan, have students hold their own StudySync® TV discussions. Afterwards, briefly share with the whole class ideas that were discussed.	Ask students to jot down ideas from the StudySync® TV episode and their own discussions that might assist with their writing.
Think Questions	Think Questions may be discussed and answered as a class, using the text as support.	Think Questions may be discussed and answered in pairs or small groups before reviewing correct answers with the entire class.	Think Questions may be answered individually, using the text as support.

Teacher's Edition

Skills	Project the Concept Definition video and as a group read the definition of the Skill. If there is a SkillsTV video in the Model sections of the lesson, watch and discuss as a class.	Have students work in pairs or small groups to read through the text in the Model section, stopping throughout to discuss questions and ideas. Work your way around to each group to provide feedback.	Have students individually complete the mini-assessments that conclude Skills lessons. When all students are finished, project the questions and discuss correct answers.
Close Read	Review vocabulary analysis from the First Read. Ask students to compare their context analysis of vocabulary against the actual definitions. Review key skills students will apply in the Close Read.	Close Reads can occur individually or in small groups. If assigning Close Reads for small group work, have students discuss and explain their annotations to one another as they go.	Have students reread and annotate the text in order to complete the Skills Focus questions and prepare themselves for the writing prompt that follows.
Write	Discuss the prompt as a class, making sure students understand the directions and expectations. Display the rubric for the assignment as well.	Allow students time to brainstorm ideas or discuss the prompts with their peers, referring to the text, StudySync® TV episode, and/or previous discussions.	Students individually submit responses to the assigned prompt.
Peer Review	Remind students of your expectations for the peer review process, and inform them of specific directions for this assignment.	In pairs or small groups, have students discuss what they will look for in their peers' responses, based on the directions and rubric. What will an exemplar response include? Report ideas to the whole class.	Students complete peer reviews individually, using the guidelines established.
Blasts	As a class, hold a brief discussion about the prompt. After students read the Background information, discuss the Quikpoll and Number Crunch as a class. Ask students to make predictions on how their peers will answer the QuikPoll, and how the results might differ if answered by another class, age group, etc.	Students should read the Background section in small groups and record notes in their handbooks. Have students discuss questions and ideas that came up as they read. Ask students to split up the Research Links, so that each student researches 2-3 sites and then reports the information back to their peers.	Students may read the Background information individually, as well as the information from several Research Links. After discussing the information with their peers, they should craft their 140-character response to the prompt and complete 5 or more peer reviews.

studysync®

Teacher's Edition

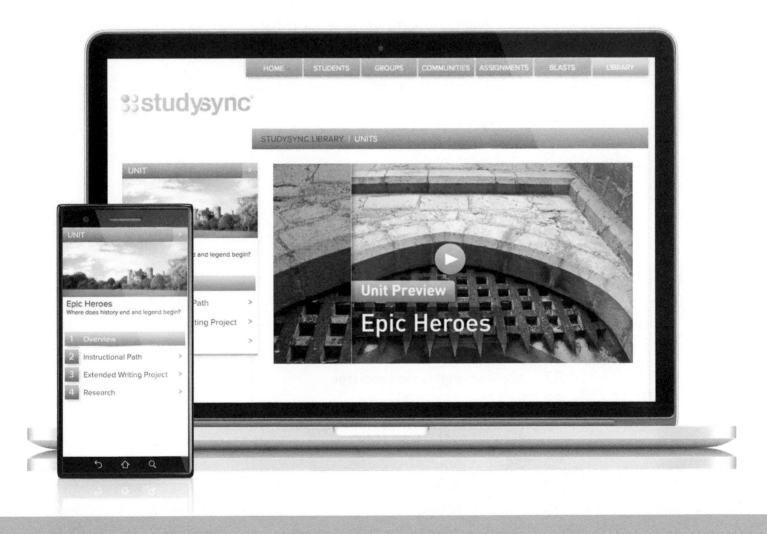

Where does history end and legend begin?

Epic Heroes

Epic Heroes

OVERVIEW MATERIALS

INSTRUCTIONAL PATH

EXTENDED WRITING PROJECT

RESEARCH

FULL-TEXT STUDY

Overview Materials

Epic Heroes

OVERVIEW

UNIT TITLE

Epic Heroes

UNIT DRIVING QUESTION

Where does history end and legend begin?

UNIT OVERVIEW

Where does history end and legend begin? How do legendary tales affect the way we understand historical people and events? In this Grade 12 unit, which explores epics and legends from the Anglo-Saxon period of England through today, students will examine these questions.

The unit begins with an excerpt from the oldest written Old English poem, *Beowulf*, which presents the archetype of the epic hero. *Beowulf* is followed by an excerpt from *Grendel*, a modern novel that shows the monster's side of Beowulf's story. Other selections include texts by the such varied writers as Venerable Bede, Geoffrey Chaucer, T. H. White, Sir Thomas Malory, and J. R. R. Tolkien, as well as contemporary analyses of the legends.

Blasts on contemporary issues show students how legends and history continue to influence national identities today, and an Extended Writing Project guides students through the process of developing narratives with heroes of their own.

TEXTS

Beowulf	Epic
Grendel	Novel
The Ecclesiastical History of the English People	Christian History
The Canterbury Tales	Poetry
The Once and Future King	Novel
Le Morte d'Arthur	Romance
Conversation with Geoffrey Ashe re: King Arthur	Interview
Unsolved Mysteries of History	History
The Lord of the Rings	Epic Fantasy Novel
DC Comics: Sixty Years of the World's Favorite Comic Book Heroes	Non-Fiction

FULL-TEXT STUDY

Beowulf

EXEMPLAR TEXTS

The Canterbury Tales

ASSIGNMENT TYPES

Blasts: 8
First Reads: 10
Reading Skills: 15
Close Reads: 10
Extended Writing Project Prompts: 5
Writing Skills: 8

STANDARDS FOCUS

RL.11-12.1, RL.11-12.2, RL.11-12.3, RL.11-12.4, RL.11-12.6, RL.11-12.7
RI.11-12.1, RI.11-12.3
W.11-12.3.A, W.11-12.3.B, W.11-12.3.C, W.11-12.3.D, W.11-12.3.E, W.11-12.4, W.11-12.5, W.11-12.6, W.11-12.7, W.11-12.8, W.11-12.9, W.11-12.10
SL.11-12.1, SL.11-12.2, SL.11-12.3, SL.11-12.4, SL.11-12.5, SL.11-12.6
L.11-12.1.A, L.11-12.1.B, L.11-12.2.A, L.11-12.2.B, L.11-12.3.A, L.11-12.4.A, L.11-12.4.B, L.11-12.4.C, L.11-12.4.D, L.11-12.5.A, L.11-12.6

KEY READING SKILLS

Story Elements
Word Meaning
Figurative Language
Media
Theme
Informational Text Elements
Textual Evidence
Setting
Point of View
Story Elements

 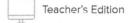

KEY GRAMMAR SKILLS

First Read: Le Morte d'Arthur - Archaic Usage
First Read: Unsolved Mysteries of History - Appositives, Semicolons, and Parallelism
First Read: The Lord of the Rings - Contested Usage
Extended Writing Project: Draft - Misplaced and Dangling Modifiers
Extended Writing Project: Revise - Hyphenation Conventions
Extended Writing Project: Publish - Basic Spelling Rules Review

KEY WRITING SKILLS

Audience and Purpose
Organize Narrative Writing
Narrative Sequencing
Introductions
Narrative Techniques
Conclusions
Descriptive Details
Precise Language

EXTENDED WRITING PROJECT

Stories give students the opportunity to experience lives outside of their own. In this unit featuring epic heroes, students not only imagine what the life of a hero or heroine might be like through reading, but also by writing their own hero narratives in the Extended Writing Project. Students have specific writing skills modeled for their instruction and the chance to review them as they write their narratives. The writing process itself is broken down into steps and explained in short lessons that require student practice as they build to the published work.

ADDITIONAL TEXTS

These additional texts from the StudySync library are related to the unit theme and/or time period. Teachers can choose to include some of these texts in addition to the texts in this unit to create a customized course of instruction for their students.
The Myths and Legends of Ancient Greece and Rome: Theseus, by E. M. Berens
The Odyssey, by Homer
Ulysses, by Alfred Lord Tennyson
Epic of Gilgamesh
Ozymandias, by Percy Bysshe Shelley
Idylls of the King, by Alfred Lord Tennyson
Self-Made Men, by Frederick Douglass
Into Thin Air, by Jon Krakauer

studysync®

GRADE 12 UNIT 1: EPIC HEROES

PURPOSE

This pacing guide will help you utilize the wealth of resources offered in each StudySync Core ELA unit. The pacing guide weaves lessons from every segment of this Core ELA unit: the Instructional Path, Extended Writing Project, Research Project, and Full-text Study.

The pacing guide presents a suggested plan to cover all content in this unit. You may cover all of these lessons in class, or you may decide to divide the assignments between in-class work and homework. Of course, no one understands your students' needs like you do, and one of the key benefits of StudySync is the ease with which you can adapt, alter, eliminate, or reorganize lessons to best meet the needs of your students. The Shortcuts and Additional Activities section at the end of this pacing guide contains recommendations to help in that regard.

ORGANIZATION

The pacing guide divides the unit into 45 days. Instructional days often have more than a single task. For example, all of the activities on row 1 are suggested to be covered on the first instructional day. Pacing is based on an assumption of 50-minute instructional days, but since schedules vary from school to school, you may need to modify the suggested pacing to fit your unique needs.

The column labeled "Full-text Study Connections" often identifies other texts in the StudySync Library that complement the chapter in the Full-text Study students are reading on a particular day. Though these comparative texts are not considered part of the 45 days of Core ELA instruction for this unit, they are listed in the pacing guide in case you would like to include additional texts as part of this unit.

There are no activities or lessons planned for the final two days of the unit, which are dedicated to assessment.

Note: This pacing guide supports the reading of either of two different translations of *Beowulf*, the anchor text of the unit. The unit includes an excerpt from the 1910 Francis B. Gummere translation. That translation may be downloaded in its entirety from the StudySync Library. However, some teachers may prefer to use the 1999 translation of *Beowulf* by Irish poet Seamus Heaney since that translation is perhaps more accessible than Gummere's for modern readers. The two translations have slightly different line breaks and counts, so depending on what edition they are reading, teachers may need to add or remove a line or two to the day's recommended reading to reach natural stopping points.

CORE ELA UNIT

DAY	INSTRUCTIONAL PATH	EXTENDED WRITING PROJECT	RESEARCH PROJECT	FULL-TEXT STUDY	FULL-TEXT STUDY CONNECTIONS
1	**UNIT PREVIEW** **BLAST** Epic Heroes		**SPEAKING & LISTENING HANDBOOK** Handbook "Research Using Various Media" Section **RESEARCH PROJECT PART I** Break students into small groups and assign each group a topic to research (see list of topics under Research tab) and begin research (in class and/or online).		
2	British Literature & History: The Anglo-Saxon Period and Middle Ages (449-1485)		**RESEARCH PROJECT PART I CONT.** Students should continue to research		
3	Literary History: The Epic and the Epic Hero Literary History: The Development of English		**RESEARCH PROJECT PART I CONT.** Students should continue to research.		
4	**FIRST READ** *Beowulf*		**RESEARCH PROJECT PART II** Groups should work collaboratively (in class and/or online) on a presentation to present their information to the class.		

DAY	INSTRUCTIONAL PATH	EXTENDED WRITING PROJECT	RESEARCH PROJECT	FULL-TEXT STUDY	FULL-TEXT STUDY CONNECTIONS
5	**SKILL** Story Elements		**RESEARCH PROJECT PART II CONT.** Students should continue working to create their presentations.		
6	**SKILL** Word Meaning		**RESEARCH PROJECT PART II CONT.** Students should continue working to create their presentations.		
7	**SKILL** Figurative Language		**SPEAKING & LISTENING HANDBOOK** "Presentation Skills" **RESEARCH PROJECT PART III** Allow a couple of groups to present to the class.		
8	**CLOSE READ** *Beowulf*		**RESEARCH PROJECT PART III CONT.** Allow a couple of groups to present to the class.		
9	**BLAST** Conflict Resolution		**RESEARCH PROJECT PART III CONT.** Allow a couple of groups to present to the class.		

DAY	INSTRUCTIONAL PATH	EXTENDED WRITING PROJECT	RESEARCH PROJECT	FULL-TEXT STUDY	FULL-TEXT STUDY CONNECTIONS
10	**FIRST READ** *Grendel*			*Beowulf* Lines 1-188 **COMPARE** to *The Anglo-Saxon Chronicle*	**LINK** to *Beowulf* – In lines 115-188 of *Beowulf*, the writer describes Grendel's first attack. Ask students to analyze how this description differs from the one presented in chapter 4 of *Grendel*.
11	**SKILL** Theme			*Beowulf* Lines 189-370 **COMPARE** Heaney and Gummere translations of *Beowulf*, lines 144-300	**LINK** to *Beowulf* – Ask students to analyze the writer's descriptions of Beowulf, Beowulf's dialogue, and Wulfgar's description of Beowulf to make inferences about the central themes of lines 189–370.
12	**SKILL** Media			*Beowulf* Lines 371–558 **COMPARE** to *On Heroes, Hero-Worship, and the Heroic in History*	**LINK** to *Beowulf* – Show students the clip of Beowulf's swimming contest with Breca from the 2007 film adaptation of *Beowulf*. In small groups, ask them to analyze the differences in the portrayal in the film and in the text. What has been changed in the film? What is the impact of that change? How is reading the text different from watching the film version?
13	**CLOSE READ** *Grendel*				
14	**FIRST READ** *The Ecclesiastical History of the English People*				

DAY	INSTRUCTIONAL PATH	EXTENDED WRITING PROJECT	RESEARCH PROJECT	FULL-TEXT STUDY	FULL-TEXT STUDY CONNECTIONS
15	**SKILL** Informational Text Elements			*Beowulf* Lines 559–789	**LINK** to *Beowulf* – After students have read about informational text elements, ask them to select a character from *Beowulf* (Beowulf, Breca, Unferth, Hrothgar, or Wealtheow) and write a diary entry about the day's events from that character's point of view using text elements appropriate for a diary entry.
16	**SKILL** Word Meaning			*Beowulf* Lines 790–989 **COMPARE** to *Grendel*	**LINK** to *Beowulf* – Ask students to consider the words the writer of *Beowulf* chooses to describe Beowulf and Grendel, like hero, monster, warrior, fiend. Ask students to examine lines 790–989 and create a list of opposing words used to describe the two characters. What is the impact of these contrasts? How do the connotations of these words contribute to that impact?
17	**CLOSE READ** *The Ecclesiastical History of the English People*				
18	**BLAST** American Idols Literary History: The Development of English			*Beowulf* Lines 990–1350 **COMPARE** to *The Fury of the Northmen*	**LINK** to *Beowulf* – After completing the Blast: American Idols, ask students compare American Celebrity Culture with the story of Finn in lines 1070–1190. What similarities and/or differences exist in the way we talk about famous people?
19	**FIRST READ** *The Canterbury Tales*				

DAY	INSTRUCTIONAL PATH	EXTENDED WRITING PROJECT	RESEARCH PROJECT	FULL-TEXT STUDY	FULL-TEXT STUDY CONNECTIONS
20	SKILL Textual Evidence	EXTENDED WRITING PROJECT Narrative Writing			
21	SKILL Figurative Language			*Beowulf* Lines 1351–1472	LINK to *Beowulf* – This portion of *Beowulf* contains many examples of figurative language. Ask students to find examples of figurative language and discuss how they impact the story.
22	CLOSE READ *The Canterbury Tales*	SKILL Audience and Purpose			
23	BLAST Mirror, Mirror on the Wall			*Beowulf* Lines 1473–1744 COMPARE to *The Myths and Legends of Ancient Greece and Rome: Theseus*	LINK to *Beowulf* – After students have completed the Blast: Mirror, Mirror on the Wall, ask them to consider the descriptions of women in *Beowulf* like Wealtheow and Grendel's mother and draw conclusions about Anglo-Saxon ideals of beauty. How is Grendel's mother described? How is Wealtheow described? Based on the differences, what can we infer?
24	FIRST READ *The Once and Future King*	SKILL Organize Narrative Writing		*Beowulf* Lines 1745–1962	LINK to *Beowulf* – How do the various kings in *Beowulf* compare to Arthur's ideas about Might and Right? Which of the two do the characters in *Beowulf* seem to value more? How do we know?
25	SKILL Point of View	EXTENDED WRITING PROJECT Prewrite			

DAY	INSTRUCTIONAL PATH	EXTENDED WRITING PROJECT	RESEARCH PROJECT	FULL-TEXT STUDY	FULL-TEXT STUDY CONNECTIONS
26	**CLOSE READ** *The Once and Future King*			*Beowulf* Lines 1963–2220	**LINK** to *Beowulf* – Both the excerpt from *The Once and Future King* and *Beowulf* contain allusions. What are the allusions in each text, and why are they included? How do they impact the reader?
27	**FIRST READ** *Le Morte d'Arthur*	**SKILL** Narrative Sequencing			
28	**SKILL** Story Elements			*Beowulf* Lines 2221–2462 **COMPARE** to "Dragons" in *Mythical and Fabulous Beasts*	**LINK** to *Beowulf* – Ask students to consider the role of archetype in *Beowulf*. First, have students review this PDF about The Archetypal Hero: in films, and then ask them to analyze how Beowulf does and does not fit the characteristics of an archetypal hero.
29	**CLOSE READ** *Le Morte d'Arthur*	**EXTENDED WRITING PROJECT** Plan			
30	**FIRST READ** "Conversation with Geoffrey Ashe"			*Beowulf* Lines 2463–2693 **COMPARE** to *The Volsung Saga* (Old Norse Poem)	**LINK** to *Beowulf* – Like the legend of King Arthur, *Beowulf* was written long after the events of the story, and as a result, scholars must discover where exactly the line between fact and fiction lies. Ask students to read this essay about the historical accuracy of *Beowulf* and this article about an archaeological excavation at the location that might have been Heorot in Denmark. Discuss the similarities that exist in how the two stories made use of contemporary features and how archaeology is playing a role in the study of each.

DAY	INSTRUCTIONAL PATH	EXTENDED WRITING PROJECT	RESEARCH PROJECT	FULL-TEXT STUDY	FULL-TEXT STUDY CONNECTIONS
31	**SKILL** Informational Text Elements			*Beowulf* Lines 2694–2945	**LINK** to *Beowulf* – Pair or group students and using the interview with Geoffrey Ashe as a model, have them write a brief interview between Wiglaf and a reporter about the events of lines 2703-2954, using the informational text elements appropriate to an interview.
32	**CLOSE READ** "Conversation with Geoffrey Ashe"	**SKILL** Introductions			
33	**FIRST READ** *Unsolved Mysteries of History*			*Beowulf* Lines 2695–3192 **COMPARE** to "*Beowulf*: The Monsters and the Critics"	**LINK** to *Beowulf* – While reading the final sections of *Beowulf*, make a list of explicit and implicit information (in notes, on the board, or on a shared Google document). Then have students articulate three inferences they made while reading based on textual evidence.
34	**SKILL** Textual Evidence	**SKILL** Narrative Techniques			
35	**CLOSE READ** *Unsolved Mysteries of History*				
36	**FIRST READ** *The Lord of the Rings*	**SKILL** Conclusions			
37	**SKILL** Setting	**EXTENDED WRITING PROJECT** Draft			

DAY	INSTRUCTIONAL PATH	EXTENDED WRITING PROJECT	RESEARCH PROJECT	FULL-TEXT STUDY	FULL-TEXT STUDY CONNECTIONS
38	**CLOSE READ** *The Lord of the Rings*				
39	**FIRST READ** *DC Comics: Sixty Years of the World's Favorite Comic Book Characters*	**SKILL** Descriptive Details			
40	**SKILL** Informational Text Elements	**EXTENDED WRITING PROJECT** Revise			
41	**CLOSE READ** *DC Comics: Sixty Years of the World's Favorite Comic Book Characters*	**SKILL** Precise Language			
42	**BLAST** The Best Movies Ever!				
43	**BLAST** Our Stories, Ourselves	**EXTENDED WRITING PROJECT** Edit, Proofread, Publish			

DAY	INSTRUCTIONAL PATH	EXTENDED WRITING PROJECT	RESEARCH PROJECT	FULL-TEXT STUDY	FULL-TEXT STUDY CONNECTIONS
44	**ASSESSMENT** StudySync Grade 12 Unit 1 Assessment				
45	**ASSESSMENT** StudySync Grade 12 Unit 1 Assessment				

SHORTCUTS AND ADDITIONAL ACTIVITIES

Shortcuts

In a perfect world, teachers would have time to cover everything, but most teachers feel as if they are in a race against the bell. There is never enough time to cover everything. If you find yourself short on time, there are places where you can trim a StudySync Unit to ensure you are covering the most important parts. Here are some suggestions for how you can shorten this unit to fit in the time you have.

1. **Replace the Research Project with a Crowdsourcing Activity:** Instead of a 9-day research project, you can make the research component of this unit an informal exploration using a crowdsourcing activity. To facilitate a crowdsourcing assignment, break students into groups, give each group a question or research topic, and allow them time to research using computers or devices to generate information about their topic. Then allow them to share what they have learned with the class by writing their information on the board or posting it to a shared Padlet Wall (or other online collaborative space).

2. **Eliminate Repeated Story Elements, Word Meaning, Informational Text Elements, Textual Evidence, and/or Figurative Language Skill Lessons:** Each unit focuses on developing specific skills. Some of these skills are repeated throughout the unit to ensure students have plenty of practice with those skills. As the old adage says, "practice makes perfect!" That said, if you are in a rush and looking to cut some of the content in a unit, you can eliminate one or two of these skill lessons and feel confident your students will still be exposed to the information they need about story elements or informational text elements.

3. **Content Cuts:** There are several different types of texts presented in a unit—excerpts from novels, nonfiction readings, short stories, and poems. If you are running out of time, you may want to eliminate a StudySync selection that focuses on a similar type of text as a previous lesson. For example, the unit contains two nonfiction excerpt about history and literature: "Conversation with Geoffrey Ashe" and Unsolved Mysteries.

Suggestions for Integrated and Multidisciplinary Lessons

The Thematic Unit for Beowulf contains several texts that link to both history and science curriculum. The Ecclesiastical History of the English People provides one explanation for how Christianity came to England, while Unsolved Mysteries of History examines the myth of King Arthur in order to determine whether or not he was real. "Conversation with Geoffrey Ashe" explains how archaeologists use scientific methods and approaches to learn more about the Anglo-Saxon world of Beowulf. An excerpt from DC Comics: Sixty Years of the World's Favorite Comic Book Heroes describes how DC Comics became one of the largest comic book publishers during the "Golden Age of Comics" in the middle of the 20th century.

In addition to the texts available in the Thematic Unit, the Full-text Unit includes The Anglo Saxon Chronicle, which presents a historical record of England's early history, as well as an excerpt from The Fury of the Northmen that tells the story of an early Viking raid that is considered the beginning of the Viking Age. The Myths and Legends of Ancient Greece and Rome: Theseus and The Volsung Saga are similar hero epics from different cultures. Finally, J.R.R. Tolkien's lecture "Beowulf: The Monsters and the Critics," which argues for the recognition of Beowulf as a piece of literature, is itself a historical document, as Tolkien was the first scholar to make such an argument. It may also help to answer students' questions of "Why do we have to read this?" All of these texts provide different answers to the unit's central question of "How do legends transform history?" by supplying examples of times when history has been transformed by legends.

In addition to these texts from the Thematic Unit for Beowulf, the'e are StudySync Blasts that link the texts and central ideas in this unit to history and science topics. The "Dissing Utopia" Blast allows students to investigate the connection between history and cultural legend in the 20th century, and research links include a psychological explanation for why teenagers love dystopias. The "Olympic Cheaters: Coping with Doping" Blast asks the question, "Is cheating in sports the new normal?" This Blast encourages students to examine our contemporary attitudes to athletic "heroes," while research links provide information about gene doping, and as a result, the Blast connects the ethics and science of performance-enhancing substances.

Books excerpted in the Full-text Unit for *Beowulf* offer a diverse array of reading opportunities, particularly for students who are interested in exploring the world of the Anglo-Saxons and Scandinavians. *The Anglo-Saxon Chronicle* and *The Ecclesiastical History of the English People* both provide early written historical accounts of those groups of people, while *The Fury of the Northmen* presents a contemporary explanation of the Viking Age. *Unsolved Mysteries of History: An Eye-Opening Investigation into the Most Baffling Events of All Time* examines multiple time periods and locations for students who want to look at history from a broader perspective. *DC Comics: Sixty Years of the World's Favorite Comic Book Heroes* offers a critical analysis of contemporary heros for students who are intrigued by the interaction of culture and heroism, but prefer a more recent period of focus. Students who prefer fiction can choose from *Grendel*, *The Once and Future King*, or Tolkien's *Lord of the Rings*. The first two present new interpretations of familiar heroes and worlds, while Tolkien invites his readers to enter into a completely new realm.

Readings outside the Full-text Unit provide a myriad of options and directions for students to further their study. *The Hobbit*, by J. R. R. Tolkien, is the prequel to the *Lord of the Rings* trilogy for students who desire to remain in Middle-earth a little longer. *The Mists of Avalon*, by Marion Zimmer Bradley, reimagines the tale of King Arthur from the perspective of the female characters while including information about the Celtic culture that existed in Britain before the acceptance of Christianity. Students who enjoyed comparing Seamus Heaney's 1999 translation of *Beowulf* with the 1910 Gummere translation might further enjoy sampling other versions of *Beowulf*. A very short list might include translations by Michael Alexander (1973 and Frederick R. Rebsamen (1991); Rebsamen's prose version, *Beowulf Is My Name*, and Gareth Hinds's dynamic graphic novel of *Beowulf*. Students who prefer nonfiction can check out Geoffrey of Monmouth's *History of the Kings of Britain*, which dates from the early 12th century and traces the genealogy of the kings of Britain back to the Trojans almost two thousand years prior. Additionally, it is one of the first texts to present the legend of King Arthur that most of us know today. While it has not been accepted as historically accurate since the 1600s, it was hugely influential in the centuries after its creation. Finally, students who prefer contemporary nonfiction might enjoy *Chaucer's Knight*, written by Terry Jones of Monty Python Fame. Jones, a medieval scholar, argues that the Knight in *The Canterbury Tales* is not the upstanding model of virtue and chivalry many perceive, but rather a mercenary presented ironically by Chaucer.

Although 12th grade students are expected to "Cite the textual evidence that most strongly supports an analysis of what the text says explicitly as well as inferences drawn from the text" (RL.11-12.1), selecting strong textual evidence and making inferences is challenging, especially when the text might be difficult to understand. These skills require students employ higher-order thinking in addition to comprehending the words on the screen. Students must read closely to pick up on clues in the text, analyze the explicit and implicit information provided, and draw conclusions based on that information. Students will benefit from explicit instruction on how to make inferences as they read. In addition to providing concrete strategies for making inferences, teachers can return to a Textual Evidence Skill Lesson from a previous unit (e.g., 11th Grade Unit 3 Textual Evidence Skill Lesson for "Theme for English B") to allow students the opportunity to practice applying strategies for making inferences with a text they've already read.

While identifying strong textual evidence to support inferences and analysis is probably nothing new for students at this level, students may struggle to find useful evidence with some of the older texts in the unit. Teachers need to ask text dependent questions that require students back up their statements with strong textual evidence. This skill requires practice. To provide students with more practice, teachers can replace a repeated skill lesson with a First Read assignment for another text or they can spend more time reviewing and discussing the Think Questions from another text in the unit. For example, *The Once and Future King* and *Le Morte d'Arthur* both follow the first Textual Evidence Skill Lesson and can be used to review this skill in depth. Remember that Think Questions 1-3 ask text dependent questions that require students to back up their statements with evidence from the text, so the First Read assignment of any text can be used to support the development of this skill if teachers focus on reviewing the responses to Think Questions 1-3.

Understanding how the use of language in a text affects the audience is an important yet challenging skill for students to master. By 12th grade students should be acquiring the skills to "analyze a case in which grasping a point of view requires distinguishing what is directly stated in a text from what is really meant" (RL.11-12.6), which will make it easier for them to engage more deeply with the texts they encounter by understanding why an author is or is not persuasive. Because understanding how authors use rhetorical strategies can be a difficult skill for students to master, students may benefit from repeated practice identifying and analyzing rhetorical arguments. Teachers can use additional texts in this unit that contain rhetorical arguments to provide students with additional practice. For example, teachers can ask students to reread *Grendel* and identify the rhetorical strategies Gardner uses to transform *Grendel* from rampaging monster to sympathetic outcast. In addition, teachers can also provide extra practice with a wide range of texts by searching the StudySync Library Skill Index for additional skill lessons that target this concept. Ideally, teachers will want to select skill lessons below the current grade level for additional practice to ensure the texts are accessible.

Read Aloud Selection

The epic poem *Beowulf* celebrates the victories of its hero, Beowulf as he fights the monster Grendel, Grendel's mother, and later in his life, a dragon. Written anonymously sometime before the 11th century, this text provides readers with an impression Anglo-Saxon life, and both the Gummere and Heaney translations recreate the alliteration and rhythm that typify Anglo-Saxon poetry. Listening to the text will help students hear how the heavy use of alliteration dominates and distinguishes each line of the poem while caesura provides a pause in the middle of each line. By reading the poem aloud, students have an opportunity to practice using expression, intonation, phrasing, punctuation, and pacing to understand Beowulf's heroic feats.

Instructional Path

Epic Heroes

BLAST:
Epic Heroes

OVERVIEW

To develop a focus for this unit, students will learn about the role of legends in the human experience and will make their first attempt at articulating a response to the unit's essential question. Students will explore research links that connect them to the importance of myths and stories in human life.

OBJECTIVES

1. Explore background information about legends and culture.
2. Research using the hyperlinks to learn about legends and the appeal of storytelling throughout history.

ELA Common Core Standards:
Reading: Informational - RI.11-12.1
Writing - W.11-12.1.A, W.11-12.1.B, W.11-12.5, W.11-12.6
Speaking & Listening - SL.11-12.1.A, SL.11-12.1.C, SL.11-12.1.D

RESOURCES

Blast Response - Student Model
Access 1 handout (Beginner)
Access 2 handout (Intermediate)
Access 4 handout (Approaching)

Please note that excerpts and passages in the StudySync® library, workbooks, and PDFs are intended as touchstones to generate interest in an author's work. The excerpts and passages do not substitute for the reading of entire texts, and StudySync® strongly recommends that teachers and students seek out and purchase the whole literary or informational work in order to experience it as the author intended. Links to online resellers are available in our digital library. In addition, complete works may be ordered through an authorized reseller by filling out and returning to StudySync® the order form enclosed in this workbook.

Teacher's Edition   27

TITLE/DRIVING QUESTION

Core Path	Access Path
Discuss. As a class read aloud the title and driving question for this Blast. These correspond to the title/driving question for the unit as a whole. Ask students what they know about myths and legends. Do they have a sense of how these stories influence their understanding of history? Remind students that they'll be returning to this question for their formal entries after they've written a draft and read and discussed the Background.	**English Learners All Levels** **Discuss a Visual.** Have students view an image of a representation of the legendary figure Paul Revere, such as this one at: http://tinyurl.com/ppvjup3. Discuss how the mural represents elements of real life as well as details that make the figure a legend, prompting students with questions such as: • What is happening in this image? • How are Paul Revere and his horse depicted in this image? • What elements of real life do you see? How might those elements have been exaggerated? • What impact do legends like that of Paul Revere have on history?
Draft. In their notebooks or on scrap paper, have students draft their initial responses to the driving question. This will provide them with a baseline response that they will update and revise as they gain more information about the topic in the Background and Research Links sections of the assignment. You may wish to review with students the Blast Response - Student Model for guidance on how to construct an effective Blast. The Blast review criteria are as follows: 1. – Response does not address the driving question or is unclear; language is vague. 2. – Response insufficiently addresses the driving question or is mostly unclear; language is mostly vague. 3. – Response somewhat addresses the driving question or is somewhat unclear; language is somewhat vague. 4. – Response adequately addresses the driving question and is clear; language is mostly precise. 5. – Response fully addresses the driving question and is clear; language is precise.	**Beginner & Intermediate** **Draft with Sentence Frame.** When drafting their initial response to the driving question, have students refer to this Blast sentence frame on their Access 1 and 2 handouts: • Legend transforms history by shaping the way we think about _____. Point out these two key features of the sentence frame: 1. The clause at the beginning of the sentence "Legend transforms history" borrows language from driving question and shows how "legend" and "history" interact. 2. Ask students to make special note of the preposition *by*, which signals to readers that the writer is going to explain how something happens.

BACKGROUND

Core Path	Access Path
Read. Have students read the Blast background to provide context for the driving question.	**Beginner & Intermediate** **Read with Support.** Have students read the Blast background to provide context for the driving question. When they encounter unfamiliar words or phrases, have students refer to the glossary on their Access 1 and 2 handouts. If there are unfamiliar words that are not included in their glossary, encourage students to check a dictionary or online reference tool, like http://dictionary.reference.com. **Approaching** **Read and Summarize.** Have students read the Blast background to provide context for the driving question. As they read, ask students to complete the fill-in-the-blank summary of the background provided on their Access 4 handout. When they encounter unfamiliar words or phrases, have students refer to the glossary on their Access 4 handout.
Discuss. Pair students and have them discuss the following questions: 1. Why does the writer share the example of "back in my day" stories? (as an example of exaggerated stories presented as true history) 2. What are legends? (traditional stories passed down through history) 3. How have legends influenced our view of ancient history? (Our understanding of the Middle Ages is based on tales of dragons and damsels in distress. Our understanding of Ancient Greece is colored by stories of Greek gods.) 4. How have legends influenced our view of our own US history? (We latch onto details that aren't entirely historical, like George Washington never telling lies.)	**Beginner** **Discuss.** Pair Beginner with Advanced (or Beyond) students and have them use the dialogue starter on their Access 1 handout to discuss the topic. Advise them to return to the dialogue and switch roles if they get stuck. **Intermediate** **Discuss.** Pair Intermediate with Advanced (or Beyond) students and have them use the dialogue starter on their Access 2 handout to discuss the topic. Advise them to return to the dialogue and switch roles if they get stuck. If their conversation is progressing smoothly, encourage them to continue the discussion beyond the dialogue starter sheet. They can expand their conversations to discuss legends they are familiar with and the impact those legends have had on history.

Core Path	Access Path
Brainstorm. Remind students about the driving question for this Blast and the driving question for this unit: Where does history end and legend begin? In their notebooks, ask students to make two columns, one for legends with which they are familiar, and one for their places of origin. After they have finished that, have them think about the legends in their charts and make a list of what the legends reveal about the values and beliefs of the culture from which they are derived. Have them review the Blast Background for an example of how this works. Here is what a chart might look:	

Legend	Origin
The myth of Persephone, Hades, and Demeter	Ancient Greece
The myth of Anansi the trickster	West Africa

RESEARCH LINKS

Core Path	Access Path
Examine and Explore. Use these questions to guide students' exploration of the research links: 1. Ask students to watch the clip "Joseph Campbell on the Importance of Mythology" from the "Excerpts from *The Power of Myth*" link. What is it about myths that might pique our interest, according to Joseph Campbell? (They are stories about the search for inner meaning. They are stories to help us figure out who we are.) Campbell says we all want to experience life. How can myths help us do that? (Myths are clues to the potential of human life.)	

Core Path	Access Path
2. Have students watch the clip "George Lucas on Mentors and Faith" from the "Excerpts from *The Power of Myth*" link. As a class discuss the impact traditional myths had on Lucas's *Star Wars* films. Do you think these traditional mythic elements made the movies more successful? Why or why not? (Answers will vary.) 3. Have students read "The Use of Myth in U.S. History." As a class, discuss the myths described in the article. Were students surprised by any of the examples given? Did they think any of the myths were true? Does it help or hurt their opinion of the Founding Fathers to know some of the famous stories are not completely true? (Answers will vary.)	

	Extend
	Research, Discuss, and Present.
	
	1. Assign each group one link to explore in depth.
	2. Ask them to discuss the information:
	    a. What are the key points?
	    b. What inferences did you make as you read?
	    c. What did you learn about this "big idea" from reading this research?
	    d. How did this help you to better understand the topic?
	    e. What questions does your group have after exploring this link?
	3. Allow students time to informally present what they learned.

	Extend **Tech Infusion** **Collaborate.** As students explore the links, have all groups use Lino (http://en.linoit.com/) to gather common elements about myths and stories. Keep this list handy throughout the unit and add to it as the class reads more legends.

QUIKPOLL

Core Path	Access Path
Participate. Answer the poll question. Have students use information from the background and research links to explain their answers.	

NUMBER CRUNCH

Core Path	Access Path
Predict, Discuss, and Click. Before students click on the number, break them into pairs and have them make predictions about what they think the number is related to. After they've clicked the number, ask students if they are surprised by the revealed information.	

CREATE YOUR BLAST

Core Path	Access Path
Blast. Ask students to write their Blast response in 140 characters or less.	**Beginner** **Blast with Support.** Have students refer back to the sentence frame on their Access 1 handout that they used to create their original Blast draft. Ask them to use this frame to write and enter their final Blast. **Intermediate** **Blast with Support.** Have students attempt to draft their Blast without the sentence frame on their Access 2 handout. If students struggle to compose their Blast draft without the sentence frame, remind them to reference it for support.

Copyright © BookheadEd Learning, LLC

Core Path	Access Path
	Beyond **Write a Claim.** Ask students to use their answer to the poll question to write a strong claim that could be used as the foundation for a piece of argumentative writing. Once students have written their claims, ask them to read the claims to a small group of their peers. This activity will provide them practice writing claims, as well as expose them to claims written by their peers.
Review. After students have completed their own Blasts, ask them to review the Blasts of their peers and provide feedback. To help students respond effectively, read and discuss the review criteria with them before they review one another's Blasts.	
	Extend **Discuss.** As a class or in groups, identify a few strong Blasts and discuss what made those responses so powerful. As a group, analyze and discuss what characteristics make a Blast interesting or effective.
	Extend **Revise.** Resend a second version of this Blast assignment to your students and have them submit revised versions of their original Blasts. Do the same responses make the Top Ten? How have the answers improved from the first submissions?

Please note that excerpts and passages in the StudySync® library, workbooks, and PDFs are intended as touchstones to generate interest in an author's work. The excerpts and passages do not substitute for the reading of entire texts, and StudySync® strongly recommends that teachers and students seek out and purchase the whole literary or informational work in order to experience it as the author intended. Links to online resellers are available in our digital library. In addition, complete works may be ordered through an authorized reseller by filling out and returning to StudySync® the order form enclosed in this workbook.

Teacher's Edition **33**

FIRST READ:
Beowulf

OVERVIEW

The epic poem *Beowulf* focuses on a series of battles involving the hero Beowulf, who comes from Geatland—a Scandinavian region in Southern Sweden—to help Denmark's King Hrothgar, whose banquet hall has been attacked by the monster Grendel. Beowulf slays Grendel, but Grendel's mother returns for revenge—slaying Hrothgar's trusted adviser, Aeschere. This excerpt picks up there, as Hrothgar addresses his people in section XX, and Beowulf responds to Hrothgar and the challenge of Grendel's mother in section XXI. The First Read gives students the opportunity to experience the text with limited context.

OBJECTIVES

1. Perform an initial reading of a text and demonstrate comprehension by responding to short analysis and inference questions with textual evidence.
2. Practice defining vocabulary words using context.
3. Participate effectively in a range of conversations and collaborations to express ideas and build upon the ideas of others.
4. Practice acquiring and using academic vocabulary correctly.

ELA Common Core Standards:
Reading: Literature - RL.11-12.1, RL.11-12.4, RL.11-12.10
Speaking & Listening - SL.11-12.1.A, SL.11-12.1.B, SL.11-12.1.C, SL.11-12.1.D, SL.11-12.2, SL.11-12.3, SL.11-12.6
Language - L.11-12.4.A, L.11-12.C, L.11-12.4.D, L.11-12.6

RESOURCES

Access 1 handout (Beginner)

Access 2 handout (Intermediate)

Access 3 handout (Advanced)

Access 4 handout (Approaching)

ACCESS COMPLEX TEXT

This excerpt from *Beowulf* picks up in the middle of the action of the epic poem. Important events, including the deaths of the king's adviser Aeschere and the monster Grendel, have already occurred. To help students understand the characters and plot of the excerpt as well as the style and form of the language used to tell the tale, use the following ideas to provide scaffolded instruction for a first reading of the more complex features of this text:

- **Genre** - *Beowulf* is an Old English epic poem. Any poem can pose a challenge to readers because of its form and the way ideas are stretched across lines and verses. Old English poems are especially difficult because they make use of alliterative verse, which made the oral poetry sound more pleasing to the ear. However, alliteration may make the poem harder to understand for struggling readers since words were chosen due to their matching initial sounds, not because they helped the poet express himself clearly. For example, in line 1331, the poet writes "when warriors clashed and we warded our heads." The meaning of the line would have been clearer if "defended" or "protected" were used to describe the action, but "warded" is chosen because it has the same initial sound as "when," "warriors," and "we."

- **Connection of Ideas** - This excerpt from *Beowulf* deals with events that have occurred previously in the poem. Struggling readers may have a hard time connecting the characters' feelings and actions with events that do not take place within the excerpt. Students may also have a difficult time connecting character names with the various epithets used to describe them. For instance, line 1387 says, "BEOWULF spake, bairn of Ecgtheow." In this line, both "Beowulf" and "bairn of Ecgtheow" refer to the same person.

- **Specific Vocabulary** - Old English terms, such as *thane* and *liegemen*, and archaic word and word endings, such as *spake*, *wot*, and *killedst*, may present a challenge to some readers.

- **Prior Knowledge** - The warrior culture of the Anglo-Saxon world is especially important to understanding the setting, plot, and characterization in *Beowulf.* Honor, loyalty, and justice were key ideas during this time.

Please note that excerpts and passages in the StudySync® library, workbooks, and PDFs are intended as touchstones to generate interest in an author's work. The excerpts and passages do not substitute for the reading of entire texts, and StudySync® strongly recommends that teachers and students seek out and purchase the whole literary or informational work in order to experience it as the author intended. Links to online resellers are available in our digital library. In addition, complete works may be ordered through an authorized reseller by filling out and returning to StudySync® the order form enclosed in this workbook.

Teacher's Edition   **35**

1. INTRODUCTION

Core Path	Access Path
Watch. As a class, watch the video preview of *Beowulf*.	**English Learners All Levels** **Fill in the Blanks.** Ask students to use their Access 1, 2, and 3 handouts to fill in the blanks of the transcript for the preview's voiceover as they watch the preview along with their classmates. Correct answers are located at the end of the lesson plan online.
Read. Individually or as a class, read the Introduction for *Beowulf*. The introduction provides context for the excerpts taken from sections XX and XXI.	**English Learners All Levels & Approaching** **Read and Listen.** Ask students to read and listen to the introduction for *Beowulf*. Have them refer to the "Introduction Glossary" on their Access 1, 2, 3, and 4 handouts for definitions of key vocabulary terms. If there are unfamiliar words that are not included in their glossary, encourage students to check a dictionary or online reference tool, like http://dictionary.reference.com.
	Extend **Discuss the Introduction.** After students read the introduction, have them use the information provided to facilitate a prereading discussion to get them thinking about the events and themes in *Beowulf*. 1. Have you ever wanted to get even for a wrong done to you? 2. How common is it for an act of violence to be returned in kind? 3. What legacy would you like to leave the world? What values and characteristics would you like people to remember you for when you are gone?

Core Path	Access Path
Build Background. In pairs or small groups, ask students to use devices to research different aspects of the Anglo-Saxon period and the epic poem *Beowulf.* Assign each group a topic to investigate: • Geography, national boundaries, and invasions in present-day Britain and Scandinavia during the Anglo-Saxon period. • Germanic traditions and folklore, including Norse myths, that precede *Beowulf* and the rise of Christianity. • The epic tradition, including *Gilgamesh*, and the *Iliad* and the *Odyssey, The Song of El-Cid*, and the *The Song of Roland* (and the roots of these works in oral storytelling). If you are in a low-tech classroom, you can provide photocopies of background materials on the Anglo-Saxon period and the epic tradition for students to read and discuss.	**Beginner & Intermediate** **Research.** Pair Beginner and Intermediate students and work with them to complete the "Research" activity on their Access 1 and 2 handouts. Have them use the questions on their Access 1 and 2 handouts as a jumping-off point. Coach students as they discuss what they've learned in their research and take notes in the chart on their Access 1 and 2 handouts. If there's time, coach students to come up with their own research questions. **Advanced & Approaching** **Research.** Pair students and have them work together to complete the "Research" activity. They should work as a team to come up with research questions, discuss what they've learned, and take notes in the chart on their Access 3 and Access 4 handouts.
	Extend **Analyze and Discuss a Quotation.** "For it is now to us itself ancient; and yet its maker was telling of things already old and weighted with regret, and he expended his art in making keen that touch upon the heart which sorrows have that are both poignant and remote. If the funeral of Beowulf moved once like the echo of an ancient dirge, far-off and hopeless, it is to us as a memory brought over the hills, an echo of an echo." Lead students in a discussion of this quote. (J. R. R. Tolkien, from "*Beowulf*: The Monsters and the Critics") 1. What do you think this quotation means? 2. How does it change your perception of *Beowulf*, to consider that at the time it was written down it already was an old tale? 3. Why would you describe *universal themes* evident in ancient and medieval literature as things that are, as Tolkien writes, "both poignant and remote"?

2. READ

Core Path	Access Path

Core Path

Preteach Special Vocabulary. Because *Beowulf* is from the Anglo-Saxon period, it contains a number of archaic words that might interfere with student comprehension. Before students read the text, explain the meaning of the following words. Or if time permits, give students the list of archaic words and have them work together to find the definitions.

Word: liegemen [line 1340]
Word Information:
liege•men \ 'lēj-men\ *noun*
Vassals - loyal followers of a lord (nobleman) who provided military service in exchange for land (archaic: Middle English)
The liegemen quickly gathered weapons when they heard of their lord's request.

Word: moorland [line 1352]
Word Information:
moor•land \ 'mur-,land\ *noun*
An area of moor, which can be dry and full of heather (low shrubs) but is usually soft, wet, and marshy ground
The hikers believed the lake was near when their boots sank into the moorland.

Word: trod [line 1356]
Word Information:
trod \'träd\ verb
Walked or proceeded
She trod through the forest.

Word: mere [line 1366]
Word Information:
mere \'mir\ noun
A body of water, usually a lake or pond (British dialect)
At the bottom of a hill, the warriors found a still mere.

Access Path

Beginner & Intermediate
Use the Text Glossaries. Before students read, direct them to the Preread Glossary on their Access 1 and 2 handouts. This section contains the Preteach Special Vocabulary words and their definitions. Explain to students that these are archaic words that are no longer common in contemporary English. Then, have students read the text. As students encounter additional unfamiliar words, direct them to the Text Glossary on their Access 1 and 2 handouts. Encourage them to add to the glossary as needed.

Advanced & Approaching
Use the Text Glossaries. Before students read, direct them to the Preread Glossary on their Access 1 and 2 handouts. This section contains the Preteach Special Vocabulary words. Have Advanced and Approaching students work along with the rest of the class to learn the definitions of these words, using a dictionary and context clues to paraphrase the definitions on their handouts. Then, have students read the text. As students encounter additional unfamiliar words, direct them to the Text Glossary on their Access 3 and 4 handouts. Encourage them to add to the glossary as needed.

Core Path	Access Path
Word: bairn [line 1387] **Word Information:** bairn \'bern\ noun Child (archaic: Middle English) *She told a story as the bairn fell asleep in her lap.* **Word: atheling** [line 1412] **Word Information:** ath•e•ling \'a-thə-liŋ\ noun Anglo-Saxon prince or lord (archaic: Middle English) *The atheling was next in line to the throne.*	
	Extend **Identify and Define.** After reading the text, compile a list of additional vocabulary words. Ask students to reference their annotations and share any vocabulary words that were unfamiliar. 1. As a class, compile a list of unknown words on the board. 2. In small groups, ask students to make predictions about what they think these words mean based on how they are used in the sentence. (Note: Students will need to read the words in context and make predictions.) 3. Each group should work together using dictionaries or devices to define the words and write the definitions in their notebooks.
Model Reading Comprehension Strategy. Before students begin reading, model the reading comprehension strategy of asking and answering questions by using this Think Aloud that talks students through the first few lines of the excerpt. First explain to your students what asking and answering questions is:	**Note:** This exercise, which extends instruction around reading comprehension strategies, should be completed when the class shifts from whole group instruction to individual work during the "Read and Annotate" exercise.

Please note that excerpts and passages in the StudySync® library, workbooks, and PDFs are intended as touchstones to generate interest in an author's work. The excerpts and passages do not substitute for the reading of entire texts, and StudySync® strongly recommends that teachers and students seek out and purchase the whole literary or informational work in order to experience it as the author intended. Links to online resellers are available in our digital library. In addition, complete works may be ordered through an authorized reseller by filling out and returning to StudySync® the order form enclosed in this workbook.

Teacher's Edition   **39**

Core Path	Access Path
Proficient readers ask themselves questions before, during, and after they read to facilitate understanding. Good readers approach a text with questions and ask new questions as they read. Explain to students how asking and answering questions will help them better comprehend the poem and help drive their discussions. • The excerpt begins in the middle of the action, so right away I have to figure out who these people are and what they're doing. I ask myself, Who is Hrothgar, and why is he so upset? • In the first line, I see that Hrothgar is called "helmet-of-Scyldings." This helps me infer that he is some sort of warrior or military leader. I keep reading and see references to "my sage adviser and stay in council." I know kings have counselors, so that helps me know that Hrothgar is the king. • Next, I try to figure out why Hrothgar is so upset. He says, "Pain is renewed / to Danish folk. Dead is Aeschere." I ask, Who is Aeschere, and why is his death so upsetting to the king? • Based on lines I've already read, I know that Aeschere is the king's adviser, but I have to keep reading to understand why his death is so painful "to Danish folk." • I read "hero famed / should be every earl as Aeschere was! / But here in Heorot a hand hath slain him / of wandering death-sprite." These lines help me infer that Aeshere was a national hero in addition to being a cherished adviser to the king. They also tell me that Aeshere was murdered. It leads me to ask myself if Hrothgar will seek revenge for Aeshere's death. I keep reading to find out.	**Beginner, Intermediate & Approaching** **Apply Reading Comprehension Strategy.** 1. To practice asking and answering questions, have students listen to the audio version of *Beowulf*. Pause the audio after the first 10 lines. Direct students to the sample questions and answers on their Access 1, 2, and 4 handouts. Encourage students to add to the list of questions or the list of details that appear in the chart. 2. Resume the audio, pausing periodically to allow students to ask new questions as well as take notes on their Access handouts, as clues to their previous questions arise. Offer guidance to help them notice answers, such as: *In lines 1352–1357, Grendel is described as a "march-stalker" and "huger than human bulk." What might that suggest about how he compares to the Danes?* 3. Once all their questions have been answered, pair students with more proficient readers and ask them to discuss the strategies they used. What led you to ask certain questions? What details answered your questions? Encourage groups to share their findings with the class.

Core Path	Access Path
Read and Annotate. Have students read and annotate the excerpt. Ask students to use the annotation tool as they read to: 1. use context clues to analyze and determine the meaning of the bolded vocabulary terms 2. ask questions about passages of the text that may be unclear or unresolved 3. identify key details, events, characters, and connections between them 4. note unfamiliar vocabulary 5. capture their reaction to the events in the text	**Beginner** **Coach the Reading.** While other students read, annotate, and discuss the text independently, work with Beginner students, listening to the audio of the text and pausing periodically or when any student has a question. Coach students in articulating their questions for the group and in highlighting and annotating the text. Have students use the Annotation Guide on the Access 1 handout to support them as they highlight and annotate the text. For further support, ask questions about the text such as: • Is there anything about the story that you don't understand? • What events have happened before the excerpt begins? • Why do you think Beowulf is the one who seeks out Grendel's mother? • What do you think Beowulf will do next? **Intermediate** **Listen to the Audio.** Have these students listen to the audio of the text and use the Text Glossary on the Access 2 handout to help them with words or phrases that may be unfamiliar. If students need help with annotating the text, have them use the Annotation Guide on the Access 2 handout. After working with the Beginner students, you may wish to check this group's progress and provide support as needed. **Advanced** **Pair with Proficient Peers.** Have Advanced students work with English proficient peers to read, annotate, and discuss the text. Have students use the Annotation Guide in the Access 3 handout to support them as they highlight and annotate the text. Encourage them to listen to the audio of the text if needed.

Please note that excerpts and passages in the StudySync® library, workbooks, and PDFs are intended as touchstones to generate interest in an author's work. The excerpts and passages do not substitute for the reading of entire texts, and StudySync® strongly recommends that teachers and students seek out and purchase the whole literary or informational work in order to experience it as the author intended. Links to online resellers are available in our digital library. In addition, complete works may be ordered through an authorized reseller by filling out and returning to StudySync® the order form enclosed in this workbook.

Teacher's Edition   41

Core Path	Access Path
	Approaching **Use the Annotation Guide.** Have students use the Annotation Guide on the Access 4 handout to support them as they highlight and annotate the text.
Discuss. In small groups or pairs, have students discuss the questions and inferences they made while reading. To help facilitate discussions, refer to Collaborative Discussions in the Speaking & Listening Handbook. 1. Why is Hrothgar particularly upset at the death of Aeschere? (Aeschere was Hrothgar's trusted adviser, "shoulder-comrade in stress of fight.") 2. What does Hrothgar offer Beowulf as a reward for hunting down Grendel's mother? (treasure, gold) 3. Besides expressing his values (righting wrongs and seeking glory, even in the face of danger) and saying that he will take on the challenge of Grendel's mother, what else can you infer about the purpose of Beowulf's speech in section XXI? (Beowulf wants to cheer up Hrothgar, saying "Sorrow not, sage! ... Rise, O realm-warder!) 4. How can "doom" be a good thing? Explain what Beowulf means in lines 1390-1393. (Beowulf is saying that we all will die, and if a warrior dies while fighting courageously for glory, then his doom is most worthy.) 5. How do they find Grendel's mother? (They follow a trail of footprints.) How does asking and answering questions help you determine this information?	**English Learners All Levels & Approaching** Use the extra time while on- and beyond-grade-level students are discussing their first reads of the text to work individually and in small groups with Approaching readers and English Learners as outlined above. Should those students complete their first reads quickly, integrate them into the on- and beyond-grade-level discussion groups. Otherwise, English Learners and Approaching readers will be given an opportunity to participate in text discussions with their peers later in the lesson. **Tech Infusion** **Beyond** **Paraphrase.** Pair students and have them use a word-processing app like Google Docs to rewrite part of the poem as prose. Have them choose a section that explains important details about the plot or characterization (for example, Section XXI, lines 1387–1400) and work together to paraphrase the text in their own words. When students complete their prose paragraphs, have them trade with another group to discuss the choices they made as they worked.
	Tech Infusion **Record.** Use a voice recording app (Voice Memo on the iPhone or Smart Voice Recorder for Androids) or Voice Thread (https://voicethread.com) to capture each group's discussion ideas.

3. SYNCTV

Core Path	Access Path
Watch. As a class, watch the SyncTV video on *Beowulf*. Remind students to listen for the way the students use academic vocabulary during their discussion. Pause the video at these key moments to discuss the information with your students. Have students review and reflect on the ideas expressed:	**Beginner & Intermediate** **Analyze the Discussion.** Have students use the "Analyze the Discussion" guide on the Access 1 and 2 handouts to identify key points in the discussion and the evidence the students use to determine those points. Sample answers are at the end of the lesson plan online.

Core Path:

1. 3:10 – Rebecca says the plot is "a chain of revenge." How does the group use textual evidence to support this point of view? Evaluate how the group uses evidence and reasoning to draw conclusions about early Scandinavian culture based on this "chain of revenge."

2. 4:43 – Jessica says, "Then clearly nobody wants to be this other dude Unferth who 'lost he his glory' because he was too scared to go down into that lake." (Explain to students that Unferth is identified in the excerpt as "bairn of Ecglaf.") Why does Jessica have this point of view? Is this a fair assessment of the character? Why or why not?

3. 6:23 – Why does the group talk about "creepy loners" and "lonely weirdos"? Is their discussion of such solitary figures, including Grendel, fair? Why or why not? Consider their reasoning, evidence, points of emphasis, and tone.

Access Path:

Advanced
Analyze Epic Heroes. Have students discuss and complete the "Epic Heroes" chart on the Access 3 handout, referring back to the SyncTV video as needed to clarify their answers. Sample answers appear at the end of the lesson plan online.

Approaching
Analyze the Discussion. Have students complete the chart on the Access 4 handout by listing textual evidence cited by the students in the video. Sample answers are at the end of the lesson plan online.

Extend
Tech Infusion
Record. Ask one student in each group to videotape the group's conversation. They can upload their videos to YouTube, share them via Google Drive, or email them to you for review. They can also play the video back and critique their own conversations to continually improve.

Please note that excerpts and passages in the StudySync® library, workbooks, and PDFs are intended as touchstones to generate interest in an author's work. The excerpts and passages do not substitute for the reading of entire texts, and StudySync® strongly recommends that teachers and students seek out and purchase the whole literary or informational work in order to experience it as the author intended. Links to online resellers are available in our digital library. In addition, complete works may be ordered through an authorized reseller by filling out and returning to StudySync® the order form enclosed in this workbook.

Teacher's Edition   **43**

4. THINK

Core Path	Access Path
Answer and Discuss. Have students complete the Think questions and then use the peer review instructions and rubric to complete two peer reviews. Refer to the sample answers at the end of the lesson plan online to discuss responses with your students.	**Beginner & Intermediate** **Sentence Frames.** Have students use the sentence frames on the Access 1 and 2 handouts to support their responses to the Think questions. If necessary, distribute sentence frames to Advanced students as well. **Approaching** **Find the Evidence.** Have students use Find the Evidence on the Access 4 handout to help them identify the evidence needed to answer the questions.
SyncTV Style Discussion. Put students into small groups and give them a prompt to discuss. Remind them to model their discussions after the SyncTV episodes they have seen. Stress the importance of using both academic language and formal English correctly and citing textual evidence in their conversations to support their ideas. To help students prepare for, strategize, and evaluate their discussions, refer to the Collaborative Discussions section of the Speaking & Listening Handbook. Discussion prompt: 1. What are some pros and cons of living by the warrior code described by Beowulf in the selection? 2. Which character has the most justification for seeking revenge? Have students review the key ideas expressed, demonstrating an understanding of multiple perspectives through reflection and paraphrasing. You may wish to have students create a video or audio recording of their SyncTV-Style Discussion.	**Beginner & Intermediate** **Use Sentence Frames.** Have these students use the sentence frames on Access 1 and 2 handouts to help them participate in the discussion. **Approaching** **Use Think Questions.** Remind these students to refer back to their answers to the Think questions to help them participate in the group discussion.

Core Path	Access Path
	Extend **Debate.** Present students with an issue from the text that can be debated. Allow students to debate the issue as a class or in smaller groups. Debate prompts: 1. Is Hrothgar a good leader? Why or why not? 2. Is Beowulf foolish for hunting Grendel's mother? Why or why not?
	Extend **Write a Claim.** Ask students to write a strong claim that clearly states their position in relation to the topic they debated. Once students have written their claims, ask them to read their claims to a small group of their peers. This activity will provide them practice writing claims, and will also expose them to claims written by their peers.

Story Elements

OVERVIEW

Story elements comprise a vital skill for students to master. This lesson plan provides follow-up questions and useful enrichments to help teachers guide students toward a usable, repeatable method for identifying and analyzing story elements.

OBJECTIVES

1. Learn the definition of story elements.
2. Practice using concrete strategies for identifying and analyzing story elements.
3. Participate effectively in a range of conversations and collaborations to express ideas and build upon the ideas of others.

   ELA Common Core Standards:
   Reading: Literature - RL.11-12.1, RL.11-12.3
   Speaking & Listening - SL.11-12.1.A, SL.11-12.1.C, SL.11-12.2

RESOURCES

Access 1 handout (Beginner)

Access 2 handout (Intermediate)

Access 3 handout (Advanced)

Access 4 handout (Approaching)

1. DEFINE

Core Path	Access Path

Watch. Watch the Concept Definition video on story elements with your students. Make sure your students know all three elements of a story—plot, character, and setting—as well as how the three elements are interrelated. Pause the video at these key moments to discuss the information with your students:

1. 0:30 – What typically occurs over the course of a story's plot? How does the action move forward, from beginning to middle to end? What changes or evolves? Discuss.

2. 0:47 – Who are some of your favorite characters from the stories you've read? What makes these characters interesting or likable? Why?

3. 1:20 – How might changing a story's setting affect both its plot and characters? What are some things an author might consider before deciding on the right setting for a particular story?

English Learners All Levels & Approaching
Match. Have students complete the matching exercise on the Access 1, 2, 3, and 4 handouts as they watch the video. Answers are located at the end of the lesson plan online.

Read and Discuss. After watching the Concept Definition video, have students read the definition of story elements. Either in small groups or as a whole class use these questions to engage students in a discussion about story elements.

1. How does a story's plot help us to determine its genre? (The relationship of plot to a story's characters and setting determine the story's unique genre.)

2. What information helps us to determine a story's setting? (Knowing the place(s) in which the action of the story takes place helps a reader determine the setting.) (Students may also identify the time period of a story as important in determining its setting.)

3. What qualities do your favorite characters from books and movies share? (Answers will vary.)

Beginner & Approaching
Complete a Chart. To prepare students to participate in the discussion, have them complete the chart on the Access 1 and 4 handouts as they read the definition. The correct answers are located at the end of the lesson plan online.

Intermediate & Advanced
Discuss Prompts. To help these students participate in the discussion, prompt them with questions that can be answered with a few words, such as:

•   What do the characters of a story do? (the actions that make up the plot)

•   If the theme of a story is its central message, how does the plot help develop theme? (what happens and how characters react to events develops the theme)

•   Which is most important to a story: the setting, plot, or characters? Why? (Answers will vary.)

Core Path	Access Path
4. Can you think of an example from a movie, TV show, or book when the setting had an impact on the plot or characters? (Answers will vary.)	**Beyond** **Discuss.** Have students select a book they've read and describe its setting. Compile a list of examples. Have students discuss how the setting of each work affects what the reader learns about the characters and plot. How might a change in setting affect not only what the reader learns, but what the characters do in the story?
	Extend **Tech Infusion** **Brainstorm.** Have the class choose a scene from a well-known movie, and list on a whiteboard or projector the following: • plot • characters • setting Then as a class or in small groups discuss how these different elements worked together to draw the viewer into the story. How effectively were the story elements in this film used?

2. MODEL

Core Path	Access Path
Read and Annotate. Have students independently read the Model section. As they read, ask students to use the annotation tool to: • highlight key points • ask questions • identify places where the Model applies the strategies laid out in the Identification and Application section • comment on the effect of story elements on the text's meaning	**Note:** During this portion of the lesson, instruction shifts from whole group to individual work. Use this time to work one-on-one or in small groups with Beginner, Intermediate, Advanced, and Approaching students.

Core Path	Access Path
	Beginner & Intermediate **Coach the Reading.** Work with these students (either individually or in small groups) to fill out the guided reading questions on the Access 1 and 2 handouts. Have Beginner students refer to the glossary on the Access 1 handout to help them determine the meaning of difficult words (note: provide the Access 1 handout glossary to Intermediate students if necessary). Let students know they'll use these answers to help participate in the discussion about the Model. Sample answers for this exercise are located at the end of the lesson plan online. **Advanced** **Identify Evidence.** Provide these students with the same instructions to read and annotate as on-grade-level and Beyond students. In addition, ask Advanced students to complete the identifying evidence exercise on the Access 3 handout. Let students know that they'll use these answers to help participate in the discussion about the Model. Sample answers for this exercise are located at the end of the lesson plan online. **Approaching** **Guided Reading.** Have students complete the guided reading questions on the Access 4 handout as they read. Let them know that they'll use these answers to help participate in the discussion about the Model. Sample answers for this exercise are located at the end of the lesson plan online.
Discuss. After students read the Model text, use these questions to facilitate a whole-group discussion that helps students understand how to determine and analyze the story elements of the passage: 1. What's the first step this Model uses to identify and analyze story elements? (Identify plot, characters, and setting.)	

Please note that excerpts and passages in the StudySync® library, workbooks, and PDFs are intended as touchstones to generate interest in an author's work. The excerpts and passages do not substitute for the reading of entire texts, and StudySync® strongly recommends that teachers and students seek out and purchase the whole literary or informational work in order to experience it as the author intended. Links to online resellers are available in our digital library. In addition, complete works may be ordered through an authorized reseller by filling out and returning to StudySync® the order form enclosed in this workbook.

Teacher's Edition   **49**

Core Path	Access Path
2. Why does the Model start by identifying plot, characters, and setting instead of just diving into looking for how action is ordered and developed? (Before beginning to analyze how action is ordered, it is first important to determine what action is happening, who the actors are, and where the action is set.)	
3. Which strategy from the Define section of this Skill lesson does the Model use to analyze how action is ordered? (Think about how the author unfolds episodes that form the plot or that reveal the nature of characters.)	
	Extend **Tech Infusion** **Prezi.** Pair or group students and assign each group in the class a different story element to focus on. Have them create a Prezi map (prezi.com) to identify the story element and analyze how it is developed. Have students work in either a timeline or map format. Ask the groups to share their findings with the class. If possible, have students use video recording on their mobile devices so they can watch their conversations and critique the content.

3. YOUR TURN

Core Path	Access Path
Assess and Explain. Have students answer the comprehension questions to test for understanding. Share the explanations for Parts A and B (located online) with your students.	

Core Path	Access Path
	Extend **Share and Discuss.** Have students complete the Your Turn section in class. Poll students (using www.polleverywhere.com or www.socrative.com) about their responses and as a class discuss the different strategies they used to determine the correct answers. Discuss other textual evidence that could be correct for Part B if it were an option (such as, "It beseems us better / friends to avenge than fruitlessly mourn them.")
	Extend **Tech Infusion** **Compile.** As a class compile a list of "Test Taking Tips" throughout the year. They can keep this list in their notebooks or the class can save a master list as a Google document to edit throughout the school year.

OVERVIEW

As students read more complex texts over the course of the year, knowing how to determine the meanings of unfamiliar words will be a key skill. This lesson plan provides follow-up questions and useful enrichments to help teachers guide students toward a usable, repeatable method for determining the meanings of unknown words.

OBJECTIVES

1. Learn the definition of word meaning.
2. Practice using concrete strategies for determining meanings of unknown words.
3. Participate effectively in a range of conversations and collaborations to express ideas and build upon the ideas of others.

ELA Common Core Standards:
Reading: Literature - RL.11-12.1, RL.11-12.4
Speaking & Listening - SL.11-12.1.A, SL.11-12.1.C, SL.11-12.2
Language: L.11-12.4.A, L.11-12.4.B

RESOURCES

Vocabulary handout: Context Clues

Access 1 handout (Beginner)

Access 2 handout (Intermediate)

Access 3 handout (Advanced)

Access 4 handout (Approaching)

1. DEFINE

Core Path	Access Path
Read and Discuss. Have students read the definition of word meaning. Either in small groups or as a whole class use these questions to engage students in a discussion about word meaning. 1. What are context clues and how are they helpful in determining word meaning? (They are the words and phrases that surround a word providing clues to the meaning of that word.) 2. What are affixes? What is the difference between suffixes and prefixes? (An affix is a group of letters added to a word to change the meaning. Suffixes come at the end of words; prefixes come at the beginning.) 3. Read the example using the word "conceive." As a class, make a list of other verbs that can change meanings using the affixes -able and -ly. Then make a list of other affixes that could be used with those words.	**Beginner & Approaching** **Complete a Chart.** To prepare students to participate in the discussion, have them complete the chart on the Access 1 and 4 handouts as they read the definition. The correct answers are located at the end of the lesson plan online. **Intermediate & Advanced** **Discuss Prompts.** To help these students participate in the discussion, prompt them with questions that can be answered with a few words, such as: • Why is flowery language appropriate for a poem? (It helps readers think about a topic in a new way.) • Why is technical language appropriate for an informational text? (It is precise and teaches readers about a topic.) • Do you prefer to read flowery or technical language? Why? (Answers will vary.) **Beyond** **Discuss.** Have students brainstorm ways to talk about a topic, first using flowery language and then using technical language. For instance, they might describe a sunrise as "the Sun popping up to say hello" and as "the moment when the Sun appears over the eastern horizon." Have students discuss how the word choice in each instance affects their understanding of the topic and the effect each has on them as a reader.
	Extend **Tech Infusion** **Brainstorm.** As a class, have students use a print or an online dictionary to create a list of common affixes and their meanings. Save this list in a Google Doc or on a class server for students to refer to throughout the year.

Please note that excerpts and passages in the StudySync® library, workbooks, and PDFs are intended as touchstones to generate interest in an author's work. The excerpts and passages do not substitute for the reading of entire texts, and StudySync® strongly recommends that teachers and students seek out and purchase the whole literary or informational work in order to experience it as the author intended. Links to online resellers are available in our digital library. In addition, complete works may be ordered through an authorized reseller by filling out and returning to StudySync® the order form enclosed in this workbook.

Teacher's Edition   53

Core Path	Access Path
	Extend **Practice.** If students struggle with using context clues to determine the meaning of unknown words, use the vocabulary handout on Context Clues for additional practice.

2. MODEL

Core Path	Access Path
Read and Annotate. Have students independently read the Model section. As they read, ask students to use the annotation tool to: • highlight key points • ask questions • identify places where the Model applies the strategies laid out in the Identification and Application section on word meaning	**Note:** During this portion of the lesson, instruction shifts from whole group to individual work. Use this time to work one-on-one or in small groups with Beginner, Intermediate, Advanced, and Approaching students. **Beginner & Intermediate** **Coach the Reading.** Work with these students (either individually or in small groups) to fill out the guided reading questions on the Access 1 and 2 handouts. Have Beginner students refer to the glossary on the Access 1 handout to help them determine the meaning of difficult words (note: provide the Access 1 handout glossary to Intermediate students if necessary). Let students know they'll use these answers to help participate in the discussion about the Model. Sample answers for this exercise are located at the end of the lesson plan online. **Advanced** **Identify Evidence.** Provide these students with the same instructions to read and annotate as on-grade-level and Beyond students. In addition, ask Advanced students to complete the identifying evidence exercise on the Access 3 handout. Let students know that they'll use these answers to help participate in the discussion about the Model. Sample answers for this exercise are located at the end of the lesson plan online.

Core Path	Access Path
	Approaching **Guided Reading.** Have students complete the guided reading questions on the Access 4 handout as they read. Let them know that they'll use these answers to help participate in the discussion about the Model. Sample answers for this exercise are located at the end of the lesson plan online.
Discuss. After students read the Model text, use these questions to facilitate a whole-group discussion that helps students understand how to determine the meanings of unknown words: 1. What's the first step this Model uses to analyze word meaning? (looks at context to determine part of speech and meaning) 2. What's the second step this Model uses to analyze word meaning? What does the "mock" chart illustrate and how does this example help you as a reader? (The second step is to analyze word parts to determine meaning and part of speech. The chart shows how one word can use affixes to have different meanings and parts of speech.) 3. What's the final step this Model uses to analyze word meaning in *Beowulf*? How do word parts help a reader with unknown words? (studies Anglo-Saxon word origins to determine the meaning of unfamiliar words)	
	Extend **Create a List.** In small groups, have students create a list of multiple-meaning words and their meanings, and have students write example sentences for each meaning. As they work, students should make flashcards with the words on one side and definitions and example sentences on the other. Students can use the flashcards to quiz each other on the multiple-meaning words, or use them as reference during writing assignments.

3. YOUR TURN

Core Path	Access Path
Assess and Explain. Have students answer the comprehension questions to test for understanding. Share the explanations for Parts A and B (located online) with your students.	
	Extend **Share and Discuss.** Have students come up with other usages of the base word *yield*. Make a list on the board. Challenge students to use affixes to make as many variations as possible. Then have students go back to the text and find other base words they can expand on.
	Extend **Tech Infusion** **Compile.** As a class compile a list of "Vocabulary Tips" throughout the school year. Students can keep this list in their notebooks, or the class can save a master list as a Google document to edit and reference for strategies to determining the meanings of vocabulary words.

OVERVIEW

Figures of speech are an important part of literature, especially in epic poems. This lesson plan provides follow-up questions and useful enrichments to help teachers guide students toward a usable, repeatable method for determining and analyzing hyperbole, a key figure of speech.

OBJECTIVES

1. Learn the definition of figurative language.
2. Practice concrete strategies for identifying figurative language.
3. Participate effectively in a range of conversations and collaborations to express ideas and build upon the ideas of others.

ELA Common Core Standards:
Reading: Literature - RL.11-12.1, RL.11-12.4
Speaking & Listening - SL.11-12.1.A, SL.11-12.1.C, SL.11-12.2
Language - L.11-12.5.A

RESOURCES

Access 1 handout (Beginner)

Access 2 handout (Intermediate)

Access 3 handout (Advanced)

Access 4 handout (Approaching)

Please note that excerpts and passages in the StudySync® library, workbooks, and PDFs are intended as touchstones to generate interest in an author's work. The excerpts and passages do not substitute for the reading of entire texts, and StudySync® strongly recommends that teachers and students seek out and purchase the whole literary or informational work in order to experience it as the author intended. Links to online resellers are available in our digital library. In addition, complete works may be ordered through an authorized reseller by filling out and returning to StudySync® the order form enclosed in this workbook.

Teacher's Edition   57

1. DEFINE

Core Path	Access Path
Watch. Watch the Concept Definition video on figurative language with your students. Make sure students understand the difference between literal and figurative language and ask them to write down the seven examples of figurative language in the video, with a definition and example for each. Pause the video at these key moments to discuss the information with your students: 1. 0:45 – What are some instances when it would help to use figurative language? When might it be better to avoid figurative language? Do you think certain genres employ figurative language more often than others? Which ones? 2. 1:29 – Can you think of any other effects of figurative language besides those mentioned in the video? What can figurative language do that literal language cannot? 3. 1:36 – How does the reader know when an author is using figurative language? Is it always obvious? Think of some of the tell-tale signs that can help us decipher when an author is using figurative language in a given text.	**English Learners All Levels & Approaching** **Complete the Sentence.** Have students complete the sentence completion exercise on the Access 1, 2, 3, and 4 handouts as they watch the video. Answers are located at the end of the lesson plan online.
Read and Discuss. After watching the Concept Definition video, have students read the definition of figurative language. Either in small groups or as a whole class use these questions to spur discussion among your students about figurative language. 1. What is figurative language and how do authors use it? What examples of figurative language can you come up with from your reading? (comparative or non-literal language used to share ideas in a fresh or imaginative way)	**Beginner & Approaching** **Fill in the Blanks.** To prepare students to participate in the discussion, have them fill in the missing words or phrases on the Access 1 and 4 handouts as they read the definition for figurative language. The correct answers are located at the end of the lesson plan online. **Intermediate & Advanced** **Discuss Prompts.** To help these students participate in the discussion, prompt them with questions that can be answered with a few words, such as: • Is figurative language meant to be taken literally? (no) • How does using figurative language help writers? (It helps them make a point.)

Core Path	Access Path
2. What is hyperbole? Have you ever used hyperbole in conversation? Why did you choose to use that figure of speech? What did it convey? (Hyperbole is a figure of speech that uses exaggeration to express strong emotion, make a point, or evoke humor; e.g., I have a million things to do before I can go out tonight.)	• What makes figures of speech interesting or fun? (Answers will vary.) **Beyond** **Discuss.** Have students brainstorm examples of similes and metaphors. Compile a list. Then discuss how each figure of speech would help a writer make a specific point or make readers think about an idea in a new and different way.
	Extend **Brainstorm.** As a class, gather more examples of hyperbole in everyday speech. (For example: "My backpack weighs a ton." "I'm so hungry I could eat everything in the cafeteria." "I need a gallon of coffee to stay awake this morning.") Challenge students to come up with as many as they can. Then have partners describe their day yesterday using as much hyperbole as possible.

2. MODEL

Core Path	Access Path
Read and Annotate. Have students independently read the Model section. As they read, ask students to use the annotation tool to: • highlight key points • ask questions • identify places where the Model applies the strategies laid out in the Identification and Application section	**Note:** During this portion of the lesson, instruction shifts from whole group to individual work. Use this time to work one-on-one or in small groups with Beginner, Intermediate, Advanced, and Approaching students.

Core Path	Access Path
	Beginner & Intermediate
	Coach the Reading. Work with these students (either individually or in small groups) to fill out the guided reading questions on the Access 1 and 2 handouts. Have Beginner students refer to the glossary on the Access 1 handout to help them determine the meaning of difficult words (note: provide the Access 1 handout glossary to Intermediate students if necessary). Let students know they'll use these answers to help participate in the discussion about the Model. Sample answers for this exercise are located at the end of the lesson plan online.
	Advanced
	Identify Evidence. Provide these students with the same instructions to read and annotate as on-grade-level and Beyond students. In addition, ask Advanced students to complete the identifying evidence exercise on the Access 3 handout. Let students know that they'll use these answers to help participate in the discussion about the Model. Sample answers for this exercise are located at the end of the lesson plan online.
	Approaching
	Guided Reading. Have students complete the guided reading questions on the Access 4 handout as they read. Let them know that they'll use these answers to help participate in the discussion about the Model. Sample answers for this exercise are located at the end of the lesson plan online.
Discuss. After students read the Model text, use these questions to facilitate a whole-group discussion that helps students understand how to identify hyperbole in the passage: 1. Why is hyperbole often used in epics and superhero stories? (Hyperbole exaggerates what is possible, like epic heroes or superheroes, who do more than a normal person could.)	

Copyright © BookheadEd Learning, LLC

Core Path	Access Path
2. What is the Model's first step in analyzing hyperbole? (identifying an example of hyperbole from the selection and explaining why the description isn't technically possible) 3. After identifying the hyperbole, how does the Model take it a step further? (analyzing how the hyperbole develops the purpose of the text by looking at two reasons why the author might have used hyperbole in the passage)	
	Extend **Tech Infusion** **Blast.** Create a Blast with a driving question that asks students to create their own new superhero and use 140 characters or less of hyperbole to describe him or her (e.g., Punctuality Man! Never a second late. Never a second early. Always on time! More regular than the Earth's rotation around the Sun! or School Spirit Girl! Cheers louder than a 747. Goes to more events than a politician during election year. Bleeds the Green and Gold!). If you have time to extend this assignment, have students continue to use hyperbole to describe their hero and write a list of impossible feats this hero could accomplish. Allow them to draw or use devices to create a comic strip about their new character.

3. YOUR TURN

Core Path	Access Path
Assess and Explain. Have students answer the comprehension questions to test for understanding. Share the explanations for Parts A and B (located online) with your students.	

Please note that excerpts and passages in the StudySync® library, workbooks, and PDFs are intended as touchstones to generate interest in an author's work. The excerpts and passages do not substitute for the reading of entire texts, and StudySync® strongly recommends that teachers and students seek out and purchase the whole literary or informational work in order to experience it as the author intended. Links to online resellers are available in our digital library. In addition, complete works may be ordered through an authorized reseller by filling out and returning to StudySync® the order form enclosed in this workbook.

Teacher's Edition   61

Core Path	Access Path
	Extend **Share and Discuss.** Ask students to rewrite each incorrect answer in Part B to include an example of hyperbole, then share their rewrites with the class. Have the class vote on which example best illustrates both hyperbole and the lair of Grendel's mother. (In a 1-to-1 class, this exercise could also be completed as a Blast.)

OVERVIEW

The epic poem *Beowulf* focuses on a series of battles involving the hero Beowulf, who comes from Geatland—a Scandinavian region in Southern Sweden—to help Denmark's King Hrothgar, whose banquet hall has been attacked by the monster Grendel. Beowulf slays Grendel, but Grendel's mother returns for revenge—slaying Hrothgar's trusted adviser, Aeschere. This excerpt picks up there, as Hrothgar addresses his people in section XX, and Beowulf responds to Hrothgar and the challenge of Grendel's mother in section XXI. The Close Read gives students the opportunity to focus on story elements, word meaning, and figures of speech, such as hyperbole.

OBJECTIVES

1. Complete a close reading of a passage of literature.
2. Practice and apply concrete strategies for identifying story elements, word meaning, and figures of speech.
3. Participate effectively in a range of conversations and collaborations to express ideas and build upon the ideas of others.
4. Prewrite, plan, and produce clear and coherent writing in response to a prompt.

   ELA Common Core Standards:
   Reading: Literature - RL.11-12.1, RL.11-12.3, RL.11-12.4
   Writing - W.11-12.4, W.11 12.5, W.11-12.6, W.11-12.9.A, W.11-12.10
   Speaking & Listening - SL.11-12.1.A, SL.11-12.1.B, SL.11-12.1.C, SL.11-12.1.D, SL.11-12.6
   Language: L.11-12.4.A, L.11-12.4.C, L.11-12.4.D, L.11-12.5.A

RESOURCES

Beowulf Vocabulary handout

Short Constructed Response - Informative/
Explanatory Student Model

Access 1 handout (Beginner)

Access 2 handout (Intermediate)

Access 3 handout (Advanced)

Access 4 handout (Approaching)

Please note that excerpts and passages in the StudySync® library, workbooks, and PDFs are intended as touchstones to generate interest in an author's work. The excerpts and passages do not substitute for the reading of entire texts, and StudySync® strongly recommends that teachers and students seek out and purchase the whole literary or informational work in order to experience it as the author intended. Links to online resellers are available in our digital library. In addition, complete works may be ordered through an authorized reseller by filling out and returning to StudySync® the order form enclosed in this workbook.

Teacher's Edition   63

1. INTRODUCTION

Core Path	Access Path
Define and Compare. Project the vocabulary words and definitions onto the board or provide students with handouts, so they can copy the vocabulary into their notebooks. Suggest that students consult general and specialized reference materials, both print and digital, to compare the precise meaning of a specific word with their initial vocabulary predictions from the First Read. Review words that students defined incorrectly to understand why they were unable to use context clues or other tools to develop usable definitions.	**Beginner & Intermediate** **Complete a Chart.** Have students complete the chart on the Access 1 and 2 handouts by using the correct word for each of the definitions. **Advanced & Beyond** **Write in Journals.** Have students write a journal entry using all of their vocabulary words. Remind them to write sentences that communicate the meaning of the words they are using. **Approaching** **Graphic Organizer.** To support students in comparing their predictions with the correct meanings, have them complete the graphic organizer on the Access 4 handout to record the vocabulary words, their initial analysis, and the definitions. Then have them write sentences using the words.
Review. Have students complete the fill-in-the blank vocabulary worksheet for this selection. Answers for the worksheet are listed online.	
	Extend **Tech Infusion** **Act and Record.** Break up the class into small groups, assign each group a vocabulary word, and ask them to design a short skit to demonstrate the meaning of the word for their peers. If possible, record skits and post them to your class YouTube Channel, so they can be reviewed.
	Extend **The Art of Translation.** Remind students that the excerpt they read has been translated from the original Old English it was written in. Have students review the following sites. If you wish, group students and have them divide the research.

Core Path	Access Path
	• Various translations: http://tinyurl.com/nnf3v3s • Side-by-side modern and Old English: http://tinyurl.com/o6s2yu3 • Notes from Seamus Heaney, who recently translated Beowulf: http://tinyurl.com/7snmpk9 • Reading of Beowulf in Old English: http://tinyurl.com/c5zxbsv Allow time for groups to share their research.
	Extend **Research.** Sutton Hoo is one of the greatest archaeological discoveries in western history. The discovery of this burial site was a literal treasure trove, and it provides glimpses of the life and riches of a warrior-king that may have been described in Beowulf. Have students research the British Museum's site on Sutton Hoo: http://tinyurl.com/ks9fg2w. Have them report on their findings using a multimedia program, such as Prezi.

2. READ

Core Path	Access Path
Model Close Reading. Project the text onto the board and model a close reading of section XX using the annotation strategies mentioned below. While modeling annotation strategies, make notes that tie the text to the focus skill and demonstrate what students are looking for as they read. Some guidance for you as you annotate for your students: • As the Skills lessons that precede this text make clear, the skills focus on story elements, word meaning, and figurative language (hyperbole). Students should annotate words and phrases in section XX that use these skills.	

Core Path	Access Path
• For instance, highlight lines 1337–1347. Identify the action that is taking place. The narration explains that Grendel was killed and then his mother vows to avenge her son's death "Now another comes, / keen and cruel, her kin to avenge." • Then, identify the use of alliteration in the following lines: "fain ... fill ... feud" (1337); "Grendel ... grimmest grasp" (1339); "ruined ... ravaged. Reft" (1341); "keen ... cruel ... kin" (1343); "faring far ... feud" (1344); "that ... thane ... think" (1345); "sorrows ... soul ... sharer" (1346); and "hardest ... heart-bales ... hand" (1347). • Point out how the alliteration creates and sustains a rhythm in the passage. • Identify instances of hyperbole in the passage. There are several overstatements that add weight to the poetry, such as the liegemen, who were "ruined and ravaged," and Grendel, who was "Reft of life," instead of just *killed* in lines 1340-1341. • Guide students to use context clues to confirm word meaning.	
Read and Annotate. Read the Skills Focus questions as a class, so your students know what they should pay close attention to as they read. Then have students read and annotate the excerpt. Ask students to use the annotation tool as they read to: 1. respond to the Skills Focus section 2. ask questions about how story element interrelate 3. make connections between context and word meanings 4. identify examples of figurative language 5. note unfamiliar vocabulary 6. capture their reaction to the images and themes found in the text	**Note:** While on-grade-level students are reading and annotating, work one-on-one or in small groups with Beginner, Intermediate, Advanced, and Approaching students to support them as they read and annotate the text. **Beginner & Intermediate** **Summarize and Analyze the Text.** Work with these students to complete the sentence frames on the Access 1 and 2 handouts (note: the sentence frames for Intermediate students on the Access 2 handout contain fewer scaffolds). They will then use the completed sentence frames to help them analyze and annotate the text by completing the Skills Focus questions. Refer to the sample Skills Focus answers to help them complete the sentence frames and annotate the text.

Core Path	Access Path
As they reread the text, remind students to use the comprehension strategy of asking and answering questions that they learned in the First Read.	**Advanced** **Work in Pairs.** Pair these students with more proficient English speakers to work together on analyzing and annotating the text to complete the Skills Focus questions. If these students need more support, have them use the sentence frames on the Access 3 handout as they work with their more proficient peers. **Approaching** **Summarize the Text.** Have these students discuss and complete the text summary on the Access 4 handout and use their summary to help them analyze and annotate the text by completing the Skills Focus questions. Correct answers for the summary are at the end of the lesson plan online. Also refer to the sample Skills Focus answers to aid students with their annotations.
Discuss. After students have read the text, use the sample responses to the Skills Focus questions at the end of the lesson plan online to discuss the reading and the process of analyzing story elements, word meanings, and figurative language (hyperbole). Make sure that students have acquired and accurately use academic-specific words and phrases related to the skill and demonstrate a command of formal English appropriate to the discussion. To help facilitate discussions, refer to Collaborative Discussions in the Speaking & Listening Handbook.	**Extend** **Pair and Share.** In small, heterogeneous groups or pairs, ask students to share and discuss their annotations with a focus on the story elements and the author's word choice as presented in the selection. You can provide students with these questions to guide their discussion: 1. What words and phrases does the poem use to describe Aeschere and Beowulf? What makes these characters similar? Cite textual evidence to support your answer. (Hrothgar describes Aeschere as "my sage adviser and stay in council / shoulder-comrade in stress of fight /... hero famed should be every earl as Aeschere was!" The description of Beowulf focuses mainly on his armor and weapons. It says, "Then girt him Beowulf / in martial mail, nor mourned for his life. / His breastplate broad and bright of hues / ... well could it ward the warrior's body / that battle should break on his breast in vain." These characters are similar because they are both portrayed as warriors.)

Core Path	Access Path
	2. What obstacles and creatures do the Danish men encounter on their quest? How does the setting influence your understanding of Beowulf as an epic hero? Cite textual evidence to support your answer. (Hrothgar's men travel "o'er stone-cliffs steep and strait defiles" and they see waves that are "hot with blood." They also see "worm-like" sea creatures and "sea-dragons." These details emphasize how dangerous the journey is and Beowulf's bravery for undertaking it.)
	3. Bravery was a key quality during the Anglo-Saxon period. How does the poet use hyperbole to accentuate this quality? Cite textual evidence to support your answer. (Answers will vary. Students may point out the description of the sword, which never "blenched it at fight / in hero's hand who held it ever." This magical sword encourages and rewards a man's bravery.)
	Extend **Literary Terms: Kenning and Alliteration.** A **kenning** is a compound word or noun phrase that identifies something or someone in a poetic way. There are a number of them in *Beowulf*. Have students focus on the one in the opening line of the excerpt, "helmet-of-Scyldings," which describes Hrothgar. Knowing that he is a king, what do you think this kenning means? (Hrothgar is the king and military leader "helmet" of the Scyldings.) Now have students identify more kennings in the excerpt. **Alliteration**—the repetition of consonant sounds, usually at the beginning of words—is a key stylistic element of *Beowulf*. Point out the repetition of "h" in line 1332: "**h**ewed the **h**elm-boars; **h**ero famed." Have students find more examples of alliteration in the excerpt, and ask them to describe the effect those examples have on the style of the selection.

Core Path	Access Path
	Extend
	Write. Have students write ten lines of verse modeling the use of kenning and alliteration in the excerpt from *Beowulf*.
	Note: Interested students may find the entirety of the Grummere translation used in StudySync available online at various sites (since it is in the public domain). Advise students that one reliable site for authoritative poetic texts along with digital resources is the Poetry Foundation: http://www.poetryfoundation.org/poem/180445

3. WRITE

Core Path	Access Path
Prewrite and Plan. Read the prompt as a class and ask students to brainstorm about how the story elements help them understand more about Anglo-Saxon culture. Remind your students to look at the excerpt and their annotations to find textual evidence to support their ideas. You may wish to review with students the Short Constructed Response - Informative/Explanatory Student Model for guidance on how to construct an effective response to the writing prompt.	**Beginner & Intermediate**
	Plan and Organize. Have students complete the prewriting activity on the Access 1 and 2 handouts and then explain their ideas to a partner before they write. Explain to students that they need to choose details, examples, or quotes from the text that support their ideas and then explain how those details support their statements. For example, students could include the first line, "HROTHGAR spake, helmet-of-Scyldings," which tells us that Hrothgar is the king. He is the speaker of section XX, so we know he is a main character. This detail about character might tell us that Anglo-Saxons were ruled by kings and that they depended on them for protection.
	Approaching
	Plan and Organize. Have students complete the prewriting activity on the Access 4 handout to organize their thoughts before they write.

Please note that excerpts and passages in the StudySync® library, workbooks, and PDFs are intended as touchstones to generate interest in an author's work. The excerpts and passages do not substitute for the reading of entire texts, and StudySync® strongly recommends that teachers and students seek out and purchase the whole literary or informational work in order to experience it as the author intended. Links to online resellers are available in our digital library. In addition, complete works may be ordered through an authorized reseller by filling out and returning to StudySync® the order form enclosed in this workbook.

Teacher's Edition   69

Core Path	Access Path
	Extend **Organize.** Encourage students to complete a graphic organizer to help them connect the story elements to elements of Anglo-Saxon culture.
	Extend **Tech Infusion** **Map.** Students can create concept maps online using https://bubbl.us. Google Drawing can also be used to design a concept map.
Discuss. Project these instructions for the peer review onto the board and review them with your class, so they know what they are looking for when they begin to provide their classmates with feedback: • How has this essay helped you understand the Anglo-Saxon worldview and culture? • Has the writer made clear and well-supported observations about Anglo-Saxon culture based on the descriptions of character, plot, and setting in the epic? • What sort of evidence did the writer use from the text to support his or her writing? • How well does the writer explain how that evidence supports his or her arguments? • Does the writer write using standard grammar and punctuation? Are there any weak spots? • What specific suggestions can you make to help the writer improve the response? • What thing(s) does this paper do especially well? After you've looked at the peer review instructions, review the rubric with students before they begin writing. Allow time for students briefly to pose and discuss any questions they may have about the peer review instructions and the rubric. Tell students how many peer reviews they will need to complete once they submit their writing.	

Core Path	Access Path
Write. Ask students to complete the writing assignment using textual evidence to support their answers. Once they have completed their writing, they should click "Submit."	
	Extend **Critique.** Project a writing sample on the board and ask the class to identify the elements of writing that are strong, as well as those that are weak or in need of improvement. Alternatively, you can put students in small groups and give them photocopies of a writing sample to collaboratively evaluate. After students have had an opportunity to evaluate student samples, work as a class to generate strategies students can use as they complete their peer reviews to ensure they are substantive.
Review. Once students complete their writing assignment, they should submit substantive feedback to two peers. Students should use their peers' feedback to improve their writing.	

OVERVIEW

To supplement their study of *Beowulf*, students will think about ways that people resolve conflict. Students will explore research links that connect them to information about conflict resolution in different times and places.

OBJECTIVES

1. Explore background information about the factors and key issues surrounding conflict resolution.
2. Research using hyperlinks to a range of information about conflict resolution, including legal codes, geopolitical peace talks and awards, and gang violence.

ELA Common Core Standards:
Reading: Informational Text - RI.11-12.1
Writing - W.11-12.1.A, W.11-12.1.B, W.11-12.5, W.11-12.6
Speaking & Listening - SL.11-12.1.A, SL.11-12.1.C, SL.11-12.D

RESOURCES

Blast Response - Student Model

Access 1 handout (Beginner)

Access 2 handout (Intermediate)

Access 4 handout (Approaching)

TITLE/DRIVING QUESTION

Core Path	Access Path
Discuss. As a class read aloud the title and driving question for this Blast. Ask students what they know about conflict resolution. Can they think of any examples in their own lives where they have had to resolve conflict? Remind students that they will be returning to this question for their formal entries after they've written a draft and read and discussed the Background.	**English Learners All Levels** **Discuss a Visual.** Have students view photographs of a prank war gone too far, such as the ones shown here that took place between juniors and seniors in high school: http://tinyurl.com/nswv2bv/. Discuss how the picture represents groups of people attempting to get revenge, prompting students with questions such as: • What is happening in these photos? • How is pulling a prank on someone a form of revenge? • How do you think the people who pulled the prank felt afterward? • What consequences likely await the people who pulled this prank?
Draft. In their notebooks or on scrap paper, have students draft their initial responses to the driving question. This will provide them with a baseline response that they will update and revise as they gain more information about the topic in the Background and Research Links sections of the assignment. You may wish to review with students the Blast Response - Student Model for guidance on how to construct an effective Blast. The Blast review criteria are as follows: 1. Response does not address the driving question or is unclear; language is vague. 2. Response insufficiently addresses the driving question or is mostly unclear; language is mostly vague. 3. Response somewhat addresses the driving question or is somewhat unclear; language is somewhat vague. 4. Response adequately addresses the driving question and is clear; language is mostly precise.	**Beginner & Intermediate** **Draft with Sentence Frame.** When drafting their initial response to the driving question, have students refer to this Blast sentence frame on their Access 1 and 2 handouts: • Yes/No, people can/cannot "get even" with someone who has harmed them because _____. Point out these two key features of the sentence frame: 1. The introductory clause "Yes/No, people can/cannot "get even" with someone who has harmed them" borrows language directly from the Blast driving question to provide a response. Point out that students will either have to choose "Yes, people can" or "No, people cannot" when they write their own Blast.

Core Path	Access Path
5. Response fully addresses the driving question and is clear; language is precise.	2. Ask students to note how the conjunction "because" invites them to state a reason for their opinions. Also, point out that "because" is not preceded by a comma, unlike other common conjunctions such as "and" or "but."

BACKGROUND

Core Path	Access Path
Read. Have students read the Blast background to provide context for the driving question.	**Beginner & Intermediate** **Read with Support.** Have students read the Blast background to provide context for the driving question. When they encounter unfamiliar words or phrases, have students refer to the glossary on their Access 1 and 2 handouts. If there are unfamiliar words that are not included in their glossary, encourage students to check a dictionary or online reference tool, like http://dictionary.reference.com. **Approaching** **Read and Summarize.** Have students read the Blast background to provide context for the driving question. As they read, ask students to complete the fill-in-the-blank summary of the background provided on their Access 4 handout. When they encounter unfamiliar words or phrases, have students refer to the glossary on their Access 4 handout.
Discuss. Pair students and have them discuss the following questions: 1. To what does "eye for eye" justice refer? (the code of Hammurabi) 2. When was the Code of Hammurabi recorded? (18th century B.C.E.) 3. What solution did people use in the Anglo-Saxon period to reduce revenge killings? (*wergild*, "man price")	**Beginner** **Discuss.** Pair Beginner with Advanced (or Beyond) students and have them use the dialogue starter on their Access 1 handout to discuss the topic. Advise them to return to the dialogue and switch roles if they get stuck.

Core Path	Access Path
4. What current societal group in the United States battles the problem of revenge killings? (gangs)	**Intermediate** **Discuss.** Pair Intermediate with Advanced (or Beyond) students and have them use the dialogue starter on their Access 2 handout to discuss the topic. Advise them to return to the dialogue and switch roles if they get stuck. If their conversation is progressing smoothly, encourage them to continue the discussion beyond the dialogue starter sheet. They can expand their conversations by discussing other examples of historical figures, celebrities, or people they know who have attempted to "get even" with someone and how that worked out.
Brainstorm. Remind students about the driving question for this Blast: Can you ever "get even"? In their notebooks, ask students to define what "getting even" means, using a web diagram to define the phrase. Then, have students collect a list of conflicts that have been about "getting even." Students should draw on their knowledge of historical conflicts and should include examples of conflicts from their personal lives. Here's a short example of how this list might look: • In WWII, Germany was partially seeking retaliation for what they believed were unfair restrictions imposed on Germany at the end of WWI. • After my mom told my three-year-old sister she couldn't stay up past her bedtime, she took a crayon and drew all over the wall in her bedroom.	

RESEARCH LINKS

Core Path	Access Path
Examine and Explore. Use these questions to guide students' exploration of the research links: 1. Have students read the History article on Hammurabi's code. Ask students what contemporary legal precedent the code included, starting with the word "presumption" (presumption of innocence) 2. Have students review the mission statement, goals, and vision sections on the Cure Violence site homepage. Ask: What claim does the site make about understanding violent behavior? (Violent behavior is a health issue that can be prevented, not the result of inherently "bad" people.) 3. Have students read one of the Success Stories on the Cure Violence page and explain how it changed their perspective on the issue.	

	Extend
	Research, Discuss, and Present.
	
	1. Assign each group one link to explore in depth.
	2. Ask them to discuss the information:
	    a. What are the key points?
	    b. What inferences did you make as you read?
	    c. What did you learn about this "big idea" from reading this research?
	    d. How did this help you to better understand the topic?
	    e. What questions does your group have after exploring this link?
	3. Allow students time to informally present what they learned.

Core Path	Access Path
	Extend **Tech Infusion** **Share.** As students explore the links, have them compile a list of strategies for conflict resolution. Have students share their findings using a site like Padlet (http://padlet.com). Use the list as a basis for a discussion about which strategy seems the most effective. Have students defend their choice.

QUIKPOLL

Core Path	Access Path
Participate. Answer the poll question. Have students use information from the background and research links to explain their answers.	

NUMBER CRUNCH

Core Path	Access Path
Predict, Discuss, and Click. Before students click on the number, break them into pairs and have them make predictions about what they think the number is related to. After they've clicked the number, ask students if they are surprised by the revealed information.	

CREATE YOUR BLAST

Core Path	Access Path
Blast. Ask students to write their Blast response in 140 characters or less.	**Beginner** **Blast with Support.** Have students refer back to the sentence frame on their Access 1 handout that they used to create their original Blast draft. Ask them to use this frame to write and enter their final Blast. **Intermediate** **Blast with Support.** Have students attempt to draft their Blast without the sentence frame on their Access 2 handout. If students struggle to compose their Blast draft without the sentence frame, remind them to reference it for support. **Beyond** **Write a Claim.** Ask students to use their answer to the poll question to write a strong claim that could be used as the foundation for a piece of argumentative writing. Once students have written their claims, ask them to read the claims to a small group of their peers. This activity will provide them practice writing claims, as well as expose them to claims written by their peers.
Review. After students have completed their own Blasts, ask them to review the Blasts of their peers and provide feedback. To help students respond effectively, read and discuss the Blast review criteria with them before they review one another's Blasts.	
	Extend **Discuss.** As a class or in groups, identify a few strong Blasts and discuss what made those responses so powerful. As a group, analyze and discuss what characteristics make a Blast interesting or effective.

Core Path	Access Path
	Extend **Revise.** Resend a second version of this Blast assignment to your students and have them submit revised versions of their original Blasts. Do the same responses make the Top Ten? How have the answers improved from the first submissions?

Please note that excerpts and passages in the StudySync® library, workbooks, and PDFs are intended as touchstones to generate interest in an author's work. The excerpts and passages do not substitute for the reading of entire texts, and StudySync® strongly recommends that teachers and students seek out and purchase the whole literary or informational work in order to experience it as the author intended. Links to online resellers are available in our digital library. In addition, complete works may be ordered through an authorized reseller by filling out and returning to StudySync® the order form enclosed in this workbook.

Teacher's Edition   79

OVERVIEW

The novel *Grendel* by John Gardner retells the Beowulf legend from the point of view of the monster Grendel. The First Read gives students the opportunity to experience the text with a limited context.

OBJECTIVES

1. Perform an initial reading of a text and demonstrate comprehension by responding to short analysis and inference questions with textual evidence.
2. Practice defining vocabulary words using context.
3. Participate effectively in a range of conversations and collaborations to express ideas and to build upon the ideas of others.
4. Practice acquiring and using academic vocabulary correctly.

   ELA Common Core Standards:
   Reading: Literature - RL.11-12.1, RL.11-12.4, RL.11-12.10
   Speaking & Listening - SL.11-12.1.A, SL.11-12.1.B, SL.11-12.1.C, SL.11-12.1.D, SL.11-12.2
   Language - L.11-12.4.A, L.11-12.4.B, L.11-12.6

RESOURCES

Access 1 handout (Beginner)

Access 2 handout (Intermediate)

Access 3 handout (Advanced)

Access 4 handout (Approaching)

ACCESS COMPLEX TEXT

This excerpt from *Grendel* communicates the monster's status as an outsider who is set apart from the lavishness and community of Hrothgar's meadhall. Grendel himself takes on the role of first-person narrator and recounts his side of the story as he observes the construction of the meadhall and has a violent encounter with Hrothgar's men. To help students understand the main character of Grendel and the internal and external conflicts he faces, use the following ideas to provide scaffolded instruction for a first reading of the more complex features of this text:

- **Genre** - This is a narrative retelling of the epic poem *Beowulf*. Students who are already familiar with the events and characters of *Beowulf* may be confused by the change in these story elements in this excerpt. In this version, Grendel is not the cruel beast he is in the epic, and Hrothgar's men are not the epic heroes readers may expect them to be.

- **Connection of Ideas** - The characterization of Grendel as the first-person narrator of this retelling is complex. He can be seen as both a protagonist and an antagonist in the text. He is the main character, but he is also critical of and trapped by his own monstrousness. For example, he says "My heart was light with Hrothgar's goodness, and leaden with grief at my own bloodthirsty ways." This juxtaposition may be challenging for readers who expect Grendel to be a cold-hearted villain.

- **Specific Vocabulary** - Complex vocabulary, such as *belligerent* and *posturing,* and figurative language, such as "the thought took seed in Hrothgar's mind," may present a challenge to some readers.

- **Prior Knowledge** - Students who are not familiar with the characters and plot of *Beowulf* may struggle to understand the characters and plot of *Grendel*. Encourage these students to revisit *Beowulf,* or provide them with a short summary.

Please note that excerpts and passages in the StudySync® library, workbooks, and PDFs are intended as touchstones to generate interest in an author's work. The excerpts and passages do not substitute for the reading of entire texts, and StudySync® strongly recommends that teachers and students seek out and purchase the whole literary or informational work in order to experience it as the author intended. Links to online resellers are available in our digital library. In addition, complete works may be ordered through an authorized reseller by filling out and returning to StudySync® the order form enclosed in this workbook.

Teacher's Edition   **81**

1. INTRODUCTION

Core Path	Access Path
Read. Individually or as a class, read the Introduction for *Grendel*. The introduction provides context for the excerpts taken from Chapter 4.	**English Learners All Levels & Approaching** **Read and Listen.** Ask students to read and listen to the introduction for *Grendel*. Have them refer to the "Introduction Glossary" on their Access 1, 2, 3, and 4 handouts for definitions of key vocabulary terms. If there are unfamiliar words that are not included in their glossary, encourage students to check a dictionary or online reference tool, like http://dictionary.reference.com.
	Extend **Make Predictions.** Based on the introduction, ask students to make predictions about how Grendel's narrative will differ from the narrative in *Beowulf*. List the predictions on the whiteboard and save the list for referencing in a subsequent lesson.
	Extend **Discuss the Introduction.** After reading the introduction, use the information provided to facilitate a prereading discussion to get students thinking about the events and themes in *Grendel*. 1. Have you ever been torn between doing the right thing and doing the wrong thing? Explain. 2. How can envy contribute to evil? 3. How do you think Grendel might be similar to his mother?
Access Prior Knowledge. Find out what your students recall about the Beowulf legends. 1. First, divide your students up into small groups. 2. Ask each group to generate a list of the information and previous knowledge your students have about *Beowulf*.	**Beginner & Intermediate** **Access Prior Knowledge.** Pair Beginner and Intermediate students, and have them complete the "Recall Details" chart on the Access 1 and 2 handouts with details that they recall from *Beowulf*. Encourage students to revisit the excerpt from *Beowulf* as needed. Have the pairs generate ideas, discuss the questions on the chart, and complete it together.

Copyright © BookheadEd Learning, LLC

Core Path	Access Path
3. Then discuss with students how some of their prior knowledge about *Beowulf* may help them understand the context of *Grendel* as they read. Ask them if they can think of any stories, songs, or movies that use a different narrator than the initial work to tell the story.	**Advanced & Approaching** **Access Prior Knowledge.** Pair Advanced and Approaching students, and have them complete the "Recall Details" story map on the Access 3 and 4 handouts with details that they recall from *Beowulf*. Encourage students to revisit the excerpt from *Beowulf* as needed. Have the pairs generate ideas, discuss the story map, and complete the map together.
	Extend **Analyze and Discuss a Quotation** "Knowledge is power. Power to do evil … or power to do good. Power itself is not evil. So knowledge itself is not evil." (*Allegiant,* Veronica Roth) 1. What do you think this quotation means? 2. Do you agree with this quotation? Why or why not? 3. How would you define *evil*?

2. READ

Core Path	Access Path
Make Predictions about Vocabulary. There are six bold vocabulary words in the text. As students read the text, ask them to make predictions about what they think each bold vocabulary word means based on the context clues in the sentence. If you are in a low-tech classroom and students are reading from printed copies or a projected text, ask students to record predictions in their notes, so they can be easily referenced in class. If your students have access to technology, they can use the annotation tool to make their predictions. It might be helpful to model this for students before they begin reading. Either using the board or projecting the actual text, focus in on the line containing the word "belligerent":	**Note:** This exercise, which extends vocabulary instruction, should be completed when the class shifts from whole group instruction to individual work during the "Read and Annotate" exercise.

Core Path	Access Path
• "He reshapes the world," I whispered, belligerent. "So his name implies. He stares strange-eyed at the mindless world and turns dry sticks to gold." Model for the class how to use the overall structure and meaning of the sentence and the sentences around it, the word's position, and other clues to define the unfamiliar vocabulary word. In this case, point out these context clues: 1. Look at the structure of the sentence. What is the subject of the sentence (I) and which word modifies it (belligerent)? The position of the word "belligerent" indicates that it is an adjective because Grendel uses it to describe himself, not his actions. 2. I see that the suffix of "belligerent," is "-ent." Other words I know ending in "-ent" are "independent" and "lenient," both words that act as adjectives. This confirms my guess that the word "belligerent" functions as an adjective. 3. There are not many context clues in the sentence, so I look at the surrounding sentences to see if they can help me determine what the word means. I scan the sentences that come before. Grendel seems to be angry at himself and at King Hrothgar. This helps me infer that "belligerent" must relate to feelings of anger. 4. Grendel says, "I hissed in the black of the forest," "I listened, tensed," and "I whispered crossly." These descriptions, along with his anger, help me determine that "belligerent" must mean "aggressive and eager to fight." 5. If I look up the meaning of the prefix "belli-," I see that it means "war." This would make sense, given the context clues pointing at anger and aggression. 6. Just to be sure, I will look up the word in the dictionary later to confirm my predicted meaning.	**Beginner, Intermediate & Approaching Pair Practice.** 1. Pair students with more proficient readers. 2. Give them an additional sentence that contains a new vocabulary word. 3. Ask the students to complete a Think Aloud using the teacher-led Make Predictions about Vocabulary activity as a model, while the proficient student actively listens. 4. The student should use the context clues in the sentence to try to determine the meaning of the new vocabulary word. 5. After the student has completed the Think Aloud and made a prediction about the word's meaning, allow time for the proficient reader to add his/her own thoughts and clarify any points of confusion. 6. Once they've completed this Think Aloud, encourage them to use a dictionary to confirm the definition of the new vocabulary word. Have them refer to the "Text Glossary" on their Access 1, 2, and 4 handouts for definitions of key vocabulary terms in the text. Encourage them to add any additional vocabulary words or idioms they find in the text and look up definitions for those words and idioms online or in a dictionary.

Core Path	Access Path
	Extend
	Identify and Define. After students have read the text, compile a list of additional vocabulary words. Ask students to reference their annotations and share any vocabulary words that were unfamiliar.
	1. As a class, compile a list of unknown words on the board.
	2. In small groups, ask students to make predictions about what they think these words mean based on how they are used in the sentence. (Note: They will need to read the words in context and make predictions.)
	3. Each group should work together using dictionaries or devices to define the words and write the definitions in their notebooks.

Model Reading Comprehension Strategy. Before students begin reading, model the reading comprehension strategy of visualizing by using this Think Aloud that talks students through the first three paragraphs of text. First explain to your students that visualizing is

forming a mental picture of something as you read and using new details from the text to add to or change the mental images you have created.

Model for students how visualizing will help them better comprehend the selection and help drive their discussions.

- In the first paragraph, I see the words "magnificent meadhall high on a hill," and a picture starts to form in my mind. The phrases "victory-seat" and "sign of the glory and justice of Hrothgar's Danes" help me imagine a massive structure where all the Danes can go and celebrate Hrothgar's successes and their pride in their country.

Note: This exercise, which extends instruction around reading comprehension strategies, should be completed when the class shifts from whole group instruction to individual work during the "Read and Annotate" exercise.

Beginner, Intermediate & Approaching
Apply Reading Comprehension Strategy.

1. Have students listen to the audio version of the excerpt from *Grendel*. As they listen to the audio recording, ask them to underline or annotate phrases that create vivid pictures in their mind as they visualize the story. Then have them complete the Visualizing chart on their Access 1, 2, and 4 handouts.

2. Once they have listened to the audio version and have their annotations, pair Beginner, Intermediate, and Approaching students with more proficient readers and ask them to describe the setting and characters of the story. What does the meadhall look like? What does Grendel look like?

3. Allow pairs time to discuss their mental images. Then ask: If you were making a painting of this scene, what part would you focus on? What colors would you use? Why?

Core Path	Access Path
• The second paragraph confirms the size and importance of the meadhall. Hrothgar calls for "woodsmen, carpenters, metalsmiths, goldsmiths—also carters, victualers, clothiers to attend to the workmen," so I can see that this was a huge project. I read that men came from all around to celebrate, and I imagine a ton of people having a good time together and showing their support for Hrothgar. • However, in the third paragraph, I see the narrator, Grendel, backing away "crablike, further into darkness." I imagine a monstrous figure obscured by night's darkness slinking away from the celebration. This image helps me infer that not everyone in the land is welcome to join Hrothgar's party. • As I continue to read, I will use the strategy of visualizing to help me to understand images and a context that is unfamiliar.	
Read and Annotate. Have students independently read and annotate the excerpt. Ask students to use the annotation tool as they read to: 1. use context clues to analyze and determine the meaning of the bolded vocabulary terms 2. ask questions about passages of the text that may be unclear or unresolved 3. identify key details, events, characters, and connections between them 4. note unfamiliar vocabulary 5. capture their reaction to the events in the text	**Beginner** **Coach the Reading.** While other students read, annotate, and discuss the text independently, work with Beginner students, listening to the audio of the text and pausing periodically or when any student has a question. Coach students in articulating their questions for the group and in highlighting and annotating the text. Have students use the Annotation Guide on the Access 1 handout to support them as they highlight and annotate the text. For further support, ask questions about the text such as: • Is there anything about the story that you don't understand? • What do you think will happen to Grendel? • Why do you think *Grendel* is the title of the story?

Core Path	Access Path
	Intermediate **Listen to the Audio.** Have these students listen to the audio of the text and use the Text Glossary on the Access 2 handout to help them with words or idioms that may be unfamiliar. If students need help with annotating the text, have them use the Annotation Guide on the Access 2 handout. After working with the Beginner students, you may wish to check this group's progress and provide support as needed. **Advanced** **Pair with Proficient Peers.** Have Advanced students work with English proficient peers to read, annotate, and discuss the text. Have students use the Annotation Guide in the Access 3 handout to support them as they highlight and annotate the text. Encourage them to listen to the audio of the text if needed. **Approaching** **Use the Annotation Guide.** Have students use the Annotation Guide on the Access 4 handout to support them as they highlight and annotate the text.
Discuss. In small groups or pairs, have students discuss the questions and inferences they made while reading. To help facilitate discussions, refer to Collaborative Discussions in the Speaking & Listening Handbook. 1. What are the Danes doing during the first part of the excerpt? (constructing a meadhall) 2. Which sentence in Paragraph 3 is the strongest evidence of the theme of good versus evil? ("My heart was light with Hrothgar's goodness, and leaden with grief at my own bloodthirsty ways.") 3. When Grendel tells the snake, "I knew him when," whom is he talking about? (Paragraph 3) (Hrothgar) 4. What does Grendel carry out of the forest? (the body of a person murdered by the Danes)	**English Learners All Levels & Approaching** Use the extra time while on- and beyond-grade-level students are discussing their first reads of the text to work individually and in small groups with Approaching readers and English Learners as outlined above. Should those students complete their first reads quickly, integrate them into the on- and beyond-grade-level discussion groups. Otherwise, English Learners and Approaching readers will be given an opportunity to participate in text discussions with their peers later in the lesson.

Core Path	Access Path
5. How did visualizing the characters and their actions help you better understand the excerpt?	**Tech Infusion** **Beyond** **Write.** What might have happened if Grendel had a chance to speak with Hrothgar before the Danes attacked him? Have students write an alternate ending to the scene, drawing inspiration from the characterization and tone of *Grendel*. Have students share their endings by publishing them on Pen.io. (http://pen.io) Pair students and have them compare and contrast the narrative choices they made.
	Extend **Tech Infusion** **Record.** Have students use a voice recording app (Voice Memo on the iPhone or Smart Voice Recorder for Androids) or VoiceThread (https://voicethread .com) to record a radio commercial that contains hyperbole. Provide the following examples of hyperbole: • "Shimmer toothpaste whitens your teeth so well that you will be offered a Hollywood contract within days!" • "Theodore's Frozen Pizza is so overwhelmingly delicious you will dream about it for months!" • Liquid Lustre shampoo will make your hair so irresistible that you will triple your number of Instagram followers!

3. THINK

Core Path	Access Path
Answer and Discuss. Have students complete the Think questions and then use the peer review instructions and rubric to complete two peer reviews. Refer to the sample answers at the end of the lesson plan online to discuss responses with your students.	**Beginner & Intermediate** **Sentence Frames.** Have students use the sentence frames on the Access 1 and 2 handouts to support their responses to the Think questions. If necessary, distribute sentence frames to Advanced students as well.

Core Path	Access Path
	Approaching **Find the Evidence.** Have students use Find the Evidence on the Access 4 handout to help them identify the evidence needed to answer the questions.
	Extend **Write a Claim.** Ask students to write a strong claim that clearly states their position of the following topic: "Grendel is a misunderstood individual who is not as bad as the Danes make him out to be." Once students have written their claims, ask them to read their claims to a small group of their peers. This activity will provide them practice writing claims, and will also expose them to claims written by their peers.

OVERVIEW

Determining the theme of a text is a difficult skill for students to master. This lesson plan provides follow-up questions and useful enrichments to help teachers guide students toward a usable, repeatable method for uncovering theme.

OBJECTIVES

1. Learn the definition of theme.
2. Practice using concrete strategies for determining theme.
3. Participate effectively in a range of conversations and collaborations to express ideas and build upon the ideas of others.

ELA Common Core Standards:

Reading: Literature - RL.11-12.1, RL.11-12.2
Speaking & Listening - SL.11-12.1.A, SL.11-12.1.C, SL.11-12.2

RESOURCES

Access 1 handout (Beginner)

Access 2 handout (Intermediate)

Access 3 handout (Advanced)

Access 4 handout (Approaching)

1. DEFINE

Core Path	Access Path
Watch. Watch the Concept Definition video on theme with your students. Ask students to write the definitions and the key evidence they can examine to determine theme in their notes. Pause the video at these key moments to discuss the information with your students: 1. 1:00 – Why would authors choose to have readers infer stories' themes? Why don't all authors just come out and state the theme like they do in fables? 2. 1:25 – What are some other real life examples of when inference skills are important? 3. 2:37 – Can you think of any evidence that might help a reader identify theme that the students in the video don't mention? Are some pieces of evidence more important for determining theme?	**English Learners All Levels & Approaching** **Match.** Have students complete the matching exercise on the Access 1, 2, 3, and 4 handouts as they watch the video. Answers are located at the end of the lesson plan online.
Read and Discuss. After watching the Concept Definition video, have students read the definition of theme. Either in small groups or as a whole class use these questions to engage students in a discussion about theme. 1. What steps does the definition give to find theme? (The reader may look at the title, the words of a character, or a descriptive line.) Why is theme so difficult to identify? (It isn't clearly stated in the story, as plot or characters are, with the exception of fables.) 2. What kinds of themes can writers express out of conflicts in stories? Can you think of any themes that are unrelated to conflict? (Answers may vary, but most themes do relate to conflict.) 3. How does the development of theme in a poem differ from a short story, a novel, or a nonfiction article? (Most poems are short and use few words, so the reader has an easier time inferring the theme, or main message.)	**Beginner & Approaching** **Fill in the Blanks.** To prepare students to participate in the discussion, have them work with partners to complete the "Fill in the Blanks" exercise on the Access 1 and 4 handouts as they read the definition. The correct answers are located at the end of the lesson plan online. **Intermediate & Advanced** **Discuss Prompts.** To help these students participate in the discussion, prompt them with questions that can be answered with a few words, such as: • What is a theme? (the author's central idea or message) • What do readers have to do to determine the theme when an author does not state it? (infer it) • What do readers need to use to determine theme in a text? (textual evidence)

Teacher's Edition

Core Path	Access Path
	Beyond **Discuss.** Have students select a book or movie and identify its theme. Compile a list of examples. Have students discuss how they determined the theme of the book or movie. Did the author or a character explicitly state the theme? If not, what textual or verbal evidence did they use to infer the theme?
	Extend **Tech Infusion** **Brainstorm.** As a class, discuss common themes found in books, movies, or TV shows. If students struggle, prompt with such universal themes as the pain of growing up or the power of love. For each common theme, ask students to give an example of a story with that theme. Alternatively, read your students a children's story and ask them to identify the theme or themes present.
	Extend **Discuss.** In small groups or as a class, discuss the following questions: • Do you think an author chooses a theme before starting to write a book? • Can a reader ever detect a theme that the author did not intend? • Can a book or movie ever not have a theme?

2. MODEL

Core Path	Access Path
Watch. Ask students to take notes on the SkillsTV video on theme in *Grendel* as you watch together. Remind students to listen for the way the students use academic vocabulary related to the definition of theme during their discussion. Pause the video at these key moments to discuss the information with your students:	**Beginner, Intermediate & Approaching** **Analyze the Discussion.** Have students watch the video again and complete the chart on the Access 1, 2, and 4 handouts as they watch the video. Sample answers for this exercise are located at the end of the lesson plan online.

Core Path

Watch. Ask students to take notes on the SkillsTV video on theme in *Grendel* as you watch together. Remind students to listen for the way the students use academic vocabulary related to the definition of theme during their discussion. Pause the video at these key moments to discuss the information with your students:

1. 0:54 – Why is it a good strategy to close-read the title and discuss the context of the story? How can these elements provide clues, either directly or indirectly, for determining the theme(s)? How well does the group use the title and context to draw conclusions about *Grendel?*

2. 2:02 – How does the presence of conflict point to the theme of a story? What conflict does the group identify? Do they use evidence effectively in their discussion? Why or why not?

3. 3:16 – What are some words or phrases the group repeats in their discussion of the excerpt? How do they use these points of emphasis to draw conclusions about the themes of *Grendel?*

Read and Annotate. Have students independently read the Model section. As they read, ask students to use the annotation tool to:
- highlight key points
- ask questions
- identify places where the Model applies the strategies laid out in the Identification and Application section on theme

Access Path

Beginner, Intermediate & Approaching
Analyze the Discussion. Have students watch the video again and complete the chart on the Access 1, 2, and 4 handouts as they watch the video. Sample answers for this exercise are located at the end of the lesson plan online.

Advanced
Journals. Have students note in their journals the strategies the students in the SkillsTV video use to determine theme.

Note: During this portion of the lesson, instruction shifts from whole group to individual work. Use this time to work one-on-one or in small groups with Beginner, Intermediate, Advanced, and Approaching students.

Beginner & Intermediate
Coach the Reading. Work with these students (either individually or in small groups) to fill out the guided reading questions on the Access 1 and 2 handouts. Have Beginner students refer to the glossary on the Access 1 handout to help them determine the meaning of difficult words (note: provide the Access 1 handout glossary to Intermediate students if necessary). Let students know they'll use these answers to help participate in the discussion about the Model. Sample answers for this exercise are located at the end of the lesson plan online.

Please note that excerpts and passages in the StudySync® library, workbooks, and PDFs are intended as touchstones to generate interest in an author's work. The excerpts and passages do not substitute for the reading of entire texts, and StudySync® strongly recommends that teachers and students seek out and purchase the whole literary or informational work in order to experience it as the author intended. Links to online resellers are available in our digital library. In addition, complete works may be ordered through an authorized reseller by filling out and returning to StudySync® the order form enclosed in this workbook.

Teacher's Edition   **93**

Core Path	Access Path
	Advanced **Identify Evidence.** Ask Advanced students to complete the identifying evidence exercise on the Access 3 handout. Let students know that they'll use these answers to help participate in the discussion about the Model. Sample answers for this exercise are located at the end of the lesson plan online. **Approaching** **Guided Reading.** Have students complete the guided reading questions on the Access 4 handout as they read. Let them know that they'll use these answers to help participate in the discussion about the Model. Sample answers for this exercise are located at the end of the lesson plan online.
Discuss. After students read the Model text, use these questions to facilitate a whole-group discussion that helps students understand how to infer the theme of the passage: 1. What's the first step this Model uses to begin looking for the passage's theme? (identifying the narrator and point of view) 2. Why does the Model start by determining the passage's point of view instead of just diving into looking for the theme? (The theme isn't stated outright, as characters or plot are.) 3. What does the Model analyze first? (character motivations) What does the Model conclude about Grendel? (He is a conflicted narrator.) 4. How does the setting of *Grendel* contribute to its theme? (The mythical setting supports stark lines of difference in epic struggles between good and evil.) 5. Look back at the selection. What other descriptions of the setting would support the Model's conclusions about theme and setting? (Descriptions such as "darkness" and "torment" suggest a sense of social isolation.) 6. In pairs or small groups, have students summarize theme, using the definition and the Identification and Application sections.	

Core Path	Access Path
	Extend **Tech Infusion** **Apply.** Pair or group students and assign each group a strategy for analyzing a text to determine theme. Here are the elements to consider: • main character and experiences • conflicts • important events Have each group apply that strategy to *Grendel.* Allow each group time to walk the rest of the class through their thought process in applying that strategy to determine theme. Then as a class, discuss which strategy was most effective for this selection and why.

3. YOUR TURN

Core Path	Access Path
Assess and Explain. Have students answer the comprehension questions to test for understanding. Share the explanations for Parts A and B (located online) with your students.	
	Extend **Tech Infusion** **Create.** Have students write the next chapter of *Grendel,* continuing the same themes they identified in this lesson. Students should use their knowledge of *Beowulf* to guide their thinking and to keep the chapter consistent with the plot. Gather all new chapters and post them on a class blog or a shared Google Drive folder for the whole class to see. Have students anonymously determine which new chapters best continue the themes determined and follow the story as they know it from *Beowulf.*

Please note that excerpts and passages in the StudySync® library, workbooks, and PDFs are intended as touchstones to generate interest in an author's work. The excerpts and passages do not substitute for the reading of entire texts, and StudySync® strongly recommends that teachers and students seek out and purchase the whole literary or informational work in order to experience it as the author intended. Links to online resellers are available in our digital library. In addition, complete works may be ordered through an authorized reseller by filling out and returning to StudySync® the order form enclosed in this workbook.

Teacher's Edition   **95**

Media

OVERVIEW

Grendel is a reimagining of the classic epic *Beowulf*. This lesson plan provides follow-up questions and enrichments to help teachers guide students toward a usable, repeatable method for analyzing two interpretations of the same story.

OBJECTIVES

1. Learn the definition of media.
2. Practice using concrete strategies for analyzing two versions of the same story.
3. Participate effectively in a range of conversations and collaborations to express ideas and build upon the ideas of others.

ELA Common Core Standards:
Reading: Literature - RL.11-12.1, RL.11-12.7
Speaking & Listening - SL.11-12.1.A, SL.11-12.1.C, SL.11-12.2

RESOURCES

Venn Diagram for *Grendel* and *Beowulf*

Access 1 handout (Beginner)

Access 2 handout (Intermediate)

Access 3 handout (Advanced)

Access 4 handout (Approaching)

1. DEFINE

Core Path	Access Path
Watch. Watch the Concept Definition video on media with your students. Have your students write down the definition of "media" and consider the many different kinds of media, as well as the role of technology in the dissemination of information. Pause the video at these key moments to discuss the information with your students:	**English Learners All Levels & Approaching** **Match.** Have students complete the matching exercise on the Access 1, 2, 3, and 4 handouts as they watch the video. Answers are located at the end of the lesson plan online.
1. 0:30 – "Media" refers to methods of communication, but what do we mean when we say "the media"? What does this term encompass? From which forms of media do you get most of your news, entertainment, etc.?	
2. 0:36 – How has technology influenced the three basic forms of communication (spoken, written, visual)? Does all communication still fall into these three basic categories, or are there new forms that have been created?	
3. 0:43 – Think about modern forms of media, including Twitter, Facebook, Instagram, etc. How are language, form, and audience experience different for each? Discuss.	
Read and Discuss. After watching the Concept Definition video, have students read the definition of media. Either in small groups or as a whole class use these questions to engage students in a discussion about media.	**Beginner & Approaching** **Complete a Chart.** To prepare students to participate in the discussion, have them complete the chart on the Access 1 and 4 handouts as they read the definition. The correct answers are located at the end of the lesson plan online.
1. How long has the medium of the ancient story been popular, according to the definition? (throughout most of human history) What is different about written stories today? (the delivery methods that readers can choose from: print, ebook, audiobook)	**Intermediate & Advanced** **Discuss Prompts.** To help these students participate in the discussion, prompt them with questions that can be answered with a few words, such as: • What is the purpose of all kinds of media? (communication)
2. What different types of media have you consumed this week? In the past year? How did they express stories and ideas differently? (Answers will vary.)	• What was invented that changed media in the middle of the 19th century? (photography, the telegraph, and the telephone)

Core Path	Access Path
3. What form of media do you find most useful to use to communicate an idea? Explain your choice. (Answers will vary.) 4. How might different types of media change your view of a character or an interpretation of a story? (Answers will vary.)	• How are current methods of media, such as texting and emailing, similar to and different from 19th-century methods of communication? (Answers will vary.) **Beyond** **Discuss.** Challenge students to brainstorm the best medium to use to communicate certain information. For example, an invitation to a party, a book review, or a scientific paper. What method would they use to communicate these messages? Who would be the audience of each message?
	Extend **Brainstorm.** As a class, ask students to list reasons they might consume media, such as to learn something new, to catch up with friends, and so on. Write these reasons on the board. Then ask students which medium is best to accomplish each goal and why. Discuss the pros and cons students mention as they make claims for each medium.

2. MODEL

Core Path	Access Path
Read and Annotate. Have students independently read the Model section. As they read, ask students to use the annotation tool to: • highlight key points • ask questions • identify places where the Model applies the strategies laid out in the Identification and Application section on media	**Note:** During this portion of the lesson, instruction shifts from whole group to individual work. Use this time to work one-on-one or in small groups with Beginner, Intermediate, Advanced, and Approaching students.

Core Path	Access Path
	Beginner & Intermediate
	Coach the Reading. Work with these students (either individually or in small groups) to fill out the guided reading questions on the Access 1 and 2 handouts. Have Beginner students refer to the glossary on the Access 1 handout to help them determine the meaning of difficult words (note: provide the Access 1 handout glossary to Intermediate students if necessary). Let students know they'll use these answers to help participate in the discussion about the Model. Sample answers for this exercise are located at the end of the lesson plan online.
	Advanced
	Identify Evidence. Provide these students with the same instructions to read and annotate as on-grade-level and Beyond students. In addition, ask Advanced students to complete the identifying evidence exercise on the Access 3 handout. Let students know that they'll use these answers to help participate in the discussion about the Model. Sample answers for this exercise are located at the end of the lesson plan online.
	Approaching
	Guided Reading. Have students complete the guided reading questions on the Access 4 handout as they read. Let them know that they'll use these answers to help participate in the discussion about the Model. Sample answers for this exercise are located at the end of the lesson plan online.
Discuss. After students read the Model text, use these questions to facilitate a whole-group discussion that helps students understand how to analyze two versions of the same story:	
1. What distinction does the Model make between the two Grendels? (Gardner's Grendel is a more sympathetic portrayal.)	

Please note that excerpts and passages in the StudySync® library, workbooks, and PDFs are intended as touchstones to generate interest in an author's work. The excerpts and passages do not substitute for the reading of entire texts, and StudySync® strongly recommends that teachers and students seek out and purchase the whole literary or informational work in order to experience it as the author intended. Links to online resellers are available in our digital library. In addition, complete works may be ordered through an authorized reseller by filling out and returning to StudySync® the order form enclosed in this workbook.

Teacher's Edition   99

Core Path	Access Path
2. Why does the Model present the last paragraph of the novel excerpt? What does it illustrate? (It illustrates a fight scene from Grendel's perspective. Grendel comes off as an accidental killer, only protecting himself.) 3. How is Gardner's description of Grendel different from the one in the passage from *Beowulf*? (*Beowulf's* Grendel is an "accursed" monster who no one ever got close to. Gardner represents Grendel's point of view.)	
	Extend **Compare and Contrast.** Pair or group students. Have students review both *Beowulf* and *Grendel* to compare Grendel's attitude toward the men in *Grendel* with the men's attitude toward monsters in *Beowulf.* Have students complete a Venn diagram, citing textual evidence to support their conclusions. When students have finished their diagrams, discuss as a class. What do the similarities and differences between how the monsters and men see each other show us? What theme in *Grendel* does this comparison develop?

3. YOUR TURN

Core Path	Access Path
Assess and Explain. Have students answer the comprehension questions to test for understanding. Share the explanations for Parts A and B (located online) with your students.	

Core Path	Access Path
	Extend **Tech Infusion** **Record.** If students have trouble understanding poetry such as *Beowulf* quickly enough for a testing setting, encourage them to practice reading it aloud to learn how to understand the line breaks and punctuation. Have students read the passage in the Your Turn section aloud and record it on devices. Then have students play the recording back, rerecording if there are fluency errors. Students should listen to this recording to get a feeling of the poem's rhythm and syntax.
	Extend **Analyze Multiple Interpretations of a Story.** Find a movie version of *Beowulf* and have students watch the scene in which Grendel attacks the meadhall. Then have students write responses to the following questions: 1. How does the movie scene interpret the source text? 2. What do the similarities and differences suggest about the different time periods and cultures in which the source text and the movie were produced? 3. How does this movie scene compare to the presentation of the meadhall attack in the novel *Grendel*? 4. What do the similarities and differences suggest about the theme, or central idea, of each version?

Please note that excerpts and passages in the StudySync® library, workbooks, and PDFs are intended as touchstones to generate interest in an author's work. The excerpts and passages do not substitute for the reading of entire texts, and StudySync® strongly recommends that teachers and students seek out and purchase the whole literary or informational work in order to experience it as the author intended. Links to online resellers are available in our digital library. In addition, complete works may be ordered through an authorized reseller by filling out and returning to StudySync® the order form enclosed in this workbook.

Teacher's Edition   **101**

Core Path	Access Path
	Alternatively, you may have students form groups to write their own scene of the meadhall attack. They should use both excerpts from *Beowulf* and *Grendel* as their source material. Before they write, students should decide what interpretation of Grendel they plan to convey and provide a one-paragraph explanation about their interpretation of the character and how their interpretation reflects a theme. Then have student groups exchange scenes. Ask each student to write a response to these question:

1. How does the scene interpret the source material?

2. What are the similarities and differences between the scene and the source material?

3. What do these similarities and differences suggest about the choices that the writers made? How do these choices relate to the theme?

OVERVIEW

The novel *Grendel* by John Gardner retells the Beowulf legend from the point of view of the monster Grendel. The Close Read gives students the opportunity to focus on analyzing theme and comparing two interpretations of a story.

OBJECTIVES

1. Guide students through a close reading of a passage of literature.
2. Practice and apply concrete strategies for determining theme and comparing media in an excerpt from the novel *Grendel* (compared with an excerpt from the poem *Beowulf*).
3. Participate effectively in a range of conversations and collaborations to express ideas and build upon the ideas of others.
4. Prewrite, plan, and produce clear and coherent writing in response to a prompt.

ELA Common Core Standards: :
Reading: Literature - RL.11-12.1, RL.11-12.2, RL.11-12.4, RL.11-12.7
Writing - W.11-12.4, W.11-12.5, W.11-12.6, W.11-12.9.A, W.11-12.10
Speaking & Listening - SL.11-12.1.A, SL.11-12.1.B, SL.11-12.1.C, SL.11-12.1.D, SL.11-12.6
Language - L.11-12.4.A, L.11-12.4.C, L.11-12.4.D, L.11-12.5.A, L.11-12.6

RESOURCES

Grendel Vocabulary handout
Access 1 handout (Beginner)
Access 2 handout (Intermediate)
Access 3 handout (Advanced)
Access 4 handout (Approaching)

Please note that excerpts and passages in the StudySync® library, workbooks, and PDFs are intended as touchstones to generate interest in an author's work. The excerpts and passages do not substitute for the reading of entire texts, and StudySync® strongly recommends that teachers and students seek out and purchase the whole literary or informational work in order to experience it as the author intended. Links to online resellers are available in our digital library. In addition, complete works may be ordered through an authorized reseller by filling out and returning to StudySync® the order form enclosed in this workbook.

Teacher's Edition   103

1. INTRODUCTION

Core Path	Access Path
Define and Compare. Project the vocabulary words and definitions onto the board or provide students with handouts, so they can copy the vocabulary into their notebooks. Suggest that students consult general and specialized reference materials, both print and digital, to compare the precise meaning of a specific word with their initial vocabulary predictions from the First Read. Review words that students defined incorrectly to understand why they were unable to use context clues or other tools to develop usable definitions.	**Beginner & Intermediate** **Complete a Chart.** Have students complete the chart on the Access 1 and 2 handouts by writing the correct word for each of the definitions. **Advanced & Beyond** **Write in Journals.** Have students write a journal entry using all of their vocabulary words. Remind them to write sentences that communicate the meaning of the words they are using. **Approaching** **Graphic Organizer.** To support students in comparing their predictions with the correct meanings, have them complete the graphic organizer on the Access 4 handout to record the vocabulary words, their initial analysis, and the definitions. Then have them write sentences using the words.
Review. Have students complete the fill-in-the-blank vocabulary worksheet for this selection. Answers for the worksheet are listed online.	
	Extend **Tech Infusion** **Act and Record.** Break students into small groups, assign each group a vocabulary word, and ask them to design a short skit to demonstrate the meaning of the word for their peers. If possible, record skits and post them to a class YouTube Channel, so they can be reviewed.
	Extend **Create.** Write the word on one side of an index card and use a dictionary to verify the part of speech and definition on the other side of the card. Use these flashcards to review and memorize the words.

Core Path	Access Path
	Extend **Role Reversal.** Have students think about other stories that could be told from the perspective of an antagonist, antihero, or minor character in a well-known work. (Suggest the Joker from *Batman* as a starter.) Ask them to write a plot synopsis for the work told from a new perspective. Have them clarify how the new work would be different from the original.

2. READ

Core Path	Access Path
Model Close Reading. Project the text onto the board and model a close reading of the first three paragraphs using the annotation strategies mentioned below. While modeling annotation strategies, make notes that tie the text to the focus skill and demonstrate what students are looking for as they read. Some guidance for you as you annotate for your students: • As the Skills lesson that precedes this text makes clear, works of literature can have more than one theme, and themes are often revealed through the resolution of conflicts. Students should annotate words and phrases that convey the theme or themes most important to understanding *Grendel*. • In the next several paragraphs, remind students to consider how Gardner's descriptions in the novel *Grendel* compare and contrast with those in the poem *Beowulf*. • How do the differing genre forms of *Grendel* and *Beowulf* affect their presentations of the story? Annotate words and phrases that demonstrate particular features of *Grendel's* genre.	

Core Path	Access Path
• A significant difference between *Beowulf* and *Grendel* are the interpretations of the main character. Annotate words and phrases that show some of these key differences.	
Read and Annotate. Read the Skills Focus questions as a class, so your students know what they should pay close attention to as they read. Then have students read and annotate the excerpt. Ask students to use the annotation tool as they read to: 1. respond to the Skills Focus section 2. ask questions about which interpretation of the main character is most believable 3. make connections between the details of plot, setting, and characters in relation the story's themes 4. identify key differences in the two genres 5. note unfamiliar vocabulary and use context to uncover word meanings 6. capture their reaction to the ideas and examples in the text As they reread the text, remind students to use the comprehension strategy of visualizing that they learned in the First Read.	**Note:** While on-grade level students are reading and annotating, work one-on-one or in small groups with Beginner, Intermediate, Advanced, and Approaching students to support them as they read and annotate the text. **Beginner & Intermediate** **Summarize and Analyze the Text.** Work with these students to complete the sentence frames on the Access 1 and 2 handouts (note: the sentence frames for Intermediate students on the Access 2 handout contain fewer scaffolds). They will then use the completed sentence frames to help them analyze and annotate the text by completing the Skills Focus questions. Refer to the sample Skills Focus answers to help them complete the sentence frames and annotate the text. **Advanced** **Work in Pairs.** Pair these students with more proficient English speakers to work together on analyzing and annotating the text to complete the Skills Focus questions. If these students need more support, have them use the sentence frames on the Access 3 handout as they work with their more proficient peers.
	Approaching **Summarize the Text.** Have these students discuss and complete the text summary on the Access 4 handout and use their summary to help them analyze and annotate the text by completing the Skills Focus questions. Correct answers for the summary are at the end of the lesson plan online. Also refer to the sample Skills Focus answers to aid students with their annotations.

Core Path	Access Path
Discuss. After students have read the text, use the sample responses to the Skills Focus questions at the end of the lesson plan online to discuss the reading and the process of determining how themes build into a complex account. Make sure that students have acquired and accurately use academic-specific words and phrases related to the skill and demonstrate a command of formal English appropriate to the discussion. To help facilitate discussions, refer to Collaborative Discussions in the Speaking & Listening Handbook.	**Extend** **Pair and Share.** In small, heterogeneous groups or pairs, ask students to share and discuss their annotations with a focus on the themes and the differing points of view presented in *Beowulf* and in *Grendel*. You can provide students with these questions to guide their discussion: 1. Why does Hrothgar want to build a great meadhall? Are his motives selfless or selfish? Why? Cite specific textual evidence to support your statements. (Hrothgar wants to build the meadhall "as a sign of the glory and justice of Hrothgar's Danes." He wants to use the meadhall as a place to "sit and give treasures out." This makes him seem generous. However, he also sees the meadhall as a symbol of his own enduring legacy—"And so his sons would so after him, and his sons' sons, to the final generation"—which is selfish and vain.) 2. What words and phrases does Grendel use to describe Hrothgar and the Danes? How do these words and phrases compare to the ones he uses to describe himself? (At first, it seems as if Grendel uses positive terms to describe the Danes and negative ones to describe himself. For instance, Grendel mentions Hrothgar's "goodness" and describes the Danes as "smiling, peaceable" during the celebration. He describes himself as "crablike" and "cross." He mentions feeling grief at his own "bloodthirsty ways." However, after he is attacked in the meadhall, he compares the Danes to dogs and remarks that his is "shocked" by the fact that "they could kill [him].")

Core Path	Access Path
	3. Based on details in the text, who do you think is more monstrous: Grendel or the Danes? Why? How do the varying degrees of monstrousness help develop the themes of the text? Give evidence to support your opinion. (Answers will vary. Some may say the Danes are more monstrous because they have killed one of their own men and then attack Grendel. Others may say that Grendel is more monstrous because he cannot control his own strength and "bloodthirsty ways." The varying degrees of monstrousness help develop the ambiguity between good and evil by showing that everyone is the story shows both qualities.)
	Extend **Tech Infusion** **Record.** Use a voice recording app (Voice Memo on the iPhone or Smart Voice Recorder for Androids) or VoiceThread (https://voicethread.com) to capture each group's ideas.
	Extend **Create.** Ask students to create a collage using images and words taken from magazines that they believe reflect themes address the "outsider." Alternatively, they can use an online tool, like Glogster (http://edu.glogster.com) or Google Drawing, to create a virtual collage with a mix of text and media. Invite students to present their collages for the class explaining why they selected particular words and images.

3. WRITE

Core Path	Access Path
Prewrite and Plan. Read the prompt as a class and ask students to brainstorm about outsiders in art and literature; then have them loop back to the novel *Grendel*. Remind your students to look at the excerpt and their annotations to find textual evidence to support their ideas.	**Beginner & Intermediate** **Plan and Organize.** Have students complete the prewriting activity on the Access 1 and 2 handouts and then explain their ideas to a partner before they write. Explain to students that they need to choose details, examples, or quotes from the text that support their ideas and then explain how those details support their statements. For example, students could include the line, "I listened, huddled in the darkness, tormented, mistrustful. I knew them, had watched them ...," which shows that Grendel is an outsider, literally observing the Danes from the outside. **Approaching** **Plan and Organize.** Have students complete the prewriting activity on the Access 4 handout to organize their thoughts before they write.
	Extend **Organize.** Encourage students to complete a graphic organizer to organize their ideas before they type their responses.
	Extend **Tech Infusion** **Map.** Students can create concept maps online using https://bubbl.us. Google drawing can also be used to design a concept map.
Discuss. Project these instructions for the peer review onto the board and review them with your class, so they know what they are looking for when they begin to provide their classmates with feedback: • How has this essay helped you understand how and why Grendel is an outsider?	

Please note that excerpts and passages in the StudySync® library, workbooks, and PDFs are intended as touchstones to generate interest in an author's work. The excerpts and passages do not substitute for the reading of entire texts, and StudySync® strongly recommends that teachers and students seek out and purchase the whole literary or informational work in order to experience it as the author intended. Links to online resellers are available in our digital library. In addition, complete works may be ordered through an authorized reseller by filling out and returning to StudySync® the order form enclosed in this workbook.

Teacher's Edition   109

Core Path	Access Path
• Did the writer use his or her understanding of theme to explore what Gardner expresses about outsiders? • What sort of evidence did the writer use from the text to support his or her writing? • How well does the writer explain how that evidence supports his or her arguments? • Does the writer write using standard grammar and punctuation? Are there any weak spots? • What specific suggestions can you make to help the writer improve the response? • What thing(s) does this paper do especially well? After you've looked at the peer review instructions, review the rubric with students before they begin writing. Allow time for students briefly to pose and discuss any questions they may have about the peer review instructions and the rubric. Tell students how many peer reviews they will need to complete once they submit their writing.	
Write. Ask students to complete the writing assignment using textual evidence to support their answers. Once they have completed their writing, they should click "Submit."	
	Extend **Critique.** Project a writing sample on the board and ask the class to identify the elements of writing that are strong, as well as those that are weak or in need of improvement. Alternatively, you can put students in small groups and give them photocopies of a writing sample to collaboratively evaluate. After students have had an opportunity to evaluate student samples, work as a class to generate strategies students can use as they complete their peer reviews to ensure they are substantive.
Review. Once students complete their writing assignment, they should submit substantive feedback to two peers.	

OVERVIEW

The medieval chronicle *The Ecclesiastical History of the English People* by the Venerable Bede explains how Christianity came to England. The First Read gives students the opportunity to experience the text with limited context.

OBJECTIVES

1. Perform an initial reading of a text and demonstrate comprehension by responding to short analysis and inference questions with textual evidence.
2. Practice defining vocabulary words using context.
3. Participate effectively in a range of conversations and collaborations to express ideas and to build upon the ideas of others.
4. Practice acquiring and using academic vocabulary correctly.

ELA Common Core Standards: :
Reading: Informational - RI.11-12.1, RI.11-12.2, RI.11-12.4, RI.11-12.6, RI.11-12.10
Writing - W.11-12.7
Speaking & Listening - SL.11-12.1.A, SL.11-12.1.B, SL.11-12.1.C, SL.11-12.1.D, SL.11-12.2
Language - L.11-12.4.A, L.11-12.6

RESOURCES

Access 1 handout (Beginner)

Access 2 handout (Intermediate)

Access 3 handout (Advanced)

Access 4 handout (Approaching)

Please note that excerpts and passages in the StudySync® library, workbooks, and PDFs are intended as touchstones to generate interest in an author's work. The excerpts and passages do not substitute for the reading of entire texts, and StudySync® strongly recommends that teachers and students seek out and purchase the whole literary or informational work in order to experience it as the author intended. Links to online resellers are available in our digital library. In addition, complete works may be ordered through an authorized reseller by filling out and returning to StudySync® the order form enclosed in this workbook.

Teacher's Edition   **111**

ACCESS COMPLEX TEXT

This excerpt from *The Ecclesiastical History of the English People* explains how the Anglo-Saxon people of England came to embrace Christianity. The text explains how the king embraced the new religion after his counselors renounced their old religion. To help students understand this religious conversion, use the following ideas to provide scaffolded instruction for a first reading of the more complex features of this text:

- **Purpose** - As a monk, the Venerable Bede's purpose and point of view in the excerpt are explicitly biased toward Christianity. Students may struggle to understand why the Anglo-Saxons seem so willing to replace their religion without debate.

- **Organization** - Longer paragraphs contain multiple ideas, and dialogue is not broken out into individual paragraphs. While the excerpt is mostly arranged chronologically, it jumps from event to event within the same paragraphs, often without transitions.

- **Specific Vocabulary** - Archaic terms such as *henceforth, thanes, idols,* and *girded* may present a challenge to some readers.

- **Prior Knowledge** - Students may not know that England was not always a majority-Christian country. They may struggle to understand why the religious conversion of a king is a major event and why all his counselors need to convert as well.

1. INTRODUCTION

Core Path	Access Path
Read. Individually or as a class, read the introduction for *The Ecclesiastical History of the English People*. The introduction provides context for the excerpt taken from "The Anglo-Saxons Embrace Christianity." Explain to students that the text was translated because the author wrote the text in Latin, as was typical of the religious writing of the time.	**English Learners All Levels & Approaching** **Read and Listen.** Ask students to read and listen to the introduction for *The Ecclesiastical History of the English People*. Have them refer to the "Introduction Glossary" on their Access 1, 2, 3, and 4 handouts for definitions of key vocabulary terms. If there are unfamiliar words that are not included in their glossary, encourage students to check a dictionary or online reference tool, like http://dictionary.reference.com.

Core Path	Access Path
Build Background. Put students into small groups and have them find research and list answers to the following questions: 1. Who were the Anglo-Saxons, and how did they come to rule England? 2. What was the political structure of England in the 500s and 600s? 3. What was the role of the Christian church in early medieval England and Europe? When students have completed their lists, discuss their answers as a class.	**Beginner & Approaching** **Build Background.** Pair Beginner and Approaching students, and have them discuss what they learned about the Anglo-Saxon people from reading *Beowulf*. Ask students to think about these questions to guide their research of the Anglo-Saxons. 1. Why did the Anglo-Saxons come to England? 2. What were the rulers in the Anglo-Saxon society called? 3. What was the most important value of the Anglo-Saxons? **Intermediate & Advanced** **Build Background.** Pair Intermediate and Advanced students, and have them discuss what they learned about the Anglo-Saxon people from reading *Beowulf*. Ask students to think about these questions to guide their research of the Anglo-Saxons. 1. Who worked to convert the Anglo-Saxons to Christianity? 2. What kinds of beliefs did the Anglo-Saxons hold before becoming Christians? 3. How did Christianity affect the literary traditions of the Anglo-Saxons?
	Extend **Vocabulary.** Have students skim the text and locate the bolded vocabulary words. Ask students to provide definitions for words they know and look up unknown words in a print or online dictionary to verify their meanings. Ask: What do most of these terms have in common? What clues do these terms provide about the content of this chronicle? (The terms are mostly related to religion or religious places.)

Please note that excerpts and passages in the StudySync® library, workbooks, and PDFs are intended as touchstones to generate interest in an author's work. The excerpts and passages do not substitute for the reading of entire texts, and StudySync® strongly recommends that teachers and students seek out and purchase the whole literary or informational work in order to experience it as the author intended. Links to online resellers are available in our digital library. In addition, complete works may be ordered through an authorized reseller by filling out and returning to StudySync® the order form enclosed in this workbook.

Teacher's Edition   **113**

Core Path	Access Path
	Extend **Discuss.** The Introduction says that the early Christian church was highly influential in the development of English civilization. As a class, discuss the role religion should have in a government or a country. What effects should a leader's religion have on his/her country? How has the role of religion in government changed over history?

2. READ

Core Path	Access Path
Make Predictions about Vocabulary. There are five bold vocabulary words in the text. As students read the text, ask them to make predictions about what they think each bold vocabulary word means based on the context clues in the sentence. If you are in a low-tech classroom and students are reading from printed copies or a projected text, ask students to write meanings in their notes, so they can be easily referenced in class. If your students have access to technology, have them use the annotation tool to make their predictions. It might be helpful to model this for students before they begin reading. Select either one of the five vocabulary words or another term in the selection unfamiliar to students. Either using the board or projecting the actual text, focus in on the sentence that uses the word "consecrated":	**Note:** This exercise, which extends vocabulary instruction, should be completed when the class shifts from whole group instruction to individual work during the "Read and Annotate" exercise. **Beginner, Intermediate & Approaching Pair Practice.** 1. Pair students with more proficient readers. 2. Give them an additional sentence that contains a new vocabulary word. 3. Ask the students to complete a Think Aloud using the teacher-led Make Predictions about Vocabulary activity as a model, while the proficient student actively listens. 4. The student should use the context clues in the sentence to try to determine the meaning of the new vocabulary word.
• He said, however, that he would confer about this with his loyal chief men and his counsellors so that, if they agreed with him, they might all be consecrated together in the waters of life.	

Copyright © BookheadEd Learning, LLC

Core Path	Access Path
Model for the class how to use the overall structure and meaning of the sentence and the sentences around it, the word's position, and other clues to define the unfamiliar vocabulary word. In this case, point out these context clues: 1. Based on its word ending (*-ed*), I can tell that "consecrated" is a verb, and based on its location in the sentence (following the verb "be"), I can tell that it is a verb acting as an adjective, which makes it a participle. I know that participles are used like adjectives to describe nouns, so I reread the sentence looking for context clues. 2. The phrase "together in the waters of life" follows "consecrated" in the sentence. This phrase makes me think of baptism, which makes sense within the religious context of the text. 3. Based on its placement in the sentence and this context, I can infer that "consecrated" means "officially made or declared as sacred through a religious ceremony." Model using a print or online dictionary to check your definition.	5. After the student has completed the Think Aloud and made a prediction about the word's meaning, allow time for the proficient reader to add his/her own thoughts and clarify any points of confusion. 6. Once they've completed this Think Aloud, encourage them to use a dictionary to confirm the definition of the new vocabulary word. Have them refer to the "Text Glossary" on their Access 1, 2, and 4 handouts for definitions of key vocabulary terms in the text. Encourage them to add any additional vocabulary words or idioms they find in the text and look up definitions for those words and idioms online or in a dictionary.

Please note that excerpts and passages in the StudySync® library, workbooks, and PDFs are intended as touchstones to generate interest in an author's work. The excerpts and passages do not substitute for the reading of entire texts, and StudySync® strongly recommends that teachers and students seek out and purchase the whole literary or informational work in order to experience it as the author intended. Links to online resellers are available in our digital library. In addition, complete works may be ordered through an authorized reseller by filling out and returning to StudySync® the order form enclosed in this workbook.

Teacher's Edition   **115**

Core Path	Access Path
Model Reading Comprehension Strategy. Before students begin reading, model the reading comprehension strategy of summarizing by using this Think Aloud that talks students through the second paragraph of text. First explain to your students that summarizing is *a process of selecting, organizing, and synthesizing the most important elements in a text.* Model for students how summarizing will help them better comprehend the selection and will help drive their discussions. • After I read the text, I reread it with the goal of condensing what it says into a few sentences. • I try to separate the main idea from the less important details. Often the main idea is stated at the beginning of the text. In this case, the subtitle "The Anglo-Saxons Embrace Christianity" gives me a clue about the main idea of the passage. The main idea is that King Edwin and his advisors decided to become Christians. I scan the rest of the text to find the main reasons why. • In the second paragraph, I see that Paulinus convinces Edwin by pointing out that God has already helped the king succeed and by saying "If from henceforth you are willing to follow His will … He will also rescue you from the everlasting torments of the wicked and make you a partaker with Him of His eternal kingdom of heaven." Based on this I can begin my summary by saying Edwin converted to Christianity because he sought salvation. • I can continue my summary by adding sentences that state the main ideas of the remaining paragraphs.	**Note:** This exercise, which extends instruction around reading comprehension strategies, should be completed when the class shifts from whole group instruction to individual work during the "Read and Annotate" exercise. **Beginner, Intermediate & Approaching** **Apply Reading Comprehension Strategy.** 1. Have Beginner and Intermediate students listen to the audio version of the excerpt from *The Ecclesiastical History of the English People*. After each paragraph, stop the recording, and have students turn to a partner one proficiency level above or below them. Have pairs orally summarize the key information in the paragraph they just heard. 2. Once they have worked together to create an oral summary, have pairs write the summary down. Tell students that, at this point, they should make sure that they are only including the most important information, and that a summary of a paragraph should not be more than a few sentences. 3. Allow pairs time to share their summaries with another group. Did they include the same information? Which details could be removed from the summary without losing the most important ideas?

Core Path

Read and Annotate. Read and annotate the excerpt. Ask students to use the annotation tool as they read to:

1. use context clues to analyze and determine the meaning of the bolded vocabulary terms

2. ask questions about passages of the text that may be unclear or unresolved

3. identify key details, events, and people, and connections between them

4. note unfamiliar vocabulary

5. capture their reaction to the events in the text

Access Path

Beginner
Coach the Reading. While other students read, annotate, and discuss the text independently, work with Beginner students, listening to the audio of the text and pausing periodically or when any student has a question. Coach students in articulating their questions for the group and in highlighting and annotating the text. Have students use the Annotation Guide on the Access 1 handout to support them as they highlight and annotate the text.

For further support, ask questions about the text such as:

- Is there anything about the text that you don't understand?

- What reasons did Paulinus and Coifi give for abandoning the old religion?

- What surprised you about the events in the text? Why?

Intermediate
Listen to the Audio. Have these students listen to the audio of the text and use the Text Glossary on the Access 2 handout to help them with words or idioms that may be unfamiliar. If students need help with annotating the text, have them use the Annotation Guide on the Access 2 handout. After working with the Beginner students, you may wish to check this group's progress and provide support as needed.

Advanced
Pair with Proficient Peers. Have Advanced students work with English proficient peers to read, annotate, and discuss the text. Have students use the Annotation Guide in the Access 3 handout to support them as they highlight and annotate the text. Encourage them to listen to the audio of the text if needed.

Approaching
Use the Annotation Guide. Have students use the Annotation Guide on the Access 4 handout to support them as they highlight and annotate the text.

Please note that excerpts and passages in the StudySync® library, workbooks, and PDFs are intended as touchstones to generate interest in an author's work. The excerpts and passages do not substitute for the reading of entire texts, and StudySync® strongly recommends that teachers and students seek out and purchase the whole literary or informational work in order to experience it as the author intended. Links to online resellers are available in our digital library. In addition, complete works may be ordered through an authorized reseller by filling out and returning to StudySync® the order form enclosed in this workbook.

Teacher's Edition   117

Core Path	Access Path
Discuss. Have small groups or pairs of students discuss the questions and inferences they made while reading. To help facilitate discussions, refer to Collaborative Discussions in the Speaking & Listening Handbook.	**English Learners All Levels & Approaching** Use the extra time while on- and beyond-grade-level students are discussing their first reads of the text to work individually and in small groups with Approaching readers and English Learners as outlined above. Should those students complete their first reads quickly, integrate them into the on- and beyond-grade-level discussion groups. Otherwise, English Learners and Approaching readers will be given an opportunity to participate in text discussions with their peers later in the lesson.

Core Path

1. What finally led King Edwin to embrace Christianity? (Paulinus pointed out the gifts God already bestowed on the king and promised eternal life if the king converted.)

2. Why did King Edwin ask Paulinus to call his council? (He wanted to give them the opportunity to be consecrated with him.)

3. Who is Coifi, and what was his response to King Edwin's conversion? (Coifi is the chief of the priests. His response was to say that the old religion had never really offered any benefit to the king.)

4. What reasons do the king's councilmen give in favor of Christianity? (The councilmen suggest that, if this unknown religion can offer more than their present life, they should embrace it.)

5. Why does Coifi go to Goodmanham and what does he do there? What is symbolic about his choices? (He decides to destroy or "profane" the altars and shrines of other idols.)

6. How does summarizing the text help you determine the answers to these questions? (Answers may vary.)

Access Path

Tech Infusion
Beyond
Brainstorm. Pair students and ask them to predict how the "common people" might respond to the destruction of their shrines and the new religion. How would they expect people to react? Would Bede describe the response objectively? Students who have access to a collaborative tool such as Padlet (https://padlet.com/) may enjoy brainstorming in that medium.

Extend
Discuss. After students have read the text, ask them to make a list of or highlight words and phrases in the selection used to describe or define the Christian God. Use this list as a starting point to discuss how the Christian God is depicted.

1. What does this word choice reveal about the author?

2. What does it reveal about the role of Christianity in Anglo-Saxon England?

3. In what ways would you expect the descriptions to be similar or different if this text were written today?

Core Path	Access Path
	Extend **Connect to History.** Bede's text describes Coifi profaning the idols of the old religion. Destruction of idols, religious sites, and other symbols of religions has happened throughout history whenever a new religion or new political order wants to assert power. It is often called iconoclasm. Instruct small groups of students to research examples of iconoclasm in different parts of the world. You may wish to assign groups to continents or historical eras to ensure diverse topics. Have students take notes on the event to answer the following questions: 1. What was the political atmosphere before the iconoclasm took place? 2. What group committed the acts, and what was its stated reasoning? 3. What was the result of the iconoclasm? Did the offending group stay in power? Have each group present their findings. In the presentations, have students make direct connections to the text.
	Extend **Tech Infusion** **Create.** Have students use Google Drawing (https://docs.google.com/drawings) or Glogster (http://edu.glogster.com) to create posters of their researched historical event. If possible, direct students to include photographs or artwork done during or about the event.

3. THINK

Core Path	Access Path
Answer and Discuss. Have students complete the Think questions and then use the peer review instructions and rubric to complete two peer reviews. Refer to the sample answers at the end of the lesson plan online to discuss responses with your students.	**Beginner, Intermediate & Advanced** **Sentence Frames.** Have students use the sentence frames on the Access 1, 2, and 3 handouts to support their responses to the Think questions. **Approaching** **Find the Evidence.** Have students use Find the Evidence on the Access 4 handout to help them identify the evidence needed to answer the questions.
	Extend **Vocabulary.** Point out vocabulary words in the text that are used in a religious sense here but have secular multiple meanings: profane (profanity), icon, doctrine, confess, inspiration. Have students list the meaning of the words as used in the text and other meanings more often used today. Discuss how these words may have transitioned from a religious meaning to a common meaning today.

Copyright © BookheadEd Learning, LLC

OVERVIEW

Analyzing informational text elements is a key skill to help students in understanding nonfiction texts. This lesson plan provides follow-up questions and useful enrichments to help teachers guide students toward a usable, repeatable method for analyzing informational text elements.

OBJECTIVES

1. Learn the definition of informational text elements.
2. Practice using concrete strategies for analyzing informational text elements.
3. Participate effectively in a range of conversations and collaborations to express ideas and build upon the ideas of others.

ELA Common Core Standards:
Reading: Informational - RI.11-12.1, RI.11-12.3
Speaking & Listening - SL.11-12.1.A, SL.11-12.1.C, SL.11-12.2

RESOURCES

Access 1 handout (Beginner)

Access 2 handout (Intermediate)

Access 3 handout (Advanced)

Access 4 handout (Approaching)

Please note that excerpts and passages in the StudySync® library, workbooks, and PDFs are intended as touchstones to generate interest in an author's work. The excerpts and passages do not substitute for the reading of entire texts, and StudySync® strongly recommends that teachers and students seek out and purchase the whole literary or informational work in order to experience it as the author intended. Links to online resellers are available in our digital library. In addition, complete works may be ordered through an authorized reseller by filling out and returning to StudySync® the order form enclosed in this workbook.

Teacher's Edition   121

1. DEFINE

Core Path	Access Path
Watch. Watch the Concept Definition video on informational text elements with your students. Make sure your students are familiar with all the different elements shared in the video—including details, events, people, and ideas—as well as how these elements may interact over the course of a text. Pause the video at these key moments to discuss the information with your students:	**English Learners All Levels & Approaching** **Match.** Have students complete the matching exercise on the Access 1, 2, 3, and 4 handouts as they watch the video. Answers are located at the end of the lesson plan online.
1. 0:25 – Before writing things down, how do you think people remembered and communicated information? What challenges might have led to the development of a written language?	
2. 0:50 – Do you think there are any similarities between the elements of fictional and informational texts? What are they? Compare and contrast the two forms.	
3. 1:20 – For what reasons might an author "leave out" various events in an informational text? How does this challenge our understanding of certain facts or events? What can we do as readers to broaden our understanding of a topic or event?	
Read and Discuss. After watching the Concept Definition video, have students read the definition of informational text elements. Either in small groups or as a whole class use these questions to engage students in a discussion about informational text elements.	**Beginner & Approaching** **Fill in the Blanks.** To prepare students to participate in the discussion, have them complete the "Fill in the Blanks" activity on the Access 1 and 4 handouts as they read the definition. The correct answers are located at the end of the lesson plan online.
1. Which text elements are easiest to identify and understand? (main titles and chapter titles) Which are the hardest? (understanding how individuals, events, and ideas develop over the course of a text)	**Intermediate & Advanced** **Discuss Prompts.** To help these students participate in the discussion, prompt them with questions that can be answered with a few words, such as: • What text elements would you expect to see in a news article? (details or descriptions about an event, quotations from real people)

Copyright © BookheadEd Learning, LLC

Core Path	Access Path
2. What is an author's purpose? (presents readers with information) How might informational text elements support an author's purpose? (An author may blend facts and details about events, individuals, and ideas to support a particular point of view on a subject.) 3. What kind of order or sequencing do you feel is most helpful in informational texts? (Answers may vary.) 4. What strategies have you used when you're trying to present a complicated argument? (Answers may vary.)	• How is an advertisement different from an essay? (An advertisement is shorter and wants to make you buy or do something.) • How can you tell if a writer is giving straight facts or trying to persuade you of something? (Answers will vary.) **Beyond** **Discuss.** Have students look at the list of types of informational texts in the definition. In pairs, have students compare and contrast the elements they would expect to find in different types of text. For example, what would they expect to see in a diary that wouldn't appear in a biography, or vice versa? Students may want to use collaborative software like Google Docs to take notes and share their ideas.
	Extend **Brainstorm.** After watching the video, ask students to think of informational texts they've read recently and identify key individuals, events, and ideas. Compile a list of those elements on the board or in a shared Google Doc. Ask students how those elements worked together to form a central idea in the text.
	Extend **Explore Sequence.** Explore the idea of sequence in depth. In small groups, have students describe an event in a clear sequence using transitional words. If it helps, allow students to create a timeline of their event. Then have students revisit their descriptions and try rewriting them out of chronological order. Stress that the description still needs to make sense to a reader with no knowledge of the event. As a class, discuss the challenges they faced in their rewrites. Why is it difficult to describe an event out of chronological order? What elements can you use to help support your description? What choices can a writer make to create a clear sequence?

Please note that excerpts and passages in the StudySync® library, workbooks, and PDFs are intended as touchstones to generate interest in an author's work. The excerpts and passages do not substitute for the reading of entire texts, and StudySync® strongly recommends that teachers and students seek out and purchase the whole literary or informational work in order to experience it as the author intended. Links to online resellers are available in our digital library. In addition, complete works may be ordered through an authorized reseller by filling out and returning to StudySync® the order form enclosed in this workbook.

Teacher's Edition   **123**

2. MODEL

Core Path	Access Path
Watch. Ask students to take notes on the SkillsTV video on informational text elements in *The Ecclesiastical History of the English People* as you watch together. Remind students to listen for the way the students use academic vocabulary related to the definition of informational text elements during their discussion. Pause the video at these key moments to discuss the information with your students:	**Beginner, Intermediate & Approaching Analyze the Discussion.** Have students watch the video again and complete the chart on the Access 1, 2, and 4 handouts as they watch the video. Sample answers for this exercise are located at the end of the lesson plan online.
1. 0:35 – When is it necessary to look up a definition or reference in the text for understanding, as the students do here with "ecclesiastical"? When can the meaning of unfamiliar words be inferred?	**Advanced** **Journals.** Have students note in their journals the strategies the students in the SkillsTV video use to analyze informational text elements.
2. 1:38 – What does the group conclude about the order in which Bede presents information in the excerpt from *The Ecclesiastical History of the English People*? How well do the students use evidence to support this point of view?	
3. 3:40 – What other inferences can we draw from this text, based on individuals, events, or ideas? What can we infer about the author's attitude toward the subject?	
Read and Annotate. Have students independently read the Model section. As they read, ask students to use the annotation tool to: • highlight key points • ask questions • identify places where the Model applies the strategies laid out in the Identification and Application section on informational text elements	**Note:** During this portion of the lesson, instruction shifts from whole group to individual work. Use this time to work one-on-one or in small groups with Beginner, Intermediate, Advanced, and Approaching students.

Core Path	Access Path
	Beginner & Intermediate
	Coach the Reading. Work with these students (either individually or in small groups) to fill out the guided reading questions on the Access 1 and 2 handouts. Have Beginner students refer to the glossary on the Access 1 handout to help them determine the meaning of difficult words (note: provide the Access 1 handout glossary to Intermediate students if necessary). Let students know they'll use these answers to help participate in the discussion about the Model. Sample answers for this exercise are located at the end of the lesson plan online.
	Advanced
	Identify Evidence. Ask Advanced students to complete the identifying evidence exercise on the Access 3 handout. Let students know that they'll use these answers to help participate in the discussion about the Model. Sample answers for this exercise are located at the end of the lesson plan online.
	Approaching
	Guided Reading. Have students complete the guided reading questions on the Access 4 handout as they read. Let them know that they'll use these answers to help participate in the discussion about the Model. Sample answers for this exercise are located at the end of the lesson plan online.
Discuss. After students read the Model text, use these questions to facilitate a whole-group discussion that helps students understand how to analyze informational text elements in the selection:	

Discuss. After students read the Model text, use these questions to facilitate a whole-group discussion that helps students understand how to analyze informational text elements in the selection:

1. What does the Model look at first? (the title of the text and excerpt)

2. What does the author of the Model learn from the titles? (The titles provide contextual knowledge. This text is going to be about Christianity and Anglo-Saxons.)

Please note that excerpts and passages in the StudySync® library, workbooks, and PDFs are intended as touchstones to generate interest in an author's work. The excerpts and passages do not substitute for the reading of entire texts, and StudySync® strongly recommends that teachers and students seek out and purchase the whole literary or informational work in order to experience it as the author intended. Links to online resellers are available in our digital library. In addition, complete works may be ordered through an authorized reseller by filling out and returning to StudySync® the order form enclosed in this workbook.

Teacher's Edition   **125**

Core Path	Access Path
3. What does the Model identify in the first quoted paragraph? (key individuals, events, and ideas) 4. Why does the Model say Coifi's evidence for conversion is most convincing? (The "old" religion has failed him.) 5. What inference does the Model draw about the author of this text? What support does the Model have for this inference? (The author supports Christianity. The author is a monk who presents Christianity as the best choice.)	

3. YOUR TURN

Core Path	Access Path
Assess and Explain. Have students answer the comprehension questions to test for understanding. Share the explanations for Parts A and B (located online) with your students.	
	Extend **Practice.** If students struggle to identify the correct response to Part B, have them go back and reread the passage. Ask: Why does Coifi suggest abandoning the old gods? What argument does he make in favor of adopting Christianity? How does all this provide context for the meaning of *effectual*?

Copyright © BookheadEd Learning, LLC

SKILL:
Word Meaning

OVERVIEW

As students read more complex texts over the course of the year, knowing how to determine the meanings of unfamiliar words will be a key skill. This lesson plan provides follow-up questions and useful enrichments to help teachers guide students toward a usable, repeatable method for determining the meanings of unknown words.

OBJECTIVES

1. Learn the definition of word meaning.
2. Practice using concrete strategies for determining meanings of unknown words.
3. Participate effectively in a range of conversations and collaborations to express ideas and build upon the ideas of others.

ELA Common Core Standards:
Reading: Literature - RL.11-12.1, RL.11-12.4
Speaking & Listening - SL.11-12.1.A, SL.11-12.1.C, SL.11-12.2
Language: L.11-12.4.A, L.11-12.4.B

RESOURCES

Vocabulary handout: Context Clues

Access 1 handout (Beginner)

Access 2 handout (Intermediate)

Access 3 handout (Advanced)

Access 4 handout (Approaching)

Please note that excerpts and passages in the StudySync® library, workbooks, and PDFs are intended as touchstones to generate interest in an author's work. The excerpts and passages do not substitute for the reading of entire texts, and StudySync® strongly recommends that teachers and students seek out and purchase the whole literary or informational work in order to experience it as the author intended. Links to online resellers are available in our digital library. In addition, complete works may be ordered through an authorized reseller by filling out and returning to StudySync® the order form enclosed in this workbook.

Teacher's Edition 127

1. DEFINE

Core Path	Access Path
Read and Discuss. Have students read the definition of word meaning. Either in small groups or as a whole class use these questions to engage students in a discussion about word meaning. 1. What are context clues and how are they helpful in determining word meaning? (They are the words and phrases that surround a word providing clues to the meaning of that word.) 2. What are affixes? What is the difference between suffixes and prefixes? (An affix is a group of letters added to a word to change the meaning. Suffixes come at the end of words; prefixes come at the beginning.) 3. Read the example using the word "conceive." As a class, make a list of other verbs that can change meanings using the affixes *–able* and *-ly*. Then make a list of other affixes that could be used with those words.	**Beginner & Approaching** **Complete a Chart.** To prepare students to participate in the discussion, have them complete the chart on the Access 1 and 4 handouts as they read the definition. The correct answers are located at the end of the lesson plan online. **Intermediate & Advanced** **Discuss Prompts.** To help these students participate in the discussion, prompt them with questions that can be answered with a few words, such as: • Why is flowery language appropriate for a poem? (It helps readers think about a topic in a new way.) • Why is technical language appropriate for an informational text? (It is precise and teaches readers about a topic.) • Do you prefer to read flowery or technical language? Why? (Answers will vary.) **Beyond** **Discuss.** Have students brainstorm ways to talk about a topic, first using flowery language and then using technical language. For instance, they might describe a sunrise as "the Sun popping up to say hello" and as "the moment when the Sun appears over the eastern horizon." Have students discuss how the word choice in each instance affects their understanding of the topic and the effect each has on them as a reader.
	Extend **Tech Infusion** **Brainstorm.** As a class, have students use a print or an online dictionary to create a list of common affixes and their meanings. Save this list in a Google Doc or on a class server for students to refer to throughout the year.

Core Path	Access Path
	Extend **Practice.** If students struggle with using context clues to determine the meaning of unknown words, use the vocabulary handout on Context Clues for additional practice.

2. MODEL

Core Path	Access Path
Read and Annotate. Have students independently read the Model section. As they read, ask students to use the annotation tool to: • highlight key points • ask questions • identify places where the Model applies the strategies laid out in the Identification and Application section on word meaning	**Note:** During this portion of the lesson, instruction shifts from whole group to individual work. Use this time to work one-on-one or in small groups with Beginner, Intermediate, Advanced, and Approaching students. **Beginner & Intermediate** **Coach the Reading.** Work with these students (either individually or in small groups) to fill out the guided reading questions on the Access 1 and 2 handouts. Have Beginner students refer to the glossary on the Access 1 handout to help them determine the meaning of difficult words (note: provide the Access 1 handout glossary to Intermediate students if necessary). Let students know they'll use these answers to help participate in the discussion about the Model. Sample answers for this exercise are located at the end of the lesson plan online. **Advanced** **Identify Evidence.** Provide these students with the same instructions to read and annotate as on-grade-level and Beyond students. In addition, ask Advanced students to complete the identifying evidence exercise on the Access 3 handout. Let students know that they'll use these answers to help participate in the discussion about the Model. Sample answers for this exercise are located at the end of the lesson plan online.

Copyright © BookheadEd Learning, LLC

Core Path	Access Path
	Approaching **Guided Reading.** Have students complete the guided reading questions on the Access 4 handout as they read. Let them know that they'll use these answers to help participate in the discussion about the Model. Sample answers for this exercise are located at the end of the lesson plan online.
Discuss. After students read the Model text, use these questions to facilitate a whole-group discussion that helps students understand how to determine the meanings of unknown words: 1. What's the first step this Model uses to analyze word meaning? (looks at context to determine part of speech and meaning) 2. What's the second step this Model uses to analyze word meaning? What does the "mock" chart illustrate and how does this example help you as a reader? (The second step is to analyze word parts to determine meaning and part of speech. The chart shows how one word can use affixes to have different meanings and parts of speech.) 3. What's the final step this Model uses to analyze word meaning in *The Ecclesiastical History of the English People*? How do word parts help a reader with unknown words? (studies Anglo-Saxon word origins to determine the meaning of unfamiliar words)	
	Extend **Create a List.** In small groups, have students create a list of multiple-meaning words and their meanings, and have students write example sentences for each meaning. As they work, students should make flashcards with the words on one side and definitions and example sentences on the other. Students can use the flashcards to quiz each other on the multiple-meaning words, or use them as reference during writing assignments.

Copyright © BookheadEd Learning, LLC

3. YOUR TURN

Core Path	Access Path
Assess and Explain. Have students answer the comprehension questions to test for understanding. Share the explanations for Parts A and B (located online) with your students.	
	Extend **Share and Discuss.** Have students come up with other usages of the base word *yield.* Make a list on the board. Challenge students to use affixes to make as many variations as possible. Then have students go back to the text and find other base words they can expand on.
	Extend **Tech Infusion** **Compile.** As a class compile a list of "Vocabulary Tips" throughout the school year. Students can keep this list in their notebooks, or the class can save a master list as a Google document to edit and reference for strategies to determining the meanings of vocabulary words.

The Ecclesiastical History of the English People

OVERVIEW

The chronicle *The Ecclesiastical History of the English People* by the Venerable Bede explains how the Anglo-Saxons in England came to convert to Christianity. The Close Read gives students the opportunity to analyze informational text elements.

OBJECTIVES

1. Complete a close reading of a nonfiction chronicle.
2. Practice and apply concrete strategies for analyzing informational text elements in an excerpt from *The Ecclesiastical History of the English People*.
3. Participate effectively in a range of conversations and collaborations to express ideas and build upon the ideas of others.
4. Prewrite, plan, and produce clear and coherent writing in response to a prompt.

ELA Common Core Standards: :
Reading: Informational - RI.11-12.1, RI.11-12.3, RI.11-12.4
Writing - W.11-12.4, W.11-12.5, W.11-12.6, W.11-12.9.B, W.11-12.10
Speaking & Listening - SL.11-12.1.A, SL.11-12.1.B, SL.11-12.1.C, SL.11-12.1.D, SL.11-12.6
Language - L.11-12.4.A, L.11-12.4.B, L.11-12.4.C, L.11-12.4.D, L.11-12.6

RESOURCES

The Ecclesiastical History of the English People Vocabulary handout
The Ecclesiastical History of the English People Sequence Chart
Access 1 handout (Beginner)
Access 2 handout (Intermediate)
Access 3 handout (Advanced)
Access 4 handout (Approaching)

1. INTRODUCTION

Core Path	Access Path
Define and Compare. Project the vocabulary words and definitions onto the board or provide students with handouts, so they can copy the vocabulary into their notebooks. Suggest that students consult general and specialized reference materials, both print and digital, to compare the precise meaning of a specific word with their initial vocabulary predictions from the First Read. Review words that students defined incorrectly to understand why they were unable to use context clues or other tools to develop usable definitions.	**Beginner & Intermediate** **Complete a Chart.** Have students complete the chart on the Access 1 and 2 handouts by writing the correct word for each of the definitions. **Advanced & Beyond** **Write in Journals.** Have students write a journal entry using all of their vocabulary words. Remind them to write sentences that communicate the meaning of the words they are using. **Approaching** **Graphic Organizer.** To support students in comparing their predictions with the correct meanings, have them complete the graphic organizer on the Access 4 handout to record the vocabulary words, their initial analysis, and the definitions. Then have them write sentences using the words.
Review. Have students complete the fill-in-the-blank vocabulary worksheet for this selection. Answers for the worksheet are listed online.	
	Extend **Tech Infusion** **Create.** Create artwork to visually represent the vocabulary words using an iPad (Tayasui Sketches App) or Android art (SketchBook Express App).
	Extend **Tech Infusion** **Review.** Create a vocabulary review quiz using Kahoot (www.getkahoot.com). Include questions about definitions and parts of speech. Have students respond to the questions using class laptops, tablets, or mobile devices.

Core Path	Access Path
	Extend **Connect.** In the text, King Edwin tells Paulinus that he needs to discuss his conversion with his council before being baptized to convince them to convert as well. As a class, discuss the following prompt: Think about a big decision or change you've made in your life. Did you have to make that change alone? Were you able to get family and friends to support you or change with you? Discuss your experiences and how they relate to the text.

2. READ

Core Path	Access Path
Model Close Reading. Project the text onto the board and model a close reading of the first five paragraphs using the annotation strategies mentioned below. While modeling annotation strategies, make notes that tie the text to the focus skill and demonstrate what students are looking for as they read. Some guidance for you as you annotate for your students: • Point out that a good place to start when reading a chronicle is identifying the key people in the history. The author introduces two key people in the first paragraph: King Edwin and Paulinus, a bishop. Have students identify and annotate any additional characters that appear in the first four paragraphs. • Explain to the students that the first paragraph also introduces the King's conflict, a main idea in the text: "earnestly debating within himself what he ought to do and what religion he should follow."	

Core Path	Access Path
• In the second paragraph, show students the point where Paulinus tells King Edwin that the Christian god is responsible for Edwin's successes, and threatens him with "everlasting torments" if he doesn't convert. • The third paragraph continues the same sequence of events using time order words and phrases such as "When the king had heard his words." • Model finding and annotating additional words and phrases that indicate time order in the fourth and fifth paragraphs.	

Read and Annotate. Read the Skills Focus questions as a class, so your students know what they should pay close attention to as they read. Then have students read and annotate the excerpt. Ask students to use the annotation tool as they read to: 1. respond to the Skills Focus section 2. ask questions to identify key people, ideas, and events 3. make connections between the sequence of the text and at least two main ideas and how they interact and build on one another 4. note unfamiliar vocabulary 5. capture their reaction to specific ideas and examples in the text As they reread the text, remind students to use the comprehension strategy of summarizing that they learned in the First Read.	**Note:** While on-grade-level students are reading and annotating, work one-on-one or in small groups with Beginner, Intermediate, Advanced, and Approaching students to support them as they read and annotate the text. **Beginner & Intermediate** **Summarize and Analyze the Text.** Work with these students to complete the sentence frames on the Access 1 and 2 handouts (note: the sentence frames for Intermediate students on the Access 2 handout contain fewer scaffolds). They will then use the completed sentence frames to help them analyze and annotate the text by completing the Skills Focus questions. Refer to the sample Skills Focus answers to help them complete the sentence frames and annotate the text. **Advanced** **Work in Pairs.** Pair these students with more proficient English speakers to work together on analyzing and annotating the text to complete the Skills Focus questions. If these students need more support, have them use the sentence frames on the Access 3 handout as they work with their more proficient peers.

Core Path	Access Path
	Approaching **Summarize the Text.** Have these students discuss and complete the text summary on the Access 4 handout and use their summary to help them analyze and annotate the text by completing the Skills Focus questions. Correct answers for the summary are at the end of the lesson plan online. Also refer to the sample Skills Focus answers to aid students with their annotations.
Discuss. After students have read the text, use the sample responses to the Skills Focus questions at the end of the lesson plan online to discuss the reading and the process of analyzing informational text elements. Make sure that students have acquired and accurately use academic-specific words and phrases related to the skill and demonstrate a command of formal English appropriate to the discussion. For instance, point out to students that question 3 uses the academic word "analogy." Tell students that an **analogy** is similar to a metaphor and simile (all are figures of speech that compare two seemingly unlike things); however, they differ in that an analogy is more complex and can be used to support an argument. Explain to students that question 3 is asking them to describe the analogy in the text and explain how it supports the argument in favor of adopting Christianity. To help facilitate discussions, refer to Collaborative Discussions in the Speaking & Listening Handbook.	**Extend** **Pair and Share.** In small, heterogeneous groups or pairs, ask students to share and discuss their annotations with a focus on the informational text elements presented in the selection. You can provide students with these questions to guide their discussion: 1. What is the relationship between King Edwin and his counsellors? Cite specific textual evidence to support your statements. (King Edwin respects his counsellor's opinions and wants them to be saved with him. He wanted to encourage them to convert so "they might all be consecrated together in the waters of life." It's not until after his counsellors accept Christianity that he officially converts, even though he had decided to do so based on Paulinus's convincing.) 2. The profaning of the idols is a key event in the text. Why does the author choose to end the selection with it? Cite specific textual evidence to support your answer. (Student responses will vary but may include that the author wanted to use the profaning of the idols as a dramatic climax to the scene. Students may say the story of a king changing religions is not interesting or effective without the final destruction of the idols.)

Core Path	Access Path
	3. How is the writer's point of view on Christianity expressed throughout the text? How does his point of view affect your understanding or enjoyment of the text? (Bede is biased toward Christianity, using words such as "vain superstitions" to describe the old religion. Students may say they do not trust Bede's account of events because he is biased toward one side of the story.)
	Extend **Vocabulary.** Ask students to discuss with partners any words from the text they did not understand, in addition to the bolded vocabulary terms. Have students work together to form a working definition using context. Then have pairs check their definitions in a print or online dictionary.
	Extend **Write.** Provide students with the following prompt: Imagine you were one of the common people who saw Coifi and thought he was "mad." Describe the scene in the last paragraph of the text from your perspective. Remember that the common people were still following the old religion at that moment. If resources are available, allow students to blog or tweet about the events using the persona of a common person at the time of the historical chronicle.

3. WRITE

Core Path	Access Path
Prewrite and Plan. Read the prompt as a class and ask students to brainstorm about the informational text elements in *The Ecclesiastical History of the English People*. Remind students to look at the excerpt and their annotations to find textual evidence to support their ideas.	**Beginner & Intermediate** **Plan and Organize.** Have students complete the prewriting activity on the Access 1 and 2 handouts and then explain their ideas to a partner before they write. Explain to students that they need to choose details, examples, or quotes from the text that support their ideas and then explain how those details support their statements. For example, students could include the first line, "King Edwin hesitated to accept the word of God which Paulinus preached ...," which introduces two key individuals: King Edwin and Paulinus. **Approaching** **Plan and Organize.** Have students complete the prewriting activity on the Access 4 handout to organize their thoughts before they write.
	Extend **Tech Infusion** **Map.** Students can create outlines or sequence charts online using QuickLyst (https://quicklyst.appspot.com/) or MindMeiser (http://www.mindmeister.com/).
Discuss. Project these instructions for the peer review onto the board and review them with your class, so they know what they are looking for when they begin to provide their classmates with feedback: • Did the writer clearly describe the interactions and developments of the individuals, events, and ideas in the text? • How did the writer explain what these interactions and developments reveal about the Anglo-Saxons and the history of Christianity? • What sort of evidence did the writer use from the text to support his or her writing?	

Copyright © BookheadEd Learning, LLC

Core Path	Access Path
• How well does the writer explain how that evidence supports his or her arguments? • Does the writer write using standard grammar and punctuation? Are there any weak spots? • What specific suggestions can you make to help the writer improve the response? • What thing(s) does this paper do especially well? After you've looked at the peer review instructions, review the rubric with students before they begin writing. Allow time for students briefly to pose and discuss any questions they may have about the peer review instructions and the rubric. Tell students how many peer reviews they will need to complete once they submit their writing.	
Write. Ask students to complete the writing assignment, using textual evidence to support their answers. Once they have completed their writing, they should click "Submit."	
	Extend **Critique.** Remind students that they should always use the literary present tense when writing literary analysis. For example: After much debate, King Edwin *embraces* Christianity. As they review, tell students to make sure their peers use this tense correctly and consistently throughout their essays.
Review. Once students complete their writing assignment, they should submit substantive feedback to two peers. Students should use their peers' feedback to improve their writing.	

BLAST:
American Idols

OVERVIEW

To develop an understanding of the word *idol*, students will explore hero worship of celebrities in contemporary culture. Students will explore research links that connect them to information about modern celebrity culture and the role of the Internet and social media.

OBJECTIVES

1. Explore how the meaning of "idol" has changed over time and analyze celebrity culture in the United States.
2. Research using the hyperlinks to learn more about celebrities in contemporary culture.

ELA Common Core Standards:
Reading: Informational Text - RI.11-12.1
Writing - W.11-12.1.A, W.11-12.3, W.11-12.5, W.11-12.6
Speaking & Listening - SL.11-12.1.A, SL.11-12.1.C, SL.11-12.1.D

RESOURCES

Blast Response - Student Model

Access 1 handout (Beginner)

Access 2 handout (Intermediate)

Access 4 handout (Approaching)

TITLE/DRIVING QUESTION

Core Path	Access Path
Discuss. As a class, read aloud the title and driving question for this Blast. These correspond to the title/driving question for the unit as a whole. Ask students what they think about celebrity culture. Do they think people should treat celebrities as idols? Remind students that they will be returning to this question for their formal entries after they've written a draft and read and discussed the Background.	**English Learners All Levels** **Discuss a Visual.** Have students view a photograph of a long line of people waiting to see a performer, such as the one at: http://tinyurl.com/q99jws3. Discuss how the picture represents a huge commitment to seeing someone famous, prompting students with questions such as: • What is happening in this photo? • Why do you think these people would wait in such a line overnight? • Do you think it's worth the time to wait to see a singer or band you love? How long would you wait? • What are some other events that might cause dedicated people to line up like this?
Draft. In their notebooks or on scrap paper, have students draft their initial responses to the driving question. This will provide them with a baseline response that they will update and revise as they gain more information about the topic in the Background and Research Links sections of the assignment. You may wish to review with students the Blast Response - Student Model for guidance on how to construct an effective Blast. The Blast review criteria are as follows: 1. Response does not address the driving question or is unclear; language is vague. 2. Response insufficiently addresses the driving question or is mostly unclear; language is mostly vague. 3. Response somewhat addresses the driving question or is somewhat unclear; language is somewhat vague. 4. Response adequately addresses the driving question and is clear; language is mostly precise. 5. Response fully addresses the driving question and is clear; language is precise.	**Beginner & Intermediate** **Draft with Sentence Frame.** When drafting their initial response to the driving question, have students refer to this Blast sentence frame on their Access 1 and 2 handouts: • Yes/No, it's right/not right to hold people to the standard of *idol* because _____. Point out these two key features of the sentence frame: 1. The introductory clause "Yes/No, it's right/not right to hold people to the standard of *idol*" borrows language directly from the Blast driving question to provide a response. Make sure students understand they can either use the frame as "Yes, it's right" or "No, it's not right." 2. Point out that the use of the word *because* cues them to provide a reason for their opinion.

BACKGROUND

Core Path	Access Path
Read. Have students read the Blast background to provide context for the driving question.	**Beginner & Intermediate** **Read with Support.** Have students read the Blast background to provide context for the driving question. When they encounter unfamiliar words or phrases, have students refer to the glossary on their Access 1 and 2 handouts. If there are unfamiliar words that are not included in their glossary, encourage students to check a dictionary or online reference tool, like http://dictionary.reference.com. **Approaching** **Read and Summarize.** Have students read the Blast background to provide context for the driving question. As they read, ask students to complete the fill-in-the-blank summary of the background provided on their Access 4 handout. When they encounter unfamiliar words or phrases, have students refer to the glossary on their Access 4 handout.
Discuss. Pair students and have them discuss the following questions: 1. How does the Venerable Bede use the word *idol* in *The Ecclesiastical History of the English People*? (to mean a religious object worshipped as a god) 2. What other meanings of *idol* does the text explain? (*Idol* can also mean "a greatly admired person who is not criticized.") 3. What perspectives on celebrity worship does the text present? (It may be dangerous, or it may be a healthy part of teen culture.) 4. What does the example of John Hinckley, Jr., illustrate? (an extreme result of celebrity worship)	**Beginner** **Discuss.** Pair Beginner with Advanced (or Beyond) students and have them use the dialogue starter on their Access 1 handout to discuss the topic. Advise them to return to the dialogue and switch roles if they get stuck. **Intermediate** **Discuss.** Pair Intermediate with Advanced (or Beyond) students and have them use the dialogue starter on their Access 2 handout to discuss the topic. Advise them to return to the dialogue and switch roles if they get stuck. If their conversation is progressing smoothly, encourage them to continue the discussion beyond the dialogue starter sheet. They can expand their conversations to discuss positive or negative things that can come out of idolizing someone.

Copyright © BookheadEd Learning, LLC

Core Path	Access Path
Brainstorm. Remind students about the driving question for this Blast and the driving question for this unit: Is it right to hold people to the standard of idol? Ask students to imagine that they are a celebrity. They can choose any path they wish: actor, pop star, athlete, entrepreneur. Have students write a diary entry reflecting on how they are portrayed in the media. Students should think of an event that triggers the entry, such as an awards show or a bad movie review. In their diary entries, students should explore their ideas of fame. How do they feel about students looking up to them? What is good about all the media attention? What is bad? What would they change about American celebrity culture, if anything?	

RESEARCH LINKS

Core Path	Access Path
Examine and Explore. Use these questions to guide students' exploration of the research links: 1. Explore "The Culture of Celebrity." What connection does the writer make between Greek gods and modern-day celebrities? (They are outlets for our imagination. They are surrounded in myth. The Greek gods were seen as having divine powers, and we assign divine powers to celebrities.) According to the writer, what's the value of heroes? (They lift our vision above the everyday.) What is the danger of having access to too much information about celebrities? (We learn about the bad things in their lives, and so they are taken down a notch, and we don't have true idols to look up to.) What's the difference between a hero and a celebrity, according to Boorstin? (The hero is well known for achievements, whereas the celebrity is just well known.)	

Core Path	Access Path
2. Explore "Is it Safe to Worship Athletes?" What are some potential negative effects of worshiping athletes, according to Hyman and Sierra? (It can damage fans' psychological and emotional well-being. It can cause fans to lose touch with reality and their own identity and start to feel depressed.) What do Hyman and Sierra say is the solution? (They want sports franchises to stop marketing their players as heroes.)	

	Extend
	Research, Discuss, and Present.
	1. Assign each group one link to explore in depth.
	2. Ask them to discuss the information:
	   a. What are the key points?
	   b. What inferences did you make as you read?
	   c. What did you learn about this "big idea" from reading this research?
	   d. How did this help you to better understand the topic?
	   e. What questions does your group have after exploring this link?
	3. Allow students time to informally present what they learned.

	Extend **Tech Infusion** **Share.** As students explore the links, allow them to gather images that represent celebrity culture in the United States. Have groups post these photos to a Padlet (http://padlet.com/) or PicMonkey collage (http://www.picmonkey.com/).

QUIKPOLL

Core Path	Access Path
Participate. Answer the poll question. Have students use information from the background and research links to explain their answers.	

NUMBER CRUNCH

Core Path	Access Path
Predict, Discuss, and Click. Before students click on the number, break them into pairs and have them make predictions about what they think the number is related to. After they've clicked the number, ask students if they are surprised by the revealed information.	

CREATE YOUR BLAST

Core Path	Access Path
Blast. Ask students to write their Blast response in 140 characters or less.	**Beginner** **Blast with Support.** Have students refer back to the sentence frame on their Access 1 handout that they used to create their original Blast draft. Ask them to use this frame to write and enter their final Blast. **Intermediate** **Blast with Support.** Have students attempt to draft their Blast without the sentence frame on their Access 2 handout. If students struggle to compose their Blast draft without the sentence frame, remind them to reference it for support.

Please note that excerpts and passages in the StudySync® library, workbooks, and PDFs are intended as touchstones to generate interest in an author's work. The excerpts and passages do not substitute for the reading of entire texts, and StudySync® strongly recommends that teachers and students seek out and purchase the whole literary or informational work in order to experience it as the author intended. Links to online resellers are available in our digital library. In addition, complete works may be ordered through an authorized reseller by filling out and returning to StudySync® the order form enclosed in this workbook.

Teacher's Edition 145

Core Path	Access Path
	Beyond **Write a Claim.** Ask students to use their answer to the poll question to write a strong claim that could be used as the foundation for a piece of argumentative writing. Once students have written their claims, ask them to read the claims to a small group of their peers. This activity will provide them practice writing claims, as well as expose them to claims written by their peers.
Review. After students have completed their own Blasts, ask them to review the Blasts of their peers and provide feedback. To help students respond effectively, read and discuss the Blast review criteria with them before they review one another's Blasts.	
	Extend **Discuss.** As a class or in groups, identify a few strong Blasts and discuss what made those responses so powerful. As a group, analyze and discuss what characteristics make a Blast interesting or effective.
	Extend **Revise.** Resend a second version of this Blast assignment to your students and have them submit revised versions of their original Blasts. Do the same responses make the Top Ten? How have the answers improved from the first submissions?

OVERVIEW

The Canterbury Tales by Geoffrey Chaucer includes part of the Prologue, which gives details about a pilgrimage during which travelers tell tales. Also included is one of the tales, told by a character called the Wife of Bath. The First Read gives students the opportunity to experience the text with limited context.

OBJECTIVES

1. Perform an initial reading of a text and demonstrate comprehension by responding to short analysis and inference questions with textual evidence.
2. Practice defining vocabulary words using context.
3. Participate effectively in a range of conversations and collaborations to express ideas and build upon the ideas of others.

ELA Common Core Standards:

Reading: Literature - RL.11-12.1, RL.11-12.2, RL.11-12.4, RL.11-12.10

Speaking & Listening - SL.11-12.1.A, SL.11-12.1.B, SL.11-12.1.C, SL.11-12.1.D, SL.11-12.2, SL.11-12.3, SL.11-12.6

Language - L.11-12.4.A, L.11-12.4.C, L.11-12.4.D, L.11-12.6

RESOURCES

Access 1 handout (Beginner)

Access 2 handout (Intermediate)

Access 3 handout (Advanced)

Access 4 handout (Approaching)

ACCESS COMPLEX TEXT

These two excerpts from *The Canterbury Tales* are taken from the beginning of the general prologue and from "The Wife of Bath's Tale." The Prologue outlines the historical context for *The Canterbury Tales*, including the pilgrimage on which the Wife of Bath and the other pilgrims are going. "The Wife of Bath's Tale" tells the story of a disgraced knight and the lesson he learns in order to save his life. To help students understand the structure of *The Canterbury Tales* as well as the plot and characters of "The Wife of Bath's Tale," use the following ideas to provide scaffolded instruction for a first reading of the more complex features of this text:

- **Organization** - From the beginning of the Prologue alone, students might not understand that *The Canterbury Tales* are a collection of stories intended as a storytelling contest among the pilgrims on their way to Canterbury. "The Wife of Bath's Tale" is just one of many stories in this collection.

- **Genre** - *The Canterbury Tales* is told mostly in verse, as is evident by these excerpts. The poetic structure of the text may pose a challenge to struggling readers due to its syntax, form, and word choice.

- **Specific Vocabulary** - Archaic terms, such as *holt and heath, hostelry,* and *anon,* may present a challenge to some readers.

- **Prior Knowledge** - For the Prologue, students will need to be familiar with certain facets of life during the Middle Ages, including the concept of religious pilgrimages. For "The Wife of Bath's Tale," students might benefit from a short overview of King Arthur and Arthurian tradition.

Copyright © BookheadEd Learning, LLC

1. INTRODUCTION

Core Path	Access Path
Watch. As a class, watch the video preview of *The Canterbury Tales*.	**English Learners All Levels** **Fill in the Blanks.** Ask students to use their Access 1, 2, and 3 handouts to fill in the blanks of the transcript for the preview's voiceover as they watch the preview along with their classmates. Answers are located at the end of the lesson plan online.

Core Path	Access Path
Read. Individually or as a class, read the introduction for *The Canterbury Tales*. The introduction provides context for the excerpt taken from the Prologue as well as "The Wife of Bath's Tale."	**English Learners All Levels & Approaching** **Read and Listen.** Ask students to read and listen to the introduction for *The Canterbury Tales*. Have them refer to the "Introduction Glossary" on their Access 1, 2, 3, and 4 handouts for definitions of key vocabulary terms. If there are unfamiliar words that are not included in their glossary, encourage students to check a dictionary or online reference tool, like http://dictionary.reference.com.
	Extend **Make Predictions.** Based on the introduction, ask students to make predictions about the central ideas they would expect to encounter in this text.
	Extend **Discuss the Introduction.** After reading the introduction, use the information provided to facilitate a prereading discussion to get students thinking about the events and themes in *The Canterbury Tales*. 1. If you were in a storytelling contest, what topic would you write about? What genre would your story be? Why do you think this type of story would appeal to your audience? 2. How would you feel if you had to answer a question correctly or face death? 3. If you could save a person from death and receive any favor in return, what would you ask for?

Core Path	Access Path
Build Background. In pairs or small groups, ask students to use devices to research different aspects of the Middle Ages in Europe. Assign each group a topic to investigate, and ask them to create a list of key information for each topic: • Knights and Chivalry • The Catholic Church • Medieval Society • England in the 1300s • Code of Chivalry • Gender Roles If you are in a low-tech classroom, you can provide photocopied material about the Middle Ages for students to read and discuss. After students have researched their topics, discuss their findings as a class.	**Beginner & Intermediate** **Complete and Discuss the Chart.** Pair students and have them research the history of Canterbury Cathedral. Point them to a reliable website, such as the ones at http://tinyurl.com/mjxdw2m and http://tinyurl.com/aw7ygtu. Assist students as needed as they fill out their research charts on the Access 1 and 2 handouts. If time remains, encourage them to come up with their own research questions and add them to the chart. **Advanced & Approaching** **Complete and Discuss the Chart.** Pair students and have them research the history of Canterbury Cathedral. Assist students as needed as they find reliable websites and fill out their research charts on the Access 3 and 4 handouts. Some research questions have been provided for them, and students should use these as a guide to coming up with their own questions.
	Extend **Tech Infusion** **Research.** Allow students to use computers or handheld devices to surf the Web or look up information about the topic. Emphasize that they should focus on developing general information about the topic rather than a handful of specific details.
	Extend **Analyze and Discuss a Quotation** "Everything has beauty, but not everyone sees it." (Confucius) 1. What do you think this quotation means? 2. Do you agree with this quotation? Why or why not? 3. How would you define *beauty*?

2. READ

Core Path	Access Path
Make Predictions about Vocabulary. There are six bold vocabulary words in the text. As students read the text, ask them to make predictions about what they think each bold vocabulary word means based on the context clues in the sentence. If you are in a low-tech classroom and students are reading from printed copies or a projected text, ask students to record predictions in their notes, so they can be easily referenced in class. If your students have access to technology, they can use the annotation tool to make their predictions.	**Note:** This exercise, which extends vocabulary instruction, should be completed when the class shifts from whole group instruction to individual work during the "Read and Annotate" exercise.

Make Predictions about Vocabulary. There are six bold vocabulary words in the text. As students read the text, ask them to make predictions about what they think each bold vocabulary word means based on the context clues in the sentence. If you are in a low-tech classroom and students are reading from printed copies or a projected text, ask students to record predictions in their notes, so they can be easily referenced in class. If your students have access to technology, they can use the annotation tool to make their predictions.

It might be helpful to model this for students before they begin reading. Either using the board or projecting the actual text, focus in on the part of the text that uses the word "sundry":

There came at nightfall to that hostelry
Some nine and twenty in a company
Of sundry persons who had chanced to fall
In fellowship, and pilgrims were they all

Model for the class how to use the overall structure and meaning of the sentence and the sentences around it, the word's position, and other clues to define the unfamiliar vocabulary word. In this case, point out these context clues:

1. When I look at the structure of the passage, I see that the word "persons" appears after "sundry." The position of the word "sundry" indicates that it is an adjective because it appears before a noun.

2. Next, I see what other words describe the noun "persons." The phrase "who had all chanced to fall / In fellowship" tells me that these persons came together, developing a relationship just by chance. In other words, they have nothing in common but the pilgrimage on which they are about to embark.

Note: This exercise, which extends vocabulary instruction, should be completed when the class shifts from whole group instruction to individual work during the "Read and Annotate" exercise.

Beginner, Intermediate & Approaching Pair Practice.

1. Pair students with more proficient readers.

2. Give them an additional sentence that contains a new vocabulary word.

3. Ask the students to complete a Think Aloud using the teacher-led Make Predictions about Vocabulary activity as a model, while the proficient student actively listens.

4. The student should use the context clues in the sentence to try to determine the meaning of the new vocabulary word.

5. After the student has completed the Think Aloud and made a prediction about the word's meaning, allow time for the proficient reader to add his/her own thoughts and clarify any points of confusion.

6. Once they've completed this Think Aloud, encourage them to use a dictionary to confirm the definition of the new vocabulary word. Have them refer to the "Text Glossary" on their Access 1, 2, and 4 handouts for definitions of key vocabulary terms in the text. Encourage them to add any additional vocabulary words or idioms they find in the text and look up definitions for those words and idioms online or in a dictionary.

Core Path	Access Path
3. Using these context clues, I can infer that "sundry" means "various." I predict that "sundry" refers to the differences between these strangers who are brought together for a common cause. 4. When I look up the word in a dictionary to confirm my guess, I see that it is an adjective that means "made up of different things." This makes sense in the context because I can infer that strangers brought together by chance have an assorted amount of differences. Tell students that a dictionary not only provides information about a word's pronunciation, meaning, and part of speech but also about etymology (word origin) and standard usage (the correct way words should be used). You may show students how to look up the etymology of the word "sundry," which can be traced back to the Old English word "syndrig," meaning "distinct or separate."	
	Extend **Identify and Define.** Have students compile a list of additional vocabulary words as they read the text. Ask students to reference their annotations and share any vocabulary words that were unfamiliar. 1. As a class, compile a list of unknown words on the board. 2. In small groups, ask students to make predictions about what they think these words mean based on how they are used in the sentence (Note: they will need to read the words in context and make predictions). 3. Each group should work together using dictionaries or devices to define the words and write the definitions in their notebooks.

Core Path	Access Path
	Extend **Use Reference Tools to Find Pronunciations.** Have students practice the pronunciation of the vocabulary words, using merriam-webster.com as a resource. This website has, alongside each entry, an audio button that provides the pronunciation. If you are in a low-tech classroom, review the meaning of the pronunciation symbols that follow each word. Pay special attention to stress symbols and the schwa character. Remind students that there are two types of stress symbols for syllables and that the schwa character represents the vowel sound "uh," similar to a short *u*.

Model Reading Comprehension Strategy. Before students begin reading, model the reading comprehension strategy of summarizing by using the Think Aloud below that talks students through the Prologue to *The Canterbury Tales*. First explain to your students that summarizing is

determining the most important or key ideas in a text and restating them in your own words in a brief, objective, and well-organized manner.

Model for students how summarizing will help them better comprehend the selection and help drive their discussions.

- As I read the first few lines, I discover the *when* of the passage, or the time of year during which the events take place: "When April with his showers sweet with fruit / The drought of March has pierced unto the root." I now know that it is the rainy month of April.

- I keep reading and soon I learn the *who* of this passage: "And palmers to go seeking out strange strands, / To distant shrines well known in sundry lands." I am not sure of the meaning of "palmers" in this context, and so I look up its definition in the dictionary and discover that it refers to people who make a pilgrimage, or a journey, to a holy place.

Note: This exercise, which extends instruction around reading comprehension strategies, should be completed when the class shifts from whole group instruction to individual work during the "Read and Annotate" exercise.

Beginner, Intermediate & Approaching
Apply Reading Comprehension Strategy

1. Have Beginner and Intermediate students listen to the audio version of the excerpt from *The Canterbury Tales*. As they listen to the audio recording, ask them to write down key words, phrases, and details from "The Wife of Bath's Tale" in the "Summarize" activity on their Access 1, 2 and 4 handouts. Some details have been suggested for them.

2. Once they have listened to the audio version and created a list of key details, pair Beginner and Intermediate students with more proficient readers and ask them to compare these details and combine them into a few sentences that summarize the text.

3. Allow pairs time to discuss their summaries. Were there any details from the text that one partner added but another did not? If so, encourage them to discuss such details and determine whether or not they are necessary to the summary.

Core Path	Access Path
• When I see the word "pilgrimage," I think of the Pilgrims who came to America in the 17th century, and that makes sense: Pilgrims were people who went on a journey seeking religious freedom. So now I have answered the question of *what* in this passage; the palmers are going on a pilgrimage, or a journey of religious undertaking. I learn that they are going to seek the "holy blessed martyr" to give thanks for the help he gave them when they were "ill and weak." This answers my question of *why* they are making this trip.	
• I learn next *where* these palmers are traveling: "Of England they to Canterbury wend." I see that they are traveling in England. Canterbury is also mentioned, and it seems likely that it is their destination in England.	
• I also learn *how* they are traveling: "That toward Canterbury town would ride." The palmers must be riding to Canterbury, probably on horses.	
• I now know that palmers are going on a religious journey to Canterbury, England, in the month of April to give thanks to the "martyr," or person who gave his life for a holy cause, to give thanks to him for his help in their lives.	
Have students write brief summaries of the section following the Prologue, "The Wife of Bath's Tale." Remind students that the purpose of a summary is to answer as succinctly as possible the questions *who? what? where? when? why?* and *how?* and that summaries should be objective (that is, they should not contain any personal opinions).	

Core Path	Access Path
Read and Annotate. Have students read and annotate the excerpt. Ask students to use the annotation tool as they read to: 1. use context clues to analyze and determine the meaning of the bolded vocabulary terms 2. ask questions about passages of the text that may be unclear or unresolved 3. identify key details, events, characters, and connections between them 4. note unfamiliar vocabulary 5. capture their reaction to the events in the text	**Beginner** **Coach the Reading.** While other students read, annotate, and discuss the text independently, work with Beginner students, listening to the audio of the text and pausing periodically or when any student has a question. Coach students in articulating their questions for the group and in highlighting and annotating the text. Have students use the Annotation Guide on the Access 1 handout to support them as they highlight and annotate the text. For further support, ask questions about the text such as: • Is there anything about the story that you don't understand? • Were you surprised by the events of "The Wife of Bath's Tale"? Why? • Do you think "The Wife of Bath's Tale" is good enough to win the contest? Why or why not? **Intermediate** **Listen to the Audio.** Have these students listen to the audio of the text and use the Text Glossary on the Access 2 handout to help them with words or idioms that may be unfamiliar. If students need help with annotating the text, have them use the Annotation Guide on the Access 2 handout. After working with the Beginner students, you may wish to check this group's progress and provide support as needed. **Advanced** **Pair with Proficient Peers.** Have Advanced students work with English proficient peers to read, annotate, and discuss the text. Have students use the Annotation Guide in the Access 3 handout to support them as they highlight and annotate the text. Encourage them to listen to the audio of the text if needed.

Core Path	Access Path
	Approaching **Use the Annotation Guide.** Have students use the Annotation Guide on the Access 4 handout to support them as they highlight and annotate the text.
Discuss. In small groups or pairs, have students discuss the questions and inferences they made while reading. To help facilitate discussions, refer to Collaborative Discussions in the Speaking & Listening Handbook. 1. Where are the people traveling and for what reason? (to Canterbury, on a pilgrimage) 2. In "The Wife of Bath's Tale," what punishment does the knight face before the queen becomes involved? (death) 3. What must the knight do for the queen to avoid punishment? (answer a question) 4. How does the "old wife" save the knight? (She gives him the answer he seeks.) 5. What does the knight mean when he says, "Take all my wealth and let my body go"? (end of fifth stanza) (He would rather be penniless than marry the old woman.) 6. How does the strategy of visualizing help you understand this excerpt from "The Wife of Bath's Tale"? (Answers will vary.)	**English Learners All Levels & Approaching** Use the extra time while on- and beyond-grade-level students are discussing their first reads of the text to work individually and in small groups with Approaching readers and English Learners as outlined above. Should those students complete their first reads quickly, integrate them into the on- and beyond-grade-level discussion groups. Otherwise, English Learners and Approaching readers will be given an opportunity to participate in text discussions with their peers later in the lesson. **Tech Infusion** **Beyond** **Brainstorm.** Pair students and ask them to brainstorm their answers to the question the knight is asked: What do women want? Students who have access to a back-channel tool such as TodaysMeet (https://todaysmeet.com/) may enjoy brainstorming in that medium.
	Extend **Spelling.** Tell students that Chaucer wrote the original text in Middle English and what they are reading is an adaptation into modern English. Have them compare the following excerpt from Middle English with the last six lines of the first stanza: And if thou kanst nat tellen it anon Yet wol I yeve thee leve for to gon a twelf-month and a day, to seche and leere An answere suffisant in this mateere And suretee wol I han, er that thou pace, Thy body for to yelden in this place.

Copyright © BookheadEd Learning, LLC

Core Path	Access Path
	Ask students to identify some of the main differences between Middle English and Modern English in this passage. (Middle English uses *thou/thee/thy* as forms of *you/your,* *-en* endings on some verbs, and many different spellings, especially for vowels) Point out that in some cases the person who adapted the work to modern English has substituted words with similar meanings to maintain rhyme within the Modern English verse. One example is the replacement of *mateere* with *grave concern,* to rhyme with *learn.*
	Extend **Tech Infusion** **Listening.** Have students listen to the re-creation of a reading of the beginning of the Prologue in Middle English from a YouTube video, such as this one: http://tinyurl.com/lvm4hor. Ask them which words they could recognize from the Modern English adaptation.

3. SYNCTV

Core Path	Access Path
Watch. As a class, watch the SyncTV video on *The Canterbury Tales.* Remind students to listen for the way the students use academic vocabulary during their discussion. Pause the video at these key moments to discuss the information with your students. Have students review and reflect on the ideas expressed: 1. 1:16 – Marcus says that the people on the pilgrimage are "searchers." What evidence from the group's discussion can be used to support this point of view?	**Beginner & Intermediate** **Analyze the Discussion.** Have students use the "Analyze the Discussion" guide on the Access 1 and 2 handouts to identify key points in the discussion and the evidence the students use to determine those points. Sample answers are at the end of the lesson plan online. **Advanced** **Identify the Key Evidence.** Have students discuss and complete the "Key Evidence" chart on the Access 3 handout, referring back to the SyncTV video as needed to clarify their answers. Sample answers appear at the end of the lesson plan online.

Teacher's Edition

Core Path	Access Path
2. 4:40 – Troy says that when the old woman tells the knight that he must marry her, the knight finds himself "shackled up again." What opposing viewpoint is Troy responding to? How effective is his use of evidence, choice of words, and tone in making his counterargument? 3. 8:31 – Do you think Troy's plan to win his girlfriend over is based on a valid interpretation of "The Wife of Bath's Tale"? Why or why not? Consider his reasoning and the details the group emphasizes in their discussion.	**Approaching** **Analyze the Discussion.** Have students complete the chart on the Access 4 handout by listing textual evidence cited by the students in the video. Sample answers are at the end of the lesson plan online.
	Extend **Tech Infusion** **Record.** Ask one student in each group to videotape their conversation. They can upload their videos to YouTube, share them via Google Drive or e-mail them to you for review. They can also play the video back and critique their own conversations to continually improve.

4. THINK

Core Path	Access Path
Answer and Discuss. Have students complete the Think questions and then use the peer review instructions and rubric to complete two peer reviews. Refer to the sample answers at the end of the lesson plan online to discuss responses with your students.	**Beginner & Intermediate** **Sentence Frames.** Have students use the sentence frames on the Access 1 and 2 handouts to support their responses to the Think questions. If necessary, distribute sentence frames to Advanced students as well. **Approaching** **Find the Evidence.** Have students use Find the Evidence on the Access 4 handout to help them identify the evidence needed to answer the questions.
SyncTV Style Discussion. Put students into small groups and give them a prompt to discuss. Remind them to model their discussions after the SyncTV episodes they have seen. Stress the importance of using both academic language and formal English correctly and citing textual evidence in their conversations to support their ideas. To help students prepare for, strategize, and evaluate their discussions, refer to the Collaborative Discussions section of the Speaking & Listening Handbook. Discussion prompt options: 1. What is the purpose of the Prologue? 2. By the end of "The Wife of Bath's Tale," has the knight earned a good life with a happy marriage? Have students review the key ideas expressed, demonstrating an understanding of multiple perspectives through reflection and paraphrasing. You may wish to have students create a video or audio recording of their SyncTV-Style Discussion.	**Beginner & Intermediate** **Use Sentence Frames.** Have these students use the sentence frames on Access 1 and 2 handouts to help them participate in the discussion. **Approaching** **Use Think Questions.** Remind these students to refer back to their answers to the Think questions to help them participate in the group discussion.

Core Path	Access Path
	Extend **Debate.** Present students with an issue from the text that can be debated. Allow students to debate the issue as a class or in smaller groups. As a class, evaluate the use of evidence, point of view, and reasoning. Debate prompts: 1. Consider both the Wife of Bath herself and the tale she tells: What are her views on the rights and role of women? Do you think Chaucer agrees with her views? Why or why not? 2. Does the knight in "The Wife of Bath's Tale" get the punishment he deserves? Why or why not?
	Extend **Write a Claim.** Ask students to write a strong claim that clearly states their position in relation to the topic they debated. Once students have written their claims, ask them to read their claims to a small group of their peers. This activity will provide them practice writing claims, as well as expose them to claims written by their peers.

SKILL:
Textual Evidence

OVERVIEW

Finding textual evidence to support claims is a vital skill for students to master. This lesson plan provides follow-up questions and useful enrichments to help teachers guide students toward a usable, repeatable method for finding textual evidence.

OBJECTIVES

1. Instruct students on the definition of textual evidence.
2. Practice using concrete strategies for identifying textual evidence.
3. Participate effectively in a range of conversations and collaborations to express ideas and build upon the ideas of others.

ELA Common Core Standards: :
Reading: Literature - RL.11-12.1, RL.11-12.2
Speaking & Listening - SL.11-12.1.A, SL.11-12.1.C, SL.11-12.2

RESOURCES

Access 1 handout (Beginner)

Access 2 handout (Intermediate)

Access 3 handout (Advanced)

Access 4 handout (Approaching)

Please note that excerpts and passages in the StudySync® library, workbooks, and PDFs are intended as touchstones to generate interest in an author's work. The excerpts and passages do not substitute for the reading of entire texts, and StudySync® strongly recommends that teachers and students seek out and purchase the whole literary or informational work in order to experience it as the author intended. Links to online resellers are available in our digital library. In addition, complete works may be ordered through an authorized reseller by filling out and returning to StudySync® the order form enclosed in this workbook.

Teacher's Edition   161

1. DEFINE

Core Path	Access Path
Watch. Watch the Concept Definition video on textual evidence with your students. Make sure students understand the purpose of finding textual evidence in an informational or literary text, as well as the difference between explicit and inferred evidence. Pause the video at these key moments to discuss the information with your students:	**English Learners All Levels & Approaching** **Match.** Have students complete the matching exercise on the Access 1, 2, 3, and 4 handouts as they watch the video. Answers are located at the end of the lesson plan online.
1. 0:56 – Why aren't authors always as explicit as possible in stating their meaning or purpose? Why do you think they often leave evidence to be inferred?	
2. 1:11 – How can readers be sure if an inference is valid? Think of a few ways to test the validity of an inference, in addition to the examples given in the video.	
3. 1:49 – Why is inference an important skill when reading both informational and literary works? How can this skill help us deepen our understanding of works in both genres?	
Read and Discuss. After watching the Concept Definition video, have students read the definition of textual evidence. Either in small groups or as a whole class use these questions to engage students in a discussion about textual evidence. Analyze some of the themes that arise. How are they strengthened by textual evidence? Do they have the same impact without support?	**Beginner & Approaching** **Complete a Chart.** To prepare students to participate in the discussion, have them complete the chart on the Access 1 and 4 handouts as they read the definition. The correct answers are located at the end of the lesson plan online.
1. Is a direct quotation stronger textual evidence than a paraphrase? (not necessarily)	**Intermediate & Advanced** **Discuss Prompts.** To help these students participate in the discussion, prompt them with questions that can be answered with a few words, such as:
2. Why does a strong inference require textual evidence? (Textual evidence determines whether an inference is valid.)	• What is textual evidence? (words, phrases, sentences, or paragraphs used to make an inference)
3. Describe a time when you used textual evidence outside of school to support a claim. (Answers will vary.)	• How does citing textual evidence help other people understand your inference? (It shows how and why you analyzed the text that way.)
	• How does textual evidence strengthen a writer's ideas? (Answers will vary.)

Core Path	Access Path
4. Can you think of a scenario in which it would be beneficial for a writer or a speaker to either omit or obscure textual evidence? (Answers will vary.)	**Beyond** **Discuss.** Have students choose a text they've read and make an inference about its theme. If needed, remind students that a theme is the text's central idea or message. Then, have students brainstorm evidence they would use to support that inference. Make a list. Would students use more direct quotations or paraphrases as support? Why? What are the benefits and drawbacks of both kinds of support?
	Extend **Brainstorm.** After the class has watched the video, ask students to think of a commercial they've seen or an advertisement they've read that used evidence to support a claim. Ask if they found the evidence to have weight, and why.
	Extend **Tech Infusion** **Research.** Have students find a newspaper online and choose a controversial issue discussed in one of the articles. They should select an article on an issue they have some prior knowledge about. Ask them to write a two-paragraph claim using two pieces of textual evidence from the article, one involving explicit evidence and one involving an inference. For low-tech classrooms, bring in printed copies of newspapers.

2. MODEL

Core Path	Access Path
Watch. Ask students to take notes on the SkillsTV video on textual evidence in *The Canterbury Tales* as you watch together. Remind students to listen for the way the students use academic vocabulary related to the definition of textual evidence during their discussion. Pause the video at these key moments to discuss the information with your students:	**Beginner, Intermediate & Approaching** **Analyze the Discussion.** Have students watch the video again and complete the chart on the Access 1, 2, and 4 handouts as they watch the video. Sample answers for this exercise are located at the end of the lesson plan online.
1. 0:44 – Where might you look in a text for key textual evidence? Why is it important to connect the evidence together to draw larger conclusions?	**Advanced** **Journals.** Have students note in their journals the strategies the students in the SkillsTV video use to find textual evidence.
2. 1:45 – Discuss the inference Olivia has made about the narrator. How well does she use evidence to support her points and link her ideas? What other evidence from the text could she have used to support her stance?	
3. 3:14 – How does the group use reasoning to determine the Wife of Bath's point of view? Why is the Wife of Bath's point of view important to understanding this story?	
Read and Annotate. Have students independently read the Model section. As they read, ask students to use the annotation tool to: • highlight key points. • ask questions. • identify places where the Model applies the strategies laid out in the Identification and Application section on textual evidence	**Note:** During this portion of the lesson, instruction shifts from whole group to individual work. Use this time to work one-on-one or in small groups with Beginner, Intermediate, Advanced, and Approaching students. **Beginner & Intermediate** **Coach the Reading.** Work with these students (either individually or in small groups) to fill out the guided reading questions on the Access 1 and 2 handouts. Have Beginner students refer to the glossary on the Access 1 handout to help them determine the meaning of difficult words (note: provide the Access 1 handout glossary to Intermediate students if necessary). Let students know they'll use these answers to help participate in the discussion about the Model. Sample answers for this exercise are located at the end of the lesson plan online.

Core Path	Access Path
	Advanced **Identify Evidence.** Ask Advanced students to complete the identifying evidence exercise on the Access 3 handout. Let students know that they'll use these answers to help participate in the discussion about the Model. Sample answers for this exercise are located at the end of the lesson plan online. **Approaching** **Guided Reading.** Have students complete the guided reading questions on the Access 4 handout as they read. Let them know that they'll use these answers to help participate in the discussion about the Model. Sample answers for this exercise are located at the end of the lesson plan online.
Discuss. After students read the Model text, use these questions to facilitate a whole-group discussion: 1. According to the second paragraph, what exactly will this Model focus on? (using textual evidence to make inferences about the characters of the knight and the hag and about the Wife of Bath's views on marriage and the competing natures of the sexes) 2. What differences between the sexes are suggested in the first passage? Support your responses with evidence from the text. (Men operate by "force" and value the "law," though they can be flexible, as demonstrated by King Arthur, who "granted life, at last, in the law's place" after being persuaded by the women. The women are naturally more merciful. Even though the knight is guilty, the women "long prayed of the king to show him grace.")	

Core Path	Access Path
3. Reread the second passage. How can you tell that the Wife of Bath has a high opinion of women? Support your responses with evidence from the text. (The Wife of Bath describes the women of the court as "noble" and "wise." The queen herself stands for "high justice.") 4. Reread the third passage. What do you think of the knight's reaction towards the hag? Do you think he is being superficial? Or do you think his reaction is justifiable? (Answers will vary.) 5. What do you think of the tale's message about men and women and what they desire in marriage? Do you think the message still holds true today? (Answers will vary.)	
	Extend **Tech Infusion** **Pair and Share.** Pair or group students and assign each group in the class a different theme. Have each group work together to find textual evidence they believe develops this theme in the text. Here are other themes: • social rank and class • the nature of beauty • reforming a criminal • magic and reality • true happiness Ask the groups to share their findings with the class. If possible, have students capture pair shares on video using their mobile devices so they can watch their conversations and critique the content.

3. YOUR TURN

Core Path	Access Path
Assess and Explain. Have students answer the comprehension questions to test for understanding. Share the explanations for Parts A and B (located online) with your students.	
	Extend **Share and Discuss.** Have students complete the Your Turn section in class. Poll students about their responses and as a class discuss the different strategies they used to determine the correct answers. Make sure students make the connection between the topic of marital fidelity included in both questions and the passages discussed in the Model.
	Extend **Tech Infusion** **Compile.** As a class, compile a list of types of textual evidence on a whiteboard or other board. Discuss which types have the most weight and which are best for supporting inferences.

SKILL:
Figurative Language

OVERVIEW

Figurative language incorporates a variety of literary techniques. This lesson plan provides follow-up questions and useful enrichments to help teachers guide students to determine and to understand various types of figurative language.

OBJECTIVES

1. Learn the definition of figurative language.
2. Practice using concrete strategies for identifying and applying figurative language.
3. Participate effectively in a range of conversations and collaborations to express ideas and build upon the ideas of others.

ELA Common Core Standards:
Reading: Literature - RL.11-12.1, RL.11-12.4
Speaking & Listening - SL.11-12.1.A, SL.11-12.1.C, SL.11-12.2
Language - L.11-12.5.A

RESOURCES

Access 1 handout (Beginner)

Access 2 handout (Intermediate)

Access 3 handout (Advanced)

Access 4 handout (Approaching)

1. DEFINE

Core Path	Access Path
Watch. Watch the Concept Definition video on figurative language with your students. Make sure students understand the difference between literal and figurative language and ask them to write down the seven examples of figurative language in the video, with a definition and an example for each. Pause the video at these key moments to discuss the information with your students:	**English Learners All Levels & Approaching** **Match.** Have students complete the matching exercise on the Access 1, 2, 3, and 4 handouts as they watch the video. Answers are located at the end of the lesson plan online.

Core Path (continued)

1. 0:45 — What are some instances when it would help to use figurative language? When might it be better to avoid figurative language? Do you think certain genres employ figurative language more often than others? Which ones?

2. 1:29 — Can you think of any other effects of figurative language besides those mentioned in the video? What can figurative language do that literal language cannot?

3. 1:36 — How does the reader know when an author is using figurative language? Is it always obvious? Think of some of the tell-tale signs that can help us decipher when an author is using figurative language in a given text.

Core Path	Access Path
Read and Discuss. After watching the Concept Definition video, have students read the definition of figurative language. Either in small groups or as a whole class use these questions to engage students in a discussion about figurative language.	**Beginner & Approaching** **Complete a Chart.** To prepare students to participate in the discussion, have them complete the chart on the Access 1 and 4 handouts as they read the definition. The correct answers are located at the end of the lesson plan online.

Core Path (continued)

1. What are some reasons why writers use figurative language? How does it add to a reader's enjoyment of the text? (Answers may vary.)

2. What is the difference between figures of speech such as similes and metaphors? (Similes use "like" or "as.")

3. Which form of figurative language is made easier to understand by reading text aloud? (sound devices)

Access Path (continued)

Intermediate & Advanced
Discuss Prompts. To help these students participate in the discussion, prompt them with questions that can be answered with a few words, such as:

- When you use figurative language to describe something, what are you doing? (comparing it to something else)

- What kind of language are writers using when they state facts as they are? (literal language)

Core Path	Access Path
4. What is an oxymoron? (a phrase in which some of the words contradict others, such as "awfully good" or "jumbo shrimp")	• Do you find literal or figurative language more interesting in prose? Why? (Answers will vary.) **Beyond** **Discuss.** Have students brainstorm ways to describe a feeling using both literal and figurative language. For example, "I am feeling very hungry" versus "I feel like I could eat a pizza the size of Texas." Then have them discuss which gives a clearer idea of the feeling. Which is more interesting? Why? When might they use literal language instead of figurative language to describe a feeling?
	Extend **Tech Infusion** **Brainstorm.** The definition of figurative language mentions language that "strikes the heart." Have students think of language that has moved them greatly, and ask them to name any figurative language connected with it. Compile the list of examples as a class using a whiteboard or projector.
	Extend **Tech Infusion** **Blast.** Create a Blast and ask students to "blast out" figurative language describing a favorite trip or vacation they have taken. The Blast could be in the form of a short poem or song lyric if they wish.

2. MODEL

Core Path	Access Path
Read and Annotate. Have students independently read the Model section. As they read, ask students to use the annotation tool to: • highlight key points • ask questions	**Note:** During this portion of the lesson, instruction shifts from whole group to individual work. Use this time to work one-on-one or in small groups with Beginner, Intermediate, Advanced, and Approaching students.

Core Path	Access Path
• identify places where the Model applies the strategies laid out in the Identification and Application section on figurative language	**Beginner & Intermediate** **Coach the Reading.** Work with these students (either individually or in small groups) to fill out the guided reading questions on the Access 1 and 2 handouts. Have Beginner students refer to the glossary on the Access 1 handout to help them determine the meaning of difficult words (note: provide the Access 1 handout glossary to Intermediate students if necessary). Let students know they'll use these answers to help participate in the discussion about the Model. Sample answers for this exercise are located at the end of the lesson plan online. **Advanced** **Identify Evidence.** Ask Advanced students to complete the identifying evidence exercise on the Access 3 handout. Let students know that they'll use these answers to help participate in the discussion about the Model. Sample answers for this exercise are located at the end of the lesson plan online. **Approaching** **Guided Reading.** Have students complete the guided reading questions on the Access 4 handout as they read. Let them know that they'll use these answers to help participate in the discussion about the Model. Sample answers for this exercise are located at the end of the lesson plan online.
Discuss. After students read the Model text, use these questions to facilitate a whole-group discussion that helps students understand how to identify figurative language: 1. How are alliteration, assonance, and consonance different? (Alliteration is the repetition of sounds at the beginning of words. Assonance is the repetition of vowel sounds within words. Consonance is the repetition of consonant sounds within words. In all three, the repetitions should occur in words that are in close proximity.)	

Core Path	Access Path
2. Under which category in the Define section does assonance appear? (sound devices) 3. The Model discusses some metaphors involving spring. What are some other figures of speech that you would use to describe your feelings about spring? (Answers will vary.) 4. The Model mentions renewal in connection with the metaphors involving spring. How might renewal also be a metaphor for the trip to Canterbury? (Some of the pilgrims may be seeking spiritual renewal.) 5. Look back at the passages in the Model. Identify an example of figurative language that is not mentioned in the discussion. (e.g., "pierced" as a metaphor for the spread of dryness; assonance of *bud/sun/run*) 6. Why might the Model cover so many different literary terms: personification, assonance, consonance, metaphor, alliteration, allusion, extended metaphor, hyperbole, poetic devices? (Figurative language is a general term covering many types of literary concepts.)	
	Extend **Tech Infusion** **Pair and Share.** Pair or group students and have each group find the text of a poem or song lyrics online. Have them use Diigo (diigo.com) to annotate the text to highlight incidences of figurative language. Ask them try to find one example of each of the following: • simile • alliteration • hyperbole • oxymoron Ask the groups to share their findings with the class. If possible, project Diigo files on the board.

3. YOUR TURN

Core Path	Access Path
Assess and Explain. Have students answer the comprehension questions to test for understanding. Share the explanations for Parts A and B (located online) with your students.	
	Extend **Share and Discuss.** Have students complete the Your Turn section in class. Ask them what connections they see between the passage in the assessment and the passages that appeared in the Model.
	Extend **Tech Infusion** **Evaluate.** Discuss the following list of strategies for answering multiple-choice questions. Ask students to indicate whether each strategy is effective, and why or why not. • Trust your instincts; your first choice has a better chance of being correct. • Cross out answers you know are not correct. • Cover up answer choices while reading the question. • Check for an "All of the above" choice before you mark one answer as correct. Ask students what other strategies they have found to be effective for multiple choice.

OVERVIEW

The anthology *The Canterbury Tales,* by Geoffrey Chaucer, consists of tales, mainly in verse, told by pilgrims traveling to Canterbury in the 1300s. The Close Read gives students the opportunity to practice using textual evidence to support inferences.

OBJECTIVES

1. Complete a close reading of the excerpts from *The Canterbury Tales*.
2. Practice and apply concrete strategies to use textual evidence to support inferences about excerpts from *The Canterbury Tales*.
3. Participate effectively in a range of conversations and collaborations to express ideas and build upon the ideas of others.
4. Prewrite, plan, and produce clear and coherent writing in response to a prompt.

ELA Common Core Standards:

Reading: Literature - RL.11-12.1, RL.11-12.2, RL.11-12.3, RL.11-12.4
Writing - W.11-12.4, W.11-12.5, W.11-12.6, W.11-12.9.A, W.11-12.10
Speaking & Listening - SL.11-12.1.A, SL.11-12.1.B, SL.11-12.1.C, SL.11-12.1.D, SL.11-12.6
Language - L.11-12.4.A, L.11-12.4.C, L.11-12.4.D, L.11-12.5.A, L.11-12.6

RESOURCES

The Canterbury Tales Vocabulary handout
 The Canterbury Tales Venn Diagram
Access 1 handout (Beginner)
Access 2 handout (Intermediate)
Access 3 handout (Advanced)
Access 4 handout (Approaching)

1. INTRODUCTION

Core Path	Access Path
Define and Compare. Project the vocabulary words and definitions onto the board or provide students with handouts, so they can copy the vocabulary into their notebooks. Suggest that students consult general and specialized reference materials, both print and digital, to compare the precise meaning of a specific word with their initial vocabulary predictions from the First Read. Review words that students defined incorrectly to understand why they were unable to use context clues or other tools to develop usable definitions.	**Beginner & Intermediate** **Complete a Chart.** Have students complete the chart on the Access 1 and 2 handouts by writing the correct word for each of the definitions. **Advanced & Beyond** **Write in Journals.** Have students write a journal entry using all of their vocabulary words. Remind them to write sentences that communicate the meaning of the words they are using. **Approaching** **Graphic Organizer.** To support students in comparing their predictions with the correct meanings, have them complete the graphic organizer on the Access 4 handout to record the vocabulary words, their initial analysis, and the definitions. Then have them write sentences using the words.
Review. Have students complete the fill-in-the-blank vocabulary worksheet for this selection. Answers for the worksheet are listed online.	
	Extend **Synonyms.** Project the vocabulary words and definitions onto the board or provide students with a handout, so they can copy the vocabulary into their notebooks. Ask students to find synonyms for the vocabulary words, writing down only those synonyms that do not appear in the definition. Then have students analyze nuances in the meanings of the synonyms.
	Extend **Tech Infusion** **Create.** Have students create artwork to visually represent the words using an iPad or Android art app such as Sketch Pad 3.

Teacher's Edition

Core Path	Access Path
	Extend **Tech Infusion** **Review.** Create a vocabulary review quiz using Socrative (http://socrative.com). Design multiple choice and/or short answer questions that require students to apply their understanding of the vocabulary, and then run the quiz.
	Extend **Word Forms.** Have students use a dictionary to find words that are directly related to the vocabulary words but are different parts of speech.
	Extend **Tech Infusion** **Create.** Create online flashcards for the vocabulary using Quizlet (http://quizlet.com) or StudyBlue (www.studyblue.com).
	Extend **Tech Infusion** **Act and Record.** Break students into small groups, assign each group a vocabulary word, and ask them to design an improv comedy sketch to demonstrate the meaning of the word for their peers. If possible, record sketches and post them to your class YouTube Channel, so they can be reviewed.
	Extend **Compose.** Ask students to write a short poem or song lyric that conveys the meaning of each vocabulary word.

2. READ

Core Path	Access Path
Model Close Reading. Project the text onto the board and model a close reading of the excerpt from the Prologue using the annotation strategies mentioned below. While modeling annotation strategies, make notes that tie the text to the focus skill and demonstrate what students are looking for as they read. Some guidance for you as you annotate for your students:	

Core Path (continued):

- Note that the beginning of the work establishes the setting, as happens in many literary works. Highlight the references to springtime and April and annotate it as "when." Then highlight the three lines beginning "In Southwark, ..." and annotate it as "where."

- Continue with the annotation "who," which should accompany the highlighting of the two lines following "There came at nightfall."

- Discuss how the Prologue is written in verse by highlighting two lines that rhyme. Also discuss the meter and the rhythm of these lines, perhaps using scansion.

- Explain that the tales comprise a series of frame stories, or stories within stories. A narrator inserts himself from time to time to help present sections of the work; highlight the four lines beginning "So had I spoken ..." as an example of the narrator's presence.

Core Path	Access Path
Read and Annotate. Read the Skills Focus questions as a class, so your students know what they should pay close attention to as they read. Then have students read and annotate the excerpt. Ask students to use the annotation tool as they read to: 1. respond to the Skills Focus section 2. ask questions about how textual evidence leads to making inferences	**Note:** While on-grade-level students are reading and annotating, work one-on-one or in small groups with Beginner, Intermediate, Advanced, and Approaching students to support them as they read and annotate the text.

Core Path	Access Path
3. identify examples of figurative language and explain how they relate to themes in the text 4. note unfamiliar vocabulary 5. capture their reaction to the ideas and examples in the text As they reread the text, remind students to use the comprehension strategy of summarizing that they learned in the First Read.	**Beginner & Intermediate** **Summarize and Analyze the Text.** Work with these students to complete the sentence frames on the Access 1 and 2 handouts (note: the sentence frames for Intermediate students on the Access 2 handout contain fewer scaffolds). They will then use the completed sentence frames to help them analyze and annotate the text by completing the Skills Focus questions. Refer to the sample Skills Focus answers to help them complete the sentence frames and annotate the text. **Advanced** **Work in Pairs.** Pair these students with more proficient English speakers to work together on analyzing and annotating the text to complete the Skills Focus questions. If these students need more support, have them use the sentence frames on the Access 3 handout as they work with their more proficient peers. **Approaching** **Summarize the Text.** Have these students discuss and complete the text summary on the Access 4 handout and use their summary to help them analyze and annotate the text by completing the Skills Focus questions. Correct answers for the summary are at the end of the lesson plan online. Also refer to the sample Skills Focus answers to aid students with their annotations.
Discuss. After students have read the text, use the sample responses to the Skills Focus questions at the end of the lesson plan online to discuss the reading and the process of finding textual evidence. Make sure that students have acquired and accurately use academic-specific words and phrases related to the skill and demonstrate a command of formal English appropriate to the discussion. To help facilitate discussions, refer to Collaborative Discussions in the Speaking & Listening Handbook.	**Extend** **Pair and Share.** In small, heterogeneous groups or pairs, ask students to share and discuss their annotations with a focus on the textual evidence presented in the selection. You can provide students with these questions to guide their discussion:

Core Path	Access Path
	1. How is the knight in "The Wife of Bath's Tale" different from the way knights are usually portrayed? Cite textual evidence to support your answer. (He commits a terrible crime and later he insults the old woman after she has saved his life. Knights are usually portrayed as heroic figures who behave nobly.) 2. In what way is the old woman a more heroic figure than the knight? Cite textual evidence to support your answer. (The knight behaves badly for much of the tale; the old woman saves the knight and is interested in true love instead of monetary reward.) 3. What seems to be the Wife of Bath's attitude toward the importance of physical beauty? (She seems to think that men are overly focused on physical beauty and that beauty can grow out of accepting people for who they are.)
	Extend **Write.** Ask students to imagine that the knight and his wife have children. Have them write a stanza, using the same meter and rhyme, in which the mother gives her children some advice.
	Extend **Present.** Have students give dramatic readings of their work from the previous activity. Record the readings if you have the appropriate technology.
	Extend **Tech Infusion** **Search.** Use dictionaries, thesauruses, and/or mobile devices to find antonyms for the last three vocabulary words. Students should record the word with at least one antonym in their notes. Student can work individually or collaboratively on this assignment.

Core Path	Access Path
	Extend **Connect.** 1. Ask students to define *beauty* in their own words and print out a photograph that can be found online and that is an example of their own notion of beauty. 2. Have students post their photographs on a board in the classroom. 3. Discuss the board as a class. How are the photographs similar and/or different? Are students surprised by the variety of examples shared? Do the examples share any commonalities?
	Extend **Create.** Ask students to use Microsoft Paint or Google Drawing to create a virtual collage with a mix of text and media that show the Canterbury Cathedral and the buildings that surround it. Text should deal with the history of the Cathedral. Invite students to present their collages for the class explaining why they selected particular texts and images.
	Extend **Research.** Have students research the concept of chivalry as it developed in the Middle Ages. Tell them to focus on the difference between the ideals of chivalry and actual behavior of knights during this era.
	Extend **Write.** Ask students to locate information about St. Thomas Becket online and write a brief biography of several paragraphs.

3. WRITE

Core Path	Access Path
Prewrite and Plan. Read the prompt as a class and ask students to brainstorm about qualities associated with witches in legends. Students can brainstorm together either as a class or in small groups to begin planning their responses. Remind your students to look at the excerpt and their annotations to find textual evidence to support their ideas.	**Beginner & Intermediate** **Plan and Organize.** Have students complete the prewriting activity cn the Access 1 and 2 handouts and then explain their ideas to a partner before they write. Explain to students that they need to choose details, examples, or quotes from the text that support their ideas and then explain how those details support their statements. For example, students could include the lines, "And, save I be, at dawn, as fairly seen / As any lady, empress, or great queen / That is between the east and the far west, / Do with my life and death as you like best," which show the old woman using magic to transform herself as a reward for the knight. **Approaching** **Plan and Organize.** Have students complete the prewriting activity on the Access 4 handout to organize their thoughts before they write.
	Tech Infusion **Map.** Students can create an outline for their responses by using Workflowy (workflowy.com).
Discuss. Project these instructions for the peer review onto the board and review them with your class, so they know what they are looking for when they begin to provide their classmates with feedback: • How has this essay helped you understand the characterization of the old woman in "The Wife of Bath's Tale"? • Did the writer list some traditional characteristic of witches, such as old, ugly, sneaky, or having the ability to perform magic? • How did he/she examine the themes of magic and redeemed behavior in the story? • What sort of evidence did the writer use from the text to support his or her writing?	

Core Path	Access Path
• How well does the writer explain how that evidence supports his or her arguments? • Did the writer make logical inferences based on the evidence? • Does the writer write using standard grammar and punctuation? Are there any weak spots? • What specific suggestions can you make to help the writer improve the response? • What thing(s) does this paper do especially well? After you've looked at the peer review instructions, review the rubric with students before they begin writing. Allow time for students briefly to pose and discuss any questions they may have about the peer review instructions and the rubric. Tell students how many peer reviews they will need to complete once they submit their writing.	
Write. Ask students to complete the writing assignment using textual evidence to support their answers. Once they have completed their writing, they should click "Submit."	
	Extend **Critique.** Put students in small groups and give them photocopies of a writing sample to collaboratively evaluate. After students have had an opportunity to evaluate student reviews to ensure they are substantive samples, work as a class to generate strategies students can use as they complete their peer reviews.
Review. Once students complete their writing assignment, they should submit substantive feedback to one peer. Students should use their peers' feedback to improve their writing.	

BLAST:
Mirror, Mirror on the Wall

OVERVIEW

To wrap up their study of *The Canterbury Tales*, students will explore one of the dilemmas that Chaucer's knight faces: choosing between someone "foul" but loyal, and someone lovely. Students will consider how much of a hold beauty has over us. Students will explore research links that connect them to everything from mathematical formulas for beauty, to studies that demonstrate that even babies recognize beauty.

OBJECTIVES

1. Explore background information about the human tendency to prize beauty above all else, which Chaucer explores in "The Wife of Bath's Tale" in *The Canterbury Tales*.
2. Research using hyperlinks to a range of information about beauty, exploring everything from the idea that there is a mathematical formula for beauty to the idea that our fascination with beauty starts in infancy.

   ELA Common Core Standards: :
   Reading: Informational Text - RI.11-12.1
   Writing - W.11-12.1.A, W.11-12.1.B, W.11-12.5, W.11-12.6
   Speaking & Listening - SL.11-12.1.A, SL.11-12.1.C, SL.11-12.1.D

RESOURCES

Access 1 handout (Beginner)

Access 2 handout (Intermediate)

Access 4 handout (Approaching)

Please note that excerpts and passages in the StudySync® library, workbooks, and PDFs are intended as touchstones to generate interest in an author's work. The excerpts and passages do not substitute for the reading of entire texts, and StudySync® strongly recommends that teachers and students seek out and purchase the whole literary or informational work in order to experience it as the author intended. Links to online resellers are available in our digital library. In addition, complete works may be ordered through an authorized reseller by filling out and returning to StudySync® the order form enclosed in this workbook.

Teacher's Edition   183

TITLE/DRIVING QUESTION

Core Path	Access Path
Discuss. As a class, read aloud the title and driving question for this Blast. These correspond to the title/driving question for the unit as a whole. This Blast relates to the knight's dilemma in "The Wife of Bath's Tale." How much was the knight influenced by beauty? Ask students what Chaucer was trying to say about beauty in "The Wife of Bath's Tale." Then, ask students how much beauty influences us today. Remind students that they will be returning to this question for their formal entries after they've written a draft and read and discussed the Background.	**English Learners All Levels** **Discuss a Visual.** Have students view a photograph of a plastic surgeon marking someone's face for surgery, such as the one at: http://tinyurl.com/ldspvbd. Discuss how the picture represents a standard of beauty, prompting students with questions such as: • What is happening in this photo? • Who decides what to do with the person's face? Where do those ideas come from? • How do you think this person's life will change after surgery? • What might cause a person to want to change their face?
Draft. In their notebooks or on scrap paper, have students draft their initial responses to the driving question. This will provide them with a baseline response that they will update and revise as they gain more information about the topic in the Background and Research Links sections of the assignment.	**Beginner & Intermediate** **Draft with Sentence Frame.** When drafting their initial response to the driving question, have students refer to this Blast sentence frame on their Access 1 and 2 handouts: • Beauty influences us the most when _____ because _____. Point out these two key features of the sentence frame: 1. The introductory clause "Beauty influences us the most when" borrows language directly from the Blast driving question and prompts students to give a time when beauty is most important. 2. Ask students to note that the word "because" prompts them to give a reason why the moment they chose is when beauty is most important.

BACKGROUND

Core Path	Access Path
Read. Have students read the Blast background to provide context for the driving question.	**Beginner & Intermediate** **Read with Support.** Have students read the Blast background to provide context for the driving question. When they encounter unfamiliar words or phrases, have students refer to the glossary on their Access 1 and 2 handouts. If there are unfamiliar words that are not included in their glossary, encourage students to check a dictionary or online reference tool, like http://dictionary.reference.com. **Approaching** **Read and Summarize.** Have students read the Blast background to provide context for the driving question. As they read, ask students to complete the fill-in-the-blank summary of the background provided on their Access 4 handout. When they encounter unfamiliar words or phrases, have students refer to the glossary on their Access 4 handout.
Discuss. Pair students and have them discuss the following questions: 1. What does the phrase "Beauty is only skin deep" mean? (It means that beauty only gets you so far. It's what's on the inside that counts.) Do you think this phrase is true? 2. What is some evidence that people around the world care about beauty, and have cared about it for a long time? (Victorian women removed ribs. American women spend $426 billion annually. Avon is huge in Brazil.) 3. How does society show a preference toward beautiful people? (called on more in class, paid more, shorter prison terms) Do you think people are aware that they are showing a preference toward beautiful people? 4. Why do you think babies are born with a preference for beauty? (maybe beauty and health are connected, maybe it's a survival-of-the-fittest thing)	**Beginner** **Discuss.** Pair Beginner with Advanced (or Beyond) students and have them use the dialogue starter on their Access 1 handout to discuss the topic. Advise them to return to the dialogue and switch roles if they get stuck. **Intermediate** **Discuss.** Pair Intermediate with Advanced (or Beyond) students and have them use the dialogue starter on their Access 2 handout to discuss the topic. Advise them to return to the dialogue and switch roles if they get stuck. If their conversation is progressing smoothly, encourage them to continue the discussion beyond the dialogue starter sheet. They can expand their conversations to discuss other examples of the effects of beauty or extreme things people do in the name of beauty.

Core Path	Access Path
Brainstorm. Remind students about the driving question for this Blast: How much does beauty influence us? Ask students to think about the human obsession with beauty. Have students create a two-column chart in their notebooks. Tell students to use this chart to create a list of different beauty crazes that have taken hold of humans throughout history. Create one column for the past and one column for today. Students can start with information from the Background, but then should draw from their prior knowledge to add to the chart. What are some things that people used to do to achieve beauty? What do people do today? Think about practices all over the world.	

The Past	Today
Victorian women removed ribs	Some women have their eyebrows removed and then drawn on.

RESEARCH LINKS

Core Path	Access Path
Examine and Explore. Use these questions to guide students' exploration of the research links: 1. Look at "The Math Behind Beauty." What did Pythagoras say about beauty? (Pythagoras said humans are drawn to the golden ratio: a/b = (a + b)/a.) What's an example of something that reflects the golden ratio? (A triangle does, if it's perfect.) What does Da Vinci's Vitruvian Man reveal about beauty? (The perfect body should have the following proportion: arm span = height; height = hand length x 10.) What does Dr. Stephen Marquardt say about a formula for beautiful faces? (He came up with a golden mask. Beautiful people's mouths were 1.618 times wider than their noses, it seemed; their noses were 1.618 times wider than the tip of their noses.) 2. Look at "Beauty Around the World." What beauty practice most surprised you? What are some examples of beauty practices that begin at a young age?	

	Extend
	Research, Discuss, and Present.
	
	1. Assign each group one link to explore in depth.
	2. Ask them to discuss the information:
	   a. What are the key points?
	   b. What inferences did you make as you read?
	   c. What did you learn about this "big idea" from reading this research?
	   d. How did this help you to better understand the topic?
	   e. What questions does your group have after exploring this link?
	3. Allow students time to informally present what they learned.

Core Path	Access Path
	Extend **Tech Infusion** **Share.** As students explore the links, allow them to crowdsource their findings using a back-channel tool like TodaysMeet (https://todaysmeet.com). Students can post the research they find individually or in groups to share with the class.

QUIKPOLL

Core Path	Access Path
Participate. Answer the poll question. Have students use information from the background and research links to explain their answers.	

NUMBER CRUNCH

Core Path	Access Path
Predict, Discuss, and Click. Before students click on the number, break them into pairs and have them make predictions about what they think the number is related to. After they've clicked the number, ask students if they are surprised by the revealed information.	

CREATE YOUR BLAST

Core Path	Access Path
Blast. Ask students to write their Blast response in 140 characters or less.	**Beginner** **Blast with Support.** Have students refer back to the sentence frame on their Access 1 handout that they used to create their original Blast draft. Ask them to use this frame to write and enter their final Blast.

Copyright © BookheadEd Learning, LLC

Core Path	Access Path
	Intermediate **Blast with Support.** Have students attempt to draft their Blast without the sentence frame on their Access 2 handout. If students struggle to compose their Blast draft without the sentence frame, remind them to reference it for support. **Beyond** **Write a Claim.** Ask students to use their answer to the poll question to write a strong claim that could be used as the foundation for a piece of argumentative writing. Once students have written their claims, ask them to read the claims to a small group of their peers. This activity will provide them practice writing claims, as well as expose them to claims written by their peers.
Review. After students have completed their own Blasts, ask them to review the Blasts of their peers and provide feedback.	
	Extend **Discuss.** As a class or in groups, identify a few strong Blasts and discuss what made those responses so powerful. As a group, analyze and discuss what characteristics make a Blast interesting or effective.
	Extend **Revise.** Resend a second version of this Blast assignment to your students and have them submit revised versions of their original Blasts. Do the same responses make the Top Ten? How have the answers improved from the first submissions?

FIRST READ:
The Once and Future King

OVERVIEW

The novel *The Once and Future King,* by T. H. White, is the story of King Arthur and his struggle to create the ideal society in medieval England. In White's retelling of the classic story, Merlyn, Arthur's magician tutor and advisor, lives backward in time and provides Arthur with insights gleaned from his "youth" in the future. The First Read gives students the opportunity to experience the text with a limited context.

OBJECTIVES

1. Perform an initial reading of a text and demonstrate comprehension by responding to short analysis and inference questions with textual evidence.
2. Practice defining vocabulary words using context.
3. Practice and apply concrete strategies for analyzing rhetoric and making inferences.
4. Identify the difference between explicit and implicit meaning.
5. Participate effectively in a range of conversations and collaborations to express ideas and build upon the ideas of others.
6. Practice acquiring and using academic vocabulary correctly.

    ELA Common Core Standards:
    Reading: Literature - RL.11-12.1, RL.11-12.2, RL.11-12.3, RL.11-12.4, RL.11-12.10
    Language - L.11-12.1, L.11-12.4, L.11-12.4.A, L.11-12.4.D, L.11-12.6
    Writing - W.11-12.6
    Speaking/Listening - SL.11-12.1, SL.11-12.1.A, SL.11-12.1.B, SL.11-12.1.C, SL.11-12.1.D, SL.11-12.2

RESOURCES

The Once and Future King Claim Concept Map

Access 1 handout (Beginner)

Access 2 handout (Intermediate)

Access 3 handout (Advanced)

Access 4 handout (Approaching)

ACCESS COMPLEX TEXT

The novel *The Once and Future King* focuses on the relationship between King Arthur and his adviser Merlyn, and the development of Arthur as a king. This excerpt is set in the court of Arthur and consists of conversations between Arthur and Merlyn about war and ruling. To help students understand the characters of King Arthur and Merlyn, use the following ideas to provide scaffolded instruction for a first reading of the more complex features of this text:

- **Genre** - *The Once and Future King* is part of a larger tradition of Arthurian literature. If students are unfamiliar with the legends of King Arthur, they might benefit from a quick overview on the topic, including details about Arthur's reign and his relationship to Merlyn (or Merlin).

- **Organization** - The excerpt is taken from the middle of a longer work and introduces characters only through dialogue and narration of their current actions. Students may have trouble understanding the relationship between King Arthur and Merlyn because of this.

- **Connection of Ideas** - Struggling readers may have trouble understanding the particular details of Merlyn's life, specifically that he is traveling backward in time and that his youth took place in the future. These students might also need help understanding the allusion to Adolf Hitler and World War II in the final paragraphs.

- **Specific Vocabulary** - Some descriptive words and phrases—such as "knobbed fingers," "speak with agitation," and "knocking about"—may present a challenge to some readers.

1. INTRODUCTION

Core Path	Access Path
Read. Individually or as a class, read the Introduction for *The Once and Future King*. The introduction provides context for the excerpts taken from Chapters VI and VIII.	**English Learners All Levels & Approaching** **Read and Listen.** Ask students to read and listen to the introduction for *The Once and Future King*. Have them refer to the "Introduction Glossary" on their Access 1, 2, 3, and 4 handouts for definitions of key vocabulary terms. If there are unfamiliar words that are not included in their glossary, encourage students to check a dictionary or online reference tool, like http://dictionary.reference.com.

Core Path	Access Path
	Extend **Make Predictions.** After reading the introduction, use the information provided to facilitate a prereading discussion to get students to make predictions about the events and themes in *The Once and Future King*. 1. What do you think "might and right" means? 2. How could that relate to power and justice? 3. In what ways might Merlyn's experiences from the future shape his actions in the story?
Access Prior Knowledge. Find out what your students already know about the King Arthur myth. Ask students to name versions of the story that they are familiar with. If many students are already familiar with the story, ask them to identify main elements of the plot. Discuss the list as a group. If appropriate and possible, ask students to find clips from Arthurian films, such as *King Arthur* (2004), Disney's *The Sword in the Stone* (1963), *Camelot* (1967), or *Monty Python and the Holy Grail* (1975), and play them for the class. Note to students that *Camelot* and *The Sword in the Stone* were based directly on T.H. White's retelling of the story.	**English Learners All Levels & Approaching** **Complete and Discuss the Chart.** Pair Beginner and Advanced students and Intermediate and Approaching students, and rather than discussing their prior knowledge of Arthurian legend, have them complete the "Imagine" exercises on the Access 1, 2, 3, and 4 handouts that ask students to consider what their own priorities would be if they were giving a king advice from the future. Have the pairs generate ideas, discuss the chart, and complete it together.
	Extend **Tech Infusion** **Post.** Use Padlet (www.Padlet.com) to allow students to post about their previous knowledge on virtual sticky notes. Encourage them to embed images and video clips, if appropriate. This makes it possible for students to share their prior knowledge and read the sticky notes shared by their peers. Project the completed Padlet wall and discuss it as a class.

2. READ

Core Path	Access Path
Make Predictions about Vocabulary. There are five bold vocabulary words in the text. As students read the text, ask them to make predictions about what they think each bold vocabulary word means based on the context clues in the sentence. If you are in a low-tech classroom and students are reading from printed copies or a projected text, ask students to record predictions in their notes, so they can be easily referenced in class. If your students have access to technology, they can use the annotation tool to make their predictions.	**Note:** This exercise, which extends vocabulary instruction, should be completed when the class shifts from whole-group instruction to individual work during the "Read and Annotate" exercise.

Core Path (continued)

It might be helpful to model this for students before they begin reading. Either using the board or projecting the actual text, focus in on the sentence that uses the word "indignation":

- Merlyn stood up, boiling with indignation.

Model for the class how to use the overall structure and meaning of the sentence and the sentences around it, the word's position, and other clues to define the unfamiliar vocabulary word. In this case, point out these context keys:

1. Look at the structure of the sentence. What is the subject of the sentence? (Merlyn) What is the first verb? (stood) The phrase "boiling with indignation" is an adverbial phrase that describes the manner in which Merlyn stood up.

2. The previous sentence states that Arthur had Merlyn's seat removed, which forced Merlyn to stand up. We can guess by this context that "indignation" is something Merlyn feels as a result of Arthur's impolite behavior.

3. One often hears the term "boiling" in association with anger or rage. Thus, we can infer that "indignation" is anger or irritation as a result of something that isn't fair.

Access Path (continued)

Beginner, Intermediate & Approaching Pair Practice.

1. Pair students with more proficient readers.

2. Give them an additional sentence that contains a new vocabulary word.

3. Ask the students to complete a Think Aloud using the teacher-led Make Predictions about Vocabulary activity as a model, while the proficient student actively listens.

4. The student should use the context clues in the sentence to try to determine the meaning of the new vocabulary word.

5. After the student has completed the Think Aloud and made a prediction about the word's meaning, allow time for the proficient reader to add his/her own thoughts and clarify any points of confusion.

6. Once they've completed this Think Aloud, encourage them to use a dictionary to confirm the definition of the new vocabulary word. Have them refer to the "Text Glossary" on their Access 1, 2, and 4 handouts for definitions of key vocabulary terms in the text. Encourage them to add any additional vocabulary words or idioms they find in the text and look up definitions for those words and idioms online or in a dictionary.

Core Path

Model Reading Comprehension Strategy. Before students begin reading, model the reading comprehension strategy of making, confirming, and revising predictions by using this Think Aloud that talks students through the first half of the text. First explain to your students why they should make predictions:

Strong readers use text and text clues, along with prior knowledge, to make logical guesses about what might be learned in material they read.

Explain to students how making, confirming, and revising predictions will help them better comprehend the selection and help drive their discussions.

- The first character's name I see in this excerpt is the King of England. I already know this text is about King Arthur, so I can assume that "King of England" refers to him. Based on my prior knowledge of Arthurian legend, I predict that Arthur will be portrayed as a strong but fair ruler.

- I read the first few paragraphs of the text to see if I can confirm my prediction. Arthur has come to visit Merlyn, but Merlyn refuses to talk with the king and insists that their meeting take place at court. Based on this interaction, I have to revise my earlier prediction. Now I predict that, even though Arthur is the king, he respects Merlyn's authority.

- I keep reading to see if this prediction is more accurate. As Arthur talks about "Might and Right," he tries to guess Merlyn's reasoning, even though the magician remains quiet. This interaction confirms my prediction that Arthur is committed to following Merlyn's teachings.

Access Path

Note: This exercise, which extends instruction around reading comprehension strategies, should be completed when the class shifts from whole-group instruction to individual work during the "Read and Annotate" exercise.

Beginner, Intermediate & Approaching Apply Reading Comprehension Strategy.

1. Pair students and have them listen to the audio version of the excerpt from *The Once and Future King*. As they listen to the audio recording, ask them to pause the recording periodically and make predictions about what the characters will do next. Have them record these predictions in the chart on their Access 1, 2, and 4 handouts.

2. After student pairs record their first predictions, have them resume the audio and listen for evidence to support or disprove their prediction. Have them record this evidence in their charts. Then ask them to revise their predictions if needed. Have them repeat this process, making new predictions, as they listen to the entire audio excerpt.

3. Allow pairs time to discuss their predictions and the evidence they found. Which of their predictions were accurate? Which were not? Why?

Core Path	Access Path
Read and Annotate. Have students independently read and annotate the excerpt. Ask students to use the annotation tool as they read to: 1. use context clues to analyze and determine the meaning of the bolded vocabulary terms 2. ask questions about passages of the text that may be unclear or unresolved 3. identify key details, events, characters, and connections between them 4. note unfamiliar vocabulary 5. capture their reaction to the events in the text	**Beginner** **Coach the Reading.** While other students read, annotate, and discuss the text independently, work with Beginner students, listening to the audio of the text and pausing periodically or when any student has a question. Coach students in articulating their questions for the group and in highlighting and annotating the text. Have students use the Annotation Guide on the Access 1 handout to support them as they highlight and annotate the text. For further support, ask questions about the text, such as: • Is there anything about the story that you don't understand? • According to the story, what's the difference between might and right? • Do you think King Arthur will take Merlyn's advice? Why or why not? **Intermediate** **Listen to the Audio.** Have these students listen to the audio of the text and use the Text Glossary on the Access 2 handout to help them with words or idioms that may be unfamiliar. If students need help with annotating the text, have them use the Annotation Guide on the Access 2 handout. After working with the Beginner students, you may wish to check this group's progress and provide support as needed. **Advanced** **Pair with Proficient Peers.** Have Advanced students work with English-proficient peers to read, annotate, and discuss the text. Have students use the Annotation Guide in the Access 3 handout to support them as they highlight and annotate the text. Encourage them to listen to the audio of the text if needed. **Approaching** **Use the Annotation Guide.** Have students use the Annotation Guide on the Access 4 handout to support them as they highlight and annotate the text.

Core Path	Access Path
Discuss. In small groups or pairs, have students discuss the questions and inferences they made while reading. To help facilitate discussions, refer to Collaborative Discussions in the Speaking & Listening Handbook.	**English Learners All Levels & Approaching** Use the extra time while on- and beyond-grade-level students are discussing their first reads of the text to work individually and in small groups with Approaching readers and English Learners as outlined above. Should those students complete their first reads quickly, integrate them into the on- and beyond-grade-level discussion groups. Otherwise, English Learners and Approaching readers will be given an opportunity to participate in text discussions with their peers later in the lesson.

Core Path

1. What is Arthur attempting to do in the first 7 paragraphs? (He's climbed 208 stairs to discuss something with Merlyn.)

2. What ends up happening? (Merlyn sends Arthur away, telling him that a king should summon his advisors, not visit them.)

3. What is happening in the exchange between Arthur and Merlyn after Merlyn is summoned to visit the king? (Arthur jokingly gets back at Merlyn by forcing him to stand in the king's presence rather than sit comfortably.)

4. What can you infer is the purpose of Arthur's monologue on Might and Right (paragraphs 16–30)? (Arthur is working through his own questions on the subject while also explaining his position on the proper use of power with his knights.)

5. What does Arthur conclude about Might versus Right? (Arthur concludes that might does not make right, or that people in power should not just do whatever they want because they can. He decides that might or power should be used only to achieve good or justice.)

6. How does the conversation between Merlyn and Kay (paragraphs 31-39) compare to Arthur's views on the use of power? (Unlike Arthur, Kay believes that people in power should be able to act aggressively or forcefully for any reason they decide, as long as they believe it's in the best interest of the people.)

7. Who is the "Austrian" from the future (Merlyn's past) that Merlyn uses as his example? (Adolf Hitler)

8. How does making, confirming, and revising predictions help you better understand the outcome of the conversation? (Answers will vary.)

Access Path

Tech Infusion
Beyond
Brainstorm. Pair students and ask them to brainstorm other historical evidence Merlyn could use to support his ideas about might and right. Students who have access to a back-channel tool such as TodaysMeet (https://todaysmeet.com/) may enjoy brainstorming in that medium.

Core Path	Access Path
Tech Infusion **Record.** Use a voice recording app (Voice Memo on the iPhone or Smart Voice Recorder for Androids) or VoiceThread (https://voicethread.com) to capture each group's ideas.	
	Extend **Annotate and Organize.** After reading, ask students to use their annotations to analyze Arthur's claim in the speech from the Chapter VI excerpt. 1. Identify relevant details that establish the main points of Arthur's argument. 2. In small groups, ask students to create a concept map to identify how the details connect to each other. Students may collaborate using a resource like MindMeister (https://www.mindmeister.com/) to create their maps. If you're in a low-tech classroom, students may use the Claim Concept Map handout. 3. Each group should present its concept map to the class. Discuss similarities and differences between the maps with the whole class.
	Extend **Crowdsource.** Ask students to reflect on the arguments made by Arthur to his knights and by Merlyn to Kay. Students should: 1. Identify the main claims made in each section. 2. Analyze the differences between the leadership style that Arthur exhibits and that of the "Austrian" that Merlyn describes to Kay. 3. Identify ways that a good leader might both protect *and* guide his or her people. 4. Post ideas about these differences to a Padlet wall (https://padlet.com/) or participate in a back-channel discussion using TodaysMeet (https://todaysmeet.com/).

3. THINK

Core Path	Access Path
Answer and Discuss. Have students complete the Think questions and then use the peer review instructions and rubric to complete two peer reviews. Refer to the sample answers at the end of the lesson plan online to discuss responses with your students.	**Beginner & Intermediate** **Sentence Frames.** Have students use the sentence frames on the Access 1 and 2 handouts to support their responses to the Think questions. If necessary, distribute sentence frames to Advanced students as well. **Approaching** **Find the Evidence.** Have students use Find the Evidence on the Access 4 handout to help them identify the evidence needed to answer the questions.
	Extend **Debate.** Present students with an issue from the text that can be debated. Allow students to debate the issue as a class or in smaller groups. Remind students to use details from the text as they make their arguments. Debate prompt: Arthur acknowledges that he must fight two battles before he can consider using might for right. Kay argues that wanting to fight a war is a good enough reason for starting one. Both of them give examples or reasons to support their claims. Side with either Arthur or Kay and debate the following question: Under what circumstances, if any, should you start a war?

OVERVIEW

Analyzing point of view in literature is an important way for students to understand the perspectives of the narrator and other characters. This lesson plan provides follow-up questions and useful enrichments to help teachers guide students toward a usable, repeatable method for using an analysis of how authors use description and dialogue to establish a character's point of view.

OBJECTIVES

1. Instruct students on the definition of Point of View.
2. Provide students with strategies for identifying point of view as they read.
3. Participate effectively in a range of conversations and collaborations to express ideas and build upon the ideas of others.

    ELA Common Core Standards: :
    Reading: Literature - RL.11-12.1, RL.11-12.6
    Speaking & Listening - SL.11-12.1, SL.11-12.1.A, SL.11-12.1.C, SL.11-12.2

RESOURCES

Access 1 handout (Beginner)

Access 2 handout (Intermediate)

Access 3 handout (Advanced)

Access 4 handout (Approaching)

Please note that excerpts and passages in the StudySync® library, workbooks, and PDFs are intended as touchstones to generate interest in an author's work. The excerpts and passages do not substitute for the reading of entire texts, and StudySync® strongly recommends that teachers and students seek out and purchase the whole literary or informational work in order to experience it as the author intended. Links to online resellers are available in our digital library. In addition, complete works may be ordered through an authorized reseller by filling out and returning to StudySync® the order form enclosed in this workbook.

Teacher's Edition   199

1. DEFINE

Core Path	Access Path
Watch. Watch the Concept Definition video on point of view with your students. Make sure students understand the different components of point of view. Pause the video at these key moments to discuss the information with your students:	**English Learners All Levels & Approaching** **Match.** Have students complete the matching exercise on the Access 1, 2, 3, and 4 handouts as they watch the video. Answers are located at the end of the lesson plan online.

Core Path

1. 0:43 – Ben talks about second person reminding him of a hypnotist, but what are some other examples of second-person point of view that you can think of? What effect does the second person and the repetition of "you" have on readers or listeners?
2. 1:50 – What are the advantages and disadvantages for writers of using the different third-person point of view options? What considerations might a writer weigh before choosing an omniscient versus an objective narrator?
3. 2:25 – How is character point of view, mentioned last in the video, distinguishable from the various types of first-, second-, and third-person narrative point of view? What other elements go into a character's point of view?

Read and Discuss. Read the introduction to the concept definition. Either in small groups or as a whole class use these questions to spur discussion among your students about point of view.

1. How do you distinguish the three narrative points of view from one another? (First-person point of view uses "I." Everything you learn about the story is filtered through his/her thoughts and impressions. Second-person point of view uses "you" and addresses the reader directly. Third-person point of view refers to "him," "her," and "them." The narrator is only an observer, not a character.)

Access Path

Beginner & Approaching
Fill in the Blank. To prepare students to participate in the discussion, have them complete the fill-in-the-blanks activity on the Access 1 and 4 handouts as they read the definition. The correct answers are located at the end of the lesson plan online.

Intermediate & Advanced
Discuss Prompts. To help these students participate in the discussion, prompt them with questions that can be answered with a few words, such as:
• What are the three points of view in a story? (third-, second-, and third-person)

Core Path	Access Path
2. What are the three different types of third-person point of view? (Third-person omniscient point of view is "all-knowing"; limited omniscient point of view reveals the thoughts and feelings of a few characters; and third-person objective point of view is when the narrator describes the actions of characters, but not their thoughts and feelings.) 3. Describe a book you have read and its narrative point of view. How did you feel it worked with the story? Would it have been more interesting if it had used a different narrative point of view? (Answers will vary.)	• How can you tell the three types of third-person point of view frcm one another? (look at pronouns, ask if you know the thoughts and feelings of all characters or just a few, see if only their actions are described) • What narrative point of view does the author of *The Once and Future King* use? (third-person) Would another narrative point of view work? (Answers will vary.) **Beyond** **Discuss.** Have students tell a short story about one of their personal experiences. Then ask them to tell a story about someone else's experience. Have them discuss the techniques they used for these two different points of view.
	Extend **Present.** Ask students to review the techniques that authors might use to indicate narrative point of view. In small groups, have students create a skit that they will present to another small group, using each of the three narrative points of view. After they have presented their skits, have their small group "audience" list the techniques they used to demonstrate their various points of view. Then have them give feedback on what worked, what didn't, and how they might make improvements.
	Extend **Debate.** Divide the class into two groups. Have students debate one of the following questions: 1. Is technology in school a distraction? 2. Should social media be accessible to children under age 13?

Please note that excerpts and passages in the StudySync® library, workbooks, and PDFs are intended as touchstones to generate interest in an author's work. The excerpts and passages do not substitute for the reading of entire texts, and StudySync® strongly recommends that teachers and students seek out and purchase the whole literary or informational work in order to experience it as the author intended. Links to online resellers are available in our digital library. In addition, complete works may be ordered through an authorized reseller by filling out and returning to StudySync® the order form enclosed in this workbook.

Teacher's Edition **201**

Core Path	Access Path
	Guide each group to carefully craft their arguments. In this exercise, encourage them to conduct research to support their statements but focus most of their attention on the language they use. Each group should have a chance to present its argument and then rebut the opposing side's claims. At the end of the activity, ask students what they noticed about point of view and how it affected the language each group used. Guide them to identify instances in which one group used a euphemism, humor, or sarcasm to gloss over a perceived weakness in its argument. Students should grasp that truly understanding an argument or text requires that a reader carefully analyze language to infer an underlying meaning.

2. MODEL

Core Path	Access Path
Read and Annotate. Have students independently read the Model section. As they read, ask students to use the annotation tool to: • highlight key points • ask questions • identify places where the Model is applying the strategies laid out in the identification and Application section on point of view.	**Note:** During this portion of the lesson, instruction shifts from whole group to individual work. Use this time to work one-on-one or in small groups with Beginner, Intermediate, Advanced, and Approaching students. **Beginner & Intermediate** **Coach the Reading.** Work with these students (either individually or in small groups) to fill out the guided reading questions on the Access 1 and 2 handouts. Have Beginner students refer to the glossary on the Access 1 handout to help them determine the meaning of difficult words (note: provide the Access 1 handout glossary to Intermediate students if necessary). Let students know they'll use these answers to help participate in the discussion about the Model. Sample answers for this exercise are located at the end of the lesson plan online.

Core Path	Access Path
	Advanced **Identify Evidence.** Ask Advanced students to complete the identifying evidence exercise on the Access 3 handout. Let students know that they'll use these answers to help participate in the discussion about the Model. Sample answers for this exercise are located at the end of the lesson plan online. **Approaching** **Guided Reading.** Have students complete the guided reading questions on the Access 4 handout as they read. Let them know that they'll use these answers to help participate in the discussion about the Model. Sample answers for this exercise are located at the end of the lesson plan online.
Discuss. After students read the Model text, use these questions to facilitate a whole group discussion that helps students understand how to analyze the point of view of the passage: 1. What is the first step this Model uses to identify how point of view is used in the passage? (The first step is determining the passage's narrative point-of-view.) 2. What is important about analyzing the point of view, according to the Model? (It provides a clue to the reader that further work will need to be done to analyze the characters' attitudes toward the subject, namely, analyzing the language for tone and bias.) 3. What techniques does the Model use to indicate character point of view? (It analyzes language and description for insight into Arthur's perspective. Then, it uses dialogue to support and expand on it.)	

Please note that excerpts and passages in the StudySync® library, workbooks, and PDFs are intended as touchstones to generate interest in an author's work. The excerpts and passages do not substitute for the reading of entire texts, and StudySync® strongly recommends that teachers and students seek out and purchase the whole literary or informational work in order to experience it as the author intended. Links to online resellers are available in our digital library. In addition, complete works may be ordered through an authorized reseller by filling out and returning to StudySync® the order form enclosed in this workbook.

Teacher's Edition   203

Core Path	Access Path
4. The Model predicts that, after a close reading of the rest of the excerpt, the language and point of view will continue to support the conclusion that Arthur wants to use his power as king to keep people from following their baser instincts and hurting each other. Do you think this prediction is valid based on the points made in the Model? If not, what textual evidence will you consider in the rest of the excerpt to support a different conclusion?	

Extend

Tech Infusion

Retell. Remind students that another feature of point of view is learning to read between the lines, or looking for information in the text that isn't directly stated. Ask students to work in pairs or small groups.

- First, in rereading the excerpt, students should note any instance in which they infer or jump to a conclusion about the characters' attitudes or the text in general. They may use VoiceThread (https://voicethread.com) or another voice recorder to record the discussion.

- Second, students should collaborate on a document (use Google Docs, if available) and retell the events of the Model text using third-person omniscient point of view or first-person (Arthur's) point of view. In this retelling, they should state overtly, using the narrator as a tool, any inferences they may have made before. For example: "'I'll just have to convince these knights that they can't go around flaunting their strength by beating up on the peasants,' Arthur thought."

- Finally, guide groups to compare their new paragraphs to the Model and discuss how the use of point of view in the Model text differs from that used in their retelling.

Ask the groups to share their findings with the class. If possible, have students capture their discussions on video using their mobile devices so they can watch their conversations and critique the content.

3. YOUR TURN

Core Path	Access Path
Assess and Explain. Have students answer the comprehension questions to test for understanding. Share the explanations for Parts A and B (located online) with your students.	
	Extend **Share and Discuss.** Have students complete the Your Turn section in class. Poll students about their responses and, as a class, discuss the different strategies they used to determine the correct answers. Make sure they understand the vocabulary used in the questions. Prompt them to look up and define "convictions" and "consequences" if needed.
	Extend **Tech Infusion** **Apply.** Ask students to look through the list of test-taking strategies they've begun to compile this year. Have them revise the list and add to it any useful strategies they observed during this activity.

SKILL: Point of View

Please note that excerpts and passages in the StudySync® library, workbooks, and PDFs are intended as touchstones to generate interest in an author's work. The excerpts and passages do not substitute for the reading of entire texts, and StudySync® strongly recommends that teachers and students seek out and purchase the whole literary or informational work in order to experience it as the author intended. Links to online resellers are available in our digital library. In addition, complete works may be ordered through an authorized reseller by filling out and returning to StudySync® the order form enclosed in this workbook.

Teacher's Edition  **205**

CLOSE READ:
The Once and Future King

OVERVIEW

The novel *The Once and Future King,* by T. H. White, is the story of King Arthur and his struggle to create the ideal society in medieval England. In White's retelling of the classic story, Merlyn, Arthur's magician tutor and advisor, lives backward in time, and provides Arthur with insights gleaned from his "youth" in the future. The Close Read gives students the opportunity to delve into the language of the text to analyze the author's rhetoric.

OBJECTIVES

1. Complete a close reading of a passage of literature.
2. Practice and apply concrete strategies for analyzing point of view in an excerpt from *The Once and Future King.*
3. Participate effectively in a range of conversations and collaborations to express ideas and build upon the ideas of others.
4. Prewrite, plan, and produce clear and coherent writing in response to a prompt.

   ELA Common Core Standards:
   Reading: Literature - RL.11-12.1, RL.11-12.4, RL.11-12.6
   Writing - W.11-12.1, W.11-12.4, W.11-12.5, W.11-12.6, W.11-12.9.A, W.11-12.10
   Speaking & Listening - SL.11-12.1, SL.11-12.1.A, SL.11-12.1.B, SL.11-12.1.C, SL.11-12.1.D, SL.11-12.5, SL.11-12.6
   Language - L.11.12.4, L.11-12.4.A, L.11-12.4.C, L.11-12.4.D

RESOURCES

The Once and Future King Vocabulary Worksheet
Access 1 handout (Beginner)
Access 2 handout (Intermediate)
Access 3 handout (Advanced)
Access 4 handout (Approaching)

1. INTRODUCTION

Core Path	Access Path
Define and Compare. Project the vocabulary words and definitions onto the board or provide students with a handout, so they can copy the vocabulary into their notebooks. Ask students to compare their initial vocabulary predictions from the First Read with the actual definitions. Review words that students defined incorrectly to understand why they were unable to use context clues or other tools to develop usable definitions.	**Beginner & Intermediate** **Complete a Chart.** Have students complete the chart on the Access 1 and 2 handouts by writing the correct word for each of the definitions. **Advanced & Beyond** **Write in Journals.** Have students write a journal entry using all of their vocabulary words. Remind them to write sentences that communicate the meaning of the words they are using. **Approaching** **Graphic Organizer.** To support students in comparing their predictions with the correct meanings, have them complete the graphic organizer on the Access 4 handout to record the vocabulary words, their initial analysis, and the definitions. Then have them write sentences using the words.
Review. Have students complete the fill-in-the-blank vocabulary worksheet for this selection. Answers for the worksheet are listed online.	
	Extend **Tech Infusion** **Create and Publish.** Create artwork to visually represent the words using an iPad or Android art app, such as Paper or Tayasui Sketches. Then have students submit their work, either by e-mailing it to you or by posting it to the class blog. If you're in a low-tech classroom, students may draw on paper, and you can post the drawings around the classroom. Guide students to leave comments about each drawing stating what they found compelling about the artwork and how it illustrated the vocabulary word.

Core Path	Access Path
	Extend **Tech Infusion** **Review.** Create a vocabulary review quiz using Kahoot (https://getkahoot.com). Design multiple-choice questions that require students to apply their understanding of the vocabulary. Then run the quiz and allow students to compete against each other to test their knowledge of the vocabulary. Scores are based on whether the answer is correct and how fast the student answers.
	Extend **Tech Infusion** **Create.** Create online flashcards for the vocabulary using Quizlet (http://quizlet.com) or StudyBlue (http://www.studyblue.com). Have students work in pairs to practice with the flash cards. End the activity by asking each student to explain an experience he or she has had that could relate to one of the vocabulary words. For instance, one student my explain that his parents **impose** a curfew on him on weekend nights.

2. READ

Core Path	Access Path
Model Close Reading. Project the text onto the board and model a close reading of the first four paragraphs using the annotation strategies mentioned below. While modeling annotation strategies, make notes that tie the text to the focus skill and demonstrate what students are looking for as they read. Some guidance for you as you annotate for your students:	

Core Path	Access Path

Core Path

- As the Skills Lesson that appeared just before this text made clear, we have to look at the language White uses to indicate the characters' points of view and attitudes. Highlight phrases such as "painfully climbed" and "panting" to show that Arthur is putting forth a lot of energy to go talk to Merlyn, and in return, Merlyn "shoos" him away and "shouts" at him to "go away!" Now we know that Arthur was perhaps trying to do Merlyn a favor because paragraph 6 tells us that Merlyn is an "old man." But Arthur's kind gesture is rebuffed. What inference can we make about the balance of power in their relationship as a result of this?

- The next few paragraphs show how Arthur reacts to this treatment from Merlyn. Arthur "summons" Merlyn, who "presents himself" formally to the "Royal Chamber," which Merlyn indicates is "better" behavior for a king. Arthur then pokes fun at Merlyn by having Merlyn's "comfortable" seat taken away by a page— whom Arthur has also "summoned" by clapping his hands. This should please Merlyn because Arthur is behaving like a king, as Merlyn wanted him to in paragraph 4, but Merlyn is now "boiling with indignation" because his chair has been taken away.

- Make sure students understand the humor used here. We know Arthur thinks it's funny, too, because he uses an "airy" tone—demonstrate what this would sound like—when he goes on to begin the conversation he would have liked to have had before, when he climbed those "two hundred and eight" stairs.

- Point out that this first scene with Arthur and Merlyn allows the reader to conclude that Arthur will be someone who wants to have serious conversations, but isn't afraid of having a little bit of fun, too.

Core Path	Access Path
Read and Annotate. Read the Skills Focus questions as a class, so your students know what they should pay close attention to as they read. Then have students read and annotate the excerpt. Ask students to use the annotation tool as they read to:	**Note:** While on-grade-level students are reading and annotating, work one-on-one or in small groups with Beginner, Intermediate, Advanced, and Approaching students to support them as they read and annotate the text.

Core Path (continued)

1. respond to the Skills Focus section

2. analyze how the author uses language to advance the central idea, point of view, or purpose

3. examine each character's use of language and note how it reveals the character's attitude or how he or she feels or thinks about a topic

4. note any persuasive or figurative language

5. note unfamiliar vocabulary

6. capture their reaction to the ideas and examples in the text.

As they reread the text, remind students to use the comprehension strategy of making, confirming, and revising predictions that they learned in the First Read.

Access Path (continued)

Beginner & Intermediate

Summarize and Analyze the Text. Work with these students to complete the sentence frames on the Access 1 and 2 handouts (note: the sentence frames for Intermediate students on the Access 2 handout contain fewer scaffolds). They will then use the completed sentence frames to help them analyze and annotate the text by completing the Skills Focus questions. Refer to the sample Skills Focus answers to help them complete the sentence frames and annotate the text.

Advanced

Work in Pairs. Pair these students with more proficient English speakers to work together on analyzing and annotating the text to complete the Skills Focus questions. If these students need more support, have them use the sentence frames on the Access 3 handout as they work with their more proficient peers.

Approaching

Summarize the Text. Have these students discuss and complete the text summary on the Access 4 handout and use their summary to help them analyze and annotate the text by completing the Skills Focus questions. Correct answers for the summary are at the end of the lesson plan online. Also refer to the sample Skills Focus answers to aid students with their annotations.

Core Path	Access Path
Discuss. After students have read the text, use the sample responses to the Skills Focus questions located at the end of the lesson plan online to discuss the reading and the process analyzing rhetoric. Make sure that students have acquired and accurately use academic-specific words and phrases related to the skill and demonstrate a command of formal English appropriate to the discussion. To help facilitate discussions, refer to Collaborative Discussions in the Speaking & Listening Handbook.	**Extend** **Pair and Share.** In small, heterogeneous groups or pairs, ask students to share and discuss their annotations with a focus on the rhetoric in the selection. You can provide students with these questions to guide their discussion: 1. How is "Might" defined in the text? How is "Right" defined in the text? What inferences did you have to make to arrive at these definitions? (After Arthur first introduces the concepts of Might and Right, he states that you shouldn't do something simply because you can. That is a good definition of Might, which is reinforced later in the excerpt, when Arthur talks about how *not* to behave. Similarly, after he introduces Might and Right, he says "I think [things] should be done because you *ought* to do them." Later, Arthur says that "people ought not to be killed," which reinforces this as a definition of Right. However, the reader has to infer what specifically falls under the category of using force for good and using force simply for its own sake. Kay seems to be having the same problem later on in the excerpt.) 2. Why do you think Might and Right are given high status as proper nouns in this text? (Might and Right are capitalized because they are important concepts, not just actions or theories. The language of the text almost treats "Might for Right" as a belief system, like Christianity, or Buddhism—something that keeps the world from "plunging into misery and chaos.")

Core Path	Access Path
	3. How does the end of the excerpt deal with the issue of "Might and Right"? Cite textual evidence to support your answer. (Kay is confused about the concepts of Might and Right, because they seem to contradict what Arthur is doing in waging war with King Lot. However, Arthur explained in the first section of the excerpt that "Lot ... [is part of] the old world, the old-fashioned order who want to have their private will ... they live by force." So it would seem that, if the excerpt went on, Merlyn might try to help Kay understand Arthur's definition of the concept.)
	Extend **Research.** Find a current news article that you think focuses on the use (or lack) of Might for Right. Ask students to bring in a copy of their own article to share. In small groups, allow students to exchange articles to read and discuss.
	Extend **Write.** Ask students to write another 3-5 paragraphs of dialogue between Kay and Merlyn. Students should try to mimic the diction, tone, and speaking style of each character. Students can continue the dialogue in any way, but may choose to have Merlyn provide more examples of strong leaders and weak leaders, or to have Kay continue to argue his position about Arthur attacking King Lot. Encourage them to be creative and to use the tools of dialogue and description to indicate character point of view in this lesson. When students have finished, obtain a copy of the unabridged *The Once and Future King* and ask students to compare their narratives to the actual story.

3. WRITE

Core Path	Access Path
Prewrite and Plan. Read the prompt as a class and ask students to brainstorm about why Arthur's speech about might and right was called the "critical moment" of Merlyn's career. Students can brainstorm together either as a class or in small groups to begin planning their responses. Remind your students to look at the excerpt and their annotations to find textual evidence to support their ideas.	**Beginner & Intermediate** **Plan and Organize.** Have students complete the prewriting activity on the Access 1 and 2 handouts and then explain their ideas to a partner before they write. Explain to students that they need to choose details, examples, or quotes from the text that support their ideas and then explain how those details support their statements. For example, students could include this line from paragraph 13: "You might say that this moment was the critical one in his career—the moment towards which he had been living backward for heaven knows how many centuries, and now he was to see for certain whether he had lived in vain." This line suggests that Merlyn wants to use his life experience to guide Arthur. **Approaching** **Plan and Organize.** Have students complete the prewriting activity on the Access 4 handout to organize their thoughts before they write.
	Extend **Organize.** Encourage students to complete a graphic organizer to organize their ideas before they type their responses.
	Extend **Tech Infusion** **Map.** Students can create concept maps online using Creately (creately.com). Google Drawings can also be used to design a concept map.

Core Path	Access Path
Discuss. Project these instructions for the peer review onto the board and review them with your class, so they know what they are looking for when they begin to provide their classmates with feedback: • Has the writer made a clear statement about why Arthur's speech was so important to Merlyn? • Has the writer explained whether or not the excerpt ever made clear whether Merlyn's goals were achieved? Does the explanation make sense? • How clear was the writer's explanation of how the language from the story helped him or her analyze the story? • Does the writer reference point of view, connotation, and use of language in this analysis? • What sort of evidence did the writer use from the text to support his or her writing? • How well does the writer explain how that evidence supports his or her arguments? • Does the writer write using standard grammar and punctuation? Are there any weak spots? • What specific suggestions can you make to help the writer improve the response? • What thing(s) does this paper do especially well? After you've looked at the peer review instructions, review the rubric with students before they begin writing. Allow time for students briefly to pose and discuss any questions they may have about the peer review instructions and the rubric. Tell students how many peer reviews they will need to complete once they submit their writing.	
Write. Ask students to complete the writing assignment using textual evidence to support their answers. Once they have completed their writing, they should click "Submit."	

Core Path	Access Path
	Extend **Critique.** Project a writing sample on the board and ask the class to identify the elements of writing that are strong, as well as those that are weak or in need of improvement. Obscure the student author's name, if needed. Alternatively, you can put students in small groups and give them photocopies of a writing sample to collaboratively evaluate. After students have had an opportunity to evaluate student samples, work as a class to generate strategies students can use as they complete their peer reviews to ensure they are substantive.
	Extend **Tech Infusion** **Critique.** Have students compile a list of the most useful strategies on a Padlet wall (https://padlet.com). Create a link to the wall from your class website or blog. Call attention to the link on your site and remind students to visit it any time they are participating in a peer review.
Review. Once students complete their writing assignment, they should submit substantive feedback to two peers.	

Le Morte d'Arthur

OVERVIEW

The fifteenth-century legend *Le Morte d'Arthur* was written hundreds of years after the Arthurian legends became popular in England and France. In this selection, Sir Thomas Malory recounts the final battle and death of King Arthur. The First Read gives students the opportunity to experience the text with a limited context.

OBJECTIVES

1. Perform an initial reading of a text and demonstrate comprehension by responding to short analysis and inference questions with textual evidence.
2. Practice defining vocabulary words using context.
3. Participate effectively in a range of conversations and collaborations to express ideas and build upon the ideas of others.
4. Practice acquiring and using academic vocabulary correctly.

ELA Common Core Standards:
Reading: Literature - RL.11-12.1, RL.11-12.4, RL.11-12.10
Language - L.11-12.1.A, L.11-12.4.B, L.11-12.4.D, L.11-12.6
Speaking & Listening - SL.11-12.1, SL.11-12.1.B, SL.11-12.1.C, SL.11-12.2

RESOURCES

Grammar handout: Archaic Usage

Access 1 handout (Beginner)

Access 2 handout (Intermediate)

Access 3 handout (Advanced)

Access 4 handout (Approaching)

ACCESS COMPLEX TEXT

In this excerpt from *Le Morte d'Arthur*, the author describes the events leading up to Arthur's final battle. To help students understand the main character of King Arthur and the story elements the author employs to create a complex narrative, use the following ideas to provide scaffolded instruction for a first reading of the more complex features of this text:

- **Connection of Ideas** - As they read, students may need to make inferences and synthesize information in order to understand the characters and their actions. The characters' traits and motivations are often shown through their words and deeds, rather than stated outright by the author.

- **Prior Knowledge** - Some students may not be familiar with the legends surrounding King Arthur and his knights, including concepts such as the code of chivalry. In addition, the story balances on the edge of history and legend; much of the story seems historically plausible, while other parts seem to embody pure fantasy.

- **Specific Vocabulary** - Antiquated terms—such as "beholden," "hither," and "yonder"—may present a challenge to some readers.

1. INTRODUCTION

Core Path	Access Path
Read. Individually or as a class, read the Introduction for *Le Morte d'Arthur*. The introduction provides context for the selection.	**English Learners All Levels & Approaching** **Read and Listen.** Ask students to read and listen to the introduction for *Le Morte d'Arthur*. Have them refer to the "Introduction Glossary" on their Access 1, 2, 3, and 4 handouts for definitions of key vocabulary terms. If there are unfamiliar words that are not included in their glossary, encourage students to check a dictionary or online reference tool, such as http://dictionary.reference.com.
	Extend **Make Predictions.** Based on the introduction and the title of the selection, have students make predictions about what they think the text will be about. What aspects of the Arthurian legend might the text include? What themes do they expect to encounter?

Please note that excerpts and passages in the StudySync® library, workbooks, and PDFs are intended as touchstones to generate interest in an author's work. The excerpts and passages do not substitute for the reading of entire texts, and StudySync® strongly recommends that teachers and students seek out and purchase the whole literary or informational work in order to experience it as the author intended. Links to online resellers are available in our digital library. In addition, complete works may be ordered through an authorized reseller by filling out and returning to StudySync® the order form enclosed in this workbook.

Teacher's Edition   **217**

Core Path	Access Path
	Extend
	Discuss the Introduction. The introduction describes the text as a "romance," but medieval romance is not what students likely think of today when they think of romance novels. Explain that the word "romance" comes from the Latin "romanice," meaning "vernacular" or "common language." These medieval romances were poems written in the vernacular instead of Latin. While medieval romances included love affairs (like most books and movies today), they also included chivalry, adventure, and magic elements.
	Have small groups of students research examples of medieval French romance stories. Then discuss the following questions:
	1. What elements do these stories have in common?
	2. What surprised you about the stories you found?
	3. What audience do you think these romances were written for? Why?
	4. How is the definition of French romance different from our modern day romances?
Access Prior Knowledge. Review what your students already know about King Arthur's character and beliefs. As a class or in small groups, generate a list (on the board or on paper) of instances where he applies his ideal of "Might versus Right." What specific stories do they know? Who are the characters involved? After compiling a list, ask students to share where "good versus evil" fits in with Arthur's ideal. Keep it in mind as you read the selection.	**Beginner**
	Might versus Right. Pair students, and rather than discussing King Arthur specifically, have them complete the "Might versus Right" exercise on the Access 1 handouts that asks students to consider the meanings of "Might" and "Right" and how people use these forces in real life. Have the pairs generate ideas, discuss the questions, and complete them together.
	Intermediate & Advanced
	Critical Thinking. Pair Intermediate and Advanced students, and rather than discussing King Arthur specifically, have them complete the "Critical Thinking" exercises on the Access 2 and 3 handouts that ask students to consider "Might versus Right." Have the pairs generate ideas, discuss the questions, and complete them together.

Core Path	Access Path
	Approaching **Pair and Discuss.** 1. First, ask individuals to imagine a schoolyard bully picking on a smaller, younger student. 2. Have pairs discuss the situation and give their ideas about "Might versus Right" in such a scenario. Which person has the "might"? Is this person "right" in his or her actions? 3. After they've finished their discussion, have students complete the "Critical Thinking" exercise on the Access 4 handout.

2. READ

Core Path	Access Path
Make Predictions about Vocabulary. There are six bold vocabulary words in the text. As students read the text, ask them to use context to make a preliminary determination of the meaning of each bold vocabulary word. If you are in a low-tech classroom and students are reading from printed copies or a projected text, ask students to record meanings in their notes, so they can be easily referenced in class. If your students have access to technology, they can use the annotation tool to note their meanings. It might be helpful to model this for students before they begin reading. Either using the board or projecting the actual text, focus in on the sentence that uses the word "brandished": • And there came an arm and a hand above the water which caught it and shook and **brandished** it thrice and then vanished with the sword into the water. Model for the class how to use word parts as well as the overall structure and meaning of the sentence and the sentences around it, the word's position, and other contextual clues to define the unfamiliar vocabulary word. In this case, point out these clues:	**Note:** This exercise, which extends vocabulary instruction, should be completed when the class shifts from whole-group instruction to individual work during the "Read and Annotate" exercise. **Beginner, Intermediate & Approaching** **Pair Practice.** 1. Pair students with more proficient readers. 2. Give them an additional sentence that contains a new vocabulary word. 3. Ask the students to complete a Think Aloud using the teacher-led Make Predictions about Vocabulary activity as a model, while the proficient student actively listens. 4. The student should use the context clues in the sentence to try to determine the meaning of the new vocabulary word. 5. After the student has completed the Think Aloud and made a prediction about the word's meaning, allow time for the proficient reader to add his/her own thoughts and clarify any points of confusion.

Core Path	Access Path
• A quick analysis of the word "brandished" reveals two things: the suffix *-ed* tells me that the word is most likely a verb, and the verb is in the past tense. • From looking at the word's context in the sentence and examining its word parts, I can determine the meaning of the word. • The text says an arm came up from the water and "shook and brandished" the sword, so "brandished" must be something done with a weapon such as a sword. • The word "brandished" is paired with in this quotation is "shook," which I know is a verb. This tells me my prediction that "brandished" is a verb is likely correct. • I think "brandished" must mean "shook or waved a weapon in a menacing or celebratory way." This would seem to work in the original context of the sentence. • This seems like enough to understand the sentence, but I'll make sure to look the word up in the dictionary later on to confirm my predicted meaning.	6. Once they've completed this Think Aloud, encourage them to use a dictionary to confirm the definition of the new vocabulary word. Have them refer to the "Text Glossary" on their Access 1, 2, and 4 handouts for definitions of key vocabulary terms in the text. Encourage them to add any additional vocabulary words or idioms they find in the text and look up definitions for those words and idioms online or in a dictionary.

Model Reading Comprehension Strategy. Before students begin reading, model the reading comprehension strategy of rereading by using this Think Aloud that talks students through the first paragraph. First explain to students why rereading is valuable:

Strong readers understand that they may miss important points during a first read of a complex text.

Explain to students how rereading will help them better comprehend the story and help drive their discussions.

• I'll quickly read through the first paragraph to get a feel for the story. The first paragraph contains several long sentences, and the dream sequence is confusing.

Note: This exercise, which extends instruction around reading comprehension strategies, should be completed when the class shifts from whole-group instruction to individual work during the "Read and Annotate" exercise.

Beginner, Intermediate & Approaching Apply Reading Comprehension Strategy.

1. Have Beginner and Intermediate students listen to the audio version of the excerpt from *Le Morte d'Arthur*. As they listen to the audio recording, ask them to jot down a list of key words, phrases, and ideas that they understand as the recording plays.

2. Once they have listened to the audio version and created their lists, pair Beginner and Intermediate students with more proficient readers and ask them to share their notes. Did they write down the same words, phrases, and ideas?

Core Path	Access Path
• I'm going to take a step back and reread the first sentence. I know this paragraph is describing King Arthur's dream. It starts out as a good dream, with Arthur dressed in "the richest cloth of gold." • Then the dream turns. On the second read I can picture Arthur looking down into the "hideous deep black water" under his chair. Rereading helped me to understand the ominous tone of this paragraph.	3. Allow pairs time to discuss their lists. Then play the audio version of the excerpt again and have students make a second list of key words, phrases, and ideas. Have students return to their pairs and compare their new lists to the old ones. Have them discuss which ideas, events, or characters became clearer the second time they listened to the text and what new aspects of the text they noticed.

Read and Annotate. Read and annotate the excerpt. Ask students to use the annotation tool as they read to

1. use context clues to analyze and determine the meaning of the bolded vocabulary terms

2. ask questions about passages of the text that may be unclear or unresolved

3. identify key details, events, characters, and connections between them

4. note unfamiliar vocabulary

5. capture their reaction to the events in the text.

AdvancedBeginner Coach the Reading. While other students read, annotate, and discuss the text independently, work with Beginner students, listening to the audio of the text and pausing periodically or when any student has a question. Coach students in articulating their questions for the group and in highlighting and annotating the text. Have students use the Annotation Guide on the Access 1 handout to support them as they highlight and annotate the text.

For further support, ask questions about the text such as:
• Who are the main characters in the story? Which characters are fighting together or against each other?

• What vision does Arthur have? How does he react to the vision at first? How does he react to the vision at the end of the battle?

• Why did Arthur want his sword to be thrown into the lake?

Intermediate
Listen to the Audio. Have these students listen to the audio of the text and use the Text Glossary on the Access 2 handout to help them with words or idioms that may be unfamiliar. If students need help with annotating the text, have them use the Annotation Guide on the Access 2 handout. After working with the Beginner students, you may wish to check this group's progress and provide support as needed.

Core Path	Access Path
	Advanced **Pair with Proficient Peers.** Have Advanced students work with English-proficient peers to read, annotate, and discuss the text. Have students use the Annotation Guide in the Access 3 handout to support them as they highlight and annotate the text. Encourage them to listen to the audio of the text if needed. **Approaching** **Use the Annotation Guide.** Have students use the Annotation Guide on the Access 4 handout to support them as they highlight and annotate the text.
Discuss. In small groups or pairs, have students discuss the questions and inferences they made while reading. To help facilitate discussions, refer to Collaborative Discussions in the Speaking & Listening Handbook. 1. What two dreams does King Arthur have at the beginning of the selection? What do these dreams represent? (He dreamed first of a great threat to his life, suggested by "serpents and worms and wild beasts, foul and horrible." His second dream came in the form of a warning from Sir Gawain, who urged him not to battle Sir Mordred or he would surely lose his life.) 2. How does the battle begin? What is the result? (A knight draws his sword to slay an adder on the ground and all take that as a sign to begin battle.) 3. Who is Mordred and what is his relationship to Arthur? What happens to him? (Mordred is Arthur's illegitimate son who wages final battle against him. He is killed by Arthur.)	**English Learners All Levels & Approaching** Use the extra time while on- and beyond-grade-level students are discussing their first reads of the text to work individually and in small groups with Approaching readers and English Learners as outlined above. Should those students complete their first reads quickly, integrate them into the on- and beyond-grade-level discussion groups. Otherwise, English Learners and Approaching readers will be given an opportunity to participate in text discussions with their peers later in the lesson. **Tech Infusion** **Beyond** **Research.** Pair students and ask them to research the principles of heroism and morality associated with King Arthur (chivalry, loyalty, bravery, Right before Might, defending the weak, and so on).

Core Path	Access Path
4. What does Arthur ask Sir Bedivere to do? (Arthur asks Sir Bedivere to throw his sword into the water nearby.) What is Bedivere's response? (He lies twice to Arthur before obeying his final command.) What do Bedivere's actions represent? (They represent greed.) 5. Who greets Arthur from the barge? (Three queens and other women wearing black hoods.) Reread that section of the selection. How do they act? (They "wept and shrieked.") What does this imply about Arthur's future? (Their actions imply that he will die.)	

Core Path	Access Path
Grammar, Usage, and Mechanics. Distribute the handout on archaic usage. Review with students the information provided on the handout. Have students complete the practice exercise. (The answers to the exercise appear online.) Then encourage students to analyze archaic usage in *Le Morte d'Arthur*. Ask students what connotations the words "thee," "thy," and "thou" have. (Students may mention Shakespeare or a formal, old-fashioned means of addressing others.) Have students reread the text and examine the use of pronouns. 1. Which characters use *thee/thou/thy*? (only King Arthur) 2. Which characters use *you/your*? (all of the other characters) 3. What can you infer about these pronouns based on the usage in this selection? (*You* and *your* were more formal second person pronouns at the time the text was written, used to address royalty.)	**Beginner & Intermediate** **Work with the Teacher.** Remind students that "thou," "thee," and "thy" are second-person pronouns. They serve the same purposes as pronouns they already know and use: "you" as a subject, "you" as an object, and "your" as a possessive pronoun. "Thou" is the second-person subject pronoun, "thee" is the second-person object pronoun, and "thy" is the possessive pronoun. Write the following statement on the board: *You should help your friend because he helped you.* Have students circle the second-person pronouns. (You, your, you) Ask: Which pronoun is used as a subject? (the first *You*) Which pronoun is an object? (the second *you*) Which word is a possessive pronoun? (your) Call on volunteers to replace each pronoun with "thee," "thy," or "thou." (Thou should help thy friend because he helped thee.) As needed, write additional example sentences on the board and have students identify and replace each second-person pronoun with the correct archaic pronoun. Then work with them to complete the practice exercise.

Core Path	Access Path
	Advanced & Beyond **Extend the search.** Challenge these students to work in pairs or small groups to find examples of "you" and "your" in the text, and to rewrite these sentences using "thee," "thy," and "thou." For example: *Thus God hath given me leave to warn you away from your death becomes Thus God hath given me leave to warn thee away from thy death.* **Approaching** **Analyze an example.** If students need more support with archaic second-person pronouns, call their attention to these words in paragraph 15: *Good lord, remember your night's dream and what the spirit of Sir Gawain told you last night. God in His great goodness hath preserved you so far.* Help students identify and replace each instance of "your" and "you" with archaic pronouns: *Good lord, remember thy night's dream and what the spirit of Sir Gawain told thee last night. God in His great goodness hath preserved thee so far.* As needed, provide additional examples, including sentences with "you" as a subject pronoun. Call on students to rewrite the sentences using the three archaic pronouns. Then have students complete the practice exercise.
	Extend **Explore Images.** The Arthurian legends have been popular in visual art since the time of the medieval romances. Divide students into three groups and assign each a famous period of Arthurian art: • medieval tapestries • Victorian paintings • 20th-century engravings and illustrations Have students find examples of Arthurian images from their given time period. Then, as a class, discuss similarities and differences between the images.

Core Path	Access Path
	Extend **Tech Infusion** **Create.** Have students use Prezi (https://prezi.com) to create a timeline of Arthurian art. Direct students to include images as well as the title, date, and artist for each work.

3. THINK

Core Path	Access Path
Answer and Discuss. Have students complete the Think questions and then use the peer review instructions and rubric to complete two peer reviews. Refer to the sample answers at the end of the lesson plan online to discuss responses with your students.	**Beginner & Intermediate** **Sentence Frames.** Have students use the sentence frames on the Access 1 and 2 handouts to support their responses to the Think questions. If necessary, distribute sentence frames to Advanced students as well. **Approaching** **Find the Evidence.** Have students use Find the Evidence on the Access 4 handout to help them identify the evidence needed to answer the questions.
	Extend **Debate.** Present students with the following question from the text: Was King Arthur's death inevitable, or could he have saved himself? Why or why not? Allow students to debate the issue as a class or in smaller groups. Remind students to always refer to evidence from the text to support their opinions.

OVERVIEW

Analyzing story elements and archetypes in a text can be a challenging process. This lesson plan provides follow-up questions and useful enrichments to help teachers guide students toward a usable, repeatable strategy for analyzing story elements and using them to identify and analyze archetypes.

OBJECTIVES

1. Learn the definition of story elements and archetypes.
2. Analyze story elements and archetypes.
3. Participate effectively in a range of conversations and collaborations to express ideas and build upon the ideas of others.

    ELA Common Core Standards:
    Reading: Literature - RL.11-12.1, RL.11-12.2, RL.11-12.3
    Speaking & Listening - SL.11-12.1, SL.11-12.1.A, SL.11-12.1.C, SL.11-12.2

RESOURCES

Access 1 handout (Beginner)

Access 2 handout (Intermediate)

Access 3 handout (Advanced)

Access 4 handout (Approaching)

1. DEFINE

Core Path	Access Path
Watch. Watch the Concept Definition video on story elements with your students. Make sure your students know all three elements of a story—plot, character, and setting—as well as how the three elements are interrelated. Pause the video at these key moments to discuss the information with your students:	**English Learners All Levels & Approaching** **Fill in the Blank.** Have students complete the fill-in-the-blank exercise on the Access 1, 2, 3, and 4 handouts as they watch the video. Answers are located at the end of the lesson plan online.
1. 0:30 – What typically occurs over the course of a story's plot? How does the action move forward, from beginning to middle to end? What changes or evolves? Discuss.	
2. 0:47 – Who are some of your favorite characters from the stories you've read? What makes these characters interesting or likable? Why?	
3. 1:20 – How might changing a story's setting affect both its plot and characters? What are some things an author might consider before deciding on the right setting for a particular story?	
Read and Discuss. Read the introduction to the definition of story elements. Either in small groups or as a whole class, use these questions to spur discussion among your students about story elements.	**Beginner & Approaching** **Complete the Sentences.** To prepare students to participate in the discussion, have them complete the sentence-completion exercise on the Access 1 and 4 handouts as they read the definition. The correct answers are located at the end of the lesson plan online.
1. What three basic elements does the instruction provide? (plot, character, setting) Define each one.	**Intermediate & Advanced** **Discuss Prompts.** To help these students participate in the discussion, prompt them with questions that can be answered with a few words, such as:
2. Have you ever read a story or seen a movie that lacked one or more of these elements?	• What is the plot of a story? (what happens) What are the characters? (the people in the story) What is the setting? (the time and place where the action occurs)
3. Think about the literature you've read over your high school career. Which had the most memorable characters, plots, or settings?	• What is a story that is very memorable for you? What was the most memorable: the plot, the setting, or the characters? (Answers will vary.)
	• Could a story be complete without a key story element, such as characters? Why or why not? (Answers will vary.)

Core Path	Access Path
4. Archetypes are universal symbols, themes, or character types. What universal story elements can you think of from movies or books? (If students have trouble, start the discussion by prompting with these archetypal themes: love conquers all, death and resurrection, an epic quest; Archetypal characters: the hero, the wise old man, the fool who turns out to be wise)	**Beyond** **Discuss.** Have students select a book they've read and describe its characters. Compile a list of examples. Have students discuss how the characters of each work are affected by the plot and/or setting, and whether they affect the plot through their own actions. Are any of the characters listed archetypes? What traits do they exhibit that show they are a specific kind of archetype?
	Extend **Tech Infusion** **Brainstorm.** Choose one archetypal character or theme to focus on. Then compile a list of books, movies, or TV shows that include this archetype. Encourage students to think of examples that may not be obviously literary (such as Yoda from *Star Wars* as the wise old man archetype). Compile this list of examples as a class using a whiteboard or a Padlet wall (http://padlet.com). Discuss elements that connect all these stories.
	Extend **Explore.** Choose a text previously read and analyzed by the whole class. Put students in small groups and have them discuss how changing one story element, such as the setting, would have significantly changed the text, and why. Have students discuss why the author made the choices he or she did.

2. MODEL

Core Path	Access Path
Read and Annotate. Have students independently read the Model section. As they read, ask students to use the annotation tool to: • highlight story elements • ask questions	**Note:** During this portion of the lesson, instruction shifts from whole-group to individual work. Use this time to work one-on-one or in small groups with Beginner, Intermediate, Advanced, and Approaching students.

Core Path	Access Path
• identify places where the Model applies the strategies laid out in the Define section on story elements.	**Beginner & Intermediate** **Coach the Reading.** Work with these students (either individually or in small groups) to fill out the guided reading questions on the Access 1 and 2 handouts. Have Beginner students refer to the glossary on the Access 1 handout to help them determine the meaning of difficult words (note: provide the Access 1 handout glossary to Intermediate students if necessary). Let students know they'll use these answers to help participate in the discussion about the Model. Sample answers for this exercise are located at the end of the lesson plan online. **Advanced** **Identify Evidence.** Ask Advanced students to complete the identifying evidence exercise on the Access 3 handout. Let students know that they'll use these answers to help participate in the discussion about the Model. Sample answers for this exercise are located at the end of the lesson plan online. **Approaching** **Guided Reading.** Have students complete the guided reading questions on the Access 4 handout as they read. Let them know that they'll use these answers to help participate in the discussion about the Model. Sample answers for this exercise are located at the end of the lesson plan online.
Discuss. After students read the Model text, use these questions to facilitate a whole group discussion that helps students understand how to analyze story elements: 1. What's the first step this Model uses to begin analyzing story elements? Why does the Model start there? (It starts by identifying the characters, setting, and plot, because you can't analyze until you know what you're analyzing.)	

Core Path	Access Path
2. Which strategy from the Define section does the Model use in paragraph 3? (analyze author's choices in-depth) 3. Why does the Model focus on King Arthur's dreams in paragraphs 3 and 4? (These dreams are important elements of plot and act as foreshadowing. They also begin to introduce the idea of fate in the passage.) 4. The Model introduces the idea of Arthur as an archetypal hero, based on the role of fate in his life. Can you think of other heroes who fit these criteria? (e.g., Perseus, Harry Potter) 5. Look back at the passage. What other elements of the archetypal hero are mentioned in the Model? Do these support the Model's idea that King Arthur is a hero? ("let me know what that noise in the field betokens ..." Yes, this passage shows King Arthur's selflessness, which supports the idea that he is a hero.)	
	Extend **Tech Infusion** **Pair and Share.** Pair or group students. Have students review the Model and mark the textual evidence the author uses to support his or her claim about fate. Then have groups or pairs return to the selection and find more evidence the author of the Model could have used to support his/her analysis. Ask the groups to share their findings with the class. If possible, have students capture pair shares on video using mobile devices or tablets so they can watch their conversations and critique the content.

3. YOUR TURN

Core Path	Access Path
Assess and Explain. Have students answer the comprehension questions to test for understanding. Share the explanations for Parts A and B (located online) with your students.	
	Extend **Share and Discuss.** Have students complete the Your Turn section in class. Poll students about their responses and as a class discuss the different strategies they used to determine the correct answers. Make sure students understand that sending Sir Lucan to respond to cries from the field when Arthur is dying shows Arthur's compassion.

Le Morte d'Arthur

OVERVIEW

This excerpt from the early modern prose retelling of the Arthurian legend—*Le Morte d'Arthur* by Sir Thomas Malory—details the final battle and death of King Arthur. The Close Read gives students the opportunity to analyze story elements and the use of archetypes in the text.

OBJECTIVES

1. Guide students through a close reading of early modern literature.
2. Provide students a usable framework for analyzing story elements in an excerpt from *Le Morte d'Arthur*.
3. Participate effectively in a range of conversations and collaborations to express ideas and build upon the ideas of others.
4. Prewrite, plan, and produce clear and coherent writing in response to a prompt.

ELA Common Core Standards:
Reading: Literature - RL.11-12.1, RL.11-12.2, RL.11-12.3, RL.11-12.4
Writing - W.11-12.4, W.11-12.5, W.11-12.6, W.11-12.9.A, W.11-12.10
Speaking & Listening - SL.11-12.1, SL.11-12.1.A, SL.11-12.1.B, SL.11-12.1.C, SL.11-12.1.D, SL.11-12.6
Language - L.11-12.4, L.11-12.4.A, L.11-12.4.C, L.11-12.4.D

RESOURCES

Le Morte d'Arthur vocabulary worksheet
Le Morte d'Arthur Character trait chart
Short Constructed Response - Argumentative
Student Model
Access 1 handout (Beginner)
Access 2 handout (Intermediate)
Access 3 handout (Advanced)
Access 4 handout (Approaching)

1. INTRODUCTION

Core Path	Access Path
Define and Compare. Project the vocabulary words and definitions onto the board or provide students with a handout, so they can copy the vocabulary into their notebooks. Ask students to compare their initial vocabulary definitions from the First Read with the actual definitions. Review words that students defined incorrectly to understand why they were unable to use context clues or other tools to develop usable definitions.	**Beginner & Intermediate** **Complete a Chart.** Have students complete the chart on the Access 1 and 2 handouts by writing the correct word for each of the definitions. **Advanced & Beyond** **Write in Journals.** Have students write a journal entry using all of their vocabulary words. Remind them to write sentences that communicate the meaning of the words they are using. **Approaching** **Graphic Organizer.** To support students in comparing their predictions with the correct meanings, have them complete the graphic organizer on the Access 4 handout to record the vocabulary words, their initial analysis, and the definitions. Then have them write sentences using the words.
Review. Have students complete the vocabulary worksheet (see Resources at the end of the lesson plan online). Answers will vary. Check student sentences to make sure each student demonstrates understanding of the vocabulary words.	
	Extend **Tech Infusion** **Create.** Have students create vocabulary cards using StudyBlue (https://www.studyblue.com/) or another online publishing tool. Instruct students to include the following elements on each card: • the word • the part of speech • the definition • a sentence from the text that contains the word • an image that illustrates the word

Core Path	Access Path
	Extend **Search.** Have students use dictionaries, thesauruses, and/or mobile devices to find a synonym and antonym for each vocabulary word. Students should record the word with at least one synonym and antonym in their notes. Encourage students to find synonyms and antonyms that might appear in a more contemporary text. Students can work individually or collaboratively on this assignment.

2. READ

Core Path	Access Path
Model Close Reading. Project the text onto the board and model a close reading of the first four paragraphs using the annotation strategies mentioned below. While modeling annotation strategies, make notes that tie the text to the focus skill and demonstrate what students are looking for as they read. Some guidance for you as you annotate for your students: • As the Skills lesson that precedes this text explains, King Arthur's dreams are an example of foreshadowing. The first paragraph is filled with strong, negative words including "hideous," "wild," "foul," and " horrible." • In the next two paragraphs, Arthur wakes up and falls back asleep. He sees his knight Sir Gawain. It "seemed to the king that Sir Gawain actually came," but Sir Gawain says "when I was a living man," indicating that he is still dead. • Sir Gawain verbalizes the warning from Arthur's first dream: "if ye fight to morn with Sir Mordred, as ye have both agreed, doubt ye not that ye shall be slain." • Gawain warns Arthur to "in no wise persons with him." In this text, "wise" means "way" and "persons" means "hand-to-hand, or one-on-one, combat." His warning is clear: No matter what, do not fight Sir Mordred.	

Copyright © BookheadEd Learning, LLC

Core Path	Access Path
Read and Annotate. Read the Skills Focus questions as a class, so your students know what they should pay close attention to as they read. Then have students read and annotate the excerpt. Ask students to use the annotation tool as they read to: 1. respond to the Skills Focus section 2. identify and distinguish between plot, character, and setting 3. analyze the author's choices regarding setting, how the plot or action is ordered, and how characters are developed to understand how the author builds a complete story 4. identify how each story element impacts the others 5. look for the use of archetypes, or universal characters, symbols, or themes 6. note unfamiliar vocabulary 7. capture their reaction to the ideas and examples in the text. As they reread the text, remind students to use the comprehension strategy of rereading that they learned in the First Read.	**Note:** While on-grade-level students are reading and annotating, work one-on-one or in small groups with Beginner, Intermediate, Advanced, and Approaching students to support them as they read and annotate the text. **Beginner & Intermediate** **Summarize and Analyze the Text.** Work with these students to complete the sentence frames on the Access 1 and 2 handouts (note: the sentence frames for Intermediate students on the Access 2 handout contain fewer scaffolds). They will then use the completed sentence frames to help them analyze and annotate the text by completing the Skills Focus questions. Refer to the sample Skills Focus answers to help them complete the sentence frames and annotate the text. **Advanced** **Work in Pairs.** Pair these students with more proficient English speakers to work together on analyzing and annotating the text to complete the Skills Focus questions. If these students need more support, have them use the sentence frames on the Access 3 handout as they work with their more proficient peers. **Approaching** **Summarize the Text.** Have these students discuss and complete the text summary on the Access 4 handout and use their summary to help them analyze and annotate the text by completing the Skills Focus questions. Correct answers for the summary are at the end of the lesson plan online. Also refer to the sample Skills Focus answers to aid students with their annotations.
Discuss. After students have read the text, use the sample responses to the Skills Focus questions at the end of the lesson plan online to discuss the reading and the process of analyzing the story elements.	**Extend** **Pair and Share.** In small, heterogeneous groups or pairs, ask students to share and discuss their annotations with a focus on the story elements presented in the selection.

Core Path	Access Path
Make sure that students have acquired and accurately use academic-specific words and phrases related to the skill and demonstrate a command of formal English appropriate to the discussion. To help facilitate discussions, refer to Collaborative Discussions in the Speaking & Listening Handbook.	You can provide students with these questions to guide their discussion:

Access Path questions:

1. How do character traits play an important role in the plot? Cite specific textual evidence to support your statements. (Answers will vary. Sample response: King Arthur's bravery and sense of justice makes him continue fighting, even though he knows he may die: "Now betide me death, betide me life," said the king, "now that I see him yonder alone, he shall never escape my hands!" Sir Bedivere's greed causes him to delay throwing the sword into the lake: "If I throw this rich sword into the water, thereof shall never come good, but only harm and loss.")

2. What role does fate play in the story? (Throughout the story, clues are given that Arthur is fated to die at Mordred's hand. He tries to avoid this fate by making a treaty, but the battle happens anyway.)

3. The story happens in the distant past in England. How does this time period affect the characters and/or plot? (Answers will vary. Sample response: People during that time had strong religious faith, which is shown by many of the characters. In addition, kings and knights were expected to show loyalty, bravery, and duty, all of which are demonstrated in the selection.)

Extend

Research. Some scholars believe King Arthur's three requests to Sir Bedivere can be read as an allusion to the three denials of Peter, Jesus's apostle. In small groups, students should research the biblical story and then compare and contrast the two episodes. As students compare, have them keep in mind what human weaknesses Peter and Bedivere show, what each denial means to Jesus and Arthur, and the final outcome of the denials.

Core Path	Access Path
	Extend **Connect.** The stories of King Arthur and the Round Table were first told over a thousand years ago, yet they continue to be popular. Have students create a timeline of King Arthur in popular culture in the twentieth and twenty-first centuries. Instruct students to find books, movies, TV shows, and any other forms of media that retell the Arthurian legend. Then discuss as a class why the Arthurian legends have such staying power. Why do people still want to read about something so far from their twenty-first-century experience?

3. WRITE

Core Path	Access Path
Prewrite and Plan. Read the prompt as a class and ask students to brainstorm about story elements in *Le Morte d'Arthur.* Students can brainstorm together either as a class or in small groups to begin planning their responses. Remind your students to look at the excerpt and their annotations to find textual evidence to support their ideas. You may wish to review with students the Short Constructed Response - Argumentative Student Model for guidance on how to construct an effective response to the writing prompt.	**Beginner & Intermediate** **Plan and Organize.** Have students complete the prewriting activity on the Access 1 and 2 handouts and then explain their ideas to a partner before they write. Explain to students that they need to choose details, examples, or quotes from the text that support their ideas and then explain how those details support their statements. For example, to support their conclusion that the author describes Arthur in a heroic light, students could include the following line from the text: "King Arthur rode steadily throughout the army of Sir Mordred many times and did full nobly, as a noble king should." **Approaching** **Plan and Organize.** Have students complete the prewriting activity on the Access 4 handout to organize their thoughts before they write.

Please note that excerpts and passages in the StudySync® library, workbooks, and PDFs are intended as touchstones to generate interest in an author's work. The excerpts and passages do not substitute for the reading of entire texts, and StudySync® strongly recommends that teachers and students seek out and purchase the whole literary or informational work in order to experience it as the author intended. Links to online resellers are available in our digital library. In addition, complete works may be ordered through an authorized reseller by filling out and returning to StudySync® the order form enclosed in this workbook.

Teacher's Edition   237

Core Path	Access Path
	Extend **Analyze the Prompt.** As a class, reread the prompt. Have students make a list of all the elements they need to include in their essay. Have students use this list to begin gathering ideas and textual evidence.
	Extend **Organize.** Encourage students to complete a character trait graphic organizer (see Resources) before they begin writing.

Discuss. Project these instructions for the peer review onto the board and review them with your class, so they know what they are looking for when they begin to provide their classmates with feedback:

- How has this essay helped you understand King Arthur's character? Has the writer examined his dialogue, actions, and responses to other characters?

- Did the writer effectively use his or her understanding of story elements to add to his or her analysis?

- What claim did the writer make as to which traits make Arthur an archetypal hero? How well supported was the claim?

- What sort of evidence did the writer use from the text to support his or her writing?

- How well does the writer explain how that evidence supports his or her arguments?

- Does the writer write using standard grammar and punctuation? Are there any weak spots?

- What specific suggestions can you make to help the writer improve the response?

- What thing(s) does this paper do especially well?

After you've looked at the peer review instructions, review the rubric with students before they begin writing. Allow time for students briefly to pose and discuss any questions they may have about the peer review instructions and the rubric. Tell students how many peer reviews they will need to complete once they submit their writing.

Core Path	Access Path
Write. Ask students to complete the writing assignment using textual evidence to support their answers. Once they have completed their writing, they should click "Submit."	
	Extend **Critique.** Project a writing sample on the board and highlight the textual evidence. Model questions to ask to determine if the textual evidence supports the author's claims well. For example: • What point is th s quotation making? • Does the point make sense in the context of the selection? • What is the author's claim? • Does this quotation support that claim? Is there a better example in the text that the author could have used? Work as a class to generate strategies students can use as they complete their peer reviews to ensure quotations provide strong support.
Review. Once students complete their writing assignment, they should submit substantive feedback to two peers.	

Conversation with Geoffrey Ashe re: King Arthur

OVERVIEW

The interview "Conversation with Geoffrey Ashe" presents an Arthurian scholar's perspective on the search for the real King Arthur. The First Read gives students the opportunity to experience the text with a limited context.

OBJECTIVES

1. Perform an initial reading of a text and demonstrate comprehension by responding to short analysis and inference questions with textual evidence.
2. Practice defining vocabulary words using context.
3. Participate effectively in a range of conversations and collaborations to express ideas and build upon the ideas of others.
4. Practice acquiring and using academic vocabulary correctly.

   ELA Common Core Standards:
   Reading: Informational - RI.11-12.1, RI.11-12.4, RI.11-12.10
   Writing - W.11-12.7
   Speaking & Listening - SL.11-12.1, SL.11-12.1.B, SL.11-12.1.C, SL.11-12.1.D, SL.11-12.2
   Language - L.11-12.4.A, L.11-12.4.D, L.11-12.6

RESOURCES

Access 1 handout (Beginner)

Access 2 handout (Intermediate)

Access 3 handout (Advanced)

Access 4 handout (Approaching)

ACCESS COMPLEX TEXT

This excerpt from an interview between Arthurian scholar Geoffrey Ashe and a writer for Britannia.com explores the historical and archaeological evidence used to study who the "real" King Arthur was. To help students understand the topics discussed, use the following ideas to provide scaffolded instruction for a close reading of the more complex features of this text:

- **Genre** - Students may struggle with the interview format. Point out that the italicized questions are asked by the interviewer and the roman text is Geoffrey Ashe's response.

- **Organization** - Because an interview is a transcript of a conversation, it may not follow as clear an organizational structure as an informational text. Students may struggle to follow the connection of ideas.

- **Prior Knowledge** - Students may require a map to understand references to British geography, such as Somerset and Cornwall. Students may need to be reminded of the relationship between England, Scotland, and Wales, and also that the Roman Empire stretched from Italy to England.

1. INTRODUCTION

Core Path	Access Path
Read. Individually or as a class, read the introduction for "Conversation with Geoffrey Ashe." The introduction explains who Geoffrey Ashe is and what he studies.	**English Learners All Levels & Approaching** **Read and Listen.** Ask students to read and listen to the introduction for "Conversation with Geoffrey Ashe." Have them refer to the "Introduction Glossary" on their Access 1, 2, 3, and 4 handouts for definitions of key vocabulary terms. If there are unfamiliar words that are not included in their glossary, encourage students to check a dictionary or online reference tool, such as http://dictionary.reference.com.
	Extend **Make Predictions.** Based on the introduction, ask students to make predictions about the central ideas they would expect to encounter in this text.

Core Path	Access Path
	Extend **Discuss the Introduction.** After reading the introduction, use the information provided to facilitate a prereading discussion to get students thinking about the text structure of "Conversation with Geoffrey Ashe." 1. What other interviews have you seen or read recently? 2. What type of person do you associate interviews with? What does that say about Geoffrey Ashe? 3. What advantages does the interview format have over other types of articles? What disadvantages does it have?
Build Background. In pairs or small groups, ask students to use devices to research the field of archaeology. Ask students to find answers to the following questions: • What does an archaeologist study? • What techniques do archaeologists use in the field? • What recent discoveries have archaeologists made? If you are in a low-tech classroom, you can provide photocopies of news articles about archaeology for students to read and discuss.	**English Learners All Levels** **Discuss and Complete the Chart.** Put students into mixed proficiency groups, and rather than discussing archaeology, have them complete the "Build Background" exercises on the Access 1, 2, and 3 handouts that ask students to think about why historians might want to study legends. Have the groups discuss each question, generate ideas, and complete the chart together. **Approaching** **Brainstorm.** 1. First, ask students to brainstorm a list of legends and myths from a variety of cultures. Allow students to work in pairs if they wish. If students struggle, start their thinking by suggesting Greek mythology, Norse mythology (Thor), and Native American trickster tales. 2. Have students use their lists to answer the first three questions on the "Build Background" chart on the Access 4 handout. 3. Then have students form small groups and complete the rest of the chart together.

2. READ

Core Path	Access Path
Make Predictions about Vocabulary. There are six bold vocabulary words in the text. As students read the text, ask them to make predictions about what they think each bold vocabulary word means based on the context clues in the sentence. If you are in a low-tech classroom and students are reading from printed copies or a projected text, ask students to record predictions in their notes, so they can be easily referenced in class. If your students have access to technology, they can use the annotation tool to make their predictions.	**Note:** This exercise, which extends vocabulary instruction, should be completed when the class shifts from whole-group instruction to individual work during the "Read and Annotate" exercise.

Core Path (continued)

It might be helpful to model this for students before they begin reading. Either using the board or projecting the actual text, focus in on the sentence that uses the word "milieu":

- So, with the Arthur story, characters in a milieu which the authors knew quite well to be ancient were still dressed up as knights and ladies appropriate to the twelfth or thirteenth century.

Model for the class how to use the overall structure and meaning of the sentence and the sentences around it, the word's position, and other clues to define the unfamiliar vocabulary word. In this case, point out these context clues:

1. Look at the structure of the sentence. A "milieu" is something or someplace the characters are described as being "in." That tells me that the word is a noun.

2. I can use my background knowledge about story elements to figure out that "milieu" probably has something to do with setting, as that is what characters in a story are in.

3. The end of the sentence discusses how the characters are dressed and what century they are in. Both of those are elements of setting.

4. I will check my preliminary determination in a dictionary. I see that "milieu" means "the physical or social setting in which something happens." My prediction was correct.

Access Path (continued)

Beginner, Intermediate & Approaching Pair Practice.

1. Pair students with more proficient readers.

2. Give them an additional sentence that contains a new vocabulary word.

3. Ask the students to complete a Think Aloud using the teacher-led Make Predictions about Vocabulary activity as a model, while the proficient student actively listens.

4. The student should use the context clues in the sentence to try to determine the meaning of the new vocabulary word.

5. After the student has completed the Think Aloud and made a prediction about the word's meaning, allow time for the proficient reader to add his/her own thoughts and clarify any points of confusion.

6. Once they've completed this Think Aloud, encourage them to use a dictionary to confirm the definition of the new vocabulary word. Have them refer to the "Text Glossary" on their Access 1, 2, and 4 handouts for definitions of key vocabulary terms in the text. Encourage them to add any additional vocabulary words or idioms they find in the text and look up definitions for those words and idioms online or in a dictionary.

Core Path	Access Path
	Extend **Identify and Define.** After reading the text, compile a list of additional vocabulary words. Ask students to reference their annotations and share any vocabulary words that were unfamiliar. 1. As a class, compile a list of unknown words on the board. 2. In small groups, ask students to make predictions about what they think these words mean based on how they are used in the sentence. (Note: They will need to read the words in context and make predictions.) 3. Each group should work together using print or online dictionaries to define the words and write the definitions in their notebooks.
Model Reading Comprehension Strategy. Before students begin reading, model the reading comprehension strategy of summarizing by using this Think Aloud that talks students through the first question and answer in the text. First explain to your students that summarizing is: *a process in which students select, organize, and synthesize the most important elements in a text* Explain to students how summarizing will help them better comprehend the selection and help drive their discussions. • The first question and answer contain a lot of information. To help me remember it, I'll summarize the passage. • A summary should contain only the central idea and most important details. In this passage, there are two central ideas: Arthur appeals to "a wide variety of interests," and Arthur's golden age is a dream people want to believe in. • My summary is this: Arthur's story has been an enduring legend because he appeals to "a wide variety of interests." In addition, his golden age of courage is a dream that people want to believe in.	**Note:** This exercise, which extends instruction around reading comprehension strategies, should be completed when the class shifts from whole-group instruction to individual work during the "Read and Annotate" exercise. **Beginner, Intermediate & Approaching** **Apply Reading Comprehension Strategy.** 1. Have students complete the sentence frames that guide the summarization of each question and Ashe's response in "Conversation with Geoffrey Ashe." Refer students to the Summary Sentence Frames on their Access 1, 2, and 4 handouts. Sample answers are provided at the end of the lesson plan online. 2. Then have students pair up in order to discuss their summaries. Visit each pair of students and ask which specific vocabulary words helped them better understand the questions and answers in order to check reading comprehension. Are there any words or phrases that further confuse or complicate their summarization?

Core Path	Access Path
Read and Annotate. Read and annotate the excerpt. Ask students to use the annotation tool as they read to: 1. use context clues to analyze and determine the meaning of the bolded vocabulary terms 2. ask questions about passages of the text that may be unclear or unresolved 3. identify key details, events, individuals, and connections between them 4. note unfamiliar vocabulary 5. capture their reaction to the ideas presented in the text.	**Beginner** **Coach the Reading.** While other students read, annotate, and discuss the text independently, work with Beginner students, listening to the audio of the text and pausing periodically or when any student has a question. Coach students in articulating their questions for the group and in highlighting and annotating the text. Have students use the Annotation Guide on the Access 1 handout to support them as they highlight and annotate the text. For further support, ask questions about the text, such as: • Is there anything about the interview that you don't understand? • Why does Geoffrey Ashe think the Arthurian stories are so popular? Do you agree? • What can archaeology reveal about King Arthur? **Intermediate** **Listen to the Audio.** Have these students listen to the audio of the text and use the Text Glossary on the Access 2 handout to help them with words or idioms that may be unfamiliar. If students need help with annotating the text, have them use the Annotation Guide on the Access 2 handout. After working with the Beginner students, you may wish to check this group's progress and provide support as needed. **Advanced** **Pair with Proficient Peers.** Have Advanced students work with English-proficient peers to read, annotate, and discuss the text. Have students use the Annotation Guide in the Access 3 handout to support them as they highlight and annotate the text. Encourage them to listen to the audio of the text if needed. **Approaching** **Use the Annotation Guide.** Have students use the Annotation Guide on the Access 4 handout to support them as they highlight and annotate the text.

Core Path	Access Path
Discuss. In small groups or pairs, have students discuss the questions and inferences they made while reading. To help facilitate discussions, refer to Collaborative Discussions in the Speaking & Listening Handbook.	**English Learners All Levels & Approaching** Use the extra time while on- and beyond-grade-level students are discussing their first reads of the text to work individually and in small groups with Approaching readers and English Learners as outlined above. Should those students complete their first reads quickly, integrate them into the on- and beyond-grade-level discussion groups. Otherwise, English Learners and Approaching readers will be given an opportunity to participate in text discussions with their peers later in the lesson.
1. Who was Finn MacCool? How is he different from King Arthur?	
2. How did later English monarchs respond to the Arthurian legends?	
3. Why do most readers picture Arthur in the Middle Ages? Why is that image incorrect?	**Tech Infusion**
4. Where is Cadbury Castle? Why is it important?	**Beyond**
5. Why does Ashe think of Ambrosius Aurelianus and other historical figures often held up as "real" Arthurs?	**Discuss.** Pair students and ask them to discuss the following question: Did reading this article enhance or detract from your enjoyment of the Arthurian legend? Why? Students who have access to a back-channel tool such as TodaysMeet (https://todaysmeet.com/) may enjoy sharing their ideas in that medium.
6. Summarize the interview. What are Geoffrey Ashe's main ideas?	
	Extend **Research.** In small groups, have students conduct research to find out more about Dr. Ralegh Radford's work at Cadbury Castle. What exactly did he and his team find there? What clues (in addition to those shared by Ashe) tie the site to King Arthur? What do critics say about the connection? If possible, have students find images of what was uncovered at the site.
	Extend **Tech Infusion** **Share.** Have groups share their findings and images in a collaborative Google Doc that the whole class can access.

3. THINK

Core Path	Access Path
Answer and Discuss. Have students complete the Think questions and then use the peer review instructions and rubric to complete two peer reviews. Refer to the sample answers at the end of the lesson plan online to discuss responses with your students.	**Beginner & Intermediate** **Sentence Frames.** Have students use the sentence frames on the Access 1 and 2 handouts to support their responses to the Think questions. If necessary, distribute sentence frames to Advanced students as well. **Approaching** **Find the Evidence.** Have students use Find the Evidence on the Access 4 handout to help them identify the evidence needed to answer the questions.
	Extend **Research.** Ashe discusses Riothamus, a British warrior king who took an army to Gaul, modern-day France. Have students conduct research on sea travel in the fifth century. Then as a group, discuss the following questions: • What would a fifth-century sea trip have entailed? • Why might so many historians have dismissed Geoffrey of Monmouth's claims that King Arthur conquered lands away from Britain? • Based on what you learned in your research, would you have volunteered in Riothamus's attack on Gaul?

OVERVIEW

Analyzing the text elements—key individuals, ideas, and events—in an informational selection is a key step in understanding the text. This lesson plan provides follow-up questions and useful enrichments to help teachers guide students toward a usable, repeatable method for analyzing text elements.

OBJECTIVES

1. Learn the definition of informational text elements
2. Practice using concrete strategies for analyzing the development of individuals, events, and ideas in a text.
3. Participate effectively in a range of conversations and collaborations to express ideas and build upon the ideas of others.

ELA Common Core Standards:
Reading: Informational - RI.11-12.1, RI.11-12.3
Speaking & Listening - SL.11-12.1, SL.11-12.1.A, SL.11-12.1.C, SL.11-12.2

RESOURCES

Access 1 handout (Beginner)

Access 2 handout (Intermediate)

Access 3 handout (Advanced)

Access 4 handout (Approaching)

1. DEFINE

Core Path	Access Path
Watch. Watch the Concept Definition video on informational text elements with your students. Make sure your students are familiar with all the different elements shared in the video—including details, events, people, and ideas—as well as how these elements may interact over the course of a text. Pause the video at these key moments to discuss the information with your students: 1. 0:25 – Before writing things down, how do you think people remembered and communicated information? What challenges might have led to the development of a written language? 2. 0:50 – Do you think there are any similarities between the elements of fictional and informational texts? What are they? Compare and contrast the two forms. 3. 1:20 – For what reasons might an author "leave out" various events in an informational text? How does this challenge our understanding of certain facts or events? What can we do as readers to broaden our understanding of a topic or event?	**English Learners All Levels & Approaching** **Fill in the Blanks.** Have students complete the fill-in-the-blanks exercise on the Access 1, 2, 3, and 4 handouts as they watch the video. Answers are located at the end of the lesson plan online.
Read and Discuss. After watching the Concept Definition video, have students read the definition of informational text elements. Either in small groups or as a whole class use these questions to spur discussion among your students about informational text elements. 1. What kinds of informational text elements would you expect to find in other kinds of complex nonfiction text, such as cookbooks, instruction manuals, or legal contracts? (Cookbooks contain recipes and usually photos. Instruction manuals contain detailed instructions and often diagrams or illustrations. Legal contracts contain agreements with specific terms.)	**Beginner & Approaching** **Complete a Chart.** To prepare students to participate in the discussion, have them complete the chart on the Access 1 and 4 handouts as they read the definition. The correct answers are located at the end of the lesson plan online. **Intermediate & Advanced** **Discuss Prompts.** To help these students participate in the discussion, prompt them with questions that can be answered with a few words, such as:

Core Path	Access Path
2. What elements make up an informational text? How do they work together? (Although the exact elements may vary, an informational text usually contains facts and details related to historical, scientific, and cultural topics. These elements work together to support an author's argument or convey an idea.) 3. What do you, as a reader, need to examine to understand a text's central idea? (all the text elements) 4. What is the purpose of this text? How does the author's use informational text elements to relate the purpose of the text? (The purpose of this text is to examine the historical King Arthur. Ashe uses historical facts and details to support his argument about the historical Arthur.)	• What kinds of information do informational texts contain? (information or ideas about real people, places, things, and events) • What might some writers try to persuade readers to do? (accept a specific point of view about a subject) • Why do the main informational text elements vary depending on the type of text it is? (Answers will vary.) **Beyond** **Discuss.** Have students select two different informational texts they've read on the same subject, such as a textbook and an article about World War II. Pair students and have them discuss the differences in how information was presented. What elements did one include that the other did not? What effect do these choices have on the reader?
	Extend **Brainstorm.** After watching the video, ask students to think about how writers might use informational text elements differently to serve different purposes. For example, have students think about how an argumentative text might present ideas differently than a purely informative text. Compile a list of ways authors might use text elements differently on the board or on a collaborative Google Doc.
	Extend **Explore.** Take a familiar story from the news or a recent school event. Have students write the basic facts of the event—the who, what, where, when, why—on individual notecards. As a class or in small groups, have students explore different ways the information could be organized to make a coherent text. Discuss the effects of these differences.

2. MODEL

Core Path	Access Path
Read and Annotate. Have students independently read the Model section. As they read, ask students to use the annotation tool to: • highlight key points. • ask questions. • identify places where the Model is applying the strategies laid out in the Identification and Application section on informational text elements.	**Note:** During this portion of the lesson, instruction shifts from whole-group to individual work. Use this time to work one on one or in small groups with Beginner, Intermediate, Advanced, and Approaching students. **Beginner & Intermediate** **Coach the Reading.** Work with these students (either individually or in small groups) to fill out the guided reading questions on the Access 1 and 2 handouts. Have Beginner students refer to the glossary on the Access 1 handout to help them determine the meaning of difficult words (note: provide the Access 1 handout glossary to Intermediate students if necessary). Let students know they'll use these answers to help participate in the discussion about the Model. Sample answers for this exercise are located at the end of the lesson plan online. **Advanced** **Identify Evidence.** Ask Advanced students to complete the identifying evidence exercise on the Access 3 handout. Let students know that they'll use these answers to help participate in the discussion about the Model. Sample answers for this exercise are located at the end of the lesson plan online. **Approaching** **Guided Reading.** Have students complete the guided reading questions on the Access 4 handout as they read. Let them know that they'll use these answers to help participate in the discussion about the Model. Sample answers for this exercise are located at the end of the lesson plan online.

Core Path	Access Path
Discuss. After students read the Model text, use these questions to facilitate a whole group discussion that helps students understand how to analyze the informational text elements of the passage: 1. What does the Model do first, before jumping into key informational text elements? (identifies the interviewer and interviewee in the text) 2. What idea does the Model begin by examining? (Ashe's idea on why the King Arthur stories are still popular) 3. How does Ashe build that idea? (Ashe first points out the staying power of Arthur, then suggests a reason why, and then supports that reason with evidence from contemporary authors.) 4. What does the Model say the text introduces next to support this key idea? (a key individual: Geoffrey of Monmouth; a key event: the spread of the Arthurian legends to the rest of Europe)	
	Extend **Tech Infusion** Discuss. In small groups, have students discuss other text elements Ashe could have used to develop his key idea about the appeal of Arthur. Then discuss the effects of Ashe's (and the interviewer's) choices and how the use of different elements might change the text. Ask the groups to share their findings with the class via a TodaysMeet (www.todaysmeet.com) back channel or a shared Google document.

3. YOUR TURN

Core Path	Access Path
Assess and Explain. Have students answer the comprehension questions to test for understanding. Share the explanations for Parts A and B (located online) with your students.	
	Extend **Revise.** Have students revisit their last writing assignment done in class. How could they apply their knowledge about informational text elements to their own writing? What elements could make their writing stronger? Have students take notes on possible revisions.

Conversation with Geoffrey Ashe re: King Arthur

OVERVIEW

The interview "Conversation with Geoffrey Ashe" presents a British cultural historian's opinion on the Arthurian legend and its historical basis. The Close Read gives students the opportunity to analyze the informational text elements used in the text.

OBJECTIVES

1. Complete a close reading of an interview.
2. Practice analyzing the development of ideas in "Conversation with Geoffrey Ashe."
3. Participate effectively in a range of conversations and collaborations to express ideas and build upon the ideas of others.
4. Prewrite, plan, and produce clear and coherent writing in response to a prompt.

   ELA Common Core Standards:
   Reading: Informational - RI.11-12.1, RI.11-12.2, RI.11-12.3, RI.11-12.4
   Writing - W.11-12.4, W.11-12.5, W.11-12.6, W.11-12.9.B, W.11-12.10
   Speaking & Listening - SL.11-12.1, SL. 11-12.1.A, SL. 11-12.1.B, SL. 11-12.1.C, SL. 11-12.1.D, SL. 11-12.6
   Language - L.11-12.4.A, L.11-12.4.C, L.11-12.4.D

RESOURCES

"Conversation with Geoffrey Ashe" Vocabulary Worksheet

"Conversation with Geoffrey Ashe" Graphic Organizer

Access 1 handout (Beginner)

Access 2 handout (Intermediate)

Access 3 handout (Advanced)

Access 4 handout (Approaching)

1. INTRODUCTION

Core Path	Access Path
Define and Compare. Project the vocabulary words and definitions onto the board or provide students with a handout, so they can copy the vocabulary into their notebooks. Ask students to compare their initial vocabulary predictions from the First Read with the actual definitions. Review words that students defined incorrectly to understand why they were unable to use context clues or other tools to develop usable definitions.	**Beginner & Intermediate** **Complete a Chart.** Have students complete the chart on the Access 1 and 2 handouts by writing the correct word for each of the definitions. **Advanced & Beyond** **Write in Journals.** Have students write a journal entry using all of their vocabulary words. Remind them to write sentences that communicate the meaning of the words they are using. **Approaching** **Graphic Organizer.** To support students in comparing their predictions with the correct meanings, have them complete the graphic organizer on the Access 4 handout to record the vocabulary words, their initial analysis, and the definitions. Then have them write sentences using the words.
Review. Have students complete the fill-in-the-blank vocabulary worksheet for this selection. Answers for the worksheet are listed online.	
	Extend **Review.** Have students use a dictionary or thesaurus to find synonyms or antonyms for the vocabulary words. Write the vocabulary words, synonyms, and antonyms on individual notecards and play a memory card-matching game to review the words.
	Extend **Tech Infusion** **Create.** Have students create online flashcards for the vocabulary words using Quizlet (http://quizlet.com) or StudyBlue (www.studyblue.com).

2. READ

Core Path	Access Path
Model Close Reading. Project the text onto the board and model a close reading of the first five paragraphs using the annotation strategies mentioned below. While modeling annotation strategies, make notes that tie the text to the focus skill and demonstrate what students are looking for as they read. Some guidance for you as you annotate for your students: • The first paragraph in this interview is in italics. That tells me that the interviewer, Britannia.com, is talking. The paragraphs in roman, or normal font, are Geoffrey Ashe. • The interviewer chooses the first topic: Why are the King Arthur stories so popular? Ashe begins his answer with why they became popular in the Middle Ages: "they appealed to a wide variety of interests." He continues on to say why they are still popular: "It's something we would like to believe in." • The second question begins with a what-if about Geoffrey of Monmouth, "Without him, would we have even heard of Arthur?" Ashe dodges the question a bit, as "risky." • To support the idea about the importance of Geoffrey of Monmouth, Ashe cites the example of Finn MacCool, a similar legendary character, who was not mentioned by Geoffrey of Monmouth, and never gained the popularity of Arthur.	

Core Path	Access Path
Read and Annotate. Read the Skills Focus questions as a class, so your students know what they should pay close attention to as they read. Then have students read and annotate the excerpt. Ask students to use the annotation tool as they read to: 1. respond to the Skills Focus section 2. look for key details in the text that clarify specific events, people, and ideas 3. identify transition words and phrases that signal interactions between individuals, ideas, or events 4. note other features in the text, such as charts and graphs, that might provide additional information that does not appear in the text 5. note any unfamiliar vocabulary 6. capture their reaction to the ideas and examples in the text. As they reread the text, remind students to use the comprehension strategy of summarizing that they learned in the First Read.	**Note:** While on-grade-level students are reading and annotating, work one on one or in small groups with Beginner, Intermediate, Advanced, and Approaching students to support them as they read and annotate the text. **Beginner & Intermediate** **Summarize and Analyze the Text.** Work with these students to complete the sentence frames on the Access 1 and 2 handouts (note: the sentence frames for Intermediate students on the Access 2 handout contain fewer scaffolds). They will then use the completed sentence frames to help them analyze and annotate the text by completing the Skills Focus questions. Refer to the sample Skills Focus answers to help them complete the sentence frames and annotate the text. **Advanced** **Work in Pairs.** Pair these students with more proficient English speakers to work together on analyzing and annotating the text to complete the Skills Focus questions. If these students need more support, have them use the sentence frames on the Access 3 handout as they work with their more proficient peers. **Approaching** **Summarize the Text.** Have these students discuss and complete the text summary on the Access 4 handout and use their summary to help them analyze and annotate the text by completing the Skills Focus questions. Correct answers for the summary are at the end of the lesson plan online. Also refer to the sample Skills Focus answers to aid students with their annotations.

Core Path	Access Path
Discuss. After students have read the text, use the sample responses to the Skills Focus questions at the end of the lesson plan online to discuss the reading and the process of analyzing informational text elements. Make sure that students have acquired and accurately use academic-specific words and phrases related to the skill and demonstrate a command of formal English appropriate to the discussion. To help facilitate discussions, refer to Collaborative Discussions in the Speaking & Listening Handbook.	**Extend** **Pair and Share.** In small, heterogeneous groups or pairs, ask students to share and discuss their annotations with a focus on the informational text elements in the selection. You can provide students with these questions to guide their discussion: 1. How did Arthur go from a Briton legend to a world famous story? Cite specific textual evidence to support your statements. (Arthur's story was spread to the rest of Europe by Geoffrey of Monmouth's *History of the Kings of Britain*. He has stayed popular thanks to his "vitality" and the universal dream of a "golden age.") 2. What can archaeology teach scholars about Arthur? Is that where scholars should focus their attention? Cite specific textual evidence to support your answer. (Archaeology may never reveal anything else about Arthur himself, but it can teach scholars more about the time period. Student responses to the second question will vary.) 3. Ashe says Arthur may be a "composite" of many real people. Do you think Arthur was a real historical figure? Support your opinion with evidence from the interview. (Student answers will vary but may cite information about the Dark Ages, Riothamus, or Cadbury Castle.)

Core Path	Access Path
	Extend **Search.** Pair students and ask them to go through the text and identify unknown words and phrases. Have students use a print or online dictionary to determine each word's meaning as it is used in the text. As a class, discuss the words and phrases each pair identified.
	Extend **Connect.** Ashe says that King Arthur might be a "composite," or a combination of many different real people. As a class, think about famous real people from United States history. Have students answer the following question: If you were going to make a composite American version of Arthur, which people and which accomplishments from U.S. history would you mix together to create one? Then have students write a short character sketch of their own American Arthurs. Make sure each student bases his or her character on real historical events and people. As a class, discuss what common elements students used in their character sketches. Make a list of what an American legend would do or has done.

3. WRITE

Core Path	Access Path
Prewrite and Plan. Read the prompt as a class and ask students to brainstorm about the development of ideas in "Conversation with Geoffrey Ashe." Remind your students to look at the excerpt and their annotations to find textual evidence to support their ideas.	**Beginner & Intermediate** **Plan and Organize.** Have students complete the prewriting activity on the Access 1 and 2 handouts and then explain their answers to a partner before they write. Explain to students that they need to choose details, examples, or quotes from the text that support their ideas and then explain how those details support their statements. For example, students might conclude that Ashe's central idea is that archaeology is a valuable pursuit for Arthurian scholars. To support that idea, students could include these sentences from paragraph 14: "Archaeology may never prove anything about Arthur personally ... What archaeology can do, and certainly will, is tell us more about the Dark Age Britain where his legend originated. In doing so, it can shed light on the literary process itself." **Approaching** **Plan and Organize.** Have students complete the prewriting activity on the Access 4 handout to organize their thoughts before they write.
	Extend **Organize.** Encourage students to complete a graphic organizer to organize their ideas before they type their responses (see Resources at the end of the lesson plan online).
	Extend **Tech Infusion** **Map.** Students can create graphic organizers online using https://bubbl.us. Google Drawing can also be used to design a graphic organizer.

Core Path	Access Path
Discuss. Project these instructions for the peer review onto the board and review them with your class, so they know what they are looking for when they begin to provide their classmates with feedback: • How has this essay helped you understand how Geoffrey Ashe's ideas build over the course of the interview? • Did the writer explain the interviewer's role in prompting and moving forward the conversation? Does that explanation make sense? • Did the writer explain Ashe's ideas about the persistence of the Arthur legend, how the myth came to be seen as medieval, and the role of archaeology in studying Arthur? Were any key ideas missing? • What sort of evidence did the writer use from the text to support his or her writing? • How well does the writer explain how that evidence supports his or her arguments? • Does the writer write using standard grammar and punctuation? Are there any weak spots? • What specific suggestions can you make to help the writer improve the response? • What thing(s) does this paper do especially well? After you've looked at the peer review instructions, review the rubric with students before they begin writing. Allow time for students briefly to pose and discuss any questions they may have about the peer review instructions and the rubric. Tell students how many peer reviews they will need to complete once they submit their writing.	
Write. Ask students to complete the writing assignment using textual evidence to support their answers. Once they have completed their writing, they should click "Submit."	

Core Path	Access Path
	Extend **Critique.** Project a writing sample on the board and ask the class to identify the target purpose and audience of the text. Discuss whether the text is appropriate for that purpose and audience. Work as a class to generate strategies students can use as they complete their peer reviews to check for appropriate purpose and audience.
Review. Once students complete their writing assignment, they should submit substantive feedback to two peers.	

OVERVIEW

The excerpt from *Unsolved Mysteries of History,* by Paul Aron, digs into the history surrounding King Arthur to ask one question: Was King Arthur real? The First Read gives students the opportunity to experience the text with a limited context.

OBJECTIVES

1. Perform an initial reading of a text and demonstrate comprehension by responding to short analysis and inference questions with textual evidence.
2. Practice defining vocabulary words using context.
3. Participate effectively in a range of conversations and collaborations to express ideas and build upon the ideas of others.
4. Annotate the text and make predictions about unknown vocabulary.

ELA Common Core Standards:
Reading: Informational - RI.11-12.1, RI.11-12.2, RI.11-12.4, RI.11-12.10
Writing - W.11-12.7
Speaking & Listening - SL.11-12.1, SL.11-12.1.A, SL.11-12.1.B, SL.11-12.1.C, SL.11-12.1.D
Language - L.11-12.3.A, L.11-12.4.B, L.11-12.4.D, L.11-12.6

RESOURCES

Unsolved Mysteries of History Sequence Chart

Grammar handout: Appositives, Semicolons, and Parallelism

Access 1 handout (Beginner)

Access 2 handout (Intermediate)

Access 3 handout (Advanced)

Access 4 handout (Approaching)

ACCESS COMPLEX TEXT

This excerpt from *Unsolved Mysteries of History* explores the question "Who was King Arthur?" The author traces both the legend and the historical accounts back as far as possible to answer this question. To help students understand this history of the Arthurian legend, use the following ideas to provide scaffolded instruction for a first reading of the more complex features of this text:

- **Genre** - Though this excerpt is from an informational text, the author chooses to use a casual tone. Students may wish to discuss the effects of this choice on the text and on their opinion of the author's trustworthiness.

- **Organization** - This history is not presented in strictly chronological order. The author begins with the history of the Arthurian legend, then goes back to trace the history of the "real" King Arthur. Students may benefit from creating timelines as they read to reorganize the information.

- **Prior Knowledge** - Some readers may need clarification on the historical relationship between the Britons, the Anglo-Saxons, the Romans, and the Welsh.

1. INTRODUCTION

Core Path	Access Path
Read. Individually or as a class, read the Introduction for *Unsolved Mysteries of History*. The introduction provides context for the selection.	**English Learners All Levels & Approaching Read and Listen.** Ask students to read and listen to the introduction for *Unsolved Mysteries of History*. Have them refer to the "Introduction Glossary" on their Access 1, 2, 3, and 4 handouts for definitions of key vocabulary terms. If there are unfamiliar words that are not included in their glossary, encourage students to check a dictionary or online reference tool, such as http://dictionary.reference.com.

Core Path	Access Path
	Extend **Discuss the Introduction.** After reading the introduction, use the information provided to facilitate a prereading discussion to get students thinking about the ideas in *Unsolved Mysteries of History*: 1. Based on the Arthurian legends we've read so far in this unit, does King Arthur seem like a real person? Why or why not?. 2. Is it important to you that Arthur is real, or do you enjoy the stories more as pure fiction?
Build Background. In small groups, ask students to use computers or tablets to research early British history. Assign each group a time period: • Pre-Roman occupation • Roman occupation • Post-Roman occupation • Anglo-Saxon period Come back together as a class and discuss each group's findings. If you are in a low-tech classroom, you can provide photocopies of articles about British history for students to read and discuss.	**Beginner** **Complete and Discuss the Chart.** In small groups, rather than researching and discussing early British history, have students complete the "Build Background" exercises on the Access 1 handout that ask students to consider what they know about the legend of King Arthur. Have the pairs generate ideas, discuss the chart, and complete it together. **Intermediate & Advanced** **Complete and Discuss the Chart.** Pair Intermediate and Advanced students, and rather than researching and discussing early British history, have them complete the "Build Background" exercises on the Access 2 and 3 handouts that ask students to consider what they know about the legend of King Arthur. Have the pairs generate ideas, discuss the chart, and complete it together. **Approaching** **Draw Responses.** 1. First, ask students to think about what they know about King Arthur. Then have them create a list of characteristics. Allow students to work in pairs if they wish. 2. Have students use their lists to draw a character sketch of what they think King Arthur might have looked like. 3. After they've completed their drawings, have students complete the "Build Background" exercise on the Access 4 handout.

Please note that excerpts and passages in the StudySync® library, workbooks, and PDFs are intended as touchstones to generate interest in an author's work. The excerpts and passages do not substitute for the reading of entire texts, and StudySync® strongly recommends that teachers and students seek out and purchase the whole literary or informational work in order to experience it as the author intended. Links to online resellers are available in our digital library. In addition, complete works may be ordered through an authorized reseller by filling out and returning to StudySync® the order form enclosed in this workbook.

Teacher's Edition   **265**

Core Path	Access Path
	Extend
	Analyze and Discuss a Quote. "While the question of Arthur's historicity is critical to the historian and intriguing to anyone interested in the legends, there is a sense in which it does not matter. Real or not, Arthur has inspired a vast cultural tradition, which is manifested in poetry, fiction, drama, music, art, film, and popular culture, and has been adapted to the concerns of each succeeding age that reinterprets the tradition." (Alan Lupack, General Editor of the Camelot Project, University of Rochester)
	1. Restate the quote in your own words.
	2. Do you agree with Lupack? Why or why not?
	3. Would you go searching for the real Arthur?

2. READ

Core Path	Access Path
Make Predictions about Vocabulary. There are six bold vocabulary words in the text. As students read the text, ask them to make predictions about what they think each bold vocabulary word means based on the context clues in the sentence. If you are in a low-tech classroom and students are reading from printed copies or a projected text, ask students to record predictions in their notes, so they can be easily referenced in class. If your students have access to technology, they can use the annotation tool to make their predictions.	**Note:** This exercise, which extends vocabulary instruction, should be completed when the class shifts from whole-group instruction to individual work during the "Read and Annotate" exercise.
It might be helpful to model this for students before they begin reading. Either using the board or projecting the actual text, focus in on the sentence that uses the word "notoriously":	**Beginner, Intermediate & Approaching**
	1. Pair students with more proficient readers.
	2. Give them an additional sentence that contains a new vocabulary word.
	3. Ask the students to complete a Think Aloud using the teacher-led Make Predictions about Vocabulary activity as a model, while the proficient student actively listens.
• His notoriously disorganized material didn't help, either; the cleric himself described his approach as "making one heap" of all he found.	4. The student should use the context clues in the sentence to try to determine the meaning of the new vocabulary word.

Copyright © BookheadEd Learning, LLC

Core Path	Access Path
Model for the class how to use the overall structure and meaning of the sentence and the sentences around it, the word's position, and other clues to define the unfamiliar vocabulary word. In this case, point out these context clues:	5. After the student has completed the Think Aloud and made a prediction about the word's meaning, allow time for the proficient reader to add his/her own thoughts and clarify any points of confusion.

Core Path

Model for the class how to use the overall structure and meaning of the sentence and the sentences around it, the word's position, and other clues to define the unfamiliar vocabulary word. In this case, point out these context clues:

1. Look at the structure of the sentence. The word "notoriously" appears in front of an adjective (disorganized) and ends in -*ly*. This indicates that "notoriously" is an adverb, or a word that describes an adjective.

2. We can use the clues in the sentence to conclude that "notoriously" has a negative connotation. It describes the word "disorganized." Later in the sentence, the author describes the material as a "heap."

3. Earlier in the paragraph, the author asks, "But can Nennius be trusted?" indicating that the author is questioning Nennius and his "disorganized material." The author mentions other historians, which indicates that many people know Nennius's quirks.

4. Based on these clues, I can guess that "notoriously" means well known, but in a negative way.

Access Path

5. After the student has completed the Think Aloud and made a prediction about the word's meaning, allow time for the proficient reader to add his/her own thoughts and clarify any points of confusion.

6. Once they've completed this Think Aloud, encourage them to use a dictionary to confirm the definition of the new vocabulary word. Have them refer to the "Text Glossary" on their Access 1, 2, and 4 handouts for definitions of key vocabulary terms in the text. Encourage them to add any additional vocabulary words or idioms they find in the text and look up definitions for those words and idioms online or in a dictionary.

Model Reading Comprehension Strategy. Before students begin reading, model the reading comprehension strategy of summarizing by using this Think Aloud that talks students through the first few paragraphs in the text. First explain to your students that summarizing is:

a process in which students select, organize, and synthesize the most important elements in a text

Note: This exercise, which extends instruction around reading comprehension strategies, should be completed when the class shifts from whole group instruction to individual work during the "Read and Annotate" exercise.

Beginner, Intermediate & Approaching Apply Reading Comprehension Strategy.

1. Have Beginner and Intermediate students read or listen to the excerpt from Unsolved Mysteries of History. As they finish reading each paragraph or section, ask them to try to answer the questions *who? what? where? when? why?* and *how?* Encourage them to answer as many of the questions for each paragraph or section in the time allowed.

Core Path	Access Path
Explain to students how summarizing will help them better comprehend the selection and help drive their discussions. • In the first paragraph, the author introduces Geoffrey of Monmouth. The central idea about him is that he gets "much of the credit" for the invention of the Arthurian legend. That's an important detail that should be in a summary. • Then the author retells Geoffrey of Monmouth's version of the Arthur story. Most of the details here are interesting, but they would not go in a summary. • Once I've identified all of the most important facts and details, I'll summarize the section briefly and objectively in my own words: The legend of King Arthur began with Welsh cleric Geoffrey of Monmouth's The History of the Kings of Britain, which detailed a fifth-century king named Arthur who conquered various groups trying to overtake Britain. Have students write brief summaries for the rest of the selection. Remind students that the purpose of a summary is to answer as succinctly as possible the questions *who? what? where? when? why?* and *how?*, and that summaries should be objective (that is, they should not contain any personal opinions).	2. Once they have finished reading and answering the questions, pair Beginner and Intermediate students with more proficient readers and ask them to discuss their responses. Have students use their responses to identify the most important details of each paragraph. 3. Then allow pairs time to use these details to create one-sentence summaries for each paragraph or section. Remind students that although some details might be interesting, they should not all go in a summary. Also, summaries should be in their own words, but they should not include personal opinions.
Read and Annotate. Read and annotate the excerpt. Ask students to use the annotation tool as they read to 1. use context clues to analyze and determine the meaning of the bolded vocabulary terms 2. ask questions about passages of the text that may be unclear or unresolved 3. identify key details, events, individuals, and connections between them 4. note unfamiliar vocabulary 5. capture their reaction to the events in the text.	**Beginner** **Coach the Reading.** While other students read, annotate, and discuss the text independently, work with Beginner students, listening to the audio of the text and pausing periodically or when any student has a question. Coach students in articulating their questions for the group and in highlighting and annotating the text. Have students use the Annotation Guide on the Access 1 handout to support them as they highlight and annotate the text.

Core Path	Access Path
	For further support, ask questions about the text such as:
	• Is there anything about this selection that you don't understand?
	• Does this selection help you understand why it is difficult to answer the question "Who was King Arthur?" Why or why not?
	• Which writer cited in the text do you think tells the most complete or accurate story about King Arthur? Why?
	Intermediate
	Listen to the Audio. Have these students listen to the audio of the text and use the definitions on the Access 2 handout to help them with words or idioms that may be unfamiliar. If students need help with annotating the text, have them use the Annotation Guide on the Access 2 handout. After working with the Beginner students, you may wish to check this group's progress and provide support as needed.
	Advanced
	Pair with Proficient Peers. Have Advanced students work with English-proficient peers to read, annotate, and discuss the text. Have students use the Annotation Guide in the Access 3 handout to support them as they highlight and annotate the text. Encourage them to listen to the audio of the text if needed.
	Approaching
	Use the Annotation Guide. Have students use the Annotation Guide on the Access 4 handout to support them as they highlight and annotate the text.

Core Path	Access Path
Discuss. In small groups or pairs, have students discuss the questions and inferences they made while reading. To help facilitate discussions, refer to Collaborative Discussions in the Speaking & Listening Handbook.	**English Learners All Levels & Approaching** Use the extra time while on- and beyond-grade-level students are discussing their first reads of the text to work individually and in small groups with Approaching readers and English Learners as outlined above. Should those students complete their first reads quickly, integrate them into the on- and beyond-grade-level discussion groups. Otherwise, English Learners and Approaching readers will be given an opportunity to participate in text discussions with their peers later in the lesson.
1. Who is Geoffrey of Monmouth and what was his contribution to the Arthurian legend? (He was a Welsh cleric and teacher who wrote *The History of the Kings of Britain*.)	
2. Describe the Arthurian legend as Geoffrey of Monmouth tells it. Does it seem like a true story? (During an invasion that has destroyed much of the country, a wizard arrives with prophecies of a king who will save Britain. When he comes to the throne, he makes many conquests but loses his own wife. After slaying the traitor, Arthur is last seen leaving, wounded, for the Isle of Avalon.)	**Tech Infusion** **Beyond** **Visualize.** Invite students to track the evolution of the Arthurian legend through a visual display. Encourage students to search online for representations of King Arthur from across the centuries. Then have them display the digital images on a social media site such as Pinterest (www .pinterest.com) to share with the rest of the class. Remind students to add captions and source information.
3. How did the Arthurian legend evolve? (Initially told by Welsh bards, the story of Arthur changed slightly each time it was told.)	
4. What did sources before Geoffrey of Monmouth say about Arthur and other British warrior kings? (They inherited new enemies each time they made a conquest.)	
5. Why is it so difficult to trace the history of the real Arthur? (The written accounts did not appear until 300 years after the actual events. Their accuracy was deeply questionable.)	
6. Summarize the excerpt in your own words. What is Aron's central idea? (The real King Arthur is difficult to find due to lack of records.)	

Core Path	Access Path
Grammar, Usage, and Mechanics. Distribute the handout on appositives, semicolons, and parallelism. Review with students the information provided on the handout. Ask students, what is the appositive in the first sentence? ("an insurance company executive") Then ask, Which noun do the appositives provide additional information about? (Wallace Stevens) Then ask students, What is parallel in the second sentence? (the names of three poets: Williams Carlos Williams, Wallace Stevens, and T.S. Eliot; and the use of appositives after each poet's name: "a doctor," "an insurance company executive," and "a banker") Explain to students that parallel construction helps to succinctly express the similarities that the writer is trying to point out about the three poets.	**Beginner & Intermediate** **Work with the Teacher.** Remind these students that an appositive is a noun or pronoun placed next to another noun or pronoun to give more information about it.
Finally, encourage students to apply what they have learned by analyzing the use of appositives, semicolons, and parallelism in the following sentence from the selection:	Write the following statement on the board: *Three writers who added to the legend of King Arthur are Robert Wace, a Frenchman; Chrétien de Troyes, another Frenchman; and Wolfram von Eschenbach, a German.*
By the end of the Middle Ages, Arthur's fifth-century foot soldiers had become knights on horses; his fortified hills had become grand castles; and his court had become Camelot, a chivalric utopia.	Ask: What are the appositives in this sentence? ("a Frenchman," "another Frenchman," and "a German")
1. What is the appositive in the sentence and what does it modify? ("a chivalric utopia," modifying Camelot)	Remind students that a semicolon is used to separate three or more items in a series when at least one item contains commas. Ask students to identify how many semicolons are in the sentence above. (2) Then remind students that parallelism is the intentional repetition of certain words, phrases, or sentence structures for a particular effect.
2. Why are there semicolons used in this sentence? (because there are three items in the series and the last item contains a comma)	Ask: What is repeated in this sentence to create parallelism? (the names of the three writers and the three appositives)
3. What words are repeated in the items to create parallelism? ("had become" is repeated)	**Advanced & Beyond** **Extend the search.** Challenge these students to work in pairs or small groups to find appositives, semicolons, and parallelism in the text, and to note how effectively these work together to provide information and summarize the author's main points.
4. Do you think this use of parallelism is effective? Explain. (Possible response: I think it is effective because the use of parallelism clearly summarizes the changes that had occurred in the legend of Arthur to make it seem more grand.)	

Core Path	Access Path
	Approaching **Analyze an example.** If students need more support identifying appositives, semicolons, and parallelism in the text, call their attention to examples throughout the text. For example, ask: What is the appositive in the third sentence of paragraph 2? (a young wizard) What noun does this modify? (Merlin) Encourage students to recognize how this structure helps the author succinctly express ideas. For example, point out that "Merlin is a young wizard. Merlin arrives on the scene with prophecies of a kin who will save Britain" takes much longer to say.
	Extend **Determine Sequence.** Aron's history is not written in chronological order. After reading, have students complete a sequence chart to understand the order of the events described in the text. Have pairs compare their charts to check their answers. (See Resources at the end of the lesson online.)
	Extend **Write.** The author of this text describes historians who may or may not provide trustworthy accounts of British history because they were writing at least 50 years after the events happened. Have students choose an event from U.S. history that happened at least 50 years ago. Without doing any additional research on the topic, have students write a short "history" of the event. When they're finished, have students trade papers with a partner and fact check each other's work. As a class, discuss how close each "history" got to the real event. Are any of the histories reliable? What important information was missed entirely or misrepresented?

3. THINK

Core Path	Access Path
Answer and Discuss. Have students complete the Think questions and then use the peer review instructions and rubric to complete two peer reviews. Refer to the sample answers at the end of the lesson plan online to discuss responses with your students.	**Beginner & Intermediate** **Sentence Frames.** Have students use the sentence frames on the Access 1 and 2 handouts to support their responses to the Think questions. If necessary, distribute sentence frames to Advanced students as well. **Approaching** **Find the Evidence.** Have students use Find the Evidence on the Access 4 handout to help them identify the evidence needed to answer the questions.
	Extend **Imagine.** Have students imagine they could sit down with one of the historians described in the text. As a class, brainstorm questions they would ask the historians. List the questions on the board or on a shared Google Doc. Refer to this list during the Close Read.

Textual Evidence

OVERVIEW

Using and understanding textual evidence is a key part of literary analysis. This lesson plan provides follow-up questions and useful enrichments to help teachers guide students toward an understanding of how and why to use textual evidence.

OBJECTIVES

1. Learn the definition of textual evidence.
2. Practice using textual evidence and background knowledge to make inferences.
3. Participate effectively in a range of conversations and collaborations to express ideas and build upon the ideas of others.

   ELA Common Core Standards: :
   Reading: Literature - RL.11-12.1, RL.11-12.2
   Speaking & Listening - SL.11-12.1.A, SL.11-12.1.C, SL.11-12.2

RESOURCES

Access 1 handout (Beginner)

Access 2 handout (Intermediate)

Access 3 handout (Advanced)

Access 4 handout (Approaching)

1. DEFINE

Core Path	Access Path
Watch. Watch the Concept Definition video on textual evidence with your students. Make sure students understand the purpose of finding textual evidence in an informational or literary text, as well as the difference between explicit and inferred evidence. Pause the video at these key moments to discuss the information with your students:	**English Learners All Levels & Approaching** **Fill in the Blank.** Have students complete the fill-in-the-blank exercise on the Access 1, 2, 3, and 4 handouts as they watch the video. Answers are located at the end of the lesson plan online.
1. 0:50 – Why aren't authors always as explicit as possible in stating their meaning or purpose? Why do you think they often leave evidence to be inferred?	
2. 1:11 – How can readers be sure if an inference is valid? Think of a few ways to test the validity of an inference, in addition to the examples given in the video.	
3. 1:49 – Why is inference an important skill when reading both informational and literary works? How can this skill help us deepen our understanding of works in both genres?	
Read and Discuss. After watching the Concept Definition video, have students read the definition of textual evidence. Either in small groups or as a whole class, use these questions to spur discussion among your students about textual evidence.	**Beginner & Approaching** **Complete a Chart.** To prepare students to participate in the discussion, have them complete the chart on the Access 1 and 4 handouts as they read the definition. The correct answers are located at the end of the lesson plan online.
1. What is an inference? How can making inferences help you as a reader understand a text? (An inference is a logical guess about what is not explicitly stated by the author. Inferences help the reader to understand the text on a deeper level by connecting their prior knowledge to the information they are reading.)	**Intermediate & Advanced** **Discuss Prompts.** To help these students participate in the discussion, prompt them with questions that can be answered with a few words, such as: • What is an inference? (a logical guess)
2. In what way can textual evidence or inferences help you to understand moments in the text where the author leaves matters uncertain? (Making inferences helps the reader to draw conclusions about matters that are uncertain by examining characters, setting, and plot events.)	• What should you use to help you make inferences when you analyze a text? (textual evidence and prior knowledge) • What are some examples of textual evidence? (facts, details, quotations, statistics)

Please note that excerpts and passages in the StudySync® library, workbooks, and PDFs are intended as touchstones to generate interest in an author's work. The excerpts and passages do not substitute for the reading of entire texts, and StudySync® strongly recommends that teachers and students seek out and purchase the whole literary or informational work in order to experience it as the author intended. Links to online resellers are available in our digital library. In addition, complete works may be ordered through an authorized reseller by filling out and returning to StudySync® the order form enclosed in this workbook.

Teacher's Edition 275

Core Path	Access Path
3. Can you think of a scenario in which it would be beneficial for an author or a speaker to either omit or obscure textual evidence?	**Beyond** **Discuss.** Have students think of another informational text they've read and describe how textual evidence helped them analyze and draw conclusions about the text. Then have students discuss the strengths and weaknesses of different kinds of textual evidence. Which did they find best supported their inferences and why?
	Extend **Discuss.** After watching the video, remind students that they make inferences all the time in everyday life. Ask: When was the last time you knew a friend or family member was angry based on what he or she did not say? Then ask students if they have ever misunderstood a text or message because of something the sender left out. Discuss student responses.
	Extend **Solve.** Explain to students that solving riddles is a form of making inferences based on the clues presented. Do an Internet search and find some grade-appropriate riddles for the class. Put students in small groups and give each a riddle to solve. Have each group record its thought process, taking specific notes on what background knowledge they use to solve the puzzle and what information they use from the question itself.

2. MODEL

Core Path	Access Path
Read and Annotate. Have students independently read the Model section. As they read, ask students to use the annotation tool to: • highlight key points • ask questions	**Note:** During this portion of the lesson, instruction shifts from whole-group to individual work. Use this time to work one on one or in small groups with Beginner, Intermediate, Advanced, and Approaching students.

Copyright © BookheadEd Learning, LLC

Core Path	Access Path
• identify places where the Model is applying the strategies laid out in the Identification and Application section on textual evidence.	**Beginner & Intermediate** **Coach the Reading.** Work with these students (either individually or in small groups) to fill out the guided reading questions on the Access 1 and 2 handouts. Have Beginner students refer to the glossary on the Access 1 handout to help them determine the meaning of difficult words (note: provide the Access 1 handout glossary to Intermediate students if necessary). Let students know they'll use these answers to help participate in the discussion about the Model. Sample answers for this exercise are located at the end of the lesson plan online. **Advanced** **Identify Evidence.** Ask Advanced students to complete the identifying evidence exercise on the Access 3 handout. Let students know that they'll use these answers to help participate in the discussion about the Model. Sample answers for this exercise are located at the end of the lesson plan online. **Approaching** **Guided Reading.** Have students complete the guided reading questions on the Access 4 handout as they read. Let them know that they'll use these answers to help participate in the discussion about the Model. Sample answers for this exercise are located at the end of the lesson plan online.
Discuss. After students read the Model text, use these questions to facilitate a whole group discussion that helps students understand how to infer information from the passage: 1. Where does the Model recommend a reader start before making any inferences? (examine the author's word choice) 2. Why does the Model recommend starting there? (because it provides insight into the author's attitude and ideas) 3. What does the Model conclude about the author's attitude? (The author's tone is informal.) 4. What inference does the Model draw based on the tone? (The author doesn't take the story too seriously and doesn't expect the reader to either.)	

Core Path	Access Path
5. Why does the Model call attention to the phrase "isle of Avalon"? (The author puts this phrase in quotation marks to call attention to the euphemism.)	
	Extend **Pair and Share.** If students have trouble with the idea of making inferences, display a three-column chart with the headings "Textual Evidence," "Background Knowledge," and "Inference." (See Resources.) Explain that students can use a chart like this one to work out their thinking and make valid inferences.

3. YOUR TURN

Core Path	Access Path
Assess and Explain. Have students answer the comprehension questions to test for understanding. Share the explanations for Parts A and B (located online) with your students.	
	Extend **Tech Infusion** **Explore.** On a whiteboard or on individual students' devices, pull up maps of Europe today and in the Middle Ages. Point out the close proximity of England, France, and Germany. Explain that ideas hardly moved quickly between these areas (relative to today), but that trade and disputes kept the areas in regular contact. Ask students to research the modes of communication used during the Middle Ages. • How was information communicated? • How long did this communication take? • What impact did this form of communication have on the information sent and received?

OVERVIEW

The excerpt from *Unsolved Mysteries of History*, by Paul Aron, explains how specific people in the Middle Ages shaped the legend of King Arthur. The Close Read gives students the opportunity to use textual evidence to support analysis and inferences from an informational text.

OBJECTIVES

1. Complete a close reading of an informational text.
2. Write an analysis based on textual evidence taken from an excerpt from Unsolved Mysteries of History.
3. Participate effectively in a range of conversations and collaborations to express ideas and build upon the ideas of others.
4. Prewrite, plan, and produce clear and coherent writing in response to a prompt.

   ELA Common Core Standards:
   Reading - Informational - RI.11-12.1, RI.11-12.2, RI.11-12.4, RI.11-12.7
   Writing - W.11-12.4, W.11-12.5, W.11-12.6, W.11-12.9.B, W.11-12.10
   Speaking & Listening - SL.11-12.1, SL.11-12.1.A, SL.11-12.1.B, SL.11-12.1.C, SL.11-12.1.D, SL.11-12.6
   Language - L.11-12.4.A, L.11-12.4.D, L.11-12.6

RESOURCES

Unsolved Mysteries of History Vocabulary Worksheet

Access 1 handout (Beginner)

Access 2 handout (Intermediate)

Access 3 handout (Advanced)

Access 4 handout (Approaching)

1. INTRODUCTION

Core Path	Access Path
Define and Compare. Project the vocabulary words and definitions onto the board or provide students with handouts so they can copy the vocabulary into their notebooks. Suggest that students consult general and specialized reference materials, both print and digital, to compare the precise meaning of a specific word with their initial vocabulary predictions from the First Read. Review words that students defined incorrectly to understand why they were unable to use context clues to develop usable definitions.	**Beginner & Intermediate** **Complete a Chart.** Have students complete the chart on the Access 1 and 2 handouts by writing the correct word for each of the definitions. **Advanced & Beyond** **Write in Journals.** Have students write a journal entry using all of their vocabulary words. Remind them to write sentences that communicate the meaning of the words they are using. **Approaching** **Graphic Organizer.** To support students in comparing their predictions with the correct meanings, have them complete the graphic organizer on the Access 4 handout to record the vocabulary words, their initial analysis, and the definitions. Then have them write sentences using the words.
Review. Have students complete the fill-in-the-blank vocabulary worksheet for this selection. Answers for the worksheet are listed online.	
	Extend **Write.** Ask students to write a short story about King Arthur using all the selection vocabulary words. Make sure students are using the basic facts of Arthur's story, but allow them to vary the details as needed.

Core Path	Access Path
	Extend **Tech Infusion** **Review.** Have students create their own vocabulary review sentences. Ask students to write a sentence for each word that clearly uses context to demonstrate the meaning of the word. Using Google Docs, have students replace the vocabulary word with a blank and share their sentences with a peer to complete. Have students review each other's files and discuss any errors.
	Extend **Explore.** Place students in small groups. Have groups use a print or online dictionary to identify patterns of word changes that change the meaning or part of speech for the vocabulary words (e.g., "utopia," "utopian"). Students should discuss the meanings of each word and how the meanings relate to each other.
	Extend **Tech Infusion** **Create.** Have students use Powtoon (http://www.powtoon.com/) or other animation software to animate their stories.

2. READ

Core Path	Access Path
Model Close Reading. Project the text onto the board and model a close reading of the first five paragraphs using the annotation strategies mentioned below. While modeling annotation strategies, make notes that tie the text to the focus skill and demonstrate what students are looking for as they read. Some guidance for you as you annotate for your students:	

- The first sentence clearly sets up the topic of the excerpt: "The legend of King Arthur—in stark contrast to the actual man—is easy to track back to its origins." The author will trace the legend of King Arthur, but also discuss the real man behind the stories.

- At the start of the second paragraph, Aron says, "The story, as Geoffrey tells it" calling into the question Geoffrey's reliability as a source.

- In the next several paragraphs, the author briefly retells Geoffrey of Monmouth's version of the Arthurian legend. The author's tone is light and breezy as he hurries through the tale. Phrases like "Merlin steps in to help out" and "Fast forward about fifteen years" demonstrate his light, informal tone.

- Paragraph 6 wraps up the summary. The author ties the story back into "real" history by reminding readers that "Anglo-Saxons eventually do conquer Arthur's Britons." This return to history explains Arthur's popularity with a conquered people.

Core Path	Access Path
Read and Annotate. Read the Skills Focus questions as a class, so your students know what they should pay close attention to as they read. Then have students read and annotate the excerpt. Ask students to use the annotation tool as they read to:	**Note.** While on-grade-level students are reading and annotating, work one-on-one or in small groups with Beginner, Intermediate, Advanced, and Approaching students to support them as they read and annotate the text.

Core Path:

1. respond to the Skills Focus section

2. analyze textual evidence to understand intent, meaning, and context

3. examine textual evidence to determine its validity

4. make inferences by looking for related series of facts

5. note unfamiliar vocabulary

6. capture their reaction to the ideas and examples in the text.

As they reread the text, remind students to use the comprehension strategy of summarizing that they learned in the First Read.

Access Path:

Beginner & Intermediate
Summarize and Analyze the Text. Work with these students to complete the sentence frames on the Access 1 and 2 handouts (note: the sentence frames for Intermediate students on the Access 2 handout contain fewer scaffolds). They will then use the completed sentence frames to help them analyze and annotate the text by completing the Skills Focus questions. Refer to the sample Skills Focus answers to help them complete the sentence frames and annotate the text.

Advanced
Work in Pairs. Pair these students with more proficient English speakers to work together on analyzing and annotating the text to complete the Skills Focus questions. If these students need more support, have them use the sentence frames on the Access 3 handout as they work with their more proficient peers.

Approaching
Summarize the Text. Have these students discuss and complete the text summary on the Access 4 handout and use their summary to help them analyze and annotate the text by completing the Skills Focus questions. Correct answers for the summary are at the end of the lesson plan online. Also refer to the sample Skills Focus answers to aid students with their annotations.

Core Path	Access Path
Discuss. After students have read the text, use the sample responses to the Skills Focus questions at the end of the lesson plan online to discuss the reading and the process of reading and making inferences supported by textual evidence. Make sure that students have acquired and accurately use academic-specific words and phrases related to the skill and demonstrate a command of formal English appropriate to the discussion. To help facilitate discussions, refer to Collaborative Discussions in the Speaking & Listening Handbook	**Extend** **Pair and Share.** In small, heterogeneous groups or pairs, ask students to share and discuss their annotations with a focus on the point of view presented in the selection. You can provide students with these questions to guide their discussion: 1. The early writers of British history were Welsh clerics or monks. How do their histories support the legend of King Arthur as we know it today? Cite specific textual evidence to support your statements. (The Welsh monk Gildas wrote about a British victory at Mount Badon in 500: "In *The Ruin of Britain,* written only about fifty years after that, Gildas described the battle and the two generations of relative peace and prosperity that followed." The author notes that although the facts are sketchy, this interregnum could perhaps be considered the time of Camelot.)

Core Path	Access Path
	2. The author mentions that Britons "yearned for a return to a golden age when they ruled the land." How is this yearning reflected in the Arthurian legends of the Middle Ages? Cite specific textual evidence to support your statements. (The non-British medieval writers added details and characters so that "by the end of the Middle Ages, Arthur's fifth-century foot soldiers had become knights on horses; his fortified hills had become grand castles; and his court had become Camelot, a chivalric utopia." The elements the non-British writers added to the story allowed Englishman Thomas Malory to combine them into a sweeping mythology that has forever captured his nation, as well as the world.) 3. The author states that classic myths "can transcend almost any sort of border," noting the variations and references to the Arthurian legend in modern times and outside of England. Do you agree with this statement? Why or why not? Are there other classic myths that might also fit this statement? (Answers will vary.)
	Extend **Discuss.** As a class, brainstorm events in U.S. history that commonly appear in works of fiction, such as the Civil War or the Great Depression. Steer students toward topics that are at least 50 years old. Then discuss how fictional representations of these events vary from the actual events. Ask: Why do authors choose to write about these events? What do the fictional representations add to the collective knowledge of a time period?

Core Path	Access Path
	Extend **Research.** The author mentions the novel *The Mists of Avalon*, by Marion Zimmer Bradley, and the musical (and film) *Camelot* as examples of the Arthurian legend overcoming borders. Have students find other examples of the Arthurian legend in modern life. Encourage students to think outside books and movies (for example, the King Arthur Flour company or Merlin auto repair shops). As a class, discuss what the Arthurian legend brings to these texts and companies. Why is the legend so persistent? Why do companies want to be associated with it?

3. WRITE

Core Path	Access Path
Prewrite and Plan. Read the prompt as a class and ask students to brainstorm a conclusion they can draw about early British history and literature based on the information in *Unsolved Mysteries of History*. Remind your students to look at the excerpt and their annotations to find textual evidence to support their ideas.	**Beginner & Intermediate** **Plan and Organize.** Have students complete the prewriting activity on the Access 1 and 2 handouts and then explain their ideas to a partner before they write. Explain to students that they need to choose details, examples, or quotes from the text that support their ideas and then explain how those details support their statements. For example, to support the idea that the varying histories of King Arthur make it difficult to determine fact from fiction, students could include the following line from the text: "It was impossible to tell whether the oral tradition they recounted was the actual history of fifth-century Britain." **Approaching** **Answer Prewriting Questions.** Have students complete the prewriting questions on the Access 4 handout to summarize their thoughts before they write.

Core Path	Access Path
	Extend **Organize.** Encourage students to create an outline to organize their ideas before they type their responses.
Discuss. Project these instructions for the peer review onto the board and review them with your class, so they know what they are looking for when they begin to provide their classmates with feedback: • Has the writer drawn a conclusion about early British history and literature? Is the conclusion well supported by textual evidence? • Has the writer included a clear statement of how this conclusion enhances or enriches an understanding of the Arthurian legend? • What sort of evidence does the writer use from the text to support his or her writing? • How well does the writer explain how that evidence supports his or her ideas? • Does the writer write using standard grammar and punctuation? Are there any weak spots? • What specific suggestions can you make to help the writer improve the response? • What thing(s) does this paper do especially well? After you've looked at the peer review instructions, review the rubric with students before they begin writing. Allow time for students briefly to pose and discuss any questions they may have about the peer review instructions and the rubric. Tell students how many peer reviews they will need to complete once they submit their writing.	
Write. Ask students to complete the writing assignment using textual evidence to support their answers. Once they have completed their writing, they should click "Submit."	

Core Path	Access Path
	Extend **Spelling.** Remind students that their computer's spell-check will not catch all spelling mistakes. Many typos and homophone errors get past the spell-check because the computer only recognizes spelling errors, not usage errors. Have students read their peers' papers closely for spelling and homophone errors.
Review. Once students complete their writing assignment, they should submit substantive feedback to a peer.	

OVERVIEW

The Lord of the Rings is one of the most famous works in the literary subgenre of fantasy. J. R. R. Tolkien's work consists of three parts: *The Fellowship of the Ring, The Two Towers,* and *The Return of the King.* The story is set in a fictional place called Middle-earth. This excerpt is taken from the very start of the novel. It features a conversation between Frodo, a hobbit, and Gandalf, a wizard. The First Read gives students the opportunity to experience the text with a limited context.

OBJECTIVES

1. Perform an initial reading of a text and demonstrate comprehension by responding to short analysis and inference questions with textual evidence.
2. Practice defining vocabulary words using context.
3. Participate effectively in a range of conversations and collaborations to express ideas and build upon the ideas of others.
4. Practice acquiring and using academic vocabulary correctly.
5. Demonstrate an understanding of textual evidence and setting.
6. Practice and apply concrete strategies for identifying setting.

ELA Common Core Standards:
Reading: Literature - RL.11-12.1, RL.11-12.2, RL.11-12.3, RL.11-12.4, RL.11-12.10
Speaking & Listening - SL.11-12.1, SL.11-12.1.A, SL.11-12.1.B, SL.11-12.1.C, SL.11-12.1.D, SL.11-12.2, SL.11-12.3, SL.11-12.6
Language - L.11-12.1.A, L.11-12.1.B, L.11-12.3, L.11-12.4.A, L.11-12.4.C, L.11-12.4.D, L.11-12.1.B, L.11-12.4.D, L.11-12.6

RESOURCES

Grammar Handout: Contested Usage

Access 1 handout (Beginner)

Access 2 handout (Intermediate)

Access 3 handout (Advanced)

Access 4 handout (Approaching)

Please note that excerpts and passages in the StudySync® library, workbooks, and PDFs are intended as touchstones to generate interest in an author's work. The excerpts and passages do not substitute for the reading of entire texts, and StudySync® strongly recommends that teachers and students seek out and purchase the whole literary or informational work in order to experience it as the author intended. Links to online resellers are available in our digital library. In addition, complete works may be ordered through an authorized reseller by filling out and returning to StudySync® the order form enclosed in this workbook.

Teacher's Edition   **289**

ACCESS COMPLEX TEXT

In this excerpt from *The Lord of the Rings*, Gandalf teaches Frodo about the power and lure of the One Ring. To help students understand the main characters of Frodo and Gandalf, and the internal and external conflicts they face, use the following ideas to provide scaffolded instruction for a first reading of the more complex features of this text:

- **Genre** - *The Lord of the Rings* is a fantasy novel, set in a world that operates differently from our own. Students who are unfamiliar with the world Tolkien has created may struggle to understand how a simple piece of jewelry could yield such power.

- **Organization** - The excerpt consists mainly of dialogue between Frodo and Gandalf. Dialogue tags will help students keep track of who is talking in most paragraphs, but they will have to infer who is speaking in some parts of the excerpt.

- **Connection of Ideas** - Because this excerpt is taken from Chapter II of the novel, students may have trouble understanding some narrative elements, including the relationship between characters, the importance of Frodo's quest, and how previous events have influenced the plot so far.

1. INTRODUCTION

Core Path	Access Path
Watch. As a class, watch the video preview of *The Lord of the Rings*.	**English Learners All Levels** **Fill in the Blanks.** Ask students to use their Access 1, 2, and 3 handouts to fill in the blanks of the transcript for the preview's voiceover as they watch the preview along with their classmates. Answers are located at the end of the lesson plan online.
Read. Individually or as a class, read the Introduction for *The Lord of the Rings*. The introduction provides context for the excerpt taken from *The Fellowship of the Ring*.	**English Learners All Levels & Approaching** **Read and Listen.** Ask students to read and listen to the introduction for *The Lord of the Rings*. Have them refer to the "Introduction Glossary" on their Access 1, 2, 3, and 4 handouts for definitions of key vocabulary terms. If there are unfamiliar words that are not included in their glossary, encourage students to check a dictionary or online reference tool, such as http://dictionary.reference.com.

Core Path	Access Path
	Extend **Make Predictions.** Based on the introduction, ask students to make predictions about the central ideas they would expect to encounter in this text.
	Extend **Discuss the Introduction.** After reading the introduction, use the information provided to facilitate a prereading discussion to get students thinking about the events and themes in *The Lord of the Rings*. 1. How is fantasy different from science fiction? 2. Who are some famous wizards you know of from other works? 3. What kinds of objects are often magical in literary works of fantasy?
Access Prior Knowledge. Find out how many students have seen Peter Jackson's movie adaptation of *The Lord of the Rings*. As a class, generate a list (on the board or on paper) of phrases or sentences that describe the Shire, where Frodo lives. Then discuss what they recall about the character traits of Frodo, especially in the first movie, *The Lord of the Rings: The Fellowship of the Ring*.	**Beginner & Approaching** **Research and Discuss.** 1. Pair Beginner and Approaching students and assist them in using devices to look up images of the Shire as depicted in the movie adaptations of *The Lord of the Rings* and *The Hobbit*. 2. Have students review the images and discuss what it would be like to live in such a setting. 3. Students may conduct their discussion independently, or if they struggle, have them use the sentence frames on their Access 1 and 4 handouts.

Core Path	Access Path
	Intermediate & Advanced **Complete and Discuss the Chart.** Pair Intermediate and Advanced students, and rather than discussing what they already know about the Shire and Frodo Baggins, have them look up images of the Shire as depicted in the movie adaptations of *The Lord of the Rings* and *The Hobbit*. Then have them complete the "Imagine" exercises on the Access 2 and 3 handouts that ask students to consider what it would be like to live in the Shire. Have the pairs generate ideas, discuss the chart, and complete it together.
	Extend **Tech Infusion** **Post.** Use a Padlet (www.Padlet.com) wall with an image of a movie poster for *The Lord of the Rings: The Fellowship of the Ring* to allow students to synchronously or asynchronously post their previous knowledge on virtual sticky notes. This makes it possible for students to share their prior knowledge and read the sticky notes shared by their peers.
	Extend **Analyze and Discuss a Quotation.** "All we have to decide is what to do with the time that is given us." (J. R. R. Tolkien) 1. What do you think this quotation means? 2. Do you agree with this quotation? Why or why not? 3. How would you define a person's main purpose in life?

Copyright © BookheadEd Learning, LLC

2. READ

Core Path	Access Path

Core Path

Make Predictions about Vocabulary. There are five bold vocabulary words in the text. As students read the text, ask them to make predictions about what they think each bold vocabulary word means based on the context clues in the sentence. If you are in a low-tech classroom and students are reading from printed copies or a projected text, ask students to record predictions in their notes, so they can be easily referenced in class. If your students have access to technology, they can use the annotation tool to make their predictions.

It might be helpful to model this for students before they begin reading. Either using the board or projecting the actual text, focus in on the sentence that uses the word "stayed": "It was Pity that stayed his hand."

Model for the class how to use the overall structure and meaning of the sentence and the sentences around it, the word's position, and other clues to define the unfamiliar vocabulary word. In this case, point out these context clues:

1. I already know the verb "stay" means "to remain in the same place." I reread the sentence with this meaning in mind: "It was Pity that remained his hand." That does not make sense, so the precise meaning of "stayed" must be different in this sentence.

2. I look at the surrounding sentences for context clues to help me. I notice that the word "pity" appears in the sentence that comes at the end of the previous paragraph: "What a pity that Bilbo did not stab that vile creature, when he had a chance!" From this sentence, I understand that Bilbo did not stab Gollum. Stabbing is an action that is done by a person's hands, so I can connect this idea to the sentence that uses "stayed."

Access Path

Note: This exercise, which extends vocabulary instruction, should be completed when the class shifts from whole-group instruction to individual work during the "Read and Annotate" exercise.

Beginner, Intermediate & Approaching Pair Practice.

1. Pair students with more proficient readers.

2. Give them an additional sentence that contains a new vocabulary word.

3. Ask the students to complete a Think Aloud using the teacher-led Make Predictions about Vocabulary activity as a model, while the proficient student actively listens.

4. The student should use the context clues in the sentence to try to determine the meaning of the new vocabulary word.

5. After the student has completed the Think Aloud and made a prediction about the word's meaning, allow time for the proficient reader to add his/her own thoughts and clarify any points of confusion.

6. Once they've completed this Think Aloud, encourage them to use a dictionary to confirm the definition of the new vocabulary word. Have them refer to the "Text Glossary" on their Access 1, 2, and 4 handouts for definitions of key vocabulary terms in the text. Encourage them to add any additional vocabulary words or idioms they find in the text and look up definitions for those words and idioms online or in a dictionary.

Core Path	Access Path
3. I read the sentence again: "It was Pity that stayed his hand." If Bilbo "stayed" his hand to keep from stabbing the creature, then "stayed" must mean "stopped" or "restrained." 4. I can look up the word in a dictionary to confirm my guess. According to the dictionary, "stayed" means "stopped the advance of" or "restrained." This is consistent with my guess.	
	Extend **Identify and Define.** After students have read the text, have small groups research the following creatures using the website tolkiengateway.net: • hobbit • orc • elf • wizard • dragon • Gollum • Sauron Ask groups to print out or sketch a picture of one creature and write a paragraph-long description of it. Emphasize that the description should focus on general information about their creature and include several sensory details. Encourage them to add creative touches to their work.
	Extend **Multiple-Meaning Words.** Use the Audio Text Highlight tool to help students identify multiple-meaning words other than "stayed" that appear in the selection. 1. Ask students to search the fourth paragraph for a multiple-meaning word other than "stayed." (strike) Have them give some common meanings of "strike." (to refuse to work; to hit) Then have them identify a verb in the previous paragraph that is a context clue for the meaning of "strike" as it is used in the selection. (stab)

Core Path	Access Path
	2. Remind students that words can sometimes have both a literal meaning and a figurative meaning. Have students look at the following sentence from the middle of the eighth paragraph: "And he is bound up with the fate of the Ring." Ask students what clue indicates that Gollum is not literally bound up. (Fate is not an object.) Explain that the figurative meaning of the sentence is that Gollum's future is tied to the future of the ring. 3. Remind students that, as they read using the Audio Text Highlight tool, they can pause, repeat, or slow down the audio at any time.
Model Reading Comprehension Strategy. Before students begin reading, model the reading comprehension strategy of asking and answering questions by using this Think Aloud that talks students through the first few lines of the excerpt. First explain to your students what asking and answering questions is: *Proficient readers ask themselves questions before, during, and after they read to facilitate understanding. Good readers approach a text with questions and ask new questions as they read.* Explain to students how asking and answering questions will help them better comprehend the excerpt and help drive their discussions. • The excerpt begins in the middle of a conversation. The first sentence references "the One." This makes me ask, the One what? I keep reading to find out. • From the next couple of paragraphs, I can see that Frodo and Gandalf are worried about the One. Frodo says "But this is terrible! … Far worse than the worst that I imagined from your hints and warnings." But I still don't know what it is.	**Note:** This exercise, which extends instruction around reading comprehension strategies, should be completed when the class shifts from whole-group instruction to individual work during the "Read and Annotate" exercise. **Beginner, Intermediate & Approaching** **Apply Reading Comprehension Strategy.** 1. To practice asking and answering questions, have students listen to the audio version of the excerpt from *The Lord of the Rings* paired with the written text. As they listen to the audio recording, ask them to draw a question mark next to portions of the text where they have a question. Next, have them underline words in the text that they understand. Encourage them to use what they know to both ask questions and draw conclusions about the text. 2. Once they have listened to the audio version and created annotated areas where they have questions and understandings, pair Beginner and Intermediate students with more proficient readers and ask them to describe what they underlined and why. What words, descriptions, and ideas are familiar to them?

Core Path	Access Path
• In the third paragraph, I can see that the word Ring is also capitalized. This helps me infer that the One is a ring. But I still don't understand why Frodo and Gandalf are so worried about a piece of jewelry. I ask myself, Why is the Ring so dangerous? • I keep reading and learn that the ring is beautiful ("The gold looked very fair and pure, and Frodo thought how rich and beautiful was its colour, how perfect was its roundness.") and powerful ("With that power I should have power too great and terrible. And over me the Ring would gain a power still greater and more deadly."). • These details help me answer my question. The Ring is dangerous because it is too tempting to ignore and too powerful for most people to handle.	3. Allow pairs time to discuss the question-marked sections. Were there any details from the text that might help in their understanding? If so, encourage them to make inferences. 4. Have student pairs illustrate the setting and ideas mentioned. What might the Ring look like? What does Frodo and Gandalf's meeting look like?

Read and Annotate. Read and annotate the excerpt. Ask students to use the annotation tool as they read to

1. use context clues to analyze and determine the meaning of the bolded vocabulary terms

2. ask questions about passages of the text that may be unclear or unresolved

3. identify key details, events, characters, and connections between them

4. note unfamiliar vocabulary

5. capture their reaction to the events in the text.

Beginner
Coach the Reading. While other students read, annotate, and discuss the text independently, work with Beginner students, listening to the audio of the text and pausing periodically or when any student has a question. Coach students in articulating their questions for the group and in highlighting and annotating the text. Have students use the Annotation Guide on the Access 1 handout to support them as they highlight and annotate the text.

For further support, ask questions about the text such as:
• Is there anything about the story that you don't understand?
• Why do you think Frodo was chosen to carry the Ring?
• Why do you think *The Lord of the Rings* is the title of the series?

Core Path	Access Path
	Intermediate **Listen to the Audio.** Have these students listen to the audio of the text and use the Text Glossary on the Access 2 handout to help them with words or idioms that may be unfamiliar. If students need help with annotating the text, have them use the Annotation Guide or the Access 2 handout. After working with the Beginner students, you may wish to check this group's progress and provide support as needed. **Advanced** **Pair with Proficient Peers.** Have Advanced students work with English-proficient peers to read, annotate, and discuss the text. Have students use the Annotation Guide in the Access 3 handout to support them as they highlight and annotate the text. Encourage them to listen to the audio of the text if needed. **Approaching** **Use the Annotation Guide.** Have students use the Annotation Guide or the Access 4 handout to support them as they highlight and annotate the text.
Discuss. In small groups or pairs, have students discuss the questions and inferences they made while reading. To help facilitate discussions, refer to Collaborative Discussions in the Speaking & Listening Handbook. 1. Why has Gandalf come to speak with Frodo? (Gandalf has come to warn Frodo.) 2. Why is Frodo in danger? (He has a valuable ring.) 3. From whom can you infer that Bilbo got the ring before it was passed onto Frodo? (Gollum) 4. Why would it be a mistake for Frodo just to throw the ring away? (The Enemy might find it.) 5. What is the only way to destroy the ring? (throw it into the Cracks of Doom)	**English Learners All Levels & Approaching** Use the extra time while on- and beyond-grade-level students are discussing their first reads of the text to work individually and in small groups with Approaching readers and English Learners as outlined above. Should those students complete their first reads quickly, integrate them into the on- and beyond-grade-level discussion groups. Otherwise, English Learners and Approaching readers will be given an opportunity to participate in text discussions with their peers later in the lesson.

Please note that excerpts and passages in the StudySync® library, workbooks, and PDFs are intended as touchstones to generate interest in an author's work. The excerpts and passages do not substitute for the reading of entire texts, and StudySync® strongly recommends that teachers and students seek out and purchase the whole literary or informational work in order to experience it as the author intended. Links to online resellers are available in our digital library. In addition, complete works may be ordered through an authorized reseller by filling out and returning to StudySync® the order form enclosed in this workbook.

Teacher's Edition   297

Core Path	Access Path
6. Why must Frodo act quickly? (The Enemy is approaching.) 7. How did asking and answering questions help you better understand Frodo's quest?	**Tech Infusion** **Beyond** **Journal.** Have students use Google Docs or an online journal, such as Pen.io (http://pen.io/), to write a journal entry from Frodo's perspective. What does he have to do next? How does he feel about this? After students have published their journal entries, encourage them to read others' journal entries and discuss the similarities and differences.
Grammar, Usage, and Mechanics. Distribute the grammar handout on usage. Tell students that usage is a matter of convention and can be contested because of changes over time, as explained in the handout. Review with students how to use a reference work, such as a dictionary or handbook, to resolve issues of contested usage. Then have students complete the practice exercises. (Answers for the practice exercises appear online.) Finally, encourage students to apply what they have learned by analyzing the excerpt from *The Lord of the Rings.* Ask students: 1. What is a conjunction? (a word that connects words, phrases, clauses, or sentences) Where are conjunctions usually placed in writing and speaking? (between the words they link) Is it correct to begin a sentence with a conjunction? Why or why not? (Answers may vary. Some students may say beginning a sentence with a conjunction breaks a rule of grammar; others may point out that it is acceptable to begin a sentence with a conjunction. Encourage students to use a reference guide, such as *Merriam-Webster's Dictionary of English Usage* if they are unsure.)	**Beginner & Intermediate** **Work with the Teacher.** Remind these students that a conjunction is a word that connects other words, phrases, clauses, and sentences. Common conjunctions include "and," "but," and "or." Also review with students that beginning a sentence with a conjunction is a point of contention in standard English. Some people think it is okay; others believe it to be a grammatical error. Write the following statement on the board: *Will missed a week of school because he was sick. But he studied hard and got an "A" on the math test anyway.* Ask: What kind of word does the second sentence begin with? (the conjunction "but") How does this word link ideas between sentences? (It shows that the second sentence contrasts with the first one. Will missed school, so it would make sense that a test would be a challenge, "but" he was able to do well.) Allow time for students to discuss how conjunctions can link ideas between sentences. Then have these students participate in the short lesson above with Approaching students. Then work with them to complete the Usage Handout.

Core Path	Access Path
2. Find an example in the excerpt from *The Lord of the Rings* where Tolkien begins a sentence with a conjunction. ("And he has at last heard, I think, of *hobbits* and the *Shire*.") How does the conjunction function in this sentence? (e.g., The conjunction "and" is used to link the information Gandalf is giving Frodo. Gandalf says that the enemy knows the ring is the One "and" that he had heard of hobbits and the Shire.) 3. Why do you think Tolkien begins some sentences with conjunctions? What effect does this choice have on the text? (Answers will vary.) Remind students that they can resolve questions of usage in their own writing by consulting references such as *Garner's Modern Usage,* as needed.	**Advanced & Beyond** **Extend the search.** Challenge these students to work in pairs or small groups to find all the conjunctions in the passage and discuss how they connect ideas in the text. **Approaching** **Analyze an example.** If students need more support identifying conjunctions, call their attention to these words in paragraph 8: "Many that live deserve death. And some that die deserve life." Ask: Which of these words is a conjunction? How does the conjunction help connect ideas between these two sentences? Encourage students to recognize that the conjunction "and" highlights the comparison Gandalf is making in this paragraph. Then have students complete the Usage Handout.

3. SYNCTV

Core Path	Access Path
Watch. As a class, watch the SyncTV video on *The Lord of the Rings*. Remind students to listen for the way the students use academic vocabulary during their discussion. Pause the video at these key moments to discuss the information with your students. Have students review and reflect on the ideas expressed: 1. 1:25 – Why does Tyler summarize the events that led to Frodo's becoming the owner of the ring? How well does he use text evidence and link ideas to help move the discussion along? 2. 3:50 – The group infers that the Ring cannot be used to do good. Why? How valid is this stance? Evaluate their premise and the text evidence they use to support it.	**Beginner & Intermediate** **Analyze the Discussion.** Have students use the "Analyze the Discussion" guide on the Access 1 and 2 handouts to identify key points in the discussion and the evidence the students use to determine those points. Sample answers are at the end of the lesson plan online. **Advanced** **Analyze Good versus Evil.** Have students discuss and complete the "Good versus Evil" chart on the Access 3 handout, referring to the SyncTV video as needed to clarify their answers. Sample answers appear at the end of the lesson plan online.

Core Path	Access Path
3. 6:05 – Regarding the temptation of the Ring, Tyler says, "I'm only human. That's why these guys are heroes." What does he mean by this statement? How does the group's reasoning and points of emphasis help advance Tyler's point of view?	**Approaching** **Analyze the Discussion.** Have students complete the chart on the Access 4 handout by listing textual evidence cited by the students in the video. Sample answers are at the end of the lesson plan online.
	Tech Infusion **Record.** Ask one student in each group to videotape their conversation. They can upload their videos to YouTube, share them via Google Drive, or email them to you for review. They can also play the video back and critique their own conversations to continually improve.

4. THINK

Core Path	Access Path
Answer and Discuss. Have students complete the Think questions and then use the peer review instructions and rubric to complete two peer reviews. Refer to the sample answers at the end of the lesson plan online to discuss responses with your students.	**Beginner & Intermediate** **Sentence Frames.** Have students use the sentence frames on the Access 1 and 2 handouts to support their responses to the Think questions. If necessary, distribute sentence frames to Advanced students as well. **Approaching** **Find the Evidence.** Have students use Find the Evidence on the Access 4 handout to help them identify the evidence needed to answer the questions.
SyncTV Style Discussion. Place students into small groups and give them a prompt to discuss. Remind them to model their discussions after the SyncTV episodes they have seen. Stress the importance of citing textual evidence in their conversations to support their ideas.	**Beginner & Intermediate** **Use Sentence Frames.** Have these students use the sentence frames on Access 1 and 2 handouts to help them participate in the discussion.

Core Path	Access Path
To help students prepare for, strategize, and evaluate their discussions, refer to the Collaborative Discussions section of the Speaking & Listening Handbook. Discussion prompt: 1. Should Frodo keep the ring instead of trying to destroy it? Why or why not? 2. What evidence is there that Frodo might struggle to be the "good guy" of this story? Have students review the key ideas expressed, demonstrating an understanding of multiple perspectives through reflection and paraphrasing. You may wish to have students create a video or audio recording of their SyncTV-Style Discussion.	**Approaching** **Use Think Questions.** Remind these students to refer to their answers to the Think questions to help them participate in the group discussion.
	Extend **Debate.** Present students with an issue from the text that can be debated. Allow students to debate the issue as a class or in smaller groups. Debate prompts: 1. Should Frodo try to find someone else to take the ring? Why or why not? 2. If you had the chance to kill Gollum, as Bilbo once did, would you have taken it? Why or why not?
	Extend **Write a Claim.** Ask students to write a strong claim that clearly states their position in relation to the topic they debated. Once students have written their claims, ask them to read their claims to a small group of their peers. This activity will provide them practice writing claims, and it will also expose them to claims written by their peers.

OVERVIEW

Analyzing a conversation for details about a setting often requires the use of inference. This lesson plan provides follow-up questions and useful enrichments to help teachers guide students toward a usable, repeatable method for gathering details about setting.

OBJECTIVES

1. Infer details about setting by analyzing dialogue.
2. Practice using concrete strategies for identifying setting.
3. Participate effectively in a range of conversations and collaborations to express ideas and build upon the ideas of others.

ELA Common Core Standards:

Reading: Literature - RL.11-12.1, RL.11-12.3, RL.11-12.4

Speaking & Listening - SL.11-12.1, SL.11-12.1.A, SL.11-12.1.C SL.11-12.2, SL.11-12.3

RESOURCES

Access 1 handout (Beginner)

Access 2 handout (Intermediate)

Access 3 handout (Advanced)

Access 4 handout (Approaching)

1. DEFINE

Core Path	Access Path
Watch. Watch the Concept Definition video on setting with your students. Have your students write down the definition of setting and what it encompasses, and make sure they understand how a story's setting can influence its plot, characters, and theme(s). Pause the video at these key moments to discuss the information with your students:	**English Learners All Levels & Approaching** **Match.** Have students complete the matching exercise on the Access 1, 2, 3, and 4 handouts as they watch the video. Answers are located at the end of the lesson plan online.

Core Path (continued):

1. 0:30 – How might the "emotional conditions" of a setting influence a story? Give an example or two of a setting that contains certain emotional conditions that would affect either characters or plot.

2. 1:04 – Think of another simple plot like the example given in the video. Now, think of two different settings where it could take place: one that would benefit its characters, and another that would lead to conflict. Which of the two settings sounds like it would make for a more interesting story? Why?

3. 1:22 – How does your own setting influence you? Imagine yourself in a place that would lead to more conflict, as well as one that would lessen the conflict. How would these different settings change your day-to-day life?

Core Path	Access Path
Read and Discuss. After watching the Concept Definition video, have students read the definition of setting. Either in small groups or as a whole class, use these questions to spur discussion among your students about setting.	**Beginner & Approaching** **Complete a Chart.** To prepare students to participate in the discussion, have them complete the chart on the Access 1 and 4 handouts as they read the definition. The correct answers are located at the end of the lesson plan online.

Core Path (continued):

1. Which is a more important element of setting, place or time? Why?

2. What are some memorable settings from other works you've read?

3. Can you think of a time when you watched a movie with an unusual setting and had to make inferences about it? What were they?

Core Path	Access Path
	Intermediate & Advanced **Discuss Prompts.** To help these students participate in the discussion, prompt them with questions that can be answered with a few words, such as: • What is a setting? (the time and place where a story takes place) • What does an author create with setting elements? (mood) • How might a story with an unfamiliar setting be different from one with a familiar setting? (Answers will vary.) **Beyond** **Discuss.** Have students start to think about how setting impacts the plot and mood of *The Lord of the Rings*. Ask them to consider how the story would be different if it were set somewhere else. What if Frodo lived in contemporary New York City instead of the Shire? What if Tolkien based the setting on the future, instead of the Anglo-Saxon period? Encourage them to come up with their own suggestions for different settings.
	Extend **Brainstorm.** After watching the video, ask students to select a book they've read and describe the setting in that book. Compile this list of examples as a class using a whiteboard or projector. Make sure students give information about the time as well as the place.
	Extend **Synthesize.** Assign students to small groups and have them discuss where they would like to be in ten years. Ask them to provide descriptive details about the places they would like to be, including their home and workplace.

2. MODEL

Core Path	Access Path
Read and Annotate. Have students independently read the Model section. As they read, ask students to use the annotation tool to: • highlight key points • ask questions • identify places where the Model applies the strategies laid out in the Identification and Application section on setting.	**Note:** During this portion of the lesson, instruction shifts from whole-group to individual work. Use this time to work one-on-one or in small groups with Beginner, Intermediate, Advanced, and Approaching students. **Beginner & Intermediate** **Coach the Reading.** Work with these students (either individually or in small groups) to fill out the guided reading questions on the Access 1 and 2 handouts. Have Beginner students refer to the glossary on the Access 1 handout to help them determine the meaning of difficult words (note: provide the Access 1 handout glossary to Intermediate students if necessary). Let students know they'll use these answers to help participate in the discussion about the Model. Sample answers for this exercise are located at the end of the lesson plan online. **Advanced** **Identify Evidence.** Ask Advanced students to complete the identifying evidence exercise on the Access 3 handout. Let students know that they'll use these answers to help participate in the discussion about the Model. Sample answers for this exercise are located at the end of the lesson plan online. **Approaching** **Guided Reading.** Have students complete the guided reading questions on the Access 4 handout as they read. Let them know that they'll use these answers to help participate in the discussion about the Model. Sample answers for this exercise are located at the end of the lesson plan online.

Core Path	Access Path
Discuss. After students read the Model text, use these questions to facilitate a whole-group discussion that helps students understand how to infer the setting from the conversation:	

1. What object does the first paragraph focus on first to try to identify what kind of place is Middle-earth? (Frodo's ring)

2. Why does this object provide evidence that Frodo and Gandalf are living in an imaginary world? (The ring has magical powers.)

3. Which strategy from the Define section of this Skill lesson does this Model use to determine setting? (The Model makes inferences about the places described in the paragraphs from the details provided.)

4. How is the evidence highlighted in the second paragraph different from the evidence in the first model? (The evidence in the second Model shows that there are elements of Middle-earth that also appear in the real world.)

5. How is the content of the second paragraph similar to the content of the first paragraph? (It comes from the same conversation between Frodo and Gandalf, and it discusses the danger that Frodo faces.)

6. How does the figurative language in the first part of the Skills Model (first excerpt from *The Lord of the Rings*) compare to the figurative language discussed in the second part of the Skills Model (the second excerpt from the text)? (The first excerpt in the Model presents imagery of fire, which creates an ominous mood; the second excerpt in the Model has an image of sunlight, which creates a mood of optimism.)

Core Path	Access Path
	Extend **Tech Infusion** **Pair and Share.** Pair students and have partners examine a text for information about setting. You can select texts from this unit or other texts you have in the classroom. Assign pairs questions from the following list: • Is the setting stated or implied? • When does the story take place? • Where does the story take place? • How does the author use setting to develop the plot? • How do the characters respond to the setting? Ask the groups to share their findings with the class.

3. YOUR TURN

Core Path	Access Path
Assess and Explain. Have students answer the comprehension questions to test for understanding. Share the explanations for Parts A and B (located online) with your students.	
Assess. Have students answer the comprehension questions to test for understanding.	**Extend** **Tech Infusion** **Quiz Game.** Have students work in pairs to write one additional Comprehend question based on the passage. Create a Google Form to collect the student-generated questions (and answers). Then use those questions to create a quiz using Socrative (www.Socrative.com). You can run this quiz as a Space Race and allow groups to compete against each other to correctly answer questions.

Please note that excerpts and passages in the StudySync® library, workbooks, and PDFs are intended as touchstones to generate interest in an author's work. The excerpts and passages do not substitute for the reading of entire texts, and StudySync® strongly recommends that teachers and students seek out and purchase the whole literary or informational work in order to experience it as the author intended. Links to online resellers are available in our digital library. In addition, complete works may be ordered through an authorized reseller by filling out and returning to StudySync® the order form enclosed in this workbook.

Teacher's Edition   **307**

OVERVIEW

The Lord of the Rings is a three-part fantasy that follows the quest of the hobbit Frodo Baggins to destroy a ring filled with evil magic. The Close Read gives students the opportunity to infer details about the setting and analyze figurative language.

OBJECTIVES

1. Complete a close reading of a passage of literature.
2. Practice and apply concrete strategies for identifying setting and figurative language.

ELA Common Core Standards: :
Reading: Literature - RL.11-12.1, RL.11-12.2, RL.11-12.3, RL.11-12.4
Writing - W.11-12.3.A, W.11-12.3.B, W.11-12.4, W.11-12.5, W.11-12.6, W.11-12.9.A, W.11-12.10
Speaking & Listening - SL.11-12.1, SL.11-12.2, SL.11-12.4
Language - L.11-12.4, L.11-12.4.A, L.11-12.4.C, L.11-12.4.D, L.11-12.5

RESOURCES

The Lord of the Rings Vocabulary Worksheet
The Lord of the Rings Graphic Organizer
Short Constructed Response - Narrative Student Model
Access 1 handout (Beginner)
Access 2 handout (Intermediate)
Access 3 handout (Advanced)
Access 4 handout (Approaching)

1. INTRODUCTION

Core Path	Access Path
Define and Compare. Project the vocabulary words and definitions onto the board or provide students with handouts so they can copy the vocabulary into their notebooks. Suggest that students consult general and specialized reference materials, both print and digital, to compare the precise meaning of a specific word with their initial vocabulary predictions from the First Read. Review words that students defined incorrectly to understand why they were unable to use context clues to develop usable definitions.	**Beginner & Intermediate** **Complete a Chart.** Have students complete the chart on the Access 1 and 2 handouts by writing the correct word for each of the definitions. **Advanced & Beyond** **Write in Journals.** Have students write a journal entry using all of their vocabulary words. Remind them to write sentences that communicate the meaning of the words they are using. **Approaching** **Graphic Organizer.** To support students in comparing their predictions with the correct meanings, have them complete the graphic organizer on the Access 4 handout to record the vocabulary words, their initial analysis, and the definitions. Then have them write sentences using the words.
Review. Have students complete the fill-in-the-blank vocabulary worksheet for this selection. Answers for the worksheet are listed online.	
	Extend **Tech Infusion** **Create.** Create online flashcards for the vocabulary words using StudyBlue (www.studyblue.com) or Quizlet (http://quizlet.com).
	Extend **Word Forms.** Have students write sentences for these variant forms of three of the vocabulary words: peril (noun), stay (noun), forge (verb). Ask them to look up the definitions online as needed.

Core Path	Access Path
	Extend **Tech Infusion** **Act and Record.** Break up the class into small groups, assign each group a vocabulary word, and ask them to design a short skit to demonstrate the meaning of the word for their peers. If possible, record skits and post them to your class YouTube Channel, so they can be reviewed.

2. READ

Core Path	Access Path
Model Close Reading. Project the text onto the board and model a close reading of the first seven paragraphs using the annotation strategies mentioned below. While modeling annotation strategies, make notes that tie the text to the focus skill and demonstrate what students are looking for as they read. Some guidance for you as you annotate for your students: • As the Skills lesson that precedes this text makes clear, the details of the setting must be inferred from details in the conversation between Frodo and Gandalf. • Note that Frodo reacts with terror to Gandalf's news that the Enemy has found out about hobbits and the Shire. Frodo says, "'But this is terrible!' cried Frodo. 'Far worse than the worst that I imagined from your hints and warnings. O Gandalf, best of friends, what am I to do? For now I am really afraid.'" We can infer that Frodo must have a close connection to these two things. • Identifying the types of creatures that live in Middle-earth can help us establish that it is an imaginary world. For example, we can determine Gollum's significance by identifying details such as "vile creature" and "ownership of the Ring."	

Core Path	Access Path
• In paragraph seven, Frodo mentions an association of Elves with Gandalf and compares Gollum to an Orc. It can be inferred that the first two are protagonists and the last two are antagonists.	

Read and Annotate. Read the Skills Focus questions as a class, so your students know what they should pay close attention to as they read. Then have students read and annotate the excerpt. Ask students to use the annotation tool as they read to:

1. respond to the Skills Focus section
2. determine the setting by looking at key details
3. examine verb tenses to identify when the action is taking place
4. look for details that show how the characters react to the setting
5. note unfamiliar vocabulary
6. capture their reaction to the ideas and examples in the text

As they reread the text, remind students to use the comprehension strategy of asking and answering questions that they learned in the First Read.

Note: While on-grade-level students are reading and annotating, work one-on-one or in small groups with Beginner, Intermediate, Advanced, and Approaching students to support them as they read and annotate the text.

Beginner & Intermediate
Summarize and Analyze the Text. Work with these students to complete the sentence frames on the Access 1 and 2 handouts (note: the sentence frames for Intermediate students on the Access 2 handout contain fewer scaffolds). They will then use the completed sentence frames to help them analyze and annotate the text by completing the Skills Focus questions. Refer to the sample Skills Focus answers to help them complete the sentence frames and annotate the text.

Advanced
Work in Pairs. Pair these students with more proficient English speakers to work together on analyzing and annotating the text to complete the Skills Focus questions. If these students need more support, have them use the sentence frames on the Access 3 handout as they work with their more proficient peers.

Approaching
Summarize the Text. Have these students discuss and complete the text summary on the Access 4 handout and use their summary to help them analyze and annotate the text by completing the Skills Focus questions. Correct answers for the summary are at the end of the lesson plan online. Also refer to the sample Skills Focus answers to aid students with their annotations.

Core Path	Access Path
Discuss. After students have read the text, use the sample responses to the Skills Focus questions at the end of the lesson plan online to discuss the reading and the process of identifying the setting. Make sure that students have acquired and accurately use academic-specific words and phrases related to the skill and demonstrate a command of formal English appropriate to the discussion. To help facilitate discussions, refer to Collaborative Discussions in the Speaking & Listening Handbook.	**Extend** **Pair and Share.** In small, heterogeneous groups or pairs, ask students to share and discuss their annotations with a focus on the setting in the selection. You can provide students with questions to guide their discussion: 1. Where does the conversation between Frodo and Gandalf takes place? (Frodo's house in the Shire) How do you know? (At the end, Frodo walks to the window and pulls back the curtains.) 2. Before Frodo, who were the previous two owners of the ring? Cite textual evidence that helps you infer this information. (Bilbo and Gollum; Frodo says, "… even if Bilbo could not kill Gollum, I wish he had not kept the Ring. I wish he had never found it, and that I have never got it!") 3. Why is the Ring so dangerous? What text evidence supports this inference? (The Ring is dangerous because it holds power over anyone who uses it. Gandalf says, "'And over me the Ring would gain a power still greater and more deadly.' His eyes flashed and his face was lit as by a fire within. 'Do not tempt me! For I do not wish to become like the Dark Lord himself.'")
	Extend **Tech Infusion** **Song.** Have partners create a rap or other song featuring the vocabulary words. Use a voice-recording app (Voice Memo on the iPhone or Smart Voice Recorder for Androids) or VoiceThread (https://voicethread.com) to capture each pair's singing performance.

Core Path	Access Path
	Extend **Research.** Peter Jackson filmed his movie adaptation of *The Lord of the Rings* in New Zealand, his native country. Have students research the geography of New Zealand to determine why it made a good setting for the various storylines of Tolkien's work. Have them list their findings on the board.

3. WRITE

Core Path	Access Path
Prewrite and Plan. Read the prompt as a class and ask students to brainstorm about the setting in *The Lord of the Rings*. Remind your students to look at the excerpt and their annotations to find textual evidence to support their ideas. You may wish to review with students the Short Constructed Response - Narrative Student Model for guidance on how to construct an effective response to the writing prompt.	**Beginner & Intermediate** **Plan and Organize.** Have students complete the prewriting activity on the Access 1 and 2 handouts and then explain their ideas to a partner before they write. Explain to students that they need to choose details, examples, or quotes from the text that support their ideas and then explain how those details support their statements. For example, students could cite Gandalf's fear that the Ring would gain control over him to support their idea that Frodo might develop the same fear. **Approaching** **Plan and Organize.** Have students complete the prewriting activity on the Access 4 handout to organize their thoughts before they write.
	Extend **Organize.** Encourage students to complete a sequence chart to organize their ideas before they type their narrative (see Resources at the end of the lesson plan online).

Core Path	Access Path
Discuss. Project these instructions for the peer review onto the board and review them with your class, so they know what they are looking for when they begin to provide their classmates with feedback: • How has this narrative helped you understand what the Shire looks like? • How closely does the narrative match the characterization of Tolkien's characters? • How well does the writer use description and figurative language to develop the plot of the narrative? • What sort of evidence does the writer use from the text to support his or her writing? • Does the writer write using standard grammar and punctuation? Are there any weak spots? • What specific suggestions can you make to help the writer improve the response? • What thing(s) does this paper do especially well? After you've looked at the peer review instructions, review the rubric with students before they begin writing. Allow time for students briefly to pose and discuss any questions they may have about the peer review instructions and the rubric. Tell students how many peer reviews they will need to complete once they submit their writing.	
Write. Ask students to complete the writing assignment using textual evidence to support their answers. Once they have completed their writing, they should click "Submit."	

Core Path	Access Path
	Extend **Critique.** Project a writing sample on the board and ask the class to identify the elements of writing that are strong, as well as those that are weak or in need of improvement. After students have had an opportunity to evaluate student samples, work as a class to generate strategies students can use as they complete their peer reviews to ensure they are substantive.
Review. Once students complete their writing assignment, they should submit substantive feedback to two peers.	

OVERVIEW

The nonfiction text *DC Comics: Sixty Years of the World's Favorite Comic Book Heroes*, by Les Daniels, explores the history of one of the major players in U.S. comic books and superhero culture. The First Read gives students the opportunity to experience the text with a limited context.

OBJECTIVES

1. Perform an initial reading of a text and demonstrate comprehension by responding to short analysis and inference questions with textual evidence.
2. Practice defining vocabulary words using context.
3. Participate effectively in a range of conversations and collaborations to express ideas and build upon the ideas of others.
4. Practice acquiring and using academic vocabulary correctly.

ELA Common Core Standards:
Reading: Informational Text - RI.11-12.1, RI.11-12.4, RI.11-12.10
Speaking & Listening - SL.11-12.1.A, SL.11-12.1.B, SL.11-12.1.C, SL.11-12.1 SL.11-12.2
Language - L.11-12.4.A, L.11-12.4.D, L.11-12.6

RESOURCES

Access 1 handout (Beginner)

Access 2 handout (Intermediate)

Access 3 handout (Advanced)

Access 4 handout (Approaching)

ACCESS COMPLEX TEXT

This excerpt from *DC Comics: Sixty Years of the World's Favorite Comic Book Heroes* is an informational text about the history of DC Comics and the competition the company inspired. The text is organized chronologically and begins in 1939 with the introduction of the superheroes Superman and Batman. To help students understand the relationship of people, ideas, and events, use the following ideas to provide scaffolded instruction for a first reading of the more complex features of this text:

- **Purpose** - Though the purpose of this informational text is to inform readers about the history of DC Comics, the author does not present an unbiased point of view. Daniels sides with DC when presenting information about the copyright lawsuits through words such as "a deliberate imitation of Superman" and "suspiciously close to Superman."

- **Organization** - The author uses sequence to present historical facts but departs from strict chronological order to show relationships between people and events. Readers need to know that the events occurred in order over a period of time and also were related in cause-effect and comparison-contrast ways.

- **Specific Vocabulary** - Idioms and slang expressions, such as duked it out and decked out, may present a challenge to some readers. Figurative language, such as "flooding the newsstands with a cascade of costumed characters," may also need explanation.

1. INTRODUCTION

Core Path	Access Path
Read. Individually or as a class, read the Introduction for *DC Comics: Sixty Years of the World's Favorite Comic Book Heroes*. The introduction provides context for the excerpt taken from "DC Inspires a Horde of Heroes."	**English Learners All Levels & Approaching Read and Listen.** Ask students to read and listen to the introduction for *DC Comics: Sixty Years of the World's Favorite Comic Book Heroes*. Have them refer to the "Introduction Glossary" on their Access 1, 2, 3, and 4 handouts for definitions of key vocabulary terms. If there are unfamiliar words that are not included in their glossary, encourage students to check a dictionary or online reference tool, like http://dictionary.reference.com.

Copyright © BookheadEd Learning, LLC

Core Path	Access Path
	Extend **Make Predictions.** Based on the introduction, ask students to make predictions about the central ideas they would expect to encounter in this text.
Access Prior Knowledge. Find out what your students already know about comic books and superheroes. As a class or in small groups, generate a list (on the board or on paper) of superheroes you know. Put a star next to heroes from the DC universe, if known. After compiling a list, ask students to share where their previous knowledge came from—movies? TV shows? comics? family member? Discuss.	**Beginner & Intermediate** **Complete and Discuss the Interview.** Pair Intermediate and Advanced students. Have them interview each other. They can use Access handouts 2 and 3 for the interview. Students can add their own interview questions. **Advanced** **Compare and Discuss Superheroes** Using the questions on the Access 3 handouts, have students discuss similarities and differences between their two superheroes. **Approaching** **Create a Superhero.** Ask students to work in pairs and to write a short paragraph about a superhero from their imaginations. Have students use the Access handout 4, which has questions to help them write a paragraph.
	Extend **Analyze and Discuss a Quote.** "Superheroes fill a gap in the pop culture psyche, similar to the role of Greek mythology. There isn't really anything else that does the job in modern terms." (Christopher Nolan, writer/ director of *The Dark Knight*) 1. What is the writer saying here? 2. Can you restate this quote using your own words? 3. Do you agree with this quote? Why or why not?

2. READ

Core Path	Access Path
Make Predictions about Vocabulary. There are five bold vocabulary words in the text. As students read the text, ask them to make predictions about what they think each bold vocabulary word means based on the context clues in the sentence. Have students use the annotation tool to make their predictions.	**Note:** This exercise, which extends vocabulary instruction, should be completed when the class shifts from whole group instruction to individual work during the "Read and Annotate" exercise.

Make Predictions about Vocabulary. There are five bold vocabulary words in the text. As students read the text, ask them to make predictions about what they think each bold vocabulary word means based on the context clues in the sentence. Have students use the annotation tool to make their predictions.

It might be helpful to model this for students before they begin reading. Either using the board or projecting the actual text, focus in on the sentence that uses the word "remanded":

- The Supreme Court declared the case valid and remanded it to the lower courts.

Model for the class how to use these context clues to guess the meanings of the word:

1. Look at the structure of the sentence. What is the subject (Supreme Court)? What does the subject do (declared and remanded)? "Remanded" is a past tense verb. It's a little confusing, but the Supreme Court is the one doing the action.

2. The sentence is about a legal case, and "remanded" is something the judges of the Supreme Court did in the case. That tells me that "remanded" is likely a legal term.

3. The phrase "to the lower courts" explains what "remanded" means. It means to send a case from a higher court, such as the Supreme Court, to a lower district court.

4. Let's verify this definition using a dictionary to check the exact definition.

Access Path

Note: This exercise, which extends vocabulary instruction, should be completed when the class shifts from whole group instruction to individual work during the "Read and Annotate" exercise.

Beginner, Intermediate & Approaching Pair Practice.

1. Pair students with more proficient readers.
2. Give them an additional sentence that contains a new vocabulary word.
3. Ask the students to complete a Think Aloud using the teacher-led Make Predictions about Vocabulary activity as a model, while the proficient student actively listens.
4. The student should use the context clues in the sentence to try to determine the meaning of the new vocabulary word.
5. After the student has completed the Think Aloud and made a prediction about the word's meaning, allow time for the proficient reader to add his/her own thoughts and clarify any points of confusion.
6. Once they've completed this Think Aloud, encourage them to use a dictionary to confirm the definition of the new vocabulary word. Have them refer to the "Text Glossary" on their Access 1, 2, and 4 handouts for definitions of key vocabulary terms in the text. Encourage them to add any additional vocabulary words or idioms they find in the text and look up definitions for those words and idioms online or in a dictionary.

Core Path	Access Path
Model Reading Comprehension Strategy. Before students begin reading, model the reading comprehension strategy of summarizing by using this Think Aloud that talks students through the first few paragraphs in the text. First explain to your students that summarizing is *a process in which students select, organize, and synthesize the most important elements in a text* Model for students how summarizing will help them better comprehend the selection and help drive their discussions. • When I read the first paragraph, I see that the first sentence introduces a main idea: Superman and Batman were game changers in the comic book industry. That's an important thing to include in a summary. • In the next paragraph, the author gives evidence for this idea: competitors directly copied Superman (and were sued). This evidence belongs in my summary, but I won't include specifics of the new characters.	**Note:** This exercise, which extends instruction around reading comprehension strategies, should be completed when the class shifts from whole group instruction to individual work during the "Read and Annotate" exercise. **Beginner, Intermediate & Approaching** **Apply Reading Comprehension Strategy.** 1. Have these students listen to the audio of *DC Comics: Sixty Years of the World's Favorite Comic Book Heroes* and complete the Summary Sentence Frames on the Access 1, 2, and 4 handouts. Sample answers are provided at the end of the lesson plan online. Pause the audio as needed to allow students to complete the frames. 2. Have students write short summaries of the selection using their sentence frames. 3. Then, have students pair up in order to discuss their summaries. Visit each pair of students and ask which specific vocabulary words help them understand the text and its key ideas. Are there any words or phrases that further confuse or complicate their summarization?
Read and Annotate. Have students independently read and annotate the excerpt. Ask students to use the annotation tool as they read to: 1. use context clues to analyze and determine the meaning of the bolded vocabulary terms 2. ask questions about passages of the text that may be unclear or unresolved 3. identify key information, events, individuals, and connections between them 4. note unfamiliar vocabulary	**Beginner** **Coach the Reading.** While other students read, annotate, and discuss the text independently, work with Beginner students, listening to the audio of the text and pausing periodically or when any student has a question. Have students use the Text Glossary on the Access 1 handout to help them with words or idioms that may be unfamiliar. Coach students in articulating their questions for the group and in highlighting and annotating the text. Have students use the Annotation Guide on the Access 1 handout to support them as they highlight and annotate the text.

Core Path	Access Path
	For further support, ask questions about the text such as:
	• Is there anything about comic book heroes that you don't understand?
	• What do you think is the future of comic book heroes?
	• Why do you think the phrase "DC Inspires" is in the section title?
	Intermediate **Listen to the Audio.** Have these students listen to the audio of the text and use the Text Glossary on the Access 2 handout to help them with words or idioms that may be unfamiliar. If students need help with annotating the text, have them use the Annotation Guide on the Access 2 handout. After working with the Beginner students, you may wish to check this group's progress and provide support as needed.
	Advanced **Pair with Proficient Peers.** Have Advanced students work with English proficient peers to read, annotate, and discuss the text. Have students use the Annotation Guide in the Access 3 handout to support them as they highlight and annotate the text. Encourage them to listen to the audio of the text if needed.
	Approaching **Use the Annotation Guide.** Have students use the Annotation Guide on the Access 4 handout to support them as they highlight and annotate the text.

Core Path	Access Path
Discuss. In small groups or pairs, have students discuss the questions and inferences they made while reading. To help facilitate discussions, refer to Collaborative Discussions in the Speaking & Listening Handbook.	**English Learners All Levels & Approaching** Use the extra time while on- and beyond-grade-level students are discussing their first reads of the text to work individually and in small groups with Approaching readers and English Learners as outlined above. Should those students complete their first reads quickly, integrate them into the on- and beyond-grade-level discussion groups. Otherwise, English Learners and Approaching readers will be given an opportunity to participate in text discussions with their peers later in the lesson.

Core Path

1. What is DC and how is it related to superheroes? (DC is a comic book company that invented Superman and Batman.)

2. What was the comic book scene in the early 1940s like? (There were a lot of new superheroes because comic books were so popular.)

3. Why was DC Comics so quick to sue its rivals? What does that tell you about comic books and superheroes? (Superheroes and comic books made a lot of money for their companies. Superheroes also have similar traits, characteristics, and abilities, but companies want to protect their intellectual property.) How did DC continue to build its stack of superheroes in the 1950s and on? (buying characters from folded companies)

4. What do the characters described in this selection have in common? How are they different from each other? (Most of the characters described are tough and powerful men. Many have superpowers, while a few are simply heroes without special powers.)

5. Summarize the selection. What is the author's main idea? What key details does he provide to support that main idea?

Access Path

Tech Infusion
Beyond
Brainstorm. Pair students and ask them to brainstorm for other heroes that might be developed into comic book characters with unusual powers or names, using the descriptions of the Human Torch, the Sub-Mariner, and Blue Beetle as a guide. Students who have access to a back-channel tool such as TodaysMeet (https://todaysmeet.com) may enjoy brainstorming in that medium.

Core Path	Access Path

	Extend
	
	Understand Syntax. Use the Audio Text Highlight tool to help students identify and understand the author's use of complex sentences.
	
	1. Ask students to read the first three paragraphs (making this longer or shorter depending on your group of students) and identify examples of complex sentences.
	
	2. As a class or in small groups, discuss:
	
	   a. What do you notice about the writer's style of writing?
	
	   b. Why types of conjunctions does the writer use? What types of clauses does the writer use often?
	
	   c. Do different types of complex sentences have a different purpose and/or impact?
	
	   d. How does the writer use syntax to convey meaning?
	
	Remind students that as they read using the Audio Text Highlight tool, they can pause, repeat, or slow down the audio at any time.

	Extend **Explore Images.** Have students use devices to find pictures of the superheroes discussed in the selections. If possible, students should look for images from the time period discussed in the selection. Remind students that the art is as important to a good comic book as the story or text. As a class, examine the images. • What traits do the superheroes all seem to have in common? • How are they different? • Do the characters look the way students pictured while reading the selection? Why or why not? • How do pictures of the same characters change over time? What inferences can we make about society based on these changes?

Please note that excerpts and passages in the StudySync® library, workbooks, and PDFs are intended as touchstones to generate interest in an author's work. The excerpts and passages do not substitute for the reading of entire texts, and StudySync® strongly recommends that teachers and students seek out and purchase the whole literary or informational work in order to experience it as the author intended. Links to online resellers are available in our digital library. In addition, complete works may be ordered through an authorized reseller by filling out and returning to StudySync® the order form enclosed in this workbook.

Teacher's Edition   323

3. THINK

Core Path	Access Path
Answer and Discuss. Have students complete the Think questions and then use the peer review instructions and rubric to complete two peer reviews. Refer to the sample answers at the end of the lesson plan online to discuss responses with your students.	**Beginner & Intermediate** **Sentence Frames.** Have students use the sentence frames on the Access 1 and 2 handouts to support their responses to the Think questions. If necessary, distribute sentence frames to Advanced students as well. **Approaching** **Find the Evidence.** Have students use Find the Evidence on the Access 4 handout to help them identify the evidence needed to answer the questions.
	Extend **Debate.** Present students with an issue from the text that can be debated. Allow students to debate the issue as a class or in smaller groups. Debate prompts: 1. Should DC have been able to sue competitors for having superheroes similar to their characters? Why or why not? 2. How can a court determine if an idea for a character is truly original? What criteria should that character meet?

Informational Text Elements

OVERVIEW

Analyzing the sequence and development of events in an informational text aids student understanding of the topic. This lesson plan provides follow-up questions and useful enrichments to help teachers guide students in how to analyze events in a nonfiction text.

OBJECTIVES

1. Review the definition of informational text elements.
2. Practice using concrete strategies for analyzing the relationships between events.
3. Participate effectively in a range of conversations and collaborations to express ideas and build upon the ideas of others.

   ELA Common Core Standards:
   Reading: Informational - RI.11-12.1, RI.11-12.3
   Speaking & Listening - SL.11-12.1.A, SL.11-12.1.C, SL.11-12.2

RESOURCES

Access 1 handout (Beginner)

Access 2 handout (Intermediate)

Access 3 handout (Advanced)

Access 4 handout (Approaching)

Please note that excerpts and passages in the StudySync® library, workbooks, and PDFs are intended as touchstones to generate interest in an author's work. The excerpts and passages do not substitute for the reading of entire texts, and StudySync® strongly recommends that teachers and students seek out and purchase the whole literary or informational work in order to experience it as the author intended. Links to online resellers are available in our digital library. In addition, complete works may be ordered through an authorized reseller by filling out and returning to StudySync® the order form enclosed in this workbook.

Teacher's Edition   325

1. DEFINE

Core Path	Access Path
Watch. Watch the Concept Definition video on informational text elements with your students. Make sure your students are familiar with all the different elements shared in the video-including details, events, people, and ideas-as well as how these elements may interact over the course of a text. Pause the video at these key moments to discuss the information with your students:	**English Learners All Levels & Approaching** **Fill in the Blanks.** Have students complete the fill-in-the-blanks exercise on the Access 1, 2, 3, and 4 handouts as they watch the video. Answers are located at the end of the lesson plan online.
1. 0:25 – Before writing things down, how do you think people remembered and communicated information? What challenges might have led to the development of a written language?	
2. 0:50 – Do you think there are any similarities between the elements of fictional and informational texts? What are they? Compare and contrast the two forms.	
3. 1:20 – For what reasons might an author "leave out" various events in an informational text? How does this challenge our understanding of certain facts or events? What can we do as readers to broaden our understanding of a topic or event?	
Read and Discuss. After watching the Concept Definition video, have students read the definition of informational text elements. Either in small groups or as a whole class use these questions to spur discussion among your students about informational text elements.	**Beginner & Approaching** **Complete a Chart.** To prepare students to participate in the discussion, have them complete the chart on the Access 1 and 4 handouts as they read the descriptions in the left column. The correct answers are located at the end of the lesson plan online.
1. In what order did the author present the people, events, and ideas?	
2. What kinds of relationships can an author build between events? How can an author express these relationships?	
3. Can you think of an informational text you've read that presented events in an unconventional way? Was it successful?	
4. What kind of order or sequencing do you feel is most helpful in informational texts?	

Core Path	Access Path
	Intermediate & Advanced **Discuss Prompts.** To help these students participate in the discussion, prompt them with questions that can be answered with a few words, such as: • What do informational texts present readers with? (information or ideas about real people, places, things, and events) • What are some examples of informational texts? (biography, diary, interview, article, report, advertisement, letter, editorial, essay, proposal, and speech) • In what way does the type of text influence the elements a writer chooses? (Answers will vary.) **Beyond** **Discuss.** Have students select an informational text they've read and describe the elements and features that make it an informational text. Compile a list of examples. Have students discuss why each selection belongs in the category of informational texts. Could the information be conveyed in another genre, such as a fictional story?
	Extend **Annotate.** If students have trouble with the idea of relationships between events, model annotation strategies students can use while reading. Project a text on the board. Model using different colors to highlight or underline related events, and write notes explaining what connects the events.

Teacher's Edition **327**

2. MODEL

Core Path	Access Path
Read and Annotate. Have students independently read the Model section. As they read, ask students to use the annotation tool to: • highlight key points. • ask questions. • identify places where the Model is applying the strategies laid out in the Identification and Application section on informational text elements.	**Note:** During this portion of the lesson, instruction shifts from whole group to individual work. Use this time to work one-on-one or in small groups with Beginner, Intermediate, Advanced, and Approaching students. **Beginner & Intermediate** **Coach the Reading.** Work with these students (either individually or in small groups) to fill out the guided reading questions on the Access 1 and 2 handouts. Have Beginner students refer to the glossary on the Access 1 handout to help them determine the meaning of difficult words (note: provide the Access 1 handout glossary to Intermediate students if necessary). Let students know they'll use these answers to help participate in the discussion about the Model. Sample answers for this exercise are located at the end of the lesson plan online. **Advanced** **Identify Evidence.** Ask Advanced students to complete the identifying evidence exercise on the Access 3 handout. Let students know that they'll use these answers to help participate in the discussion about the Model. Sample answers for this exercise are located at the end of the lesson plan online. **Approaching** **Guided Reading.** Have students complete the guided reading questions on the Access 4 handout as they read. Let them know that they'll use these answers to help participate in the discussion about the Model. Sample answers for this exercise are located at the end of the lesson plan online.

Core Path	Access Path
Discuss. After students read the Model text, use these questions to facilitate a whole group discussion that helps students understand informational text elements: 1. What does the Model explain before jumping into the analysis? (It explains why history texts tend to use chronological order.) 2. What are signal words and phrases? How does an author use them? (They are words and phrases that indicate sequence or relationships.) 3. According to the Model, why does Daniels break chronological order at one point? (He does this to clarify the relationships between events.)	
	Extend **Tech Infusion** **Compile.** Pair or group students and have each group use devices or computers to make a list of signal words and phrases. Have each group add their list to a communal Google Doc or TitanPad (https://titanpad.com/) document. Sort the list by possible relationships between events, such as cause-effect or comparison. Have students add to the list throughout the year as they encounter signal words and phrases in the selections they read.

3. YOUR TURN

Core Path	Access Path
Assess and Explain. Have students answer the comprehension questions to test for understanding. Share the explanations for Parts A and B (located online) with your students.	
	Extend **Organize.** If students have trouble analyzing the relationship between events in the text, have students complete a graphic organizer to organize their thinking.

OVERVIEW

DC Comics: Sixty Years of the World's Favorite Comic Book Heroes by Les Daniels explores the explosion of superheroes in U.S. comic books in the middle of the twentieth century by focusing on DC Comics. The Close Read gives students the opportunity to analyze the relationship between events.

OBJECTIVES

1. Complete a close reading of an informational text.
2. Practice and apply concrete strategies for analyzing informational text elements in an excerpt from *DC Comics: Sixty Years of the World's Favorite Comic Book Heroes*.
3. Participate effectively in a range of conversations and collaborations to express ideas and build upon the ideas of others.
4. Prewrite, plan, and produce clear and coherent writing in response to a prompt.

   ELA Common Core State Standards:
   Reading: Informational Text - RI.11-12.1, RI.11-12.3, RI.11-12.4
   Writing - W.11-12.4, W.11-12.5, W.11-12.6, W.11-12.9.B, W.11-12.10
   Speaking & Listening - SL.11-12.1.A, SL.11-12.1.B, SL.11-12.1.C, SL.11-12.1.D, SL.11-12.6
   Language - L.11-12.4.A, L.11-12.4.C, L.11-12.4.D

RESOURCES

DC Comics: Sixty Years of the World's Favorite Comic Book Heroes Vocabulary Worksheet

Access 1 handout (Beginner)

Access 2 handout (Intermediate)

Access 3 handout (Advanced)

Access 4 handout (Approaching)

Please note that excerpts and passages in the StudySync® library, workbooks, and PDFs are intended as touchstones to generate interest in an author's work. The excerpts and passages do not substitute for the reading of entire texts, and StudySync® strongly recommends that teachers and students seek out and purchase the whole literary or informational work in order to experience it as the author intended. Links to online resellers are available in our digital library. In addition, complete works may be ordered through an authorized reseller by filling out and returning to StudySync® the order form enclosed in this workbook.

Teacher's Edition   331

1. INTRODUCTION

Core Path	Access Path
Define and Compare. Project the vocabulary words and definitions onto the board or provide students with a handout, so they can copy the vocabulary into their notebooks. Ask students to compare their initial vocabulary predictions from the First Read with the actual definitions. Review words that students defined incorrectly to understand why they were unable to use context clues or other tools to develop usable definitions.	**Beginner & Intermediate** **Complete a Chart.** Have students complete the chart on the Access 1 and 2 handouts by writing the correct word for each of the definitions. **Advanced & Beyond** **Write in Journals.** Have students write a journal entry using all of their vocabulary words. Remind them to write sentences that communicate the meaning of the words they are using. **Approaching** **Graphic Organizer.** To support students in comparing their predictions with the correct meanings, have them complete the graphic organizer on the Access 4 handout to record the vocabulary words, their initial analysis, and the definitions. Then have them write sentences using the words.
Review. Have students complete the fill in the blank vocabulary worksheet for the selection. Answers for the worksheet are listed online.	
	Extend **Tech Infusion** **Review.** Create a vocabulary review quiz using Socrative (http://socrative.com). Design multiple choice and/or short answer questions that require students to apply their understanding of the vocabulary, then run the quiz as a "Space Race" allowing groups to compete against one another to test their knowledge of the vocabulary.

Core Path	Access Path
	Extend **Practice.** Have students write a sentence that includes each vocabulary word. Then challenge students to write one sentence that uses two words, then three, and so on. Gather any sentences that use all five words and still make sense. Have the class vote on the best sentence.
	Extend **Tech Infusion** **Act and Record.** Break the class up into small groups, assign each group a vocabulary word, and ask them to design a short skit to demonstrate the meaning of the word for their peers. If possible, record skits and post them to your class YouTube Channel, so they can be reviewed.

2. READ

Core Path	Access Path
Model Close Reading. Project the text onto the board and model a close reading of the first two paragraphs using the annotation strategies mentioned below. While modeling annotation strategies, make notes that tie the text to the focus skill and demonstrate what students are looking for as they read. Some guidance for you as you annotate for your students: • As the Skills lesson that precedes this text makes clear, this selection opens with a time order phrase: "By 1939." That phrase tells the reader two things: the year Daniels will begin with and that events had been building to this point for some time. • In the rest of the first paragraph, the author sets up the events described in the excerpt: "DC had established a new genre with its superheroes, and the competition would be fast and furious."	

Core Path	Access Path
<ul><li>In paragraph 2, the author introduces DC's first "competition," Victor Fox. Daniels claims Fox decided "to write and draw a deliberate imitation of Superman called Wonder Man."</li><li>Paragraph 2 continues to introduce the first of the DC lawsuits, this one against Wonder Man.</li></ul>	

Core Path	Access Path
Read and Annotate. Read the Skills Focus questions as a class, so your students know what they should pay close attention to as they read. Then have students read and annotate the excerpt. Ask students to use the annotation tool as they read to: 1. respond to the Skills Focus section 2. ask questions 3. make connections 4. identify key information, examples, and themes 5. note unfamiliar vocabulary 6. capture their reaction to the ideas and examples in the text As they reread the text, remind students to use the comprehension strategy of summarizing that they learned in the First Read.	**Note:** While on-grade-level students are reading and annotating, work one-on-one or in small groups with Beginner, Intermediate, Advanced, and Approaching students to support them as they read and annotate the text. **Beginner & Intermediate** **Summarize and Analyze the Text.** Work with these students to complete the sentence frames on the Access 1 and 2 handouts (note: the sentence frames for Intermediate students on the Access 2 handout contain fewer scaffolds). They will then use the completed sentence frames to help them analyze and annotate the text by completing the Skills Focus questions. Refer to the sample Skills Focus answers to help them complete the sentence frames and annotate the text. **Advanced** **Work in Pairs.** Pair these students with more proficient English speakers to work together on analyzing and annotating the text to complete the Skills Focus questions. If these students need more support, have them use the sentence frames on the Access 3 handout as they work with their more proficient peers. **Approaching** **Summarize the Text.** Have these students discuss and complete the text summary on the Access 4 handout and use their summary to help them analyze and annotate the text by completing the Skills Focus questions. Correct answers for the summary are at the end of the lesson plan online. Also refer to the sample Skills Focus answers to aid students with their annotations.

Core Path	Access Path
Discuss. After students have read the text, use the sample responses to the Skills Focus questions at the end of the lesson plan online to discuss the reading and the process of analyzing informational text elements. Make sure that students have acquired and accurately use academic-specific words and phrases related to the skill and demonstrate a command of formal English appropriate to the discussion. To help facilitate discussions, refer to Collaborative Discussions in the Speaking & Listening Handbook.	**Extend** **Pair and Share.** In small, heterogeneous groups or pairs, ask students to share and discuss their annotations with a focus on the informational text elements in the selection. You can provide students with these questions to guide their discussion: 1. What does the response to the success of Superman and Batman show about the comic book industry? Cite specific textual evidence to support your statements. (The comic book industry was very profitable. When other people noticed how much money the superhero comic books were making, they wanted to publish superhero comic books and participate in the lucrative industry. The author states, "DC had established a new genre with its superheroes, and the competition would be fast and furious." and "Victor Fox, an accountant for DC, saw the sales figures and promptly opened his own office just a few floors away.") 2. Why do you think the lawsuit DC filed against Fawcett took so many years to settle? Based on details in the text, what do you think were the motives of DC and Fawcett? Cite specific evidence to support your opinion. (The lawsuit probably took so long because each side saw the advantage of winning it. Captain Marvel was making a lot of money ("Captain Marvel in his heyday was the biggest seller in the business"), so Fawcett Publications wanted to keep control, but DC wanted to regain control and the profits: "the two corporations duked it out like superheroes, and the dust didn't settle until 1953. DC editor Jack Schiff compiled a scrapbook documenting similarities, but the district court dismissed DC's complaint. DC appealed.")

Core Path	Access Path
	3. To what do you attribute the popularity of comic book heroes? What does your conclusion say about the reason people bought and read the comic books? Cite evidence to support your conclusion. (The popularity of comic book heroes demonstrates that people like to read about superheroes and their amazing powers. The author described "the double-barreled triumph of Superman and Batman." Moreover, the humor in the Captain Marvel scripts was entertaining: "the scripts developed a humorous slant in scripts provided by Otto Binder. The often obtuse hero was a 'Big Red Cheese' to his brilliant enemy Dr. Sivana, and was nearly defeated by an intellectually advanced earthworm called Mr. Mind.")
	Extend **Search.** Have students use dictionaries or other online sources to trace the etymology of each vocabulary word. Students should record the word's history in their notes. Students can work individually or collaboratively on this assignment. As a class, discuss how knowing the etymology of words can help students remember the definitions.
	Extend **Research.** Ask students to find a current news article about an intellectual property lawsuit, preferably related to a fictional character or a superhero. Ask students to bring in a copy of their article to share. In small groups, allow students to exchange articles and discuss similarities and differences between their stories and the DC Comics lawsuits described in the selection. (If multiple students find the same article, be sure to place them in different groups.)

3. WRITE

Core Path	Access Path
Prewrite and Plan. Read the prompt as a class and ask students to brainstorm about the relationship between events in *DC Comics: Sixty Years of the World's Favorite Comic Book Heroes*. Students can brainstorm together either as a class or in small groups to begin planning their responses. Remind students to look at the excerpt and their annotations to find textual evidence to support their ideas.	**Beginner & Intermediate** **Plan and Organize.** Have students complete the prewriting activity on the Access 1 and 2 handouts and then explain their ideas to a partner before they write. Explain to students that they need to choose details, examples, or quotes from the text that support their ideas and then explain how those details support their statements. For example, students could include the first line, "By 1939, the double-barreled triumph of Superman and Batman had knocked the infant comic book industry on its ear," which reveals that the selection is organized in chronological order. The year 1939 marked the beginning of DC's long history as a leader in publishing comic books featuring heroes and superheroes. **Approaching** **Plan and Organize.** Have students complete the prewriting activity on the Access 4 handout to organize their thoughts before they write.
	Extend **Review.** Review the differences between purpose (why students are writing) and audience (who they are writing for). Remind students that their purpose often can be summed up in one verb: to persuade, to explain/inform, or to entertain. Discuss examples of writing for different audiences and purposes.
Discuss. Project these instructions for the peer review onto the board and review them with your class, so they know what they are looking for when they begin to provide their classmates with feedback: • How has this essay helped you understand the relationships between the events in the text? • Did the writer use his or her understanding of signal words and phrases to support his or her analysis?	

Please note that excerpts and passages in the StudySync® library, workbooks, and PDFs are intended as touchstones to generate interest in an author's work. The excerpts and passages do not substitute for the reading of entire texts, and StudySync® strongly recommends that teachers and students seek out and purchase the whole literary or informational work in order to experience it as the author intended. Links to online resellers are available in our digital library. In addition, complete works may be ordered through an authorized reseller by filling out and returning to StudySync® the order form enclosed in this workbook.

Teacher's Edition   337

Core Path	Access Path
• Did the writer make a claim as to whether the structure effectively conveyed the relationships between the events? • What sort of evidence did the writer use from the text to support his or her writing? • How well does the writer explain how that evidence supports his or her arguments? • Does the writer write using standard grammar and punctuation? Are there any weak spots? • What specific suggestions can you make to help the writer improve the response? • What thing(s) does this paper do especially well? After you've looked at the peer review instructions, review the rubric with students before they begin writing. Allow time for students briefly to pose and discuss any questions they may have about the peer review instructions and the rubric. Tell students how many peer reviews they will need to complete once they submit their writing.	
Write. Ask students to complete the writing assignment using textual evidence to support their answers. Once they have completed their writing, they should click "Submit."	
	Extend **Critique.** While students complete their peer review, point them to an online listing of common usage errors to look out for, such as affect/effect or fewer/less. (Paul Brians's online list is useful: http://tinyurl.com/cxt92by) Remind students that computer spell checkers often will miss usage errors because the word is spelled correctly, even if it is not used correctly.
Review. Once students complete their writing assignment, they should submit substantive feedback to two peers. Students should use their peers' feedback to improve their writing.	

Copyright © BookheadEd Learning, LLC

BLAST:
The Best Movies Ever!

OVERVIEW

To continue exploring the role of superheroes in our culture, students will learn about hyperbole and superheroes. Research links explore why the superhero movie has exploded in the past decade.

OBJECTIVES

1. Learn about hyperbole and its use in superhero stories.
2. Research using the hyperlinks to learn about superhero movies in the early twenty-first century.

   ELA Common Core Standards: :
   Reading: Informational Text - RI.11-12.1
   Writing - W.11-12.1.A, W.11-12.1.B, W.11-12.5, W.11-12.6
   Speaking & Listening - SL.11-12.1.A, SL.11-12.1.C, SL.11-12.1.D
   Language - L.11-12.5.A

RESOURCES

Access 1 handout (Beginner)

Access 2 handout (Intermediate)

Access 4 handout (Approaching)

TITLE/DRIVING QUESTION

Core Path	Access Path
Discuss. As a class, read aloud the title and driving question for this Blast. Ask students what they know about superhero movies already. Do they have a sense of why these movies are so popular? Remind students that they should not immediately reply to this question. They'll be returning to this question and responding after they've read the Background and some of the Research Links.	**English Learners All Levels** **Discuss a Visual.** Have students view an image of a superhero from a movie or comic book, such as the one at: http://tinyurl.com/o3uo2bx. Discuss how the picture shows a person with both human and super-human characteristics, prompting students with questions such as: • What is happening in this photo? • What does the superhero look like? • How can you tell that the superhero is not an ordinary person? • Do you like superhero stories? Why or why not?
Draft. In their notebooks or on scrap paper, have students draft their initial responses to the driving question. This will provide them with a baseline response that they will be altering as they gain more information about the topic in the Background and Research Links sections of the assignment.	**Beginner & Intermediate** **Draft with Sentence Frame.** When drafting their initial response to the driving question, have students refer to this Blast sentence frame on their Access 1 and 2 handouts: • Superhero movies are popular because they are _____ and people like _____. Point out these two key features of the sentence frame: 1. The introductory clause "Superhero movies are popular because" borrows language directly from the Blast driving question to provide a response. 2. Ask students to make special note of both blanks in this sentence frame. First they need to provide an adjective that describes superhero movies. Then they need to explain something people like about superhero movies.

BACKGROUND

Core Path	Access Path
Read. Have students read the Blast background to provide context for the driving question.	**Beginner & Intermediate** **Read with Support.** Have students read the Blast background to provide context for the driving question. When they encounter unfamiliar words or phrases, have students refer to the glossary on their Access 1 and 2 handouts. If there are unfamiliar words that are not included in their glossary, encourage students to check a dictionary or online reference tool, like http://dictionary.reference.com. **Approaching** **Read and Summarize.** Have students read the Blast background to provide context for the driving question. As they read, ask students to complete the fill-in-the-blank summary of the background provided on their Access 4 handout. When they encounter unfamiliar words or phrases, have students refer to the glossary on their Access 4 handout.
Discuss. Pair students and have them discuss the following questions: 1. What is hyperbole? (a figure of speech that uses exaggeration to make a point) 2. What other examples of hyperbole can you think of? (Sample answer: I'm so hungry I could eat a horse!) 3. How do superheroes and comic books use hyperbole? (to emphasize how superheroes are different from the rest of us) 4. Why do you think the balance mentioned between hyperbole and human flaws is important in superhero stories? (Answers will vary.)	**Beginner** **Discuss.** Pair Beginner with Advanced (or Beyond) students and have them use the dialogue starter on their Access 1 handout to discuss the topic. Advise them to return to the dialogue and switch roles if they get stuck. **Intermediate** **Discuss.** Pair Intermediate with Advanced (or Beyond) students and have them use the dialogue starter on their Access 2 handout to discuss the topic. Advise them to return to the dialogue and switch roles if they get stuck. If their conversation is progressing smoothly, encourage them to continue the discussion beyond the dialogue starter sheet. They can expand their conversations to discuss other examples of superheroes who show both human and superhuman characteristics and why their stories are appealing.

Core Path	Access Path

Brainstorm. Remind students about the driving question for this Blast: Why are superhero movies so popular?

In their notebooks, ask students to make three columns, one for the Blast Background, one for themselves, and one for someone they know. Start with the Background and have them fill in reasons that the Blast suggests people might love superheroes. After they've finished that, have them apply the question to themselves to begin developing a list of reasons why they personally enjoy superhero movies. Lastly, have them think about someone specific they know and why that person likes superhero movies. Here's a short example of how this might look:

Background	Me	Someone I Know
The balance between powers and human traits is relatable.	I like watching superheroes struggle to fit in with society, like we all do at times.	My brother loves the big battle scenes.

RESEARCH LINKS

Core Path	Access Path
Examine and Explore. Use these questions to guide students' exploration of the research links: 1. Explore "Do Superheroes Model Damaging Gender Roles for Kids?" According to the article, how do superheroes influence the way kids play? (They make kids more likely to play with pretend weapons.) What is hypermasculinization? (It is a focus on brawn over emotions.) When DNA is taken into account, what do studies about the effects of media violence reveal? (Media violence doesn't seem to make kids more violent. It seems to be more determined by DNA.) 2. Explore "The Psychology Behind Superhero Origin Stories." What does Rosenberg believe Superhero stories show us? (How to be heroes, how to choose altruism over wealth, and how to deal with adversity) What are the three life-altering forces superheroes encounter that we can relate to? (trauma, destiny, chance)	

	Extend
	Research, Discuss, and Present.
	
	1. Assign each group one link to explore in depth.
	2. Ask them to discuss the information:
	    a. What are the key points?
	    b. What inferences did you make as you read?
	    c. What did you learn about this "big idea" from reading this research?
	    d. How did this help you to better understand the topic?
	    e. What questions does your group have after exploring this link?
	3. Allow students time to informally present what they learned.

Core Path	Access Path
	Extend **Tech Infusion** **Share.** Instruct students to look for ways that exposure to superhero stories may help us and ways it may hurt us. Have students use a site like Lino.it (en.linoit.com) to compile research findings to support each side.

QUIKPOLL

Core Path	Access Path
Participate. Answer the poll question. Have students use information from the background and research links to explain their answers.	

NUMBER CRUNCH

Core Path	Access Path
Predict, Discuss, and Click. Before students click on the number, break them into pairs and have them make predictions about what they think the number is related to. After they've clicked the number, ask students if they are surprised by the revealed information.	

CREATE YOUR BLAST

Core Path	Access Path
Blast. Ask students to write their Blast response in 140 characters or less.	**Beginner** **Blast with Support.** Have students refer back to the sentence frame on their Access 1 handout that they used to create their original Blast draft. Ask them to use this frame to write and enter their final Blast. **Intermediate** **Blast with Support.** Have students attempt to draft their Blast without the sentence frame on their Access 2 handout. If students struggle to compose their Blast draft without the sentence frame, remind them to reference it for support. **Beyond** **Write a Claim.** Ask students to use their answer to the poll question to write a strong claim that could be used as the foundation for a piece of argumentative writing. Once students have written their claims, ask them to read the claims to a small group of their peers. This activity will provide them practice writing claims, as well as expose them to claims written by their peers.
Review. After students have completed their own Blasts, ask them to review the Blasts of their peers and provide feedback.	
	Extend **Discuss.** As a class or in groups, identify a few strong Blasts and discuss what made those responses so powerful. As a group, analyze and discuss what characteristics make a Blast interesting or effective.
	Extend **Revise.** Resend a second version of this Blast assignment to your students and have them submit revised versions of their original Blasts. Do the same responses make the Top Ten? How have the answers improved from the first submissions?

BLAST:
Our Stories, Ourselves

OVERVIEW

To wrap up the unit, students will consider how legends contribute to a national identity. Research links that explore British, Malian, and American national myths and identities, as well as contemporary issues, are available.

OBJECTIVES

1. Explore background information about legends and the British national identity.
2. Research using the hyperlinks to learn more about legends in every country's national identity.

ELA Common Core Standards:
Reading: Informational Text- RI.11-12.1
Writing - W.11-12.1.A, W.11-12.2.B, W.11-12.5, W.11-12.6
Speaking & Listening - SL.11-12.1.A, SL.11-12.1.C, SL.11-12.1.D

RESOURCES

Access 1 handout (Beginner)

Access 2 handout (Intermediate)

Access 4 handout (Approaching)

TITLE/DRIVING QUESTION

Core Path	Access Path
Discuss. As a class read aloud the title and driving question for this Blast. Ask students what they know about legends and national identity. Do they have a sense of how legends influence national identities? Remind students that they should not immediately reply to this question. They'll be returning to this question and responding after they've read the Background and some of the Research Links.	**English Learners All Levels** **Discuss a Visual.** Have students view an image of King Arthur, such as the one at: http://tinyurl.com/pq7qw37. Discuss how the picture represents a legendary figure, prompting students with questions such as: • What is happening in this image? • What objects are featured? Why? • Does this depiction make Arthur seem like an epic hero? How? • How might this representation inspire a sense of pride in people who consider themselves to be descendants of the king?
Draft. In their notebooks or on scrap paper, have students draft their initial responses to the driving question. This will provide them with a baseline response that they will update and revise as they gain more information about the topic in the Background and Research Links sections of the assignment.	**Beginner & Intermediate** **Draft with Sentence Frame.** When drafting their initial response to the driving question, have students refer to this Blast sentence frame on their Access 1 and 2 handouts: • Legends influence national identity by _____. Point out these two key features of the sentence frame: 1. The introductory clause "Legends influence national identity" borrows language directly from the Blast driving question to provide a response. 2. Ask students to make special note of the preposition "by," which invites them to explain *how* they think legends influence national identity.

BACKGROUND

Core Path	Access Path
Read. Have students read the Blast background to provide context for the driving question.	**Beginner & Intermediate** **Read with Support.** Have students read the Blast background to provide context for the driving question. When they encounter unfamiliar words or phrases, have students refer to the glossary on their Access 1 and 2 handouts. If there are unfamiliar words that are not included in their glossary, encourage students to check a dictionary or online reference tool, such as http://dictionary.reference.com. **Approaching** **Read and Summarize.** Have students read the Blast background to provide context for the driving question. As they read, ask students to complete the fill-in-the-blank summary of the background provided on their Access 4 handout. When they encounter unfamiliar words or phrases, have students refer to the glossary on their Access 4 handout.
Discuss. Pair students and have them discuss the following questions: 1. How does a common history help bond a society? (because you know everyone has the same knowledge) 2. Why do people often ignore the negative aspects of history? (because it is less appealing to unite around mistakes) 3. How does the legend of King Arthur unite Great Britain? (provides a common story) 4. Why do you think it matters that King Arthur is based on a real person?	**Beginner** **Discuss.** Pair Beginner with Advanced (or Beyond) students and have them use the dialogue starter on their Access 1 handout to discuss the topic. Advise them to return to the dialogue and switch roles if they get stuck. **Intermediate** **Discuss.** Pair Intermediate with Advanced (or Beyond) students and have them use the dialogue starter on their Access 2 handout to discuss the topic. Advise them to return to the dialogue and switch roles if they get stuck. If their conversation is progressing smoothly, encourage them to continue the discussion beyond the dialogue starter sheet. They can expand their conversations to discuss other examples of legendary heroic figures, including those from American or international history and contemporary examples, such as presidents or sports stars. Ask students to consider why these figures are so inspirational.

Core Path	Access Path
Brainstorm. Remind students about the driving question for this Blast: How do legends influence national identity? In their notebooks, ask students to make a two-column chart. In the first column, have them list national myths or legends they know or have heard about. Have students think about stories they may have heard as children or around national holidays. Remind students that these myths can be entirely fictional, like the tall tales about Paul Bunyan, or stretched truth, like George Washington and the cherry tree. Then in the second column, have students note how that myth influences a national identity. Here's a short example of how this might look:	

Myth	Identity
Paul Bunyan created the Grand Canyon	Americans in the frontier are strong and exert power over nature.

RESEARCH LINKS

Core Path	Access Path
Examine and Explore. Use these questions to guide students' exploration of the research links:	

Examine and Explore. Use these questions to guide students' exploration of the research links:

1. Ask students to look at "Myth and National Identity in Nineteenth-Century Britain." What two characters does the book discuss? What different types of British people do the stories appeal to? Why is that important to study?

2. In "Myth and National Identity in Nineteenth-Century Britain," the author discusses the conflict between King Arthur's Welsh and French roots with his place as a British hero. How did scholars resolve that conflict? Why is this history important to Arthur's role in Britain's national identity?

3. Have students explore "Stuff and Nonsense." How do false stories and history make their way into museums? Why do these myths persist? Debate this in small groups or as a class.

Extend

Research, Discuss, and Present.

1. Assign each group one link to explore in depth.

2. Ask them to discuss the information:

    a. What are the key points?

    b. What inferences did you make as you read?

    c. What did you learn about this "big idea" from reading this research?

    d. How did this help you to better understand the topic?

    e. What questions does your group have after exploring this link?

3. Allow students time to informally present what they learned.

Core Path	Access Path
	Extend **Tech Infusion** **Share.** As students explore the links, encourage them to use Diigo (https://www.diigo.com/) to make notes and save annotations. Students can refer to these annotations when they write their Blasts.

QUIKPOLL

Core Path	Access Path
Participate. Answer the poll question. Have students use information from the background and research links to explain their answers.	

NUMBER CRUNCH

Core Path	Access Path
Predict, Discuss, and Click. Before students click on the number, break them into pairs and have them make predictions about what they think the number is related to. After they've clicked the number, ask students if they are surprised by the revealed information.	

CREATE YOUR BLAST

Core Path	Access Path
Blast. Ask students to write their Blast response in 140 characters or less.	**Beginner** **Blast with Support.** Have students refer to the sentence frame on their Access 1 handout that they used to create their original Blast draft. Ask them to use this frame to write and enter their final Blast. **Intermediate** **Blast with Support.** Have students attempt to draft their Blast without the sentence frame on their Access 2 handout. If students struggle to compose their Blast draft without the sentence frame, remind them to reference it for support. **Beyond** **Write a Claim.** Ask students to use their answer to the poll question to write a strong claim that could be used as the foundation for a piece of argumentative writing. Once students have written their claims, ask them to read the claims to a small group of their peers. This activity will provide them practice writing claims, as well as expose them to claims written by their peers.
Review. After students have completed their own Blasts, ask them to review the Blasts of their peers and provide feedback.	
	Extend **Discuss.** As a class or in groups, identify a few strong blasts and discuss what made those responses so powerful. As a group, analyze and discuss what characteristics make a blast interesting or effective.
	Extend **Revise.** Resend a second version of this Blast assignment to your students and have them submit revised versions of their original Blasts. Do the same responses make the Top 10? How have the answers improved from the first submissions?

Extended Writing Project

Epic Heroes

EXTENDED WRITING PROJECT:
Narrative Writing

OVERVIEW

This unit includes a variety of texts and materials that deepen students' knowledge of epic heroes and how those narratives have transformed history. For this unit's Extended Writing Project, students will be writing a hero narrative. This lesson provides students with a definition of narrative writing and its major features, as well as a sample student narrative.

OBJECTIVES

1. Discuss and demonstrate an understanding of the features of narrative writing.
2. Practice and apply concrete strategies for identifying features of narrative writing.
3. Participate effectively in a range of conversations and collaborations to express ideas and build upon the ideas of others.

ELA Common Core Standards:
Reading: Literature - RL.11-12.1, RL.11-12.2, RL.11-12.3
Reading: Informational Text - RI.11-12.1, RI.11-12.2
Writing - W.11-12.3.A, W.11-12.3.B, W.11-12.3.C, W.11-12.3.D, W.11-12.3.E, W.11-12.4, W.11-12.5, W.11-12.10
Speaking & Listening - SL.11-12.1.A, SL.11-12.1.B, SL.11-12.1.C, SL.11-12.1.D, SL.11-12.2

RESOURCES

Access 1 handout (Beginner)

Access 2 handout (Intermediate)

Access 3 handout (Advanced)

Access 4 handout (Approaching)

1. INTRODUCTION

Core Path	Access Path
Read and Discuss. Have students read the prompt to the Extended Writing Project on narrative writing. Ask them to look at the various parts of the prompt and respond to the following questions: • What is the prompt asking you to do? • What specific requirements does the prompt lay out? • What does the prompt ask you to specifically consider? • Does the prompt point you toward an example text? • Which elements of narrative writing will you need to learn more about in order to respond to the prompt? Explain to students that they will be developing their writing in stages, with time to reflect on the assignment, revise their work, and benefit from peer review. Give students an opportunity to ask any questions they may have about the prompt.	**Beginner & Intermediate** **Paraphrase.** Have students follow along with the text as they listen to the audio recording of the prompt. After they've heard the audio recording, have them fill in the blanks on their Access 1 and 2 handouts to create their own paraphrased version of the prompt. After they've completed their prompt paraphrase, have students participate in the whole class discussion of the prompt using the questions provided in the Core Path. A sample paraphrase is located in the answer key at the end of the lesson plan online. **Approaching** **Listen and Discuss.** Have students follow along with the text as they listen to the audio recording of the prompt. Then have them participate in the whole class discussion of the prompt using the questions provided in the Core Path.
Read and Annotate. Individually or as a class, read the Introduction to Narrative Writing. The introduction defines narrative writing as well as the six features of narrative writing. If you are reading the introduction as a class, encourage students to take Cornell notes defining narrative writing, identifying the purpose of narrative writing, and defining the six features of narrative writing in their own words. If they are reading online, request that they use the StudySync annotation tool to make notes about narrative writing.	**Beginner & Intermediate** **Fill in the Blanks.** As they read and listen to the introduction, have Beginner and Intermediate students work together to fill in the blanks on the Access 1 and 2 handouts. They can also refer to the introduction glossary provided on those handouts. Provide assistance and clarification as needed. Sample answers are located at the end of the lesson plan online. **Advanced & Approaching** **Identify Features of Narrative Writing.** After reading the introduction, have students list the six features of narrative writing on their Access 3 and 4 handouts in their own words.

Core Path	Access Path
If needed, divide the class into small groups. Ask each group to collaborate on writing a summary of the purpose and features of the narrative writing form to help students better understand, plan, and produce a strong narrative piece of writing. Remind students to follow the rules of collegial discussions as they exchange ideas.	
	Extend **Paraphrase.** 1. After students have read and discussed the prompt, remove the prompt from their field of vision (cover the projector, close iPads, minimize computer screens, etc.) and ask them to rewrite the prompt in their own words. Students should not put names on this paper. 2. After students have had time to rewrite the prompt, collect their work. 3. Group students and redistribute the paraphrased prompts at random. 4. In groups, students should review each paraphrased prompt. Each group should select the best paraphrased prompt and share it with the class. 5. The class can discuss the strengths and weaknesses of these prompts.

Core Path	Access Path
	Extend **Write.** Ask students to take out a sheet of paper and, at the top of the paper, write the following: 1. A celebrity they would like to have lunch with 2. Their favorite kind of car 3. A good friend outside of school Then, display the following sentence: [person from #1] gets into a [car from #2] with [person from #3] and drives around talking about music or movies. Give students 10 minutes to freewrite, using their sentence as a starting point. Remind them that their writing doesn't have to be perfect; they should **just keep writing** until the 10 minutes are up. After students have finished, give them the chance to share their ideas with a partner or the class. As a class, discuss what was challenging about the assignment (i.e., clarity, sequencing, dialogue, explanation, etc.). Remind students that these are some of the same challenges they will face when they write their narrative essay.

2. READ

Core Path	Access Path
Read and Label. Have students read the sample student narrative titled "Lady Letha, Knight of Mordred." Have students identify the six features of narrative writing in the sample and label them using the annotation tool: • setting • characters • plot • theme • point of view	**Beginner** **Coach the Reading.** While other students read, annotate, and discuss the text independently, work with Beginner students as they listen to the audio of the text and use the model glossary on the Access 1 handout. Coach students in articulating their questions for the group and in highlighting and annotating the text using the Annotation Guide on the Access 1 handout.

Core Path	Access Path
	Intermediate **Listen to the Audio.** Have Intermediate students listen to the audio of the text and use the model glossary on the Access 2 handout to help them with words or idioms that may be unfamiliar. If students need help with annotating the text, have them use the Annotation Guide on the Access 2 handout. After working with the Beginner students, you may wish to check this group's progress and provide support as needed. **Advanced** **Pair with Proficient Peers.** Have Advanced students work with English proficient peers to read, annotate, and discuss the text. You can also provide them with the model glossary from the Access 3 handout if necessary. Have these student pairs use the Annotation Guide in the Access 3 handout to support them as they highlight and annotate the text. Encourage them to listen to the audio of the text if needed. **Approaching** **Use the Annotation Guide.** Have students use the Annotation Guide or the Access 4 handout to support them as they highlight and annotate the text.
Discuss. In small groups or pairs, have students discuss the observations and annotations they made while reading. Make sure students follow the rules for collegial discussions. Have them examine the "Constructed Response - Narrative" grading rubric this Student Model was written to satisfy. Inform students that this is the same rubric that will be used to evaluate their completed Narrative Extended Writing Project. They should consider how understanding the Student Model can help them as they begin to craft their own narrative in response to the prompt.	**English Learners All Levels & Approaching** Use the extra time while on- and beyond-grade-level students are discussing their first reads of the text to work individually and in small groups with Approaching readers and English Learners as outlined above. Should those students complete their first reads quickly, integrate them into the on- and beyond-grade-level discussion groups. Otherwise Approaching readers and English Learners will be given an opportunity to participate in text discussions with their peers in future Extended Writing Project lessons.

Core Path	Access Path
	Extend **Tech Infusion** **Feature ReFocus.** Have small groups create a Prezi (www.prezi.com) that shows the plot of the model text. Students might have separate sections for exposition, rising action, climax, and falling action.

3. THINK

Core Path	Access Path
Answer and Discuss. Have students complete the Think questions. Collect papers or discuss answers as a class. Refer to the sample answers at the end of the lesson plan online.	**Beginner** **Answer Questions with Support.** Review all of the Think questions with students to clarify vocabulary and comprehension. Read question 1 aloud. Then ask students to look at the title and first paragraph and to identify the main character (Lady Letha) and what she is fighting for (Lord Mordred in a battle against King Arthur). Once you've completed this instruction with students, have them complete the remaining Think questions using the sentence frames on their Access 1 handout. **Intermediate** **Support.** Have partners review the Think questions and help one another with any terms or concepts that need to be clarified. Tell them that they may ask you about any vocabulary or concepts they cannot clarify for themselves, and then have them use the sentence frames on their Access 2 handout to assist them in writing the answers to the questions. **Advanced** **Discuss.** Have students read and answer the Think questions independently. Then have them discuss their answers to questions with an English-proficient partner. Have them share the ideas they want to develop into their own narrative, the reasons why these ideas are interesting to them, and what sources are available. They can take notes on their discussion and save them for their prewrite.

Core Path	Access Path
	Approaching **Rewrite the Think Questions.** Preview the Think questions and ask students to rewrite each question in their own words cn the Access 4 handout. Have students use their paraphrased versions of the Think questions to help them respond. Sample answers to the Think questions are located at the end of the lesson plan online.
	Extend **Identify.** Put students into small groups and ask each group to select a comic book superhero to discuss. Make a list of the character's heroic qualities. Each group might answer the following questions: • What special powers does the hero possess? • How would you describe this hero's personality? • On whose side is the hero fighting? • What ideals does the hero fight for? • Who are the hero's enemies and what is he or she trying to achieve? Allow time for each group to share their discussion details with the class.

BLAST:
Audience and Purpose

OVERVIEW

In this Blast, students will learn why it is important for writers to consider both audience and purpose when creating a hero narrative.

OBJECTIVES

1. Learn the definitions of audience and purpose in the writing of a narrative.
2. Explore background information about how writers use the elements and techniques of hero narratives when considering their audience and purpose.
3. Practice identifying an author's intended audience and the author's purpose in a model narrative.

ELA Common Core Standards:
Reading: Informational Text - RI.11-12.1
Writing - W.11-12.3.A, W.11-12.4, W.11-12.5, W.11-12.6, W.11-12.10
Speaking & Listening - SL.11-12.1.A, SL.11-12.1.C, SL.11-12.1.D, SL.11-12.2

RESOURCES

Access 1 handout (Beginner)

Access 2 handout (Intermediate)

Access 4 handout (Approaching)

TITLE/DRIVING QUESTION

Core Path	Access Path
Read and Discuss. As a class read aloud the title and driving question for this Blast: Who is the audience and what is the purpose for your hero narrative? Ask students why it might be important for writers to think about their audience who will be reading their work. Who might an audience for a narrative be? How can an author's purpose shape a hero narrative? Remind students that they should not immediately reply to these questions. They'll be returning to this question and responding after they've read the Background and explored the Model. Remind students to follow the rules for collegial discussions.	**English Learners All Levels** **Discuss a Visual.** Have students view a photograph of an audience made up of a clear group, such as the photo of construction workers listening to a speech at: http://tinyurl.com/psva65l. Discuss how the picture represents an audience, prompting students with questions such as: • Who can you see in this photo? What kinds of people are there? • Based on this audience, what do you think the speaker is talking about? • What can the speaker assume this audience knows about? • What are some other ways this audience might affect the speaker?
Draft. In their notebooks or on scrap paper, have students draft their initial responses to the driving question. This will provide them with a baseline response that they will be altering as they gain more information about the topic in the Background section of the assignment.	**Beginner & Intermediate** **Draft with Sentence Frame.** When drafting their initial response to the driving question, have students refer to this Blast sentence frame on their Access 1 and 2 handouts: • The audience for my hero narrative is _____, and my purpose is _____. Point out these two key features of the sentence frame: 1. The first half of the frame "The audience for my hero narrative is' borrows language directly from the Blast driving question and prompts students to state their audience. 2. The second half of the frame, "and my purpose is," prompts students to give their purpose. If needed, remind students that common purposes are to inform, to persuade, and to entertain.

Copyright © BookheadEd Learning, LLC

BACKGROUND

Core Path	Access Path
Read. Have students read the Blast background to provide context for the driving question: Who is the audience and what is the purpose for your hero narrative?	**Beginner & Intermediate** **Read with Support.** Have students read the Blast background to provide context for the driving question. When they encounter unfamiliar words or phrases, have students refer to the glossary on their Access 1 and 2 handouts. If there are unfamiliar words that are not included in their glossary, encourage students to check a dictionary or online reference tool, like http://dictionary.reference.com. **Approaching** **Read and Summarize.** Have students read the Blast background to provide context for the driving question. As they read, ask students to complete the fill-in-the-blank summary of the background provided on their Access 4 handout. When they encounter unfamiliar words or phrases, have students refer to the glossary on their Access 4 handout.
Discuss. Pair students and have them discuss the following questions: 1. Think about the ideas of purpose and audience in our everyday encounters. Why do we often adjust our style, tone, and content depending on with whom we are communicating? (Sample answer: The people we see each day are a kind of audience. We have different relationships with people, and different people expect different things from us. Also, our reasons for talking to different people will vary. Because of this, we adjust our style. For example, I wouldn't talk to my friend the same way I talk to my principal or to a boss, and I wouldn't share the same information.)	**Beginner** **Discuss.** Pair Beginner with Advanced (or Beyond) students and have them use the dialogue starter on their Access 1 handout to discuss the topic. Advise them to return to the dialogue and switch roles if they get stuck. **Intermediate** **Discuss.** Pair Intermediate with Advanced (or Beyond) students and have them use the dialogue starter on their Access 2 handout to discuss the topic. Advise them to return to the dialogue and switch roles if they get stuck. If their conversation is progressing smoothly, encourage them to continue the discussion beyond the dialogue starter sheet. They can expand their conversations to discuss other examples of texts or stories that change to suit the audience and purpose.

Copyright © BookheadEd Learning, LLC

Core Path	Access Path
2. What will be your primary purpose for writing a hero narrative? (to entertain) Thinking about the student Model, how might you enhance or develop your own narrative's purpose? (Sample answer: The student Model writer offered an alternative point of view to the Arthurian legend. In the same way, I might retell a famous myth or legend from the point of view of an unexpected character or offer a different focus to events in the plot.)	
3. How will you reveal your purpose to readers? (Sample answer: I will have to use engaging language to reveal a main character whose quest is clear. The language and the quest will help show why I am writing the story.)	
4. What is the relationship between audience and background knowledge when writing a hero narrative? (Knowing your audience helps a writer understand what the reader may or may not know about the subject of a story. If the audience is a general one, then specialized information or references, such as who King Arthur and Mordred are, may have to be explained.)	
5. If you want your narrative to appeal to your friends and your teacher, what are some things you should consider when you are writing? (Sample answer: I know what kinds of heroes interest me, and where I'd like to set a narrative, but that doesn't mean everyone will like it as much as I do. As I write, I have to make sure I include explanations and engaging language to keep my readers interested. In addition, I want to make sure my purpose is clear, including how much humor to use, how serious to be, and how up-to-date I am in my references.)	

Core Path	Access Path

Brainstorm. Remind students about the driving question for this Blast: Who is the audience and what is the purpose for your hero narrative?

Ask students to think about how they will appeal to their audience by answering the following questions:

- "Who will be reading my narrative?"
- "How do I think the audience will respond to a hero and his or her story?"
- "How can I present the plot, characters, and setting so that my audience will find my narrative interesting?"
- "Do I plan to make any references to other stories or heroes that my audience might not have read?"
- "What message am I trying to leave with my audience?"

Ask students to create a two-column chart that looks like the following:

Overall purpose: to entertain

Narrative elements and audience	How to make individual elements accessible to the audience
Audience for narrative	(Answers should include mention of a general audience, including the teacher and students, but may also include a more specific group.)
Main character, or the hero	(Answers should include ideas for who the hero for a story might be, based on real life or classic stories, or original.)

Core Path		Access Path
Conflict or quest that drives a plot	(Answers should identify ideas of what the hero might try to accomplish and what will make this quest hard to do.)	
Point of view, or how the story is told	(Answers should include ideas for a first or third person narrator; may also want to tell the story from the point of view of several characters.)	
References to other stories	(Answers should include how the writer might provide background information to readers, or explain ideas for updating old stories for the modern world.)	
Purpose, revealed through the theme or message	(Answers should include that the purpose is to entertain the audience; writers should include ideas for a theme or message that the audience can connect with and care about.)	

Invite students to share their brainstorming with the class and clarify any questions or concerns.

QUIKPOLL

Core Path	Access Path
Participate. Answer the poll question. Have students use information from the background to explain their answers. Remind students to follow the rules for collegial discussions.	

NUMBER CRUNCH

Core Path	Access Path
Predict, Discuss, and Click. Before students click on the number, break them into pairs and have them make predictions about what they think the number is related to. After they've clicked the number, ask students if they are surprised by the revealed information.	

CREATE YOUR BLAST

Core Path	Access Path
Blast. Ask students to write their Blast response in 140 characters or less.	**Beginner** **Blast with Support.** Have students refer back to the sentence frame on their Access 1 handout that they used to create their original Blast draft. Ask them to use this frame to write and enter their final Blast. **Intermediate** **Blast with Support.** Have students attempt to draft their Blast without the sentence frame on their Access 2 handout. If students struggle to compose their Blast draft without the sentence frame, remind them to reference it for support.

Core Path	Access Path
	Beyond **Write a Text Message.** Ask students to use their answer to the poll question to write a text message about an event for three different audiences: 1) teachers; 2) friends; and 3) members of the community. Once students have written their messages, ask them to read the different versions of the message to a small group of their peers. This activity will provide them practice writing for various audiences, as well as expose them to different approaches written by their peers.
Review. After students have completed their own Blasts, ask them to review the Blasts of their peers and provide feedback.	
	Extend **Discuss.** As a whole class or in groups, identify a few strong Blasts and discuss what made those responses so powerful. As a group, analyze and discuss what characteristics make a Blast interesting or effective.
	Extend **Revise.** Resend a second version of this Blast assignment to your students and have them submit revised versions of their original Blasts. Do the same responses make the Top 10? How have the answers improved from the first submissions?

OVERVIEW

As students move toward the prewriting stage of their Extended Writing Project, they'll need to think about how they might want to organize their writing, particularly in terms of choosing a point of view and introducing the hero and his or her quest. This lesson identifies common elements of a narrative and explains how a writer uses these elements to develop a story.

OBJECTIVES

1. Discuss and demonstrate and understanding of aspects of organizational structure in narrative writing.
2. Practice and apply concrete strategies for organizing narrative writing.
3. Participate effectively in a range of conversations and collaborations to express ideas and build upon the ideas of others.

   ELA Common Core Standards:
   Reading: Literature - RL.11-12.1, RL.11-12.3
   Reading: Informational Text - RI.11-12.1
   Writing - W.11-12.3.A, W.11-12.4, W.11-12.5
   Speaking & Listening - SL.11-12.1.A, SL.11-12.1.B, SL.11-12.1.C, SL.11-12.1.D

RESOURCES

Access 1 handout (Beginner)

Access 2 handout (Intermediate)

Access 3 handout (Advanced)

Access 4 handout (Approaching)

1. DEFINE

Core Path	Access Path
Read and Discuss. Either individually or as a class, read the Define section of the lesson. Either in small groups or as a class use these questions to spur discussion among your students about organizing narrative writing:	**Beginner** **In Your Own Words.** Have students read the definition and then use their Access 1 handouts to pause after each bullet point to rewrite the elements of organizing narrative writing in their own words. Once students have completed this activity, ask them to complete the chart on the Access 1 handout.

Core Path (continued)

1. What is a conflict in a narrative? What part does it play in the development of the narrative? (A conflict is the problem the character or characters must solve or face. The conflict and how it is resolved is key to the narration of events and character descriptions.) Can you think of examples of external conflicts in novels or movies? Internal conflicts? (Answers will vary but should include examples of that show external conflicts, such as man versus nature, man versus man, or man versus society scenarios, as well as internal conflicts, or man versus himself scenarios.)

2. What different types of narrators can a narrative have? (first person, third-person limited, third-person omniscient) What are some advantages and disadvantages of each type? (Sample answer: First-person narrators are personally invested in the outcome of the events, whereas third-person narrators are not. However, first-person narrators may not be reliable or may have biases, whereas a third-person narrator relates events without emotional connections or biases.)

3. Why is it important for authors to properly develop their characters? (An author needs to develop characters properly, meaning clearly, logically, and with helpful descriptions, to prevent confusion in audiences.)

Access Path (continued)

Intermediate
In Your Own Words. Have students read the definition of organizing narrative writing and then use their Access 2 handout to pause after each bullet point to rewrite the elements of organizing narrative writing in their own words. After they've rewritten each of the bullet points in their words, work with students to develop their own definitions of the term.

Advanced
In Your Own Words. Have Advanced students read and then discuss what they have learned about organizing narrative writing with an English-proficient partner or in mixed-proficiency groups. After their conversation, have Advanced students write the definition of organizing narrative writing on the Access 3 handout.

Core Path	Access Path
	Approaching **Restate the Definition.** Have students read the define section and then use their Access 4 handouts to restate the most important points in their own words. Clarify questions to aid students' comprehension as needed. Then have students participate in mixed-level groups with the class to discuss how to organize narrative writing. **Beyond** **Jigsaw.** If students have extra time, remind them that narratives often have two types of characters: static and dynamic. Dynamic characters change over the course of a narrative, and static characters do not. In small groups, have students discuss the following questions: • What is the purpose of a dynamic character in a text? A static character? • Why do narratives need both types of characters? • Why do people want to read or view stories with characters who change? Can you think of any books or movies with a main character who is not dynamic? Allow each group time to share their conclusions with the class.
	Extend **Discuss.** Pair or group students and have them discuss examples of stories with different types of narrators. Have each group identify a story or novel, what type of narrator it has, and what effect that narrator's choice had on the story. Have them consider how the narrative would be different with a different narrator.
	Extend **Tech Infusion** **Create.** For additional practice in creating narrators, allow groups to rewrite the stories they chose using a different type of narrator. Post these new stories on a class blog using a blogging tool such as Blogger (www.blogger.com).

2. MODEL

Core Path	Access Path
Read and Discuss. As students read the Model text use these questions to help students understand ways to organize narrative writing:	**Beginner, Intermediate & Approaching** **Identify the Elements.** Have students look closely at the chart on the Access 1, 2, and 4 handouts. Then ask them to identify each of the elements listed in the chart in "Lady Letha, Knight of Mordred." Allow students to work in pairs if they wish. Encourage students to include textual evidence to support their answers. When they have completed the chart, explain that they can use the chart as a model for the one they will complete for their own narrative in the Practice part of the lesson.

1. The Model says the student narrative uses a classic way to introduce the hero. What is it? (The hero is introduced in the story's title.) What other hero stories do this? (e.g., *Beowulf, Le Morte d'Arthur*) Why do you think this technique has been used so often by authors of this genre? (Possible response: When the focus of a narrative is on the exploits of a particular hero, it makes sense to use the hero's name in the title. In addition, when there are many stories about the same hero, as with King Arthur, fans of that hero can use such titles to seek out more stories to read.)

2. How does the Model identify the narrative's point of view? (The Model looks at the pronouns and identifies the point of view as first-person. In addition, Lady Letha's quest explains her feelings about King Arthur, and her opinion also informs the story's point of view.)

3. The Model explains how the author develops the character of Lady Letha. How does the narrative do this? (Beginning with a transition sentence and a new paragraph, the story presents a flashback of Letha remembering how she became a knight.) How else could the narrative have developed Letha's character? (Possible response: This story from the past could have been developed via dialogue with another character.)

Advanced
Identify the Parts. Have students read the Model and answer the questions on the Access 3 handout. Once they've completed the questions, pair Advanced students with more proficient students to allow them to share their answers.

Core Path	Access Path
Practice.	**Beginner**
	Write Your Character Description.
1. Ask students to review the narrative prompt for the extended writing project and think about what qualities or character traits they wish their hero or heroine to possess. Have them refer to their prewriting resources to guide them with this practice activity. They will want to use some of these ideas as they write introductory paragraphs about their central characters.	1. Prior to having them write their character descriptions, ask students to complete the chart on the Access 1 handout. Remind students to use their completed chart for "Lady Letha, Knight of Mordred" as a model.
2. Have students write their character paragraphs in both first and third person either on a piece of paper in class or online. (Note: you will need to create a Write assignment if they are going to submit their paragraphs online.) When they have finished, ask them to exchange paragraphs and provide their peers with constructive feedback.	2. After students have completed the chart, ask them to discuss with a partner what they plan to write about, clarifying any language as needed before writing their paragraphs.
	3. Then students should write their own third-person character descriptions using the sentence frames in the Apply section of the Access 1 handout.
3. Students should use their peers' feedback to improve their paragraphs and make their choices about which point of view would best suit the development of their narrative writing.	4. After students have their third-person paragraphs, have them work with a partner to write their first-person paragraphs on the blank lines at the bottom of the Access 1 handout. Clarify questions about pronouns with students as needed.
4. Students should use their peers' feedback to focus their future prewriting activities.	
	Intermediate
	Finish Sentences. Have students fill in the chart on the Access 2 handout, then complete the sentence frames below. Review their answers with them, and after making any clarifications needed, allow them to use their answers to adjust their paragraphs. Then allow them to join Advanced students to discuss and edit their paragraphs.

Core Path	Access Path
	Advanced
	Clarify and Edit. Have students refer to the writing prompt as they write their character paragraphs. Have them read both their paragraphs aloud to another Intermediate or Advanced student to check for language that needs to be clarified and to answer the following questions:
	• Have you created an interesting and complex character?
	• Does it make sense that this character is going on this quest? Why or why not?
	• Is there anything else readers should know about the character to understand the narrative?
	• Have you used grammar such as pronouns, prepositions, and subject/verb agreement correctly?
	Allow students time to make edits to their paragraphs as necessary.
	Approaching
	Complete the Chart & Complete the Fill in the Blank Character Description.
	1. Prior to having them write their character descriptions, ask students to complete the chart on the Access 4 handout.
	2. Once they have completed the chart with the information they plan to write about, allow them to use the fill in the blank character description provided on the Access 4 handout to construct a third-person character description. Remind students to complete the missing parts of the fill in the blank paragraph with information from their chart. Encourage students to add information to the chart or paragraph as needed to create a vibrant, complex main character.

Core Path	Access Path
	Extend **Discuss.** Pair or group students and have them choose a story (could be from a book or movie) with which they're all familiar. Have them identify the conflict in the story. Then have them discuss how the story would be different if the conflict never happened or was resolved quickly. Would the story still be worth reading/watching? Why or why not?
	Extend **Tech Infusion** **Write.** Challenge students to write a very short story (50 words or less) without a conflict that is still worth reading. Share all the stories on a class blog or a shared Google Document. Have students read each other's stories and determine if there really is no conflict in the story. Then have students debate whether stories like these are worth reading. If there is time, allow students to edit a classmate's super short story by adding a conflict. Tell them they must limit their additions to no more than 25 words!
	Extend **Prewrite.** Recommend that as students think of ideas for their narratives, they should start to make a list of possible motivations for their characters. If students struggle, suggest they create a cause-and-effect graphic organizer for every important action a character does. For example, if their hero is going on a journey to kill a dragon, have them ask themselves: Why is the hero doing that? If he's going for the glory, why does he seek glory? Explain that not all motivations need to be spelled out in the narrative, but could be hinted at as character development.

3. YOUR TURN

Core Path	Access Path
Assess and Explain. Have students answer the comprehension questions to test for understanding of ways to organize narrative writing. Share the explanations for Part A and B (located online) with your students.	
	Extend **Write.** Pair or group students and have them identify the point of view of other selections in the unit, such as *The Once and Future King* or *Beowulf.* Instruct groups to find textual evidence to support their identifications. Have them take one passage and write it from another point of view. Have them discuss how the narrative changes.

EXTENDED WRITING PROJECT:
Prewrite

OVERVIEW

This lesson asks students to complete a prewriting activity in preparation for writing their hero narratives. They need to start thinking about the story's hero and quest, as well as the conflict, point of view, narrator, and characters they will include in their narratives. They will identify these elements in a model and then brainstorm the narrative features of their own stories. Students will present prewriting lists for peer review and receive feedback on their prewriting ideas.

OBJECTIVES

1. Discuss and demonstrate understanding of narrative writing features.
2. Analyze the prompt and generate ideas for a hero narrative that includes a clear conflict, point of view, narrator, and characters.
3. Participate effectively in a range of conversations and collaborations to express ideas and build upon the ideas of others.

   ELA Common Core Standards:
   Reading Literature - RL.11-12.1
   Writing - W.11-12.3.A, W.11-12.4, W.11-12.5, W.11-12.9.A, W.11-12.10
   Speaking & Listening - SL.11-12.1.A

RESOURCES

Grade 12, Unit 1 Extended Writing Project: Prewrite lesson

Access 1 handout (Beginner)

Access 2 handout (Intermediate)

Copyright © BookheadEd Learning, LLC

WRITE

Core Path	Access Path
Brainstorm. As students brainstorm, have them consider the following questions to fuel their prewriting: • What makes the main character a hero? • From what point of view will the narrative be told? • What conflict will he or she face? • In what ways will this conflict challenge or change the hero? • Where will the story take place? How is the setting important to the plot? • What will happen to the hero before the conflict? What will happen after? • How will these events impact history? Remind students to look for patterns and commonalities between their notes and the selections from the unit. Then ask students to complete the following prewriting mind map brainstorm. • Have students draw three circles at the top of their paper. In each circle ask them to write the name of their hero, the setting, and the conflict they plan to write about. • Then, around those boxes, have students draw spokes (lines all around the box) and brainstorm plot elements and descriptive details for each element that could be part of the narrative. Review the rubric with students before they begin the prewriting activity. This practice will ensure they know what elements of their prewriting will be evaluated by their peer reviewers. Also, tell students how many peer reviews they will need to complete once they have finished their prewriting activity.	**Beginner & Intermediate** **Organize and Support the Prewrite.** 1. Pair students with proficient English speakers or put them in small mixed-proficiency groups. 2. Have students work together to create mind maps for their ideas. Encourage students to work together to fill in gaps, such as which setting would be appropriate for a certain type of hero. 3. Have all groups display their brainstorm charts so that all students can be inspired by each group's ideas. (Note: Beginner and Intermediate students can then use the Prewrite Worksheet on the Access 1 and 2 handouts to complete their Prewrite Worksheet for their hero narrative.) 4. Read aloud the example for "Lady Letha, Knight of Mordred" provided on the Access 1 and 2 handouts. Pause after each section to clarify any concepts related to the content or writing as necessary. Explain that they will use the completed section on "Lady Letha, Knight of Mordred" as a model for their own prewrite. 5. Have students identify their hero and the basic information about him or her information in the brainstorm chart. Provide assistance for their writing as necessary. (Note: In the Plan Lesson they will transfer this information to their Narrative Road Map.) **Advanced** **Share and Evaluate.** Ask partners to share and evaluate their finished brainstorm charts with an English-proficient partner. Have them discuss the common themes and help one another find additional details they might have missed before they move on to do their prewrite. Encourage partners to ask each other questions to flesh out all details in the chart.

Core Path	Access Path

Review. Once students complete their writing assignment, they should submit substantive feedback to three peers. Students will use the feedback to develop their writing in different stages of the writing process.
 	
Project these instructions for the peer review onto the board and review them with your class, so they know what they are looking for when they begin to provide their classmates with feedback:
• How well did he or she answer the questions presented in the prewriting activity?
 	
   • What details will the writer use to create an interesting hero and to present a problem to solve or overcome?
 	
   • Did the writer list supplementary characters and their roles?
 	
   • What makes the writer's ideas for a plot complete and compelling? Will the plot reveal the chosen theme?
 	
   • Has the writer picked a clear point of view?
 	
   • What details did the writer provide to create a setting that will strengthen the narrative?
 	
• Were there any questions from the list above that were not answered? If so, what suggestions can you provide to help your classmate answer these questions?
 	
• Does the prewriting activity address all six features of narrative writing (setting, characters, plot, conflict, theme, point of view)? Are there any elements that could be tweaked to provide a stronger narrative?	

Core Path	Access Path
	Extend **Tech Infusion** **Organize the Task.** If students struggle to form their ideas into a coherent narrative, encourage them to draw six circles on a piece of paper or use Google Drawing or MindMeister (http://www.mindmeister.com/) to create a graphic organizer. The six circles should be • setting • characters • plot • conflict • theme • point of view Have students fill in each circle with the ideas they've brainstormed. Then have them draw lines between the circles and explain the connection between each. For example, the line between "setting" and "conflict" might be described as "The knight is forced to go off to war because all of the young men in his town are required to go." When students have completed their maps, have them share their ideas with a partner and discuss any gaps in the narrative.

OVERVIEW

As students move toward the planning stage of their Extended Writing Project, they'll need to consider the sequencing of events in their hero narratives. This lesson identifies a variety of tools that writers use to develop the plot and characters, set the tone, and build toward a particular outcome.

OBJECTIVES

1. Discuss and demonstrate an understanding of narrative sequencing.
2. Practice identifying narrative sequencing and apply this understanding to a piece of narrative writing.
3. Participate effectively in a range of conversations and collaborations to express ideas and build upon the ideas of others.

ELA Common Core Standards:
Reading: Literature - RL.11-12.1, RL.11-12.3
Reading: Informational Text - RI.11-12.1
Writing - W.11-12.3.A, W.11-12.3.C
Speaking & Listening - SL.11-12.1.A, SL.11-12.1.B, SL.11-12.1.C, SL.11-12.1.D

RESOURCES

Story Structure Map Graphic Organizer
Access 1 handout (Beginner)
Access 2 handout (Intermediate)
Access 3 handout (Advanced)
Access 4 handout (Approaching)

1. DEFINE

Core Path	Access Path
Read and Discuss. Have students, either individually or as a class, read the Define section of the lesson. Either in small groups or as a class, use these questions to spur discussion among your students about narrative sequencing:	**Beginner** **In Your Own Words.** Have students read the definition and then use their Access 1 handouts to pause after each bullet point to rewrite the important points of narrative sequencing in their own words. Once students have completed this activity, ask them to complete the List the Sequence activity on the Access 1 handout.

Core Path

Read and Discuss. Have students, either individually or as a class, read the Define section of the lesson. Either in small groups or as a class, use these questions to spur discussion among your students about narrative sequencing:

1. What information do authors give in the exposition? (Sample answer: Through exposition, authors can explain characters, the setting, and the conflict. In addition, authors can provide background information so readers better understand the reasons for events to come.) Can you think of any stories, movies, etc., that don't give some of that information in the exposition? (Possible response: In Samuel Beckett's famous play *Waiting for Godot,* the audience is given no information about how the characters came to know each other or where exactly they are.)

2. What is an example of a trigger or inciting incident that sets up the plot of a movie, play, or other story you know? Explain how that incident sets the wheels of the plot in motion. (Sample answer: In the original story of King Arthur, perhaps the most important incident is the moment when Arthur, as a young man, pulls the sword from the stone. With that event, he becomes king and his legend takes off. From this moment on, he must gather knights and take a wife, and all the adventurous stories of his realm follow.)

Access Path

Beginner
In Your Own Words. Have students read the definition and then use their Access 1 handouts to pause after each bullet point to rewrite the important points of narrative sequencing in their own words. Once students have completed this activity, ask them to complete the List the Sequence activity on the Access 1 handout.

Intermediate
In Your Own Words. Have students read the definition of narrative sequencing and then use their Access 2 handout to pause after each bullet point to rewrite the important points of narrative sequencing in their own words. After they've rewritten each of the bullet points in their words, work with students to develop their own definitions of the term.

Advanced
In Your Own Words. Have Advanced students read and then discuss what they have learned about narrative sequencing with an English-proficient partner or in mixed-proficiency groups. After their conversation, have Advanced students write the definition of narrative sequencing on the Access 3 handout.

Approaching
Restate the Definition. Have students read the define section and then use their Access 4 handouts to restate the most important points in their own words. Clarify questions to aid students' comprehension as needed. Then have students participate in mixed-level groups with the class to discuss the purpose of narrative sequencing.

Core Path	Access Path
3. The definition states that the narrative sequencing authors use to frame a story usually follow a certain order: exposition, rising action, climax, falling action, resolution. Can you think of any books or movies that don't follow that order? What is the effect of such a plot? (Possible response: One example might be the movie *Rocky,* where in the beginning, Rocky is a struggling boxer with little hope. By the end of the film he has "gone the distance" and "gets the girl," which is the climax of his story. The effect of this structure on *Rocky* is that audiences have a character to get to know, learn to care about, and root for until the very end.)	**Beyond** **Create a List.** If students have extra time, have them work together to create a list of the types of elements they would expect to find in each parts of a narrative (exposition, rising action, climax, falling action, and resolution). For example, exposition would include "introduce characters" and "introduce setting." When students have finished, have them share their lists with the class. Encourage students to refer to this list as they write their narratives to help with sequencing.
4. Think of two different types of stories, plays, or novels you have read and how they differ in tone. How do the writers use narrative sequencing and language to achieve their respective tones? How, for example, does the tone of a mystery differ from the tone of a coming-of-age story? Explain your own examples. (Sample answer: The heightened language, descriptions of violence, and life-and-death struggles in *Beowulf* and *Grendel,* for example, gives those stories a serious tone. In addition, the narrators in both selections take the time to set up each event and emotion if full detail. By contrast, the tone of *The Once and Future King* is lighter. The narrative is sequenced to create a volley of ideas between the speakers. There is more dialogue, the sentences are shorter, and the descriptions are sometimes humorous, even though this is also the story of a hero.) How does an author's tone affect the reader's response to a story? (Possible response: The tone of a story can affect the way a reader feels while reading. For example, a reader might be turned off by a story with a humorous tone when he really wants to read a serious story. Also, a reader who might not think a King Arthur story would be interesting, for example, may enjoy it based on the tone of the White's writing.)	

Core Path	Access Path
	Extend **Listen.** Ask each student to select (and bring into class) a passage from a book or short story they have read and enjoyed. Put students into groups of five and ask each student to read his/her excerpt aloud for their group. Instruct students in the group to note any words or phrases that establish tone. They can use pen and paper to capture these words and phrases or post them to a TodaysMeet (www.TodaysMeet.com) back channel. After each reading, have students identify the genre of the story and list the most popular phrases they identified during the reading. At the end of the activity, ask students to point out differences between the genres and texts.
	Extend **Tech Infusion** **e-Books.** Find each student's book online—try previews from Google Books or Amazon—and project it on the whiteboard. As students identify the tone of each book, have a student volunteer annotate the projected text. Create a graphic organizer to help students classify the genres and tone of each reading.

2. MODEL

Core Path	Access Path
Read and Discuss. As students read the Model text, use these questions to help students understand narrative sequencing: 1. The Model provides an example of a plot sequencing diagram. What is included in the exposition section? (The exposition section of the student model narrative includes details from the first paragraph and the flashback paragraph.) What is incident triggers or incites the rising action? (The truce fails between Arthur and Mordred, thus setting off a final battle, which is the subject of the story.) 2. Is the characterization element—Lady Letha's backstory—necessary to the development of the rest of the plot? Why or why not? (Sample answer: The main events of the plot would have progressed without the element of backstory. However, an understanding of Lady Letha as a female knight adds a new and interesting dimension to well-known story. We also see the events from the point of view of one of Arthur's enemies, which is another twist.) 3. What is the difference between the falling action and the resolution of the story? (The falling action and resolution both happen right after the climax of the plot, but the resolution is Lady Letha's acknowledgement that she's content with dying as long as she knows she has seen an end to tyranny.) 4. How can a different sequencing of events change the outcome of the story? Have students write plot events on a plot diagram. (Answers may vary, but students should show how changing the sequence of events works within the scope of the plot diagram.)	**Beginner, Intermediate & Approaching** **Identify and Explain Narrative Elements.** Have students read the five parts of a narrative on the Access 1, 2, and 4 handouts. Have students either define the term or write what an author should include in that part of a narrative. Make sure students understand these words. Then have students write what the author of "Lady Letha, Knight of Mordred" included in each part. Explain that they can use this information to form their own narratives. **Advanced** **Identify the Parts.** Have students read the student model plot diagram and answer the questions on the Access 3 handout. Once they've completed the questions, pair Advanced students with more proficient students to allow them to share their answers.

Core Path	Access Path
Practice. Students have had a chance to think about the audience, purpose, and organization of their narratives. Now have them complete the "Story Structure Map" to organize a sequence of events, while also considering how the sequencing will affect tone. When they are finished, have them exchange their maps with a partner to offer and receive feedback.	**Beginner** **Complete Sentence Frames.** 1. Prior to having them complete their plot diagrams, ask students to complete the sentence frames on the Access 1 handout. 2. After students have answered the questions, ask them to discuss with a partner what they plan to write about, clarifying any language as needed. Encourage students to ask each other questions to make sure that all the basic elements of narrative sequence are covered. 3. Then students should complete their plot diagrams. Encourage them to refer back to the writing prompt and to the Prewrite Worksheet they completed. **Intermediate** **Finish Sentences.** Have students fill in the sentence frames in the Apply section of the Access 2 handout. Review their answers with them, and after making any clarifications needed, allow them to use their answers to complete their plot diagrams. Then allow them to join Advanced students to discuss and edit their plot diagrams. **Advanced** **Clarify and Edit.** Have students refer to their Prewrite Worksheet and the writing prompt as they complete their plot diagrams. Have them read their diagrams aloud to another Intermediate or Advanced student to check for language that needs to be clarified and to answer the following questions: • Have you set up everything in the exposition that readers need to know? • What will happen in the rising action? How will it lead seamlessly to the climax? • Does the falling action and resolution wrap up the conflict in a satisfying way? What will readers want to know at the end of the narrative? Allow students time to make edits or additions to their plot diagrams as necessary.

Core Path	Access Path
	Approaching **Finish the Sentences.** 1. Prior to having them complete their plot diagrams, ask students to complete the sentence frames on the Access 4 handout. 2. Once they have completed the statements with the information they plan to write about, have them complete the plot diagram. Encourage students to add more information as necessary to the plot diagram, and to continue to refine their ideas. 3. After they have completed their plot diagrams, have students share them with a partner. Students should explain their narratives to their partners to ensure that a reader or listener has all the information he or she would want in a narrative.
	Extend **Create.** Have students create artistic renderings of plot diagrams for other narratives in the unit. For instance, a student might choose the excerpt from *The Once and Future King* and create a graphic rendering of the narrative sequence. The main elements of the diagram should remain intact, but the student should add an artistic background, with illustrations of events in the story in place of textual explanations of the events. For example, a student might draw a picture of Arthur climbing the stairs, sweating and panting, to visit Merlyn's study as the graphic rendering of exposition. Students should be creative with their renderings. Post the drawings around the room and allow students time to view and critique their classmates' work.
	Extend **Tech Infusion** **Draw.** Allow students to use iPad or Android drawing apps, such as Paper, to complete the assignment. Once the drawings are complete, ask students to e-mail the images to you or upload them directly to the class blog. Guide students to critique each other's work by leaving comments about each picture.

Copyright © BookheadEd Learning, LLC

Core Path	Access Path
	Extend Write plot elements from several well-known stories on slips of paper. For instance, you could choose *Twilight* and write "Bella moves to Forks," "Bella and Edward meet," "Bella finds out Edward is a vampire," "Edward fights James," "Bella and Edward go to prom." Mix up the pieces of paper and hand them out randomly to students. Give students five minutes to move around the room and find others who have been assigned plot points from the same story they have. They must put themselves in order. To add a twist, have them do all of this without speaking. Finally, have each group act out the plot sequence and explain why they ordered the events the way they did.

3. YOUR TURN

Core Path	Access Path
Assess and Explain. Have students answer the comprehension questions to test for understanding. Share the explanations for Part A and B (located online) with your students.	
	Extend **Write.** Pair or group students and have them write two Your Turn questions about a different text from the unit, using the Your Turn questions from this lesson as a model. They should include multiple-choice answers to their questions. Once all groups are finished, have them trade and give their questions to other groups.

OVERVIEW

Students will gather previous prewriting lists and their previously completed Story Structure Maps to plan their hero narratives. Students will summarize their plans, present their summaries for peer review, and receive feedback on their narrative approach.

OBJECTIVES

1. Discuss and demonstrate an understanding of narrative writing skills such as organization and narrative sequencing.
2. Plan a hero narrative by summarizing of map of narrative elements and event sequences.
3. Participate effectively in a range of conversations and collaborations to express ideas and build upon the ideas of others.

   ELA Common Core Standards:
   Writing - W.11-12.3.A, W.11-12.3.C, W.11-12.5, W.11-12.6, W.11-12.10
   Speaking & Listening - SL.11-12.1.A, SL.11-12.1.B, SL.11-12.1.C, SL.11-12.1.D

RESOURCES

Grade 12, Unit 1 Extended Writing Project: Plan lesson

Access 1 handout (Beginner)

Access 2 handout (Intermediate)

Access 4 handout (Approaching)

1. WRITE

Core Path	Access Path
Discuss. As a class, review the characteristics of narrative writing. Advise students that, before they start planning their writing, they will need to answer some questions about the information they collected earlier. Read through the questions posed by the prompt: • Who is the hero of the narrative? • What conflict does the hero need to overcome? • What other characters will be in the narrative? What role do they play? • What is the setting of the narrative? How is the setting important to the narrative? • Who is telling the story? Does much the narrator know about the characters and events? • In what sequence should details be revealed to best build toward the outcome? • What do you want readers to take away from the narrative when they finish reading? Solicit two or three examples from the class and model answering the questions.	**Beginner & Intermediate** **Use Sentence Frames.** Include Beginner and Intermediate students in the whole class discussion. Then work with small groups to discuss their own writing ideas using the following questions and sentences below: • The hero of my narrative is _____. • What challenge will the hero face? What will the hero need to do to succeed? • Other characters I plan to include are _____. • The setting of my narrative is _____. The setting is important because _____. • The narrator will be _____. He/she will know _____. • Does it make the most sense for your narrative to tell the events in order? Is there another option that would work? • After reading, I want my readers to walk away with _____. Once they've had a chance to discuss their own ideas, ask them to complete the final sentence frame stating what they hope their readers will take away from their narrative.
Organize. Remind students that as part of the planning process, they should use their prewriting lists and Story Structure Maps to begin creating their summaries. Students may seek out additional plot diagrams or story maps online to help them prepare for the writing assignment.	**Note:** As the on- and beyond-grade-level students begin the organization and writing stage of this lesson, support Beginner, Intermediate, and Approaching students to ensure they understand what type of information they need to include in their narrative road maps.

Core Path	Access Path
	Beginner & Intermediate **Preview Narrative Road Map.** Give students the Narrative Road Map on the Access 1 and 2 handouts, and explain what kind of information they will write in each section. Have them review their previously completed assignments to identify and underline information and details they can use in each section of their Narrative Road Map. **Approaching** **Use Organizational Supports.** Make sure students have access to all of their previous assignments to draw upon. Then give them the Narrative Road Map on the Access 4 handout to structure their organization. Go over each of the categories. Explain that as they write they can add additional paragraphs as needed.

Write. Tell students to refer back to the ideas they compiled in the previous stage of the writing process and to transfer ideas and details from their Story Structure Map into their summaries. Point out that, as they organize their ideas, students may find it necessary to structure their narratives in a different manner than they had planned. Encourage them to adjust their Story Structure Maps as they summarize, if needed.
 	
Once they have completed their summaries, they should click "Submit."
	Beginner & Intermediate
	Write and Discuss. Remind students that they can use what they have underlined in the previous assignments, as well as the Narrative Road Map on the Access 1 and 2 handouts, to plan their writing. Have partners or small groups discuss questions about the content of their completed Narrative Road Maps such as:
	
	• Who is your hero?
	  My hero is _____.
	• What is the conflict of the narrative?
	  The conflict is _____.
	• How will the characters react to the events in this paragraph?
	  The characters will react by
	  _____.
	
	Have them make any changes necessary before submitting their writing for further peer review.

Core Path	Access Path
	Advanced **Clarify Organization.** Have students share their completed Narrative Road Map with another Advanced or English-proficient partner. Have them work together to answer the following questions about their writing and make changes if necessary: • Are the events organized in a way that makes sense? • Do the characters' actions make sense? Do they behave in a way that the reader will understand? • Are there any other details I want to include? **Approaching** **Complete a Narrative Road Map.** Provide students with the following questions to help them complete and review their Narrative Road Map on the Access 4 handout: • Did I include all the essential information a reader would need in the exposition? • Does my narrative have a clear conflict? How will the character work to solve it? • What's the climax of my story? Does it follow logically from what happened before? How will the conflict be resolved after the climax? • What do I want the reader to think after reading the resolution and the narrative as a whole?
Review. Once students complete their summary assignment, they should submit substantive feedback to three peers. Students will use the feedback to develop their writing in different stages of the writing process. Project these instructions for the peer review onto the board and review them with your class, so they know what they are looking for when they begin to provide their classmates with feedback.	

Core Path	Access Path
Read your peer's summary to see that the writer has created a clear sequence of events. Always make respectful, supportive, and thoughtful responses. Consider the following questions as you review his or her plans: • Has the writer identified a hero and noted important qualities that make this character a hero? • Has the writer identified a point of view? • Has the writer identified a quest or conflict? • Do the events of the plot follow a logical sequence and build toward a particular outcome? Are there any gaps? • What will be the story's climax? Do the events lead logically to this climax? Is the idea exciting? • What is the theme for this hero narrative? What might the writer need to think about to establish the theme more clearly? Please remember we are in the early stages of the writing process, so your feedback is important to ensure your classmates are on the right track. Keep your comments kind and supportive!	
	Extend **Plan.** If students want to include multiple plot lines in their narratives, suggest they complete a plot diagram for each character or plot line. Remind students that the plot lines should meet at or near the climax of the narrative.
	Extend **Tech Infusion** **Draw.** Have students use their Plot Diagrams to draw a short comic strip of their narratives. Remind students that comic strips can feature both description and dialogue. These comic strips can help students set a sequence and address their intended audience. Allow students to use devices with Comic Life or Make Beliefs Comix (http://www.makebeliefscomix.com/Comix/) to create their strips. Have students refer back to their comic strips during the Draft stage.

Copyright © BookheadEd Learning, LLC

OVERVIEW

As students move toward the drafting stage of their Extended Writing Project, they'll need to decide how to craft an introduction for their narratives. This lesson identifies the features of a solid introduction and explains how a writer introduces his or her ideas in a narrative. Students will write and peer edit each other's introductions.

OBJECTIVES

1. Discuss and demonstrate an understanding of the elements of a strong introduction.
2. Analyze examples of introductions in narrative writing.
3. Participate effectively in a range of conversations and collaborations to express ideas and build upon the ideas of others.

   ELA Common Core Standards:
   Reading: Literature - RL.11-12.1
   Reading: Informational Text - RI.11-12.1
   Writing - W.11-12.3.A, W.11-12.4, W.11-12.5, W.11-12.10
   Speaking & Listening - SL.11-12.1.A, SL.11-12.1.B, SL.11-12.1.C, SL.11-12.1.D
   Language - L.11-12.3.A

RESOURCES

Access 1 handout (Beginner)

Access 2 handout (Intermediate)

Access 3 handout (Advanced)

Access 4 handout (Approaching)

Please note that excerpts and passages in the StudySync® library, workbooks, and PDFs are intended as touchstones to generate interest in an author's work. The excerpts and passages do not substitute for the reading of entire texts, and StudySync® strongly recommends that teachers and students seek out and purchase the whole literary or informational work in order to experience it as the author intended. Links to online resellers are available in our digital library. In addition, complete works may be ordered through an authorized reseller by filling out and returning to StudySync® the order form enclosed in this workbook.

Teacher's Edition   395

1. DEFINE

Core Path	Access Path
Read and Discuss. Either individually or as a class, read the Define section of the lesson. Either in small groups or as a class use these questions to spur discussion among your students about introductions. Remind students to follow rules for collaborative discussions.	**Beginner** **In Your Own Words.** Have students read the definition and then use their Access 1 handouts to pause after each bullet point to rewrite the definition of introductions in their own words. Once students have completed this activity, ask them to complete the fill in the blanks activity on the Access 1 handout.
1. What purpose do introductions serve in a short narrative? (They grab the reader's attention.) How are they different from a novel or longer narrative? (An introduction in a short narrative should introduce the conflict and the main characters, unlike a longer work which can take more time.)	**Intermediate** **In Your Own Words.** Have students read the definition of introductions and then use their Access 2 handout to pause after each bullet point to rewrite the definition in their own words. After they've rewritten each of the bullet points in their words, work with students to develop their own definitions of the term.
2. The Definition contains three examples of introductions or introductory sentences. Compare and contrast the three. What different techniques do they use? How are they similar? (Sample answer: The first, from *Anna Karenina*, refers to a quality of life, happiness or unhappiness, in terms of families, which sets a specific tone and an internal conflict. The second, from "An Occurrence at Owl Creek Bridge," sets up a strong external conflict of a man about to be hanged. The third, from Orwell's *1984*, sets up an unfamiliar world with the clocks "striking thirteen." All these examples show that the authors put careful thought into setting up their narratives, with all kinds of different conflicts.)	**Advanced** **In Your Own Words.** Have Advanced students read and then discuss what they have learned about introductions with an English-proficient partner or in mixed-proficiency groups. After their conversation, have Advanced students write the definition of introductions on the Access 3 handout.
3. Based on the examples, which book or story do you want to read now? Why? (Answers will vary but should include one of the titles and an explanation of how the introduction grabbed them.)	**Approaching** **Restate the Definition.** Have students read the define section and then use their Access 4 handouts to restate the most important points in their own words. Clarify questions to aid students' comprehension as needed. Then have students participate in mixed-level groups with the class to discuss the purpose of introductions in a narrative.

Core Path	Access Path
4. What are some memorable introductions from books or movies you know? Did the rest of the book or movie live up to the introduction? Why or why not? (Answers will vary but should include a title, details from the introduction, and an explanation of how the work lived up to or didn't live up to the promise of the introduction.)	**Beyond** **Jigsaw.** If students have extra time, put them in small groups and assign each group a different kind of nonfiction narrative, such as a novel short story, movie, or play. Then have students discuss how an introduction in their narrative would be different from the other forms. • Is there something unique in your narrative that can be used for an introduction? • How does the length of a work influence the introduction? Allow each group time to share their discussions with the class.
	Extend **Write.** Invite students to write the rest of the story that begins "It was a bright cold day in April, and the clocks were striking thirteen." Encourage students to keep their stories under 300 words. Then have partners exchange stories and discuss the different directions each of the stories took.

2. MODEL

Core Path	Access Path
Read and Discuss. As students read the Model text use these questions to help students understand how to create an introduction: 1. What is *in media res*? How does it apply to the Model? (*In media res* means starting in the middle of the action. "Lady Letha, Knight of Mordred" begins this way, bringing the reader right into the beginning of a battle.)	**Beginner, Intermediate & Approaching** **Answer Questions.** Have students read the questions on the Access 1, 2, and 4 handouts. Then ask them to answer the questions the best they can using only information from the introduction of "Lady Letha, Knight of Mordred." When students are finished, have them share their answers with a partner and discuss any questions they were unable to answer, if any.

SKILL: Narrative Techniques

Core Path	Access Path
	2. After students have answered the questions, ask them to discuss with a partner what they plan to write about, clarifying any language as needed before writing their scenes.
	3. Then students should write their own scenes based on their answers to the questions. Encourage them to refer back to the writing prompt and to the Plan Worksheet they completed.
	Intermediate
	Finish Sentences. Have students answer the questions in the Apply section of the Access 2 handout. Review their answers with them, and after making any clarifications needed, allow them to use their answers to craft their scenes. Then allow them to join Advanced students to discuss and edit their scenes.
	Advanced
	Clarify and Edit. Have students refer to their Plan Worksheet and the writing prompt as they write their scenes. Have them read their paragraphs aloud to another Intermediate or Advanced student to check for language that needs to be clarified and to answer the following questions:
	• Does the scene describe one clear event?
	• Which narrative techniques are used? What's their purpose? Is there a better option to achieve the same purpose?
	• Do all narrative techniques help move the plot along or otherwise benefit the reader?
	• Have you used grammar such as pronouns, prepositions, and subject/verb agreement correctly?
	Allow students time to make edits to their scenes as necessary.

Core Path	Access Path
	Extend **View.** As a class, watch a clip from a movie with great dialogue. (Shrek and Donkey's banter in *Shrek* would work well, or the opening scene from *The Social Network*.) Discuss what makes the dialogue work well. What can students learn from the dialogue? How can they translate it to their own narratives?
	Extend **Write.** Instruct students to practice writing descriptions by writing a detailed description of the classroom. Then have students share their descriptions with a partner. Have them compare and contrast their descriptions.

3. YOUR TURN

Core Path	Access Path
Assess and Explain. Have students answer the comprehension questions to test for understanding of narrative techniques. Share the explanations for Part A and B (located online) with your students.	
	Extend **Write.** Pair or group students and have them write two Your Turn questions about a different text from the unit, using the Your Turn questions from this lesson as a model. They should include multiple-choice answers to their questions. Once all groups are finished, have them trade and give their questions to other groups.

SKILL:
Conclusions

OVERVIEW

As students move toward the drafting stage of their Extended Writing Project, they'll need to consider the manner in which they will end their narratives. This lesson identifies the variety of tools that writers use to write a strong conclusion.

OBJECTIVES

1. Discuss and demonstrate an understanding of narrative conclusions.
2. Practice concrete strategies for identifying elements of narrative conclusions and apply this understanding to an original narrative piece.
3. Participate effectively in a range of conversations and collaborations to express ideas and build upon the ideas of others.

ELA Common Core Standards:
Reading: Literature - RL.11-12.1
Reading: Informational Text - RI.11-12.1
Writing - W.11-12.3.A, W.11-12.3.E, W.11-12.4, W.11-12.5, W.11-12.10
Speaking & Listening - SL.11-12.1.A, SL.11-12.1.B, SL.11-12.1.C, SL.11-12.1.D

RESOURCES

Access 1 handout (Beginner)

Access 2 handout (Intermediate)

Access 3 handout (Advanced)

Access 4 handout (Approaching)

1. DEFINE

Core Path	Access Path
Read and Discuss. Either individually or as a class, read the Define section of the lesson. Either in small groups or as a class, use these questions to spur discussion among your students about conclusions. Remind students to follow the rules for collegial discussions.	**Beginner** **In Your Own Words.** Have students read the definition and then use their Access 1 handouts to pause after each bullet point to rewrite the components of a conclusion in their own words. Once students have completed this activity, ask them to complete the fill in the blanks activity on the Access 1 handout.

Read and Discuss. Either individually or as a class, read the Define section of the lesson. Either in small groups or as a class, use these questions to spur discussion among your students about conclusions. Remind students to follow the rules for collegial discussions.

1. The definition says that a conclusion should provide a sense of closure. What is meant by a sense of closure? (Sample answer: A "sense of closure" means that when the story is concluded, the reader has a feeling that the narrative is complete, the story is finished. There are no "loose ends" and the resolution of events and character arcs feels satisfying.) Can you think of any books you've read or movies you've seen that did not provide that sense of closure? How did it make you feel about the work as a whole? (Possible response: I have watched science fiction movies in a series, for example, where though the end of the movie resolves a conflict, the movie ends with hints of more conflicts to come. For example, sometimes a battle is won, but the enemy has lived and not been truly defeated. This leaves room for another story to come, so I don't mind those kinds of endings.)

2. What can an author or narrator add by reflecting on the events of the story in the conclusion? (Sample answer: By reflecting on events at a story's conclusion, a character leaves the reader with no doubt about how the events affected him or her. In addition, readers find out what the character has learned, if anything, as a result of the action.)

Beginner

In Your Own Words. Have students read the definition and then use their Access 1 handouts to pause after each bullet point to rewrite the components of a conclusion in their own words. Once students have completed this activity, ask them to complete the fill in the blanks activity on the Access 1 handout.

Intermediate

In Your Own Words. Have students read the definition of conclusions and then use their Access 2 handout to pause after each bullet point to rewrite the components of a strong conclusion in their own words. After they've rewritten each of the bullet points in their words, work with students to develop their own definitions of the term.

Advanced

In Your Own Words. Have Advanced students read and then discuss what they have learned about conclusions with an English-proficient partner or in mixed-proficiency groups. After their conversation, have Advanced students write the definition of conclusions on the Access 3 handout.

Approaching

Restate the Definition. Have students read the define section and then use their Access 4 handouts to restate the most important points in their own words. Clarify questions to aid students' comprehension as needed. Then have students participate in mixed-level groups with the class to discuss the elements of a strong narrative conclusion.

Please note that excerpts and passages in the StudySync® library, workbooks, and PDFs are intended as touchstones to generate interest in an author's work. The excerpts and passages do not substitute for the reading of entire texts, and StudySync® strongly recommends that teachers and students seek out and purchase the whole literary or informational work in order to experience it as the author intended. Links to online resellers are available in our digital library. In addition, complete works may be ordered through an authorized reseller by filling out and returning to StudySync® the order form enclosed in this workbook.

Teacher's Edition   **409**

Core Path	Access Path
3. The definition states that a strong conclusion needs to follow logically from the narrative. Why is this important? (Sample answer: Unless the events follow in a logical order, the story can have no real meaning. In order for a theme to emerge or for a character to grow as a result of the events, the story's conclusion must bring all the elements together in a logical way.) As a reader, how would you feel if a conclusion did not follow logically? (Possible response: When the conclusion does not logically follow what has come before, I feel that I have been investing myself emotionally in the story and characters for nothing. I also feel that the writer has not done his or her job if the ending is not logical and satisfying.)	**Beyond** **Jigsaw.** If students have extra time, have each student choose a book or a movie that had a particularly memorable conclusion, good or bad. Then put students in small groups and have them share their examples and discuss the following questions: • Is there a shared element that all strong conclusions have? If so, what is it? • If not, what makes these different conclusions strong? • What makes a conclusion bad? How does a bad conclusion leave a reader or viewer feeling? Allow each group time to share their findings with the class.
	Extend **Research.** Pair or group students and have them research the *deus ex machina* device in conclusions. Have groups answer the following questions: • What is *deus ex machina*? Where does the idea come from? • What are some criticisms of the device? • What are some contemporary examples of this device? How does the same idea manifest itself differently in modern works?

2. MODEL

Core Path	Access Path
Read and Discuss. As students read the Model text use these questions to help students understand how to craft conclusions: 1. The Model discusses the conclusion to "Lady Letha, Knight of Mordred." According to the Model, what other stories end with the death of the hero? (*Le Morte d'Arthur, Beowulf*) What stories can you think of that end with the death of a main character? (e.g., *The Fault in Our Stars, Divergent* series) 2. What descriptive details does the author of "Lady Letha, Knight of Mordred" use in the conclusion? What is the effect of this language? (Descriptive details such as "life-force" and "Through the haze of fatigue and pain" make the final battle between Arthur and Mordred dramatic.) 3. What resolution does the conclusion provide for the narrative? (Letha dies protecting Mordred.) Is it a satisfying conclusion? Why or why not? (Answers will vary but should include whether or not the conclusion is logical based on previous events, the statements made by the narrator over the course of the narrative, and the development of the theme. Answers may also include a mention of the irony that Letha will not have the fame that Arthur has.)	**Beginner, Intermediate & Approaching** **Answer the Questions.** Have students look at the questions on the Access 1, 2, and 4 handouts before reading the Model. Then ask them to answer the questions about the conclusion to "Lady Letha, Knight of Mordred." Tell students that they can use these questions to guide them in writing their own conclusions to their hero narratives. **Advanced** **Identify the Parts.** Have students read the student model conclusion and answer the questions on the Access 3 handout. Once they've completed the questions, pair Advanced students with more proficient students to allow them to share their answers.
Practice. 1. Ask students to complete a short writing assignment and apply the skills they have learned for writing a conclusion for their narratives.	**Beginner & Approaching** **Write Your Conclusion.** 1. Prior to having them write their conclusions, ask students to complete the sentence frames on the Access 1 and 4 handouts.

Core Path	Access Path
2. Remind students that they have had an opportunity to create a hero, write map to describe characters, point of view, setting, the sequence of plot events, and draft an introduction. Now students will think about how they will use these elements to create a logical conclusion. 3. Students will be able to use either this conclusion or a revised version when they write the full draft of their narratives. Point out that although their conclusions may change, having an eye toward how the hero narrative will end may help guide the writing. 4. Students can complete this draft of their conclusions on paper, or you can create a Write Assignment on StudySync, and they can submit their drafts online for anonymous peer review.	2. After students have answered the questions, ask them to discuss with a partner what they plan to write about, clarifying any language as needed before writing their conclusions. 3. Then students should write their own conclusions on the lines at the end of the Access 1 and 4 handouts, including everything from their sentence frames and discussions. Encourage them to refer back to the writing prompt and to the Plan Worksheet they completed. **Intermediate** **Finish Sentences.** Have students fill in the sentence frames in the Apply section of the Access 2 handout. Review their answers with them, and after making any clarifications needed, allow them to use their answers to write their conclusions. Then allow them to join Advanced students to discuss and edit their conclusions. **Advanced** **Clarify and Edit.** Have students refer to their Plan Worksheet and the writing prompt as they write their conclusions. Have them read their conclusion aloud to another Intermediate or Advanced student to check for language that needs to be clarified and to answer the following questions: • Does the conclusion resolve the conflict and all events of the narrative? • Does what happens to the hero follow logically from the events of the story and his or her own character traits? • Which sentence or sentences provoke an emotional response in the reader? • Which sentence or sentences provide the reader with a sentence of closure? • Have you used grammar such as pronouns, prepositions, and subject/verb agreement correctly? Allow students time to make edits to their conclusions as necessary.

Core Path	Access Path
	Extend **View.** Show clips from two movies with very different conclusions. (A Disney movie, like *Frozen*, works well for a movie with all loose ends tied up, and a movie such as *Inception* or *The Dark Knight Rises* for an open-ended conclusion.) As a class, discuss why the writers of the movie went in those directions. With what different feelings do the conclusions leave the viewers? What purpose does each ending serve?
	Extend **Analyze and Discuss a Quote.** "Ending a novel is almost like putting a child to sleep - it can't be done abruptly." (Colm Tóibín, novelist, from an <u>interview</u> in *The Guardian*) 1. What do you think this quote means? 2. Do you agree with this quote? Why or why not? 3. What challenges do you face when writing a conclusion?

3. YOUR TURN

Core Path	Access Path
Assess and Explain. Have students answer the comprehension questions to test for understanding. Share the explanations for Part A and B (located online) with your students.	
	Extend **Write.** Have students rewrite the conclusion to *Le Morte d'Arthur*, removing the possibility that Arthur is going to come back. Have students share their new conclusions with a partner and discuss the tone the new conclusion would give the text as a whole.

Please note that excerpts and passages in the StudySync® library, workbooks, and PDFs are intended as touchstones to generate interest in an author's work. The excerpts and passages do not substitute for the reading of entire texts, and StudySync® strongly recommends that teachers and students seek out and purchase the whole literary or informational work in order to experience it as the author intended. Links to online resellers are available in our digital library. In addition, complete works may be ordered through an authorized reseller by filling out and returning to StudySync® the order form enclosed in this workbook.

Teacher's Edition   **413**

EXTENDED WRITING PROJECT:
Draft

OVERVIEW

This lesson asks students to write the drafts of their hero narratives. To do so, students will use the lists and Story Structure Maps they completed in the Prewrite lesson as well as the summaries, organizers or outlines they created to help them assemble and structure a narrative. As students draft, they will focus especially on crafting an introduction that grabs the reader's attention and a conclusion that resolves the conflict. Before they submit their drafts, students should check to be sure they have fully addressed the writing prompt.

OBJECTIVES

1. Demonstrate understanding of the features of narrative writing, including narrative techniques, sequencing, introductions, and conclusions.
2. Draft a narrative that displays effective narrative techniques, well-structured event sequences, and a strong introduction and conclusion.
3. Participate effectively in a range of conversations and collaborations to express ideas and build upon the ideas of others.

   ELA Common Core Standards:
   Writing - W.11-12.3.A, W.11-12.3.B, W.11-12.3.C, W.11-12.3.E, W.11-12.4, W.11-12.5, W.11-12.6, W.11-12.10
   Speaking & Listening - SL.11-12.1.A, SL.11-12.1.B, SL.11-12.1.C, SL.11-12.1.D
   Language - L.11-12.1

RESOURCES

Grammar handout: Misplaced Modifiers
Access 1 handout (Beginner)
Access 2 handout (Intermediate)
Access 3 handout (Advanced)
Access 4 handout (Approaching)

1. WRITE

Core Path	Access Path

Core Path

Discuss. Before students begin to write, review with the class the writing prompt/directions. Have a volunteer read them aloud. Ask whether students have any questions either about the prompt or the directions. Respond to their questions, and explain the importance of addressing the prompt fully and completely. Then read aloud the peer review criteria that students will use to comment on one another's work. Students will use the feedback to develop their writing in different stages of the writing process. Point out that understanding the peer review criteria can help students focus their writing on important features of narratives.

Here are the peer review criteria for this assignment:

- How does the introduction draw the reader into the text? How effective is the introduction?

- What is the setting of the narrative? How clearly is it described?

- When is the hero introduced? Is the character well developed? Do all of his or her actions have clear motivations?

- Is the plot engaging and well paced? Are there any sections that could be sped up or slowed down?

- How does the writer build to the climax? Is the story exciting?

- How effective is the writer's conclusion? Does it effectively resolve the conflict? Are there any loose ends?

- What suggestions can you make to help the writer improve the narrative essay?

Remind students that a peer reviewer's comments are most useful when they are clear, constructive, and presented with a positive attitude. Make sure students understand your expectations for all aspects of the assignment before beginning their draft.

Access Path

Approaching & English Learners All Levels
Review Writing Draft Checklist. Read aloud the Narrative Writing Draft Checklist on the Access 1, 2, 3, and 4 handouts with students. Encourage students to circle unfamiliar words and underline anything that is confusing or unclear. Then take a few minutes to clarify unknown vocabulary, answer questions, and provide examples for any items that students do not understand. Explain that they will need to include each of these items in their writing. For each checklist item, point out an example in the student model and read it aloud.

Beyond
Critique. If students have extra time, give small groups photocopies of a narrative writing sample to collaboratively evaluate. Have them identify the elements of writing that are strong, as well as those that are weak or in need of improvement. Then ask them to generate strategies students can use when they complete their peer reviews to ensure their critiques are substantive. Have them make a list of their strategies to share with the class.

Core Path	Access Path
Organize. Remind students to refer to the plot diagram, Story Structure Map or other graphic organizer they completed in earlier Extended Writing Project lessons, as well as the sequence of events summaries they completed in the Plan lesson and drafts of their introductions and conclusions, before they begin writing. At this time, they may also want to look up the definitions of any unfamiliar vocabulary from their reading.	**Beginner & Intermediate** **Add Sequence Words to Narrative Road Map.** Before students write their draft, have them talk through their completed Essay Road Map. Have them read each paragraph or section aloud and help them identify places where they can use sequence words such as *first, then, when,* and *after* to connect ideas. Have them write the sequence words on their Narrative Road Map and then reread each section aloud with the sequence words in place.

(G) Grammar, Mechanics, and Usage. Distribute the grammar handout on misplaced modifiers. Remind students that modifiers are words or phrases that modify other words in sentences. Dangling or misplaced modifiers are confusing to readers, so writers need to correct them. Point out that dangling or misplaced modifiers often have unintended humorous consequences. Before students complete the exercise, display these examples. Guide students to make the corrections, reminding them that a phrase should be placed as closely as possible to the noun it modifies.

- Walking down the boulevard, the autumn leaves fell from the trees. (The participial phrase "Walking down the boulevard" modifies the person doing the action, not the plural noun "leaves." Correction: Walking down the boulevard, I admired the autumn leaves that fell from the trees.)

- Lying in the road, I hit a deer. (The participial phrase should modify the deer. Correction: I hit a deer [that was] lying in the road.)

- I saw the presents peeking into the closet. (The presents are probably not doing the peeking. "Peeking into the closet" modifies the speaker. Correction: Peeking into the closet, I saw the presents.)

Beginner
Support Grammar Comprehension.

1. Read the grammar handout aloud with students, pausing to clarify concepts as needed. Practice identifying modifiers in sentences using the following examples:

   a. The *harsh* wind hurt my *cold* hands.

   b. I watched the children *streaming onto the playground*.

   c. *After cooking all day long*, Valerie was ready for the dinner party.

Point out each modifier and the noun it modifies. Then rearrange the sentence to misplace the modifier. Explain why the sentence is no longer correct.

2. Work directly with small groups to complete the practice items by reading each sentence aloud and having students identify the modifier. Then help them to identify whether the modifier is misplaced or correctly placed.

3. Read students' drafts with them to help them identify modifiers and then check for misplaced or dangling modifiers by identifying the word being modified.

Core Path	Access Path
If students need more practice, have them work in small groups to do research online to locate other examples of dangling modifiers. Ask them to record two or three good examples and then make the needed corrections to share with the class. After students have completed the exercises, point out these two passages from the Student Model and ask students to identify the modifiers and explain how they are used correctly: More importantly, she supplied me with a sword that she said had special powers only for me. ("Only" modifies "for me" and is placed as close as possible to the word it modifies.) Through the haze of fatigue and pain I see the approach of the enemy king, one of the few men still able to fight. ("Through the haze of fatigue and pain" modifies the speaker, "I." At the end of the sentence, "one of the few men still able to fight" modifies "enemy king" and is placed as close as possible to the noun it modifies.) Finally, ask students to make sure as they write that all their modifiers are clear and placed correctly as they prepare to revise.	**Intermediate** **Support Grammar Comprehension.** Have Intermediate students join with Beginner students for the instruction portion of the lesson. Then allow them to work with an Advanced or English proficient partner to complete the practice items and check their drafts for misplaced or dangling modifiers. Remind students that they should be identifying the word being modified as they read their narratives. **Advanced** **Check for Correct Modifier Use.** Have Advanced students complete the practice items individually, and check and discuss their answers with an English proficient partner. Then have them check their draft for correct modifier use. Remind students that they should be identifying the word being modified as they review their narratives. **Approaching** **Partner Work.** Check in with Approaching students before they complete the grammar exercise. Ask them to explain what they understand about misplaced or dangling modifiers, and offer clarification as necessary. Allow them to complete the practice items with a partner. When they are done, have them check and discuss their answers. Have them continue working with their partner to check their drafts for correct modifier use together. Remind students that they should be identifying the word being modified as they review their essay.

Core Path	Access Path
Write. Ask students to complete the writing assignment. Once they have completed their draft, they should click "Submit."	**Beginner** **Write with Support.** Preview the Narrative Writing Draft Checklist on the Access 1 handout with students before they write. Then have students use their completed Essay Road Map to complete their draft with teacher support as needed. Before they write each paragraph, ask students to state orally what they want to say in each paragraph. They can do this in small groups with support from the teacher or in pairs with an on-level partner who can provide quality feedback. Talking through their writing before they put pen to paper will help them clarify their language and use of sequence words before they write. **Intermediate & Advanced** **Use Sequence Words.** Have students use the Narrative Writing Draft Checklist on the Access 2 and 3 handouts as they write. Remind them to focus on using sequence words to create a clear and coherent plot. They may wish to create a list of sequence words to choose from before they begin writing.
	Approaching **Use Essay Road Map to Write a Draft.** Remind students to consult all the prewriting documents they have created—plot diagram, character descriptions, and Essay Road Map—to help them craft their narratives. It may be particularly useful for Approaching students to use their Essay Road Map to structure their writing. Explain that they can follow the order of the outline they created, but in their draft they will need to add details and develop their writing. Have them use the Narrative Writing Draft Checklist on the Access 4 handout to make sure they include a strong introduction that introduces the hero and point of view, narrative techniques, clear sequence words, and a conclusion that resolves the conflict and provides readers with a sense of closure.

Copyright © BookheadEd Learning, LLC

Core Path	Access Path
Review. Once students complete their writing assignment, they should submit substantive feedback to two peers. Students should use their peers' feedback to improve their writing.	**Beginner** **Review the Checklist.** Help students to go through the Narrative Writing Draft Checklist item-by-item on the Access 1 handout to check their writing. Provide support to help them make changes as needed. **Intermediate & Advanced** **Use Checklist.** Have mixed-proficiency partners read their completed drafts aloud to one another and use the Narrative Writing Draft Checklist on the Access 2 and 3 handouts to check their writing. Remind them to check that they used sequence words appropriately and make suggestions for how plot points could be improved or clarified.
	Extend **Draft.** If students struggle to start writing their drafts because they don't have a strong idea for an introduction, suggest that students write the introduction and conclusion last. Tell students to use the Plot Diagram and start with the rising action and come back to the introduction later.
	Extend **Critique.** After students submit their drafts, pair students and have them read any dialogue they wrote aloud to each other. Have partners critique the dialogue. Does it sound natural? What works well? Where can it be improved?
	Extend **Tech Infusion** **Record.** Students can record their dialogue and play it back using Audacity (http://audacity.sourceforge.net/) or Audioboo (https://audioboo.fm/).

OVERVIEW

As students move toward the revising stage of their Extended Writing Project, they'll need to sharpen their use of descriptive details to convey a vivid sense of characters, setting, and plot events in their narratives. This lesson identifies descriptive details and shows a variety of ways that such details can enhance a narrative.

OBJECTIVES

1. Discuss and demonstrate an understanding of descriptive and telling details, including sensory language.
2. Analyze how descriptive details develop story elements and apply this understanding to an original piece of narrative writing.
3. Participate effectively in a range of conversations and collaborations to express ideas and build upon the ideas of others.

   ELA Common Core Standards:
   Reading: Literature - RL.11-12.1
   Reading: Informational Text - RI.11-12.1
   Writing - W.11-12.3.D, W.11-12.5, W.11-12.10
   Speaking & Listening - SL.11-12.1.A, SL.11-12.1.B, SL.11-12.1.C, SL.11-12.1.D
   Language - L.11-12.1.A, L.11-12.B

RESOURCES

Access 1 handout (Beginner)

Access 2 handout (Intermediate)

Access 3 handout (Advanced)

Access 4 handout (Approaching)

1. DEFINE

Core Path	Access Path
Read and Discuss. Either individually or as a class, read the Define section of the lesson. Either in small groups or as a class use these questions to spur discussion among your students about descriptive details:	**Beginner** **In Your Own Words.** Have students read the definition and then use their Access 1 handouts to pause after each bullet point to rewrite the definition of descriptive details in their own words. Once students have completed this activity, ask them to complete the fill in the blanks activity on the Access 1 handout.

Core Path

Read and Discuss. Either individually or as a class, read the Define section of the lesson. Either in small groups or as a class use these questions to spur discussion among your students about descriptive details:

1. The definition refers to the essential aspects of descriptive language. What other ways can descriptive language enhance or develop characters, setting, and plot events? (Answers will vary but should include telling details about characters, such as characters' qualities, habits, style of dress, or ways of talking; telling details about setting, such as time period, weather, the ways a place changes over the course of day, sounds, smells, air quality, and season; telling details about plot events, such as how long something lasted, how people and places were affected, and the quality of the outcome.)

2. What sort of descriptive language in headlines, movie trailers, and other "teasers" entices you to continue reading and watching? How might you use these as models in your own writing? (Answers will vary but should include examples from various media, as well as an example of how powerful details can add a missing dynamic to their hero narratives.)

3. Discuss examples of each type of sensory language. Choose one of the hero stories you have read and write a short "trailer" for the selection incorporating sensory details to entice readers. What would your trailer say? (Answers will vary but should include sensory details that describe the plot, setting, and main character, as well as the story's title.)

Access Path

Beginner
In Your Own Words. Have students read the definition and then use their Access 1 handouts to pause after each bullet point to rewrite the definition of descriptive details in their own words. Once students have completed this activity, ask them to complete the fill in the blanks activity on the Access 1 handout.

Intermediate
In Your Own Words. Have students read the definition of descriptive details and then use their Access 2 handout to pause after each bullet point to rewrite the definition of descriptive details in their own words. After they've rewritten each of the bullet points in their words, work with students to develop their own definitions of the term.

Advanced
In Your Own Words. Have Advanced students read and then discuss what they have learned about descriptive details with an English-proficient partner or in mixed-proficiency groups. After their conversation, have Advanced students write the definition of descriptive details on the Access 3 handout.

Approaching
Restate the Definition. Have students read the define section and then use their Access 4 handouts to restate the most important points in their own words. Clarify questions to aid students' comprehension as needed. Then have students participate in mixed-level groups with the class to discuss the purpose of descriptive details in a narrative.

Core Path	Access Path
	Beyond **Jigsaw.** If students have extra time, give them a simple sentence, such as *The man looked around the room.* In pairs, have students add only descriptive details to make this sentence into an engaging story. When pairs have finished, have them share their short stories with the class. Have the class vote for the best use of descriptive details.
	Extend **Sensory walk.** Give students 10 minutes to walk outside the classroom and silently observe their campus. Ask them to record the sights, sounds, smells, tastes, and feelings they observe during their sensory walk. They should record these sensory details using vibrant language that captures the detail. Remind them to be silent so they can appreciate even the smallest details. When they return to the classroom, ask them to work in small groups to share and compare their notes. What similarities or differences existed in their lists?

2. MODEL

Core Path	Access Path
Read and Discuss. As students read the Model text, use these questions to help students understand how to analyze descriptive details: 1. The Model provides an example of descriptive details about events. What sort of word form is used to describe the event? (adjective "wonderful") 2. The Model provides an example of descriptive details about setting. What literary device is used? (imagery) 3. The Model provides an example of characterization. Which kind is used? (direct) 4. The Model provides an example of descriptive details about character experiences. To which sense does the language appeal? (touch)	**Beginner, Intermediate & Approaching** **Underline Descriptive Details.** Have students reread the excerpt from "Lady Letha, Knight of Mordred" on the Access 1, 2, and 4 handouts. Then ask them to find and underline descriptive details in the excerpt. Remind students that descriptive details help them to picture the scene and understand what the characters see, hear, smell, taste, or feel. After they have their annotations, have students look closely at where the author included descriptive details and think about how they could apply descriptive details to their own narratives. **Advanced** **Identify the Parts.** Have students read the excerpt from the student model and answer the questions on the Access 3 handout. Once they've completed the questions, pair Advanced students with more proficient students to allow them to share their answers.
⚙ **Grammar, Usage, and Mechanics.** Before students revise to their essays, explain that some rules of grammar and usage can be broken or contested for the right reasons, but in order to break a rule a writer must do so by making a deliberate, informed decision. In other words, if students break a rule or convention unknowingly, their writing will look sloppy and unrevised. If they do it deliberately for effect, to add suspense to a narrative or reveal aspects of a character, they can add dimensions to their personal style of writing. For example, point out that a sentence fragment lacks a subject, a verb, or both and is technically a grammatical error. It is certainly not acceptable to use one in formal writing, such as an informational essay or a book report. But in real life, people often speak in sentence fragments, and using them in dialogue can help writers delineate a character.	**Beginner, Intermediate & Approaching** **Work with the Teacher.** Remind these students that the kind of English they use in classroom writing assignments is often different from the language they use when talking to peers. Tell students that dialogue in narratives can bend some grammar rules in order to sound natural. Write the following sentences on the board and read them out loud: "Hello, are you ready to leave? Let us go quickly," Steven said. Ask: Do these sentences sound like the way teenagers speak? (No, it is too formal. It also would use contractions and slang.) Rewrite this dialogue to make it sound more natural. (Possible response: "Hey, you ready? Let's roll," Steven said.)

Please note that excerpts and passages in the StudySync® library, workbooks, and PDFs are intended as touchstones to generate interest in an author's work. The excerpts and passages do not substitute for the reading of entire texts, and StudySync® strongly recommends that teachers and students seek out and purchase the whole literary or informational work in order to experience it as the author intended. Links to online resellers are available in our digital library. In addition, complete works may be ordered through an authorized reseller by filling out and returning to StudySync® the order form enclosed in this workbook.

Teacher's Edition   423

Core Path	Access Path
Then point out other issues of contested usage; for example, the use of the word *like* as opposed to *as if* to indicate a comparison. Write the phrases *the enemy appears out of the fog like evil ghosts* and *Nightshade moved as if it had a mind of its own,* both from the student model, on the board. Have a volunteer read both phrases aloud and then ask if the word *like* could be substituted for *as if* in the second phrase. Explain that the word *like* should be used only as a verb or as a preposition. The word *as* and the words *as if* are subordinate conjunctions when used to introduce a clause in a sentence. Remind students that a clause is a group of words with its own subject and verb, and that sentences can contain more than one clause. So *as if* is correct in the second instance as it precedes the clause *it had a mind of its own.* The word *like* would be incorrect in the second phrase, but is correct usage in the phrase *the enemy appears out of the fog like evil ghosts* as it is used as a preposition to compare two unlike things. Tell students that they can check credible online and book reference sources as needed to resolve issues of complex or contested usage. Remind them to look for books and sites from reputable publishing or educational institutions. Key words and phrases, such as "usage like versus as if," can get them started on a search.	Allow time for students to share their completed sentences. **Advanced & Beyond** **Extend the Search.** Point out to these students that "Lady Letha, Knight of Mordred" uses a formal style, which is consistent with the character of Letha and her time period. Challenge these students to work in pairs or small groups to rewrite a paragraph from the text in a style more consistent with a contemporary young woman.
Practice. Have students draft a paragraph or two of their story to include telling details and sensory language to convey a vivid picture of the experiences, events, setting, and characters in their narrative. They can write their draft on paper in the classroom or online. If they write online, create a Write Assignment in StudySync with directions.	**Beginner** **Add Descriptive Details.** 1. Prior to having them revise their paragraph, ask students to complete the chart on the Access 1 handout. 2. After students have completed the chart, ask them to discuss with a partner what details they plan to add. Have students discuss if there are other options for each sense that might work better in the paragraph.

Core Path	Access Path
Once students have completed their draft, ask them to exchange papers and provide peer feedback online. Students should focus on their peers' use of telling details and sensory language as well as their ability to create either direct or indirect characterizations. Once they have received peer feedback, students should use the comments they received to improve their writing.	3. Then students should revise their paragraph by adding at least two descriptive details from their charts. Remind students that they do not need to cover every sense in every paragraph. **Intermediate** **Finish Sentences.** Have students fill in the chart on the Access 2 handout. Review their answers with them, and after making any clarifications needed, allow them to use their answers to revise their draft. Then allow them to join Advanced students to discuss and edit their descriptive details. **Advanced** **Clarify and Edit.** Have students refer to their Plan Worksheet and the writing prompt as they revise their draft to add descriptive details. Have them read their paragraph aloud to another Intermediate or Advanced student to check for language that needs to be clarified and to answer the following questions: • Which senses do the details appeal to? • Do the descriptive details help the reader visualize the scene? • Are there more effective ways to describe a scene or object? • Have you used grammar such as commas and modifiers correctly? Allow students time to make edits to their paragraphs as necessary.

Core Path	Access Path
	Approaching **Complete the Chart & Add Descriptive Details.** 1. Prior to having them revise their drafts, ask students to complete the chart on the Access 4 handout. 2. Once they have completed the chart with descriptive details for each sense, allow them to revise their drafts. Encourage students to add at least two of the descriptive details from the chart, and to add more if it makes sense. Remind students that it can be overwhelming to a reader when a writer covers every sense in every paragraph, so they should be selective.
	Extend **Create.** 1. Pair or group students and have them choose a piece of art with which they are familiar. If they are stuck, allow them time to explore the National Gallery of Art website (www.NGA.gov) or the Louvre (www.louvre.fr/en). 2. Ask students to use descriptive details to describe the nuances of the piece of artwork they've chosen to their partner. 3. The student listening to the description should close their eyes, so the person describing the artwork is forced to use descriptive details to help their partner imagine the piece of art.

3. YOUR TURN

Core Path	Access Path
Assess and Explain. Have students answer the comprehension questions to test for understanding. Share the explanations for Part A and B (located online) with your students.	
	Extend **Discussion.** Have students focus on the image in the Your Turn passage of Mordred's army: "wilting along with that of the enemy." Have them discuss what this descriptive detail suggests about the event. (Encourage them to discuss the meaning of the word "wilting" along with the imagery and other sensory details they associate with it.)

EXTENDED WRITING PROJECT:
Revise

OVERVIEW

This lesson asks students to revise their narratives. Students will think about the steps and skills they have applied to narrative writing, and they will review the feedback they have received. They'll reread the drafts of their narratives in order to begin their revision. Students are instructed to use the descriptive details that they completed in the previous lesson.

OBJECTIVES

1. Devise a plan for making revisions to a narrative essay.
2. Revise a narrative text to improve descriptive details.
3. Participate effectively in a range of conversations and collaborations to express ideas and build upon the ideas of others.
4. Learn and practice strategies for using hyphenation correctly.

ELA Common Core Standards:
Writing - W.11-12.3.A, W.11-12.3.B, W.11-12.3.D, W.11-12.4, W.11-12.5, W.11-12.6
Speaking & Listening - SL.11-12.1.C
Language - L.11-12.1, L.11-12.2.A

RESOURCES

Grade 12, Unit 1 Extended Writing Project: Revise lesson

Grammar handout: Hyphenation Conventions

Access 1 handout (Beginner)

Access 2 handout (Intermediate)

Access 3 handout (Advanced)

Access 4 handout (Approaching)

Copyright © BookheadEd Learning, LLC

1. WRITE

Core Path	Access Path
Discuss. Before students begin to revise, review with the class the writing prompt/directions. Ask whether students have any questions either about the prompt or the revision process. Respond to their questions, and explain the importance of thoughtful, focused revisions. Then read aloud the peer review criteria that students will use to comment on one another's revision. The peer review criteria for this assignment are these: • The revision should fully address previous peer comments on issues, such as the clarity of the structure and the effectiveness of the introduction and conclusion. • The revision should sharpen the descriptive details and make them precise and vivid. • The revision should make the story more specific and describe all events and characters in a way that helps readers visualize them. • The revision should fully achieve the purpose of a narrative essay. Remind students that a peer reviewer's comments are most useful when they are clear, constructive, and presented with a positive attitude. Make sure students understand your expectations for all aspects of the assignment before beginning their revision.	**Beginner, Intermediate & Approaching** **Review the Revision Checklist.** Read aloud the Narrative Writing Revision Checklist with students. As the teacher reads each item on the checklist, students should read along on their Access 1, 2, and 4 handouts. Encourage students to circle unfamiliar words and underline anything that is confusing or unclear. Then take a few minutes to clarify unknown vocabulary, answer questions, and provide examples for any items that students do not understand. Explain to students that they will need to check their own writing for each of these items. **Advanced** **Read and Discuss.** Pair Advanced students with an on-level partner and ask them to review the Narrative Writing Revision Checklist. Allow time for them to discuss each item to ensure the students understand what they are being asked to do.

Core Path	Access Path

Core Path

(G) **Grammar, Usage, and Mechanics.** Distribute the grammar handout on hyphenation. Have students review the examples of correct hyphen usage on the handout before completing the practice exercise. (Answers for the practice exercise appear at the end of lesson plan online.) After students have completed the exercise, point out these two passages from the Student Model and ask students to explain whether the hyphen is used correctly:

While the sun rises, the fog vanishes and the glint of sunlight off the warriors' armor is like the lightning that accompanies the thunder of hundreds of sword-strikes. ("Sword-strikes" is a compound used as a noun. "Sword-strikes" is not in the dictionary, so there is no clear rule for it. However, it is clearer if hyphenated.)

We struggle in hand-to-hand combat with those knights till twilight. ("Hand-to-hand" is used as an adjective. The general rule is for adjective forms to be hyphenated, so this construction is correct.)

Access Path

Beginner
Support Grammar/Usage Comprehension.

1. Read the grammar handout aloud with students, pausing to clarify concepts as needed. Demonstrate the proper use of hyphenation conventions by using a three sample sentences: hyphens in compound words, in a series of modifiers, and with prefixes. Then have students locate more examples with one another in small groups.

2. Work directly with small groups to complete the practice items by reading the sentences aloud and having students write the word correctly, using a dictionary if necessary.

3. Read students' drafts with them to help them identify where hyphens should have been, or could be included to clarify the writing and to create increasingly detailed sentences.

Intermediate
Support Grammar/Usage Comprehension. Have Intermediate students join with Beginner students for the instruction portion of the lesson. Then allow them to work with an Advanced or English proficient partner to complete the practice items and check their drafts for correct usage of hyphens to create detailed sentences.

Advanced
Check for Correct Usage. Have Advanced students complete the practice items individually, and check and discuss their answers with an English proficient partner. Then have them check their draft for correct usage of hyphens to create more detailed sentences.

Core Path	Access Path
	Approaching **Partner Work.** Check in with Approaching students before they complete the grammar handout. Ask them to explain what they understand about hyphenation conventions. Allow them to complete the practice items with a partner. When they are done, have them check and discuss their answers. Have them continue working with their partner to check their drafts for correct usage of hyphens.
Highlight. Each student should start this activity with a copy of his or her draft either printed on paper or open in a word-processing program. Students will conduct three rereads of their own paper, each with a different focus. Students should choose two colors that they will use to mark their drafts, designating one color for vague descriptions and one for precise descriptions. Instruct them to create a key that shows the two colors they have chosen and to mark it at the top of their paper. 1. First, have students use their designated colors to mark any places where they used vague descriptions and precise descriptions. 2. Next, have students read through their drafts again. Have them look for places where they could have been more specific or used more vivid descriptions. Challenge them to find at least two places where they can improve their descriptions. They should **circle** these places with the appropriate color of highlighter. 3. Finally, instruct them to take a pen or pencil (or add comments to their drafts, if they're on a computer) and write their ideas for each section that needs improvement. If students are struggling to decide what to change, remind them to use previous peer suggestions or to work with their peers to come up with ideas.	**English Learners All Levels & Approaching Mixed-Level Partner Editing.** Have all students form mixed-level pairs in which partners vary one level up or down from one another. Then have them work together on their drafts to identify and highlight areas they need to improve when they edit their drafts.

Core Path	Access Path
	Extend **Organize.** Encourage students to complete a graphic organizer to organize their ideas before they make their revisions. (Suggest that students create a table or other organizer to keep track of their revisions relating to each writing skill lesson they have worked through up to this point.)
Write. Ask students to complete the revision including precise language and strong descriptions as needed. Once they have completed their writing, they should click "Submit."	**English Learners All Levels** **Use Checklist.** Have all English Learners use the Narrative Writing Revision Checklist to help guide their revisions. Provide additional differentiated support as indicated below. **Beginner** **Focus on Pronoun Usage.** Focus on maintaining a consistent point of view in a narrative using pronouns. Walk students through the activity on the Access 1 handout. Then have them join in the discussion of narrative writing and point of view with Intermediate students (below). Afterward, help them to check their writing for correct pronoun usage and to find and eliminate places where they have incorrectly used pronouns. **Intermediate** **Focus on Pronoun Usage.** Have Intermediate students participate in the pronoun activity on the Access 2 handout. Then display the following sentences from the student model: I feel strong, and <u>my</u> brothers-in-arms are showing great courage as <u>they</u> prepare to face the enemy this morning. <u>We</u> are to meet on the field at Camlann.

Core Path	Access Path
	Remind students that, in narrative writing, the pronouns used are a clue to the narrative point of view. If a narrative does not use a consistent point of view throughout, the reader may be confused. Help students to identify the underlined pronouns in the sentences. Explain that most of the pronouns signal a first-person point of view: *I, my, we*. Point out that the third-person pronoun *they* is used to describe a group that the narrator is not a part of and so is not a mistake.
	Discuss how the proper use of pronouns in third-person narrative point of view. Then have partners review their own writing for correct use of pronouns with teacher assistance as needed.
	Advanced **Use Descriptive Language.**
	1. Ask students to work with an English-proficient partner to identify and underline places in their essay where descriptive language could be added or revised to be made more clear or vivid.
	2. Then have them use the two-column chart on the Access 3 handout to list words students underlined in their essay that need revision and brainstorm a list of replacement and new descriptive details.
	3. Give them time to discuss which details are strongest (to help the reader visualize or understand the scene) and choose the best to include in their narrative essay.

Core Path	Access Path
	Approaching **Practice Editing.** 1. Approaching students should practice identifying instances of pronoun errors, phrases that could be replaced with more descriptive language, hyphenation errors, and places where they need to include additional sequence words, using the exercise on the Access 4 handout. 2. After they edit the example paragraph, allow them to work with an on-level partner to read through their own drafts. They should focus on identifying and underlining instances of pronoun errors, phrases that could be replaced with more descriptive language, hyphenation errors, and places where they need to include additional sequence words in their own writing. 3. Then have them make their revisions independently. Have them check their revised essay against the Narrative Revision Checklist before they submit their revision.
	Extend **Critique.** Project a writing sample on the board and ask the class to identify the elements of writing that are strong, as well as those that are weak or in need of improvement. Alternatively, you can put students in small groups and give them photocopies of a writing sample to collaboratively evaluate. After students have had an opportunity to evaluate student samples, work as a class to generate strategies students can use as they complete their peer reviews to ensure they are substantive.

Core Path	Access Path
Review. Once students complete their writing assignment, they should submit substantive feedback to two peers.	**Beginner** **Review with Teacher Support.** As a small group, help students to go through the Narrative Writing Revision Checklist on the Access 1 handout item-by-item to review one another's writing. Provide individual support to help them make changes as needed. **Intermediate & Advanced** **Use Checklist.** Have mixed-proficiency partners read their completed drafts aloud to one another and use the Narrative Writing Revision Checklist on the Access 2 and 3 handouts to check that their writing includes all of the required revisions. With teacher guidance as necessary, encourage them to suggest ways their partner could make any needed changes. **Approaching** **Use Checklist.** Have partners use the Narrative Writing Revision Checklist on the Access 4 handout to make sure their completed revisions include all the necessary elements.

BLAST:
Precise Language

OVERVIEW

As they move toward the final stage of their narrative, students will learn about how precise language improves a piece of writing.

OBJECTIVES

1. Explore background information about precise language in narrative writing.
2. Read examples of precise language in a student model essay.
3. Participate effectively in a range of conversations and collaborations to express ideas and build upon the ideas of others.

ELA Common Core Standards:

Reading: Informational Text - RI.11-12.1
Writing - W.11-12.3.A, W.11-12.3.D, W.11-12.5, W.11-12.6, W.11-12.10
Speaking & Listening - SL.11-12.1.A, SL.11-12.1.B, SL.11-12.1.C, SL.11-12.1.D, SL.11-12.2

RESOURCES

Access 1 handout (Beginner)

Access 2 handout (Intermediate)

Access 4 handout (Approaching)

TITLE/DRIVING QUESTION

Core Path	Access Path
Discuss. As a class, read aloud the title and driving question for this Blast: How can I use precise language to make my narrative more engaging? Ask students why precise language makes a story more engaging or realistic than vague language does. What do they already know about the importance of precise language in a narrative? Can they think of a good example of a vivid description from a book or story they've read? Taking into account ideas generated by their classmates, do they have a sense of how they can use precise language to make their narrative more engaging? Remind students that they'll be returning to this question and responding after they've read the Background.	**English Learners All Levels** **Discuss a Visual.** Have students view an image of a confusing or contradictory road sign, such as the one at: http://tinyurl.com/pjakpqy. Discuss how the picture represents a lack of precise language, prompting students with questions such as: • What is this sign telling people to do? • Is it clear? If not, how could it be clarified? • Why is it important for a road sign to be clear? • What are some other examples of times when precision is important?
Draft. In their notebooks or on scrap paper, have students draft their initial responses to the driving question. This will provide them with a baseline response that they will be altering as they gain more information about the topic in the Background section of the assignment.	**Beginner & Intermediate** **Draft with Sentence Frame.** When drafting their initial response to the driving question, have students refer to this Blast sentence frame on their Access 1 and 2 handouts: • One way I can use precise language to make my narrative more engaging is _____. Point out these two key features of the sentence frame: 1. The phrase "my narrative" is a clue that students should think about the narrative they are writing for this extended writing project and provide a specific answer for this text. 2. The opening phrase "one way" tells students they should only include one example in their Blast response. However, they should consider how to add precise language throughout their narrative in the editing stage.

BACKGROUND

Core Path	Access Path
Read. Have students read the Blast background to provide context for the driving question: How can I use precise language to make my narrative more engaging?	**Beginner & Intermediate** **Read with Support.** Have students read the Blast background to provide context for the driving question. When they encounter unfamiliar words or phrases, have students refer to the glossary on their Access 1 and 2 handouts. If there are unfamiliar words that are not included in their glossary, encourage students to check a dictionary or online reference tool, like http://dictionary.reference.com. **Approaching** **Read and Summarize.** Have students read the Blast background to provide context for the driving question. As they read, ask students to complete the fill-in-the-blank summary of the background provided on their Access 4 handout. When they encounter unfamiliar words or phrases, have students refer to the glossary on their Access 4 handout.
Discuss. Pair students and have them discuss the following questions: 1. What is the difference between denotation and connotation? (The "denotation" is the dictionary definition of a word; "connotation" is the feelings, associations, or images we connect with a word.) Give an example of a few words that have the same denotation but different connotations. (Answers will vary but should provide two words [e.g., "skinny" and "lean," to compare].) How might choosing words based on their connotation change the tone of a story? (Possible response: Words with a negative connotation, such as "skinny," can give a text a negative tone, whereas words with a positive connotation, such as "lean," may create a positive tone. Either tone may be appropriate, but the writer needs to understand the power of precise words.)	**Beginner** **Discuss.** Pair Beginner with Advanced (or Beyond) students and have them use the dialogue starter on their Access 1 handout to discuss the topic. Advise them to return to the dialogue and switch roles if they get stuck. **Intermediate** **Discuss.** Pair Intermediate with Advanced (or Beyond) students and have them use the dialogue starter on their Access 2 handout to discuss the topic. Advise them to return to the dialogue and switch roles if they get stuck. If their conversation is progressing smoothly, encourage them to continue the discussion beyond the dialogue starter sheet. They can expand their conversations to discuss other reasons why precise language is important in a narrative.

Core Path	Access Path
2. The background identifies examples of precise language with military connotations used in the Model. What other words in the model reinforce the military theme of the passage? (Students should point out the author's word choices with terms like "draws," "formation," and "charge." These words have military connotations.) 3. How does figurative language relate to the author's use of precise language and sensory details? (Students may say that figurative language is another way an author might choose to present images and information. In the passage, the author uses a simile to compare the enemy in the fog to evil ghosts.) 4. What other sensory details might an author provide? How would you work one of those details into this passage? (An author might also provide details that link to the other senses, such as smell, touch, and taste. The author of this passage could have provided more detail about how the grass smelled or how the mist felt on Lady Letha's face.)	
Brainstorm. Have students write a paragraph that describes a moment in a movie or story with which they are very familiar. (For instance, students might choose to describe what Elsa felt and did during the scene in the movie *Frozen* when she leaves Arendelle to build her own ice palace in the mountains.) Students should include as many sensory details and precise words as possible to describe what the character saw, felt, heard, smelled, tasted, or did, as appropriate to the scene. Next, have students underline their sensory details and use a thesaurus or dictionary to find synonyms that might provide more precise words choices to convey the sensory experiences. Have students share their work and provide feedback to each other about how the use of precise words could be improved.	

Core Path	Access Path
	Extend **Tech Infusion** **Blog.** Have students post their reviewed passages to the class blog. If possible, have students acquire—or create—images from the movie or story to accompany their posts.

QUIKPOLL

Core Path	Access Path
Participate. Answer the poll question. Have students use information from the background and research links to explain their answers.	
	Extend **Listen.** Pair or group students and have them choose a song that uses precise language or sensory details (e.g., "Royals" by Lorde, and "Lego House" by Ed Sheeran). Require students to explain why they chose each song. Ask students to quote from the lyrics in their explanations. Also require students to identify how the music enhances the descriptive details of the words. Allow students the opportunity to share their songs and rationales with other groups or the class.

NUMBER CRUNCH

Core Path	Access Path
Predict, Discuss, and Click. Before students click on the number, break them into pairs and have them make predictions about what they think the number is related to. After they've clicked the number, ask students if they are surprised by the revealed information.	

CREATE YOUR BLAST

Core Path	Access Path
Blast. Ask students to write their Blast response in 140 characters or less.	**Beginner** **Blast with Support.** Have students refer back to the sentence frame on their Access 1 handout that they used to create their original Blast draft. Ask them to use this frame to write and enter their final Blast. **Intermediate** **Blast with Support.** Have students attempt to draft their Blast without the sentence frame on their Access 2 handout. If students struggle to compose their Blast draft without the sentence frame, remind them to reference it for support. **Beyond** **Write for Sense.** Ask students to use their answer to the poll question by writing a detailed descriptive sentence using the sense they selected. Have them describe, in precise language, the same scene, such as an event at school. Once students have written their descriptions, ask them to read them to a small group of their peers. This activity will provide them practice writing details, as well as expose them to details written by their peers.
Review. After students have completed their own Blasts, ask them to review the Blasts of their peers and provide feedback.	
	Extend **Discuss.** As a whole class or in groups, identify a few strong Blasts and discuss what made those responses so powerful. As a group, analyze and discuss what characteristics make a Blast interesting or effective.

Core Path	Access Path
	Extend **Revise.** Resend a second version of this Blast assignment to your students and have them submit revised versions of their original Blasts. Do the same responses make the Top 10? How have the answers improved from the first submissions?

EXTENDED WRITING PROJECT:
Edit/Proofread/Publish

OVERVIEW

This lesson asks students to edit, proofread, and publish the revised and corrected version of their hero narrative. Students are instructed to edit for final improvements in narrative techniques, precise language, and structure, and to proofread for the correct use of grammar, spelling, and punctuation. Finally, students are encouraged to explore ways of publishing their work.

OBJECTIVES

1. Identify editing, proofreading, and publishing skills.
2. Edit and proofread text to finalize information, organization, language, and style, and to eliminate errors in grammar, punctuation, and spelling.
3. Use technology to produce and publish writing.
4. Participate effectively in a range of conversations and collaborations to express ideas and build upon the ideas of others.
5. Learn and practice strategies for following basic spelling rules.

ELA Common Core Standards:
Writing - W.11-12.3.A, W.11-12.3.B, W.11-12.3.C, W.11-12.3.D, W.11-12.3.E, W.11-12.4, W.11-12.5, W.11-12.6, W.11-12.10
Speaking & Listening - SL.11-12.1.A
Language - L.11-12.1.A, L.11-12.1.B, L.11-12.2.A, L.11-12.2.B, L.11-12.3.A

RESOURCES

Grade 12, Unit 1 Extended Writing Project: Edit/Proofread/Publish lesson

Grammar handout: Basic Spelling Rules I and II

Access 1 handout (Beginner)

Access 2 handout (Intermediate)

Access 3 handout (Advanced)

Access 4 handout (Approaching)

Please note that excerpts and passages in the StudySync® library, workbooks, and PDFs are intended as touchstones to generate interest in an author's work. The excerpts and passages do not substitute for the reading of entire texts, and StudySync® strongly recommends that teachers and students seek out and purchase the whole literary or informational work in order to experience it as the author intended. Links to online resellers are available in our digital library. In addition, complete works may be ordered through an authorized reseller by filling out and returning to StudySync® the order form enclosed in this workbook.

Teacher's Edition   **443**

1. WRITE

Core Path	Access Path
Test. Have students analyze their writing by using an online writing tool such as The Writers Diet Test (http://www.writersdiet.com/WT.php) to determine if their writing is "fit & trim" or "flabby." Students can download the "Full Diagnosis" and follow the suggestions for revision given there. Make sure students understand that the application by itself might make suggestions that do not improve the narrative. Students will need to exercise judgment as they review suggestions for changes. In particular, have them edit and proofread for the following:	**English Learners All Levels** **Use Technology to Check Clarity.** Have students conduct a check for the clarity of their writing using Hemingway (www.hemingwayapp.com). This app is designed to make the writing clear and concise. It will suggest eliminating embellishments and revising syntax for readability. Emphasize, however, that the app's suggestions may not be consistent with what the writer wishes to say. There is no substitute for the writer's own judgment.

- Correct syntax

- Understanding of grammatical conventions, aware of contested usage and the need to check reference sources as needed

- Correct use of modifiers

- Correct use of "like" and "as if," and similarly confused transitions

- Correct use of hyphens, when needed

- Errors in grammar and spelling

Core Path	Access Path
Discuss. Before students begin to edit, review with the class the writing prompt and directions. Have a volunteer read them aloud. Ask whether students have any questions either about the prompt or the process of editing and proofreading. Respond to their questions and then review criteria that can help students make final adjustments and corrections in their texts. Remind students that: • The text should reflect skill in narrative writing, including features such as a clear structure, narrative techniques, and precise word choice. • The text should have a clear plot that builds to a climax and concludes with a resolution. • The text should include narrative techniques, such as dialogue, pacing, and character development. • The text should use hyphens correctly. • The text should be free from other errors in syntax, grammar, punctuation, and spelling. Before students make final adjustments to their narratives, take a few minutes and brainstorm publishing ideas with them. Students have already been using technology to create, revise, and submit their work on StudySync, as well as to collaborate with their peers. Now, students will want to share information with one another about additional appropriate online publication opportunities, as well as about possible print outlets for their work. Ask students to collaborate on creating a list of these opportunities and outlets for their own use to help them when they are ready to publish.	**Beginner** **Use Writing Support.** Walk Beginner students through the Proofreading Checklist on the Access 1 handout item-by-item. Help them to identify and underline the sections of their narrative they will need to edit. **Intermediate** **Use Checklist.** Have Intermediate students preview the Proofreading Checklist on the Access 2 handout before they begin their final editing process. Make sure they understand everything on the checklist. As needed, help individual students identify the items on the checklist that they need to pay special attention to as they edit their narrative. **Approaching** **Support Proofreading.** Walk students through each item on the Proofreading Checklist on the Access 4 handout. Encourage students to circle unfamiliar words and underline anything that is confusing or unclear. Then take a few minutes to clarify unknown vocabulary, answer questions, and provide examples for any items that students do not understand. If you have identified individual students' challenges, circle those items on the checklist that they need to pay special attention to and provide individual support, or pair them with an on- or above-level student to make their final edits.

Core Path

(G) Grammar, Usage, and Mechanics. Distribute the grammar handout on basic spelling rules. Explain to students that understanding basic spelling rules can help them edit quickly and effectively. Have students review the examples on the handout before completing the practice exercise. (Answers for the practice exercise appear online.) After students have completed the exercise, point out these two passages from the Student Model and ask students to identify the word that follows one of the spelling rules and explain why it is spelled correctly:

Though we have been keeping Sir Mordred safe, Sir Lucan is edging closer and closer to him. ("Closer" is made up of *close + er.* "Close" has a final silent e that is dropped when a suffix that begins with a vowel, like *-er* is added.)

I feel my life force slipping away. ("Slipping" is made up of *slip + ing.* "Slip" is a one syllable word, so the final consonant needs to be doubled.)

Remind students that spelling rules change over time. For example, the former doubling of the "t" in *benefitting* is now considered nonstandard in American English, and the word is generally spelled *benefiting.* When in doubt, students should check reliable reference sources for standard spellings.

Ask students to reread their narratives to make sure that they followed all spelling rules. Remind students that a spell-checker is a valuable tool, but it does not catch all spelling errors. For example, point out that misplaced homophones such as *there, their,* and *they're* are usage errors that a spell-checker will not catch.

Access Path

Beginner & Intermediate
Identify the Silent e. Have students join in as you review the basic spelling rules with the class. Then in small groups have them complete the exercises on the Access 1 and 2 handouts by identifying the words with a silent e. Encourage them to read each word aloud several times, listening to the sound at the end of the word. Circulate among the groups, helping them identify whether the e is silent. When their work is complete, check their answers. Review any incorrect answers by reading the words aloud and helping students to identify the sound at the end.

Advanced
Work with a Partner. After the instruction, have Advanced students complete the exercise with an English proficient partner. Encourage them to check a dictionary for any words they both find challenging.

Approaching
Support Understanding. Read aloud the instruction portion of the handout with students, focusing on the rules for words with a silent e sound. Explain that when they say a word with a silent e, they will not hear an e sound. Ask: What sound do you hear at the end of the word line? (*n* sound) Have them point out the words on the worksheet that have a silent e sound. Then have them complete the exercise and check their answers with an on-level partner.

Extend
Organize. Encourage students to complete a graphic organizer to organize their editing, proofreading, and publishing task. (Suggest that students create checklist or workflow document.)

Core Path	Access Path
Write. Ask students to complete the writing assignment. Suggest, if there's time, that they set their narratives aside for a few minutes, and that they then proofread it one more time. Remind students to use the feedback they have received throughout the writing process to develop and strengthen their writing. Once they have completed their writing, they should click "Submit."	**Beginner & Intermediate** **Check Spelling and Proofread.** Before students begin proofreading, remind them of the spelling activity they just completed. Have them read through their narratives with a partner and circle any word where they think they may have spelled words incorrectly. Then have them read the circled words aloud and try to use the spelling rules they have learned to correct the spelling themselves before confirming it using a dictionary or spell checker. They can continue proofreading their narratives with a teacher or partner using the Proofreading Checklist on the Access 1 and 2 handouts. **Intermediate & Advanced** **Read Aloud to Proofread.** Explain to students that reading their work aloud is a great way to check for errors they might have otherwise missed. After students have completed their proofreading using the Proofreading Checklist, have them read their narrative aloud to an English-proficient partner. Tell them that if they stumble in their reading it may indicate a place where they need to adjust punctuation or sentence structure. Have their partner listen for correct use of grammar and suggest corrections if needed. **Approaching** **Support Writing.** Have students check their final draft against the checklist on their Access 4 handout to make sure they made all the edits needed. Ask them if they have questions or found any part of the assignment challenging. If so, provide clarification and assistance so that they can make their final edits and proofread before submitting their work.

Core Path	Access Path
	Extend **Tech Infusion** **Publish Online.** Suggest that students use Pen (http://pen.io/) to publish their narratives online instantly. Alternatively, have the class use Blogger (www.blogger.com) or Weebly (www.weebly.com) to create a Heroes blog. Encourage students to include relevant photographs or drawings with their published narratives. Students can share the blog via Facebook, Twitter, or other social media and invite friends and classmates to share their own ideas of what people can learn from heroes.

Research

Epic Heroes

TYPE

Research

TITLE

Grade 12 Unit 1: Epic Heroes

TIME

125 minutes (research and presentations)

OBJECTIVES

1. Complete topic-specific group research projects connected to the unit theme and essential question.
2. Practice and apply research strategies to produce a presentation with multimedia features.
3. Practice, apply, and reinforce the following Grades 11-12 ELA Common Core State Standards for reading literature and informational texts, writing explanatory pieces, conducting research projects, and speaking and listening:

> **Reading: Literature** - RL.11-12.3, RL.11-12.5, RL.11-12.7
> **Writing** - W.11-12.7, W.11-12.8, W.11-12.9.A-B
> **Speaking & Listening** - SL.11-12.1-6

RESOURCES

Library, online resources, links to topics

OVERVIEW

In order to better understand the cultural impact of heroes and heroines across cultures, students will research examples and impacts of heroes and heroines in media such as video, audio recordings, graphics, and books. If introduced in the first half of the unit, this research project will serve as a resource for the Extended Writing piece students will produce at the unit's close.

After the lessons for both fiction and informational texts have been taught, practiced, and applied, students should discuss story elements, themes in literature, and point of view in nonfiction.

Suggested topics for small-group research and student presentations include:

- Why do tales about legendary heroes remain popular for hundreds of years? Provide one or two examples of such heroes and explain their continuing popularity.

- How was British history changed by national heroes from the Middle Ages?

- What are some common elements from legends from different cultures? Include examples from actual legends.

- What sorts of people today should be considered heroes?

- Choose a person today who is worthy of being a legendary hero known many years from today. Explain why.

Links to some of these topics can be found on the Big Idea Blast and other Blasts throughout the unit.

REVIEW AND DISCUSS (10 MINUTES)

1. **Revisit the Big Idea Blast and Unit Preview** *(SL.11-12.1-2)*. As a group, reread the Big Idea Blast and watch the Unit Preview again. Use the following questions to guide a discussion prior to research:
   a. What is the most interesting or surprising lesson this unit has taught you about legendary heroes in medieval England and elsewhere?
   b. What themes are represented in the stories and legends you have read in this unit?
   c. What topics from the reading are you most interested to learn more about?

CONDUCTING THE RESEARCH (80 MINUTES)

1. **Break Students into Five Groups. Assign Each Group a Topic, or Let Groups Self-Select. (40 Minutes)**
   a. **Make a Research Plan** *(W.11-12.7)*. Instruct students to formulate research questions for their topic. After students prepare questions, collaborate with them on the best places to search for information, the most useful keywords to use in their search, and the type of resources available to them during the research process. Remind students that their research should focus on heroes and heroines around the world and the roles of these heroes and heroines in their cultures.
   b. **Gather Resources** *(W.11-12.8, RL.11-12.7)*. Instruct students to gather a selection of the following: print and digital text resources, video, audio recordings, graphics, and photos. Remind students to analyze and evaluate the validity of a source before using information from that source.
   c. **Review and Discuss** *(SL.11-12.1-2)*. Advise groups to assign each member a research task. Tasks should be completed and presented to the group by each member individually.

TING THE RESEARCH (80 MINUTES)

1. **Assemble the Research in Each Group (40 minutes)**
   a. **Share** *(SL.11-12.1-2)*. Instruct students in each group to share what they have learned about their individual research and why this information is important.

Copyright © BookheadEd Learning, LLC

b. **Focus** *(W.11-12.8)*. Ask students to review the information they have gathered and to select the information that is most relevant. Encourage students to revise their research questions, as needed. Each group should then create a bibliography of its resources.

c. **Write Explanations of Facts** *(W.11-12.8)*. Instruct group members to write brief explanations of any facts they uncovered during their research. These facts can be included in the group presentation.

d. **Plan a Short Presentation** *(SL.11-12.1-3, RL.11-12.3)*. Ask groups to plan a short presentation of the information they compiled. Students should follow the format below:
   i. **Title:** The title should provide information about the topic.
   ii. **Introduction:** The introduction should include a general description of the topic and research questions.
   iii. **List of Key Facts:** The list should include five to ten key facts about the subject.
   iv. **Multimedia Element** *(SL.11-12.5):* Remind students to include a visual resource (video, graphic, or photo) or a recording in their group presentation.
   v. **Conclusion:** Explain how this topic is relevant today.

PRESENT THE RESEARCH (35 MINUTES)

1. **Group Multimedia Presentations (5-7 minutes per group)**
   a. **Present** *(SL.11-12.5-6)*. Groups should take turns presenting their findings to the class. Remind students that a good presentation involves speaking clearly. This includes using appropriate grammar, an effective volume, a proper tone, and meaningful gestures to keep the audience's attention and to emphasize key points.
   b. **Summarize** *(SL.11-12.4)*. Ask groups to briefly summarize their presentations.
   c. **Question** *(SL.11-12.1.C)*. If time allows, students in the audience should ask relevant questions.

EXTENSION: RESPOND TO AND POST THE PRESENTATIONS (10 MINUTES)

1. **Write** *(W.11-12.10)*. Students should write about what they have learned from the presentations by
   a. listing three things they know now that they didn't know before; and
   b. writing a paragraph explaining how the presentations informed their understanding of heroes.

Post the Research (10 minutes) Create an area in the room where students can review the research of other groups.

Full-text Study

Epic Heroes

Beowulf

Anglo-Saxon

---

translated by
Francis B. Gummere
1910

INTRODUCTION

One of the earliest works of literature in English, the epic poem *Beowulf* tells the story of how Beowulf, a heroic Geat (from a land in what is now southern Sweden), saves the kingdom of the Danes from a family of brutal monsters. The monster Grendel, jealous of celebration, community, and fellowship, begins to raid Heorot, the Danish mead-hall, by night, devouring the men who serve King Hrothgar. Outraged by such evil and eager to prove his heroism, *Beowulf* sails from Geatland to Denmark. He kills Grendel, proving that fate (called *Wyrd* in the poem) has marked him as a great warrior and protector. Grendel's mother, avenging the death of her son, attacks the Danes at Heorot. Beowulf pursues her to her underwater lair and finally kills her with an extraordinary sword. Following his heroic achievements in Denmark, Beowulf becomes king of the Geats. After he rules for fifty years, a new challenge calls on his skill and courage: a rapacious dragon. The poem highlights important elements of early medieval society, such as clan, community, celebration of past heroes and legends, and material gifts such as rings, swords, and crowns that signalled human alliance and protection from invading forces. The monsters in the poem represent both spiritual evils and the evils that come from loneliness and isolation, from loss of clan, heritage, and family.

The author of *Beowulf* is unknown, as the poem was sung orally and then transcribed in manuscript form over a period of several centuries. The events of the poem date to the fifth century, but the only surviving manuscript copy can be dated to around 1000 C.E. Even to the poem's audiences in the ninth, tenth, and eleventh centuries, *Beowulf* would sound as it does today: a tribute to an ancient, heroic time that no longer exists, a mythic time of dragons, monsters, and legendary heroes. Although the characters of *Beowulf* live in a pagan and pre-Christian world, the poet often uses a more Christian perspective to narrate the events of the poem, showing the fusion of pagan and Christian worldviews that is essential to understanding medieval literature. The poem itself, as with the songs of other past warriors sung during the poem's feast scenes, serves to bridge the heroic past with the present by commemorating bygone times and confirming heritage. [Note: Although numerous singers, poets, and manuscript writers probably influenced the language and text of *Beowulf*, this reading guide refers to a singular poet for greater clarity.]

As students read *Beowulf*, ask them to consider how the poem presents two sets of characters: warriors and kings (Beowulf, Hrothgar, Unferth, and Wiglaf) and monsters (Grendel, Grendel's mother, the dragon). What distinguishes the heroes from the monsters? How are they similar? Do they share any values or characteristics?

USING THIS READING GUIDE

This reading guide presents lessons to support the teaching of the epic poem *Beowulf*. Organized by sections of grouped lines, the lessons preview key vocabulary words and include close reading questions tied to the Common Core State Standards. The lessons identify a key passage in each section that will help you guide students through an exploration of the essential conflicts, themes, and questions in *Beowulf*. This passage will also serve as the jumping-off point from which students will engage in their own StudySyncTV-style group discussion.

Each section of the reading guide also includes a list of comparative texts—provided in the *Beowulf* Full-text Unit in the StudySync Library—that go along with that section. For each comparative text, the reading guide includes important contextual notes and ideas for relating the text to *Beowulf*. The reading guide concludes with two writing prompts that enable students to revisit *Beowulf* both creatively and summatively, with reference to the comparative texts.

BEOWULF

TEXT SECTIONS

LINES 1–188: Trouble in the Danish Hall

The poem begins with an ode to the great Danish warrior-kings of the past, the ancestors of King Hrothgar. A monster named Grendel terrorizes Hrothgar's land and people for twelve years, with grisly and fatal raids on the Danish great hall Heorot.

LINES 189–662: A Hero Comes to Help the Danes

After hearing of Grendel's evil deeds, the Geatish warrior Beowulf travels from his native land to Hrothgar's kingdom and boasts that he will defeat the monster. The Danish warrior Unferth is jealous of Beowulf's claims, but King Hrothgar welcomes the hero.

LINES 663–1254: Hero Meets Monster

Although Grendel's demonic powers protect him from being wounded by human weapons, Beowulf defeats the monster by ripping off one of Grendel's arms. To celebrate Beowulf's triumph, the Danes hold feasts at Heorot, singing songs about great warriors of the past.

LINES 1255–1656: Grendel's Mother Wants Revenge

Furious about the death of her son, Grendel's mother leaves her underwater home and attacks Heorot, killing several Danes. Although Unferth is too afraid to fight the monster underwater, Beowulf pursues her to her lair and defeats her.

LINES 1657–1896: Gifts and Alliances

Hrothgar gives Beowulf many treasures and gifts to honor his heroic deeds. Although the two men may never see each other again, these gifts mark a new alliance between the Geats and the Danes.

LINES 1897–2468: A New Monster

Beowulf returns to his native Geatland as a hero, and when his lord King Hygelac is killed in a blood feud, Beowulf becomes king. After Beowulf rules wisely and justly for fifty years, a dragon begins to terrorize the Geat kingdom.

LINES 2469–3192: Beowulf's Heroic Fate

Beowulf fights the dragon but fails to kill him with a sword, and he suffers a chest wound. A young warrior named Wiglaf, the only Geat courageous enough to stay with Beowulf, stabs the dragon, weakening the beast and allowing Beowulf to kill it. Beowulf dies and is given a hero's funeral.

LINES 1–188: Trouble in the Danish Hall

KEY PASSAGE

144. *Thus ruled unrighteous and raged his fill*
145. *one against all; until empty stood*
146. *that lordly building, and long it bode so.*
147. *Twelve years' tide the trouble he bore,*
148. *sovran of Scyldings, sorrows in plenty,*
149. *boundless cares. There came unhidden*
150. *tidings true to the tribes of men,*
151. *in sorrowful songs, how ceaselessly Grendel*
152. *harassed Hrothgar, what hate he bore him,*
153. *what murder and massacre, many a year,*
154. *feud unfading,—refused consent*
155. *to deal with any of Daneland's earls,*
156. *make pact of peace, or compound for gold:*
157. *still less did the wise men ween to get*
158. *great fee for the feud from his fiendish hands.*
159. *But the evil one ambushed old and young*
160. *death-shadow dark, and dogged them still,*
161. *lured, or lurked in the livelong night*
162. *of misty moorlands: men may say not*
163. *where the haunts of these Hell-Runes be.*
164. *Such heaping of horrors the hater of men,*
165. *lonely roamer, wrought unceasing,*
166. *harassings heavy. O'er Heorot he lorded,*

> 167.   *gold-bright hall, in gloomy nights;*
>
> 168.   *and ne'er could the prince approach his throne,*
>
> 169.   *—'twas judgment of God,—or have joy in his hall.*

This passage describes Grendel's twelve-year reign of terror over Heorot, the great hall of Hrothgar, and the Danish kingdom. Grendel, motivated by loneliness and hatred of men, makes so many brutal raids against Heorot that the Danish people are afraid to gather there in celebration and fellowship. Although Hrothgar is a descendant of the powerful and heroic Scylding lineage, he can do nothing to appease the monster.

WHY IT'S KEY

Setting: This passage points out the significance of Heorot, the "gold-bright hall." More than just physical buildings, the great halls of the early medieval kings were sacred centers of community, where celebration always included tributes to the great heroes of the past, therefore affirming the meaning and worth of the kingdom. So much of Beowulf contrasts the isolated with the communal, and this passage shows that contrast clearly as Grendel, the "lonely roamer," causes the Hall to become silent and empty. Understanding the significance of these halls in early medieval culture can help students understand why Beowulf is inspired to travel such great distances to challenge Grendel's "unrighteous" acts. One might compare this passage to the later celebrations that occur at Heorot, after Grendel's defeat.

Alliteration: This passage establishes the poet's use of alliteration, or repeated consonant sounds at the beginning of words, a key feature of Old English poetry—"harassed Hrothgar, what hate he bore him / what murder and massacre many a year." In the original form as a poem performed or sung orally, this kind of device helped the singers remember the lines. Even in written form, the alliteration contributes to the poem's songlike quality, which connects it to the great songs of past warriors that appear throughout the text.

Central Concept: This passages provides insight into one of the poem's central question: what separates humans from the monsters that terrorize them? Here, and elsewhere in the poem, the language points to a spiritual difference between Grendel and the human characters; he is a "Hell-Rune," or sorcerer from hell; he fights not with metal weapons but with his "fiendish hands"; he is an "evil one." (At many points in the poem, he is also referred to as a descendant of Cain.) While the poem has a complicated relationship to Christianity—as the characters are pagan but the poet often refers to the Christian worldview of its audience—the overall impression is that evil has a physical presence in the world, as embodied by creatures such as Grendel.

Language: In the opening section of *Beowulf*, some Old English words appear that relate to important social and family relationships of early medieval society. The poet mentions athelings, or princes and lords, and thanes, men given land by a king or noble, who were not themselves of noble birth. Hrothgar is referred to as the *sovran* of Scyldings. An older form of the word *sovereign*, this word shows Hrothgar's status as descendant of a great line, a family fated to be kings.

YOUR STUDYSYNC® TV

Discussion Prompt: What kind of monster is Grendel, and what kind of threat does he pose to Heorot and the Danish people? If we assume that life in the early Middle Ages was more dangerous, that people were often attacked by invaders, why is Grendel such an important monster that his terror inspires an entire poem? What language or words in the passage support your ideas about the kind of monster that Hrothgar is dealing with?

Standards: RL.11-12.1, RL.11-12.4; SL.11-12.1.A, SL.11-12.1.C, SL.11-12.1.D

VOCABULARY

prowess
prow•ess *noun*
Achievement or talent in a certain profession or task
The fact that his team had won several championships proved his prowess as a coach.

endow
en•dow *verb*
To give someone property, money, or other inheritable qualities
Her mother endowed her with a strong sense of honor.

respite
res•pite *noun*
Relief or space from a challenging or stressful situation
Although the Thanksgiving holiday provided some respite, the hard work of studying began again in early December.

loathsome
loath•some *adjective*
Disgusting, hateful, or revolting
The bathroom where the pipe had burst still had a loathsome smell.

succor
suc•cor *noun*
Aid or help with a troubling, difficult, or upsetting situation
The food brought over by friends provided succor to the family while their mother recovered from surgery.

CLOSE READ

QUESTION 1: Although the main characters of the poem are Hrothgar and Beowulf, which characters' lives are described in the poem's opening lines, and why does the poet begin with stories about these characters?

Sample Answer: The poem begins by telling the stories of great Danish kings such as Scyld, Beow, and Healfdene, who are King Hrothgar's ancestors. In the world of Beowulf, heroic legends and ancestors are an important part of a person's identity.

Standards: RL.11-12.1

QUESTION 2: Why does Grendel begin attacking Heorot? What makes him so hateful toward the Danish hall? Find evidence in the poem that supports your answer.

Sample Answer: Grendel hears the joyful singing and celebrating that occurs at Heorot, and his rage about his own isolation and loneliness causes him to attack; "With envy and anger an evil spirit / endured the dole in his dark abode / that he heard each day the din of revel / high in the hall" (lines 86–9).

Standards: RL.11-12.1

QUESTION 3: Where do you see evidence in the poem of the pagan and pre-Christian religions that were an essential part of early medieval society?

Sample Answer: "Elves and evil-spirits" (112), "the giants that warred with God" (113), "altar offerings" (176), "their practice this, their heathen hope" (178–9)

Standards: RL.11-12.1

QUESTION 4: Although the characters in the poem are pagan, the poem's audience in later centuries had become more Christian. Where do you see the poet appealing to or referencing these Christian beliefs?

Sample Answer: "Since the Creator his exile doomed" (106), "Of Cain awoke all that woeful breed" (111), "Twas the Judgment of God" (169)

Standards: RL.11-12.1

COMPARATIVE TEXTS

Text: *The Anglo-Saxon Chronicle*

Compare to: *Beowulf*, Lines 1-188

Connection: *The Anglo-Saxon Chronicle* offers a rare window on the turbulent early history of England, extending from the Roman rule of Celtic Britannia to the vying of Saxon and Anglian kingdoms within the island to the incursions of Danes from across the North Sea. Students will discuss the geography and events described in *The Anglo-Saxon Chronicle*—in particular, the conversion of pagan believers like Edwin to the new Christianity—as an introduction to the location (from Britain to Denmark and southern Sweden) and times of *Beowulf*. Students will create an entry in the model of the four excerpted chronicles describing the threat of Grendel to Heorot.

Text: *Ecclesiastical History of the English People* by Bede

Compare to: *Beowulf*, Lines 86-188

Connection: In the *Ecclesiastical History of the English People*, the English monk Bede chronicles the conversion of Edwin, king of Northumbria, from paganism to Christianity in 627 C.E., after Edwin defeats his West-Saxon foes (an event recorded in the Anglo-Saxon Chronicles StudySync entry). Edwin receives an enthusiastic thumbs-up from his high priest, Coifi, who is only too willing to destroy the pagan gods he had recently promoted. This sea change in religion is shown in the Christian values invoked in *Beowulf*, despite the pagan setting—sending, in fact, a message by depicting the conquest of pagan monsters by a "Christianized" hero.

LINES 189-662: A Hero Comes to Help the Danes

KEY PASSAGE

560.   *ME thus often the evil monsters*
561.   *thronging threatened. With thrust of my sword,*
562.   *the darling, I dealt them due return!*
563.   *Nowise had they bliss from their booty then*
564.   *to devour their victim, vengeful creatures,*
565.   *seated to banquet at bottom of sea;*
566.   *but at break of day, by my brand sore hurt,*
567.   *on the edge of ocean up they lay,*
568.   *put to sleep by the sword. And since, by them*
569.   *on the fathomless sea-ways sailor-folk*
570.   *are never molested.—Light from east,*
571.   *came bright God's beacon; the billows sank,*
572.   *so that I saw the sea-cliffs high,*
573.   *windy walls. For Wyrd oft saveth*
574.   *earl undoomed if he doughty be!*
575.   *And so it came that I killed with my sword*
576.   *nine of the nicors. Of night-fought battles*
577.   *ne'er heard I a harder 'neath heaven's dome,*
578.   *nor adrift on the deep a more desolate man!*
579.   *Yet I came unharmed from that hostile clutch,*
580.   *though spent with swimming. The sea upbore me,*
581.   *flood of the tide, on Finnish land,*
582.   *the welling waters. No wise of thee*
583.   *have I heard men tell such terror of falchions,*
584.   *bitter battle. Breca ne'er yet,*
585.   *not one of you pair, in the play of war*
586.   *such daring deed has done at all*
587.   *with bloody brand,—I boast not of it!—*
588.   *though thou wast the bane of thy brethren dear,*

589.   *thy closest kin, whence curse of hell*

590.   *awaits thee, well as thy wit may serve!*

591.   *For I say in sooth, thou son of Ecglaf,*

592.   *never had Grendel these grim deeds wrought,*

593.   *monster dire, on thy master dear,*

594.   *in Heorot such havoc, if heart of thine*

595.   *were as battle-bold as thy boast is loud!*

596.   *But he has found no feud will happen;*

597.   *from sword-clash dread of your Danish clan*

598.   *he vaunts him safe, from the Victor-Scyldings.*

599.   *He forces pledges, favors none*

600.   *of the land of Danes, but lustily murders,*

601.   *fights and feasts, nor feud he dreads*

602.   *from Spear-Dane men. But speedily now*

603.   *shall I prove him the prowess and pride of the Geats,*

604.   *shall bid him battle.*

In this passage, Beowulf responds to Unferth's challenge by telling his own version of a swimming test against the warrior Breca, in which Beowulf proved the stronger swimmer and the more skilled at killing sea monsters with his sword. Beowulf questions Unferth's valor and makes a boast of his own.

WHY IT'S KEY

Central Concept: This passage reveals an important element of the early medieval hero: the hero's boast. The great warriors achieved their status not only from heroic deeds but also from having the courage to claim what they were going to accomplish in advance. In this passage, Beowulf boasts that he will defeat Grendel, but he also criticizes Unferth for falsely boasting about his prowess while failing to protect his people from the monster. That a hero should seek out danger is shown in the story Beowulf tells about the sea-monsters; he chose to undertake the swimming test, fully aware of its perils. A hero can't rest on his achievements, which explains why Beowulf wants to fight Grendel. Students might keep this in mind later, as they consider why Beowulf, though much older and weaker, decides to fight the dragon.

Character: This passage, along with all the interactions between Beowulf and Unferth, reveals important aspects of Beowulf's character. One can see his strict adherence to the heroic codes of his day: he seeks out monsters, he battles evil forces from which ordinary humans cannot defend themselves, and he doesn't tolerate other warriors, such as Unferth, who boast but can't follow through. He seems to understand the importance not only of heroic acts but also of how others tell or sing the stories of those acts, as he takes time to set the record straight about the swimming test.

Setting: As Beowulf tells this story of his earlier underwater triumphs, the reader can see how the poem depicts the ocean, and all watery realms, as places of evil and danger, inhabited by monstrous creatures outside the control of human society and culture. Only the most heroic of humans, such as Beowulf, are capable of crossing and protecting these boundaries. This distinction between the solid land on which humans live and the supernatural realms where monsters exist will help students understand Beowulf's later encounter with Grendel's mother. Students might consider the irony of how Unferth challenges Beowulf's prowess as a swimmer in this section of the poem, as he will later prove too cowardly to fight Grendel's mother underwater.

Language: Although Beowulf tells the story of Breca and the sea monsters to protect his reputation from Unferth's challenge, he also credits his success to the power of fate, or "Wyrd" as the poet calls it. While heroes are known for their individual courage and actions, their status also derives from more cosmic forces.

YOUR STUDYSYNC® TV

Discussion Prompt: Why does Beowulf talk—or "boast"—about his heroic deeds before he goes to fight Grendel? In other cultures, including our own, is boasting considered heroic? Why or why not? In what situations do we value boasting about the hard things we intend to do? Why might boasting be a difficult, challenging, or important task for a hero?

Standards: RL.11-12.1, RL.11-12.4; SL.11-12.1.A, SL.11-12.1.C, SL.11-12.1.D

VOCABULARY

assuage
as•suage *verb*
To improve a difficult situation; to decrease hurt feelings
Taking the practice tests assuaged the anxiety of the students.

henchman
hench•man *noun*
Someone who assists or works for a more powerful person, often expected to act unethically or illegally in service to his or her boss
The jewel thieves made their henchman smuggle the rubies across the border.

harangue
ha•rangue *noun*
A long speech with an attacking or critical purpose; a rant
On learning that the tableware wasn't properly cleaned, the restaurant manager made his staff stay after work while he delivered his harangue.

wane
wane *verb*
To become less in strength or size; to decrease
As the basketball game continued into a third overtime, the players' energy began to wane.

sever
sev•er *verb*
To physically separate one thing from another by cutting or slicing
To sever the fat from a piece of chicken before cooking, one must use a well-sharpened knife.

sheen
sheen *noun*
A shine or glow on the surface of something
Although the weather had cleared, the rain left a sheen on the roads.

CLOSE READ

QUESTION 1: How do the Danes react when Beowulf and his men arrive at the harbor to fight Grendel?

Sample Answer: They question the Geat hero about who he is and why he has sailed to Denmark. They're afraid of the mighty warriors who arrive in ships.

Standards: RL.11-12.1

QUESTION 2: Why does Hrothgar decide to allow Beowulf and his warriors into his kingdom?

Sample Answer: He learns of Beowulf's family heritage, and he trusts that the son of famous warriors wants to help. He knows people in Beowulf's family from an earlier time in his life.

Standards: RL.11-12.1

QUESTION 3: Does Beowulf think it possible that the monster Grendel might defeat him, or is he certain of victory? Find evidence from his conversations with Hrothgar that support your answer.

Sample Answer: Beowulf understands that Grendel might kill him. He describes what might happen in this case: "my Geatish band he will fearless eat" (444-445); "my blood-covered body he'll bear as prey" (449). He says that the outcome of the battle depends on fate: "fares Wyrd as she must" (456).

Standards: RL.11-12.1

QUESTION 4: What reason does Unferth have for doubting that Beowulf will be able to save the Danes from Grendel?

Sample Answer: Unferth has heard that Beowulf lost a swimming contest with another warrior, so Unferth thinks Beowulf is not as mighty a warrior as everyone else thinks.

Standards: RL.11-12.1

QUESTION 5: After Beowulf speaks, how do Hrothgar and his Queen Wealhtheow feel, and why do they feel this way? Give examples from the poem that support your answer.

Sample Answer: The Danish king and queen are happy to hear that Beowulf has the determination, heart, and courage that are needed to fight Grendel. They trust that he can take on the monster. Examples: "joyous then was the jewel-giver" (608), "such firm resolve" (611), "never to any man erst I trusted . . . til now to thee" (656-8), "well these words to the woman seemed, Beowulf's battle-boast" (640-1).

Standards: RL.11-12.1

COMPARATIVE TEXTS

Text: *Beowulf*, Lines 144-300 (Heaney translation)

Compare to: Lines 144-300 (Gummere translation)

Connection: Students will reread lines 144-300, from the 2000 translation by Irish poet Seamus Heaney. Heaney's translation, based on the same Anglo-Saxon text as Gummere's 1901 translation, has been described as "both direct and sophisticated, making previous versions look slightly flowery and antique by comparison." Students will draw their own conclusions from a comparison of the two translations, exploring the same themes in different modes of expression.

Text: *On Heroes* by Thomas Carlyle

Compare to: *Beowulf*, Lines 189-662

Connection: Thomas Carlyle's consideration of heroism begins with an essay on the hero as a reflection of the divine. He discourses on the wonder with which pagans, or worshippers of multiple gods and goddesses, regarded nature, a divinity especially conferred on humanity, and achieving its highest stature in hero worship. Students will apply Carlyle's ideas to the portrayal of the Anglo-Saxon hero, namely Beowulf.

Teacher's Edition

LINES 663-1254: Hero Meets Monster

KEY PASSAGE

795.   . . . Now many an earl

796.   of Beowulf brandished blade ancestral,

797.   fain the life of their lord to shield,

798.   their praised prince, if power were theirs;

799.   never they knew,—as they neared the foe,

800.   hardy-hearted heroes of war,

801.   aiming their swords on every side

802.   the accursed to kill,—no keenest blade,

803.   no farest of falchions fashioned on earth,

804.   could harm or hurt that hideous fiend!

805.   He was safe, by his spells, from sword of battle,

806.   from edge of iron. Yet his end and parting

807.   on that same day of this our life

808.   woful should be, and his wandering soul

809.   far off flit to the fiends' domain.

810.   Soon he found, who in former days,

811.   harmful in heart and hated of God,

812.   on many a man such murder wrought,

813.   that the frame of his body failed him now.

814.   For him the keen-souled kinsman of Hygelac

815.   held in hand; hateful alive

816.   was each to other. The outlaw dire

817.   took mortal hurt; a mighty wound

818.   showed on his shoulder, and sinews cracked,

819.   and the bone-frame burst. To Beowulf now

820.   the glory was given, and Grendel thence

821.   death-sick his den in the dark moor sought,

822.   noisome abode: he knew too well

823.   that here was the last of life, an end

824.   of his days on earth.—To all the Danes

825.   by that bloody battle the boon had come.

826.   From ravage had rescued the roving stranger

827.   Hrothgar's hall; the hardy and wise one

828.   had purged it anew. His night-work pleased him,

829.   his deed and its honor. To Eastern Danes

830.   had the valiant Geat his vaunt made good,

831.   all their sorrow and ills assuaged,

832.   their bale of battle borne so long,

833.   and all the dole they erst endured

834.   pain a-plenty.—'Twas proof of this,

835.   when the hardy-in-fight a hand laid down,

836.   arm and shoulder,—all, indeed,

837.   of Grendel's gripe,—'neath the gabled roof.

While Beowulf grapples with Grendel, the hero's men try to come to his defense with swords. The monster has enchanted himself, and now he cannot be cut by any man-made weapon, but Beowulf prevails, ripping off one of Grendel's arms. Near dead, Grendel slinks back to his lair.

WHY IT'S KEY

Character: This passage shows more of Beowulf's bravery and strength. Because Grendel is not human and therefore is untrained in sword-fighting, Beowulf chooses to fight him hand-to-hand. Swords, as it turns out, can't do much to harm Grendel, but the choice to fight barehanded shows the degree to which Beowulf, "the keen-souled kinsmen of Hygelac," honors his combat enemies, even when they are monstrous. The method is also further proof of Beowulf's courage and strength.

Central Concept: This passage, as well as the preceding section that narrates Grendel's final attack on Heorot, shows in sometimes gory detail the qualities that distinguish the monster from the human world he hates so much. The depth of Grendel's anger at humans is mentioned—"harmful in heart" (811)—as is his spiritual desolation—"hated of God"(811), that "hideous fiend" (804)—as well as the lonely and unholy fate that awaits the monster after death—"the fiend's domain" (809). This distinction between heroes and monsters is also heightened by the fact that a close view of Grendel's death isn't even shown in the poem, as "Grendel thence death-sick his den in the dark moor sought" (820-1). Since dying in valiant battle is further proof of their courage, Anglo-Saxon poetry honors its heroes through detailed and ceremonial descriptions of their final moments, as students will see in the final section of the poem.

Contextual Details (Weapons): This passage also shows the significant role that weapons play in Anglo-Saxon warrior culture and in *Beowulf*. The iron swords, as with any forged metal items "fashioned on earth," are proof that humans are different from monsters; *Beowulf* notes earlier that Grendel fights "unweaponed" (686). The Geats attempt to kill Grendel with "blade ancestral," showing how swords, like the family histories that are detailed at various points in the poem, are important markers of lineage, family, and warrior status. These physical tokens of past glory relate to one of the poem's underlying purposes: to connect the legendary and heroic past with the contemporary world of its audience.

Language: In this section, the poet refers on several occasions to Grendel's *gripe*, an archaic spelling of *grip*. This—his shoulder and arm—is Grendel's main tool as he terrorizes the Danes, and it is also the trophy that Beowulf retains after the battle. Some other archaic battle-related words that appear in this section and throughout the poem are *falchion* (sword) and —still-used— *doughty* (brave or courageous).

YOUR STUDYSYNC® TV

Discussion Prompt: After the fight with Grendel, both Beowulf and the Danes are pleased with the hero's "deed and its honor." Why is the fight between Beowulf and Grendel honorable? Would Grendel agree? Do you? Does the monster appear to live by the same code of conduct and values as Beowulf and the Geats? Why or why not?

Standards: RL.11-12.1, RL.11-12.4; SL.11-12.1.A, SL.11-12.1.C, SL.11-12.1.D

VOCABULARY

mettle
met•tle *noun*
Courage, perseverance, or positive attitude in the face of a difficult or challenging situation
After the tornado, the town showed its mettle when everyone worked together to rebuild the elementary school.

discern
dis•cern *verb*
To figure out or notice something that might not be obvious
A mother can sometimes discern why her baby is crying, even if others don't know.

Copyright © BookheadEd Learning, LLC

din
din *noun*
An annoying, loud, and ongoing combination of sounds.
The din from the neighbor's party made it hard for the woman to sleep.

dire
dire *adjective*
Very serious—often negative, frightening, or awful
A criminal record usually has a dire effect on one's ability to get jobs in the future.

torrent
tor•rent *noun*
A substantial flow of water or liquid, sometimes used in reference to an intense situation
The torrent of rain caused the road to flood.

throng
throng *noun*
A large number of people; a dense crowd
The rock star pushed his way through the throng of fans, not stopping for a single autograph.

CLOSE READ

QUESTION 1: How does Beowulf prepare for his battle with Grendel, and why does he make such preparations?

Sample Answer: He takes off his armor, since Grendel fights only with brute strength; he waits all night, awake, in Heorot, since he knows that the monster is due to attack.

Standards: RL.11-12.1

QUESTION 2: What emotions motivate Grendel during his attack on Heorot? What language from the poem supports your answer?

Sample Answer: Grendel appears to be very angry at the Danish people, or perhaps at human society in general: "baleful he burst in his blatant rage" (724), and "ireful he strode" (727). He also seems happy at the chance to kill Danes: "then laughed his heart" (731), "he gladly discerned" (716). He also seems scared of Beowulf: "at heart he feared, sorrowed in soul" (754).

Standards: RL.11-12.1

QUESTION 3: How do the Danes celebrate Beowulf's victory, and why do they celebrate in this way?

Sample Answer: The Danes hold a feast at Heorot, and the poet sings about Beowulf's victory and other heroic acts. They do this to honor Beowulf's deeds, and to connect him to other great heroes. They also hang Grendel's arm, or "hand-spear," from the roof, to show the strangeness of the monster and the greatness of Beowulf's accomplishment.

Standards: RL.11-12.1

QUESTION 4: What gifts does Hrothgar (sometimes called Healfdene's son) give to Beowulf in return for killing the monsters? Why does he give him these gifts?

Sample Answer: Hrothgar gives Beowulf treasure from his hoard, including a breastplate, a helmet, a flag, and a sword. These gifts signify Beowulf's greatness as a warrior, but they will also be signs of friendship between the Geats and the Danes in future battle situations.

Standards: RL.11-12.1

QUESTION 5: What gifts does Wealhtheow (Hrothgar's queen) give to Beowulf, and what is the purpose of these gifts?

Sample Answer: Wealhtheow gives Beowulf another set of armor that was once worn by Geats but is now part of the Danish wealth. These gifts are proof of Beowulf's glory as a warrior. They are also given with the expectation that he will be kind to Hrothgar and Wealhtheow's sons in the future.

Standards: RL.11-12.1

COMPARATIVE TEXTS

Text: *Grendel* by John Gardner

Compare to: *Beowulf*, lines 711-853

Connection: The story of the fateful battle between hero and monster in *Beowulf* is told from Grendel's darkly funny first-person perspective in John Gardner's *Grendel*. Grendel observes the festivities at the opening of Heorot, Hrothgar's mead-hall, bemoaning his brutish nature and stumbling across a victim of a homicide that he gets blamed for. Students will compare this sensitive, misunderstood Grendel with the purely evil monster in *Beowulf* and then analyze the different purposes of the authors.

Text: *The Fury of the Northmen* by John Marsden

Compare to: *Beowulf*, lines 915-1231

Connection: In 793 C.E., heralded by sightings of dragons, Norse Vikings came ashore on the island of Lindisfarne in northeast England, the site of a renowned monastery. The sea-raiders plundered the abbey, killing many monks. The raid is considered the beginning of the Viking Age, characterized by many similar attacks by northern raiders on British settlements over many of the next 300 years. Students will research the relationship between Scandinavians and Britons between the 8th and 11th centuries, reflected in sources such as *Beowulf* and *The Fury of the Northmen*. Students might consider the English audience of the poem; the Scandinavian characters; and the ways in which Beowulf, Hrothgar, the Danish saga-songs sung at Heorot, and Grendel's raids on Heorot all relate to or compare with Viking history and culture.

LINES 1255-1656: Grendel's Mother Wants Revenge

KEY PASSAGE

1546.   *Swift on her part she paid him back*

1547.   *with grisly grasp, and grappled with him.*

1548.   *Spent with struggle, stumbled the warrior,*

1549.   *fiercest of fighting-men, fell adown.*

1550.   *On the hall-guest she hurled herself, hent her short sword,*

1551.   *broad and brown-edged, the bairn to avenge,*

1552.   *the sole-born son.—On his shoulder lay*

1553.   *braided breast-mail, barring death,*

1554.   *withstanding entrance of edge or blade.*

1555.   *Life would have ended for Ecgtheow's son,*

1556.   *under wide earth for that earl of Geats,*

1557.   *had his armor of war not aided him,*

1558.   *battle-net hard, and holy God*

1559.   *wielded the victory, wisest Maker.*

1560.   *The Lord of Heaven allowed his cause;*

1561.   *and easily rose the earl erect.*

1562.   *'Mid the battle-gear saw he a blade triumphant,*

1563.   *old-sword of Eotens, with edge of proof,*

1564.   *warriors' heirloom, weapon unmatched,*

1565.   *—save only 'twas more than other men*

1566.   *to bandy-of-battle could bear at all—*

1567.   *as the giants had wrought it, ready and keen.*

1568.   *Seized then its chain-hilt the Scyldings' chieftain,*

1569.   *bold and battle-grim, brandished the sword,*

1570. *reckless of life, and so wrathfully smote*

1571. *that it gripped her neck and grasped her hard,*

1572. *her bone-rings breaking: the blade pierced through*

1573. *that fated-one's flesh: to floor she sank.*

1574. *Bloody the blade: he was blithe of his deed.*

1575. *Then blazed forth light. 'Twas bright within*

1576. *as when from the sky there shines unclouded*

1577. *heaven's candle.*

Grendel's mother stabs Beowulf with a knife, but his armor protects him. Heavenly forces favor Beowulf: he finds an ancient sword in Grendel's mother's treasure hoard, and he kills her with it.

WHY IT'S KEY

Character: The episode with Grendel's mother, this passage in particular, provides evidence that although the poem makes clear distinctions between monsters and heroes, the monsters are still motivated by some of the same values and social customs as the humans. A blood feud, where one avenges the death of one's kin through further violence, motivates Grendel's mother: "On the hall-guest she hurled herself, hent her short sword, broad and brown-edged, the bairn to avenge, the sole-born son" (1550-1552). Such blood feuds are referenced throughout the poem, especially in the stories of past heroes and kings.

Contextual Details (Weapons): This passage develops the sacred significance of weapons in the world of *Beowulf*. The sword that Beowulf finds has a mystical quality, due to its ancient nature and its connection to the mythic past, as well as the fortunate moment in which he finds the "warrior's heirloom, weapon unmatched." Like the poem itself, which connects mythic heroes to later English society and culture, the sword connects Beowulf to the time of the "giants." It's interesting to note that Unferth's sword Hrunting, which was lent to Beowulf prior to the combat, cannot be used in the fight. Like his sword, the cowardly Unferth isn't fit for battle with the monster.

Central Concept: Although the poem mentions the grace of God/Fate in Beowulf's battle with Grendel, the degree to which heroes' victories and monsters' defeats are determined by overarching spiritual and, more specifically, Christian forces is clearly shown in the battle with Grendel's mother. The mystical sword appears when the "Lord of Heaven allowed [Beowulf's] cause." The forged armor and weapons that protect Beowulf refer to a different "Maker" who underwrites his triumph: "holy God wielded the victory." Grendel's mother, "the fated-one," plays a less triumphant role in the spiritual battle—by virtue of her kinship connections to Cain. Although Beowulf—including the mystical sword, which appears in the underwater lair—is far too influenced by Scandinavian sagas and pre-Christian culture to be considered a formal allegory, one can also see a shift toward that later form of medieval literature, in which the overarching narratives of Christianity play a central role.

Language: This section contains some archaic water-related terms, such as *mere* and *tarn* for "lake," and *welter*, meaning "the turbulent formation of waves and currents." Knowing the definitions of these words might help students better understand the journey Beowulf makes to Grendel's mother's lair.

YOUR STUDYSYNC® TV

Discussion Prompt: Why is Beowulf able to defeat Grendel's mother in her underwater lair? Is his victory proof of his prowess as a swimmer and swordsman? Or is it owed to supernatural forces that support the rightness of his cause? Is his cause necessarily right? Is Grendel's mother justified in her attacks on Heorot?

Standards: RL.11-12.1, RL.11-12.4; SL.11-12.1.A, SL.11-12.1.C, SL.11-12.1.D

VOCABULARY

grapple
grap•ple *verb*
To fight by using just the strength of one's body; to engage in hand-to-hand combat
The two brothers began to grapple with each other on the bedroom floor over who really owned the toy.

hinder
hin•der *verb*
To stop something from happening; to delay or obstruct another's actions
Watching so many television shows may hinder Margo's ability to finish her homework.

turbid
tur•bid *adjective*
Thick or muddy, such as water or another liquid, as the result of some disturbance
The motorboat crossed the pond, leaving a turbid wake behind it.

arduous
ar•du•ous *adjective*
Involving hard work, tiring labor, or extended effort
The hikers rested after their arduous climb up the steep rock face.

perish
per•ish *verb*
To die, usually not from natural causes
Many soldiers perished at the Battle of Gettysburg

CLOSE READ

QUESTION 1: How does Hrothgar explain Grendel's mother's attack on Heorot? Use language from the poem to support your answer.

Sample Answer: Hrothgar says Grendel's mother is getting revenge for her son's death; she's acting out a blood feud between her family and the humans at Heorot: "the feud she avenged" (1337), "keen and cruel her kin to avenge" (1343), "faring far in feud of blood" (1344).

Standards: RL.11-12.1

QUESTION 2: In the culture of the Danes, what kind of places are bodies of water and their coastlines? Use language from the poem to support your answer.

Sample Answer: The people of Heorot see the water as a dangerous place; a place that is outside the control of humans; a place full of monsters; a place of strange magic: "By night is a wonder weird to see, fire on the waters" (1369–70), "'tis no happy place!" (1376), "place of fear, where thou findest out that sin-flecked being" (1382–3).

Standards: RL.11-12.1

QUESTION 3: How does Unferth (called only "bairn of Ecglaf" in this section) participate in Beowulf's quest to fight Grendel's mother in her underwater lair?

Sample Answer: Unferth is too scared to join Beowulf in the underwater battle: "Himself, though, durst not under welter of waters wager his life as loyal liegeman. So lost he his glory" (1473–5). He does lend Beowulf his sword, called "Hrunting," for use in the battle.

Standards: RL.11-12.1

QUESTION 4: In addition to bringing back the hilt of the mystical sword, what trophy does Beowulf bring back from Grendel's mother's underwater lair?

Sample Answer: He brings back the head of Grendel. The monster had returned home to die, but Beowulf has found the corpse and decapitated it.

Standards: RL.11-12.1

COMPARATIVE TEXTS

Text: *The Myths and Legends of Ancient Greece and Rome: Theseus* by E. M. Berens

Compare to: *Beowulf*, lines 663-1656

Connection: Centuries before *Beowulf*, ancient Greeks retold the adventures of their own mythical superhero, Theseus, whose path to glory was strewn with dead giants, exiled relatives, and Theseus's most notorious foe, the man-bull called the Minotaur. How does the Greek hero's feat of ending the Minotaur's reign of terror compare with Beowulf's ending of the twelve-year siege of Grendel and his mother?

Text: *DC Comics: Sixty Years of the World's Favorite Comic Book Heroes* by Les Daniels

Compare to: *Beowulf*, lines 663-1656

Connection: DC Comics introduced Superman and Batman in 1939, ushering a new age of the superhero into American popular culture. Immediately, competitors of DC created their own comic-book heroes, including Wonder Man, Captain Marvel, Captain America, the Human Torch, Sub-Mariner, Plastic Man, Blackhawk, and Blue Beetle. Students will draw on the similarities and differences between comic-book superheroes and the Anglo-Saxon hero to create a graphic adventure for Beowulf.

LINES 1657-1896: Gifts and Alliances

KEY PASSAGE

1853.   *"Thou art strong of main and in mind art wary,*

1854.   *art wise in words! I ween indeed*

1855.   *if ever it hap that Hrethel's heir*

1856.   *by spear be seized, by sword-grim battle,*

1857.   *by illness or iron, thine elder and lord,*

1858.   *people's leader,—and life be thine,—*

1859.   *no seemlier man will the Sea-Geats find*

1860.   *at all to choose for their chief and king,*

1861.   *for hoard-guard of heroes, if hold thou wilt*

1862.   *thy kinsman's kingdom! Thy keen mind pleases me*

1863.   *the longer the better, Beowulf loved!*

1864.   *Thou hast brought it about that both our peoples,*

1865.   *sons of the Geat and Spear-Dane folk,*

1866.   *shall have mutual peace, and from murderous strife,*

1867.   *such as once they waged, from war refrain.*

1868.   *Long as I rule this realm so wide,*

1869.   *let our hoards be common, let heroes with gold*

1870.   *each other greet o'er the gannet's-bath,*

1871.   *and the ringed-prow bear o'er rolling waves*

1872.   *tokens of love. I trow my landfolk*

1873.   *towards friend and foe are firmly joined,*

1874.   *and honor they keep in the olden way."*

1875.   *To him in the hall, then, Healfdene's son*

1876.   *gave treasures twelve, and the trust-of-earls*

1877.   *bade him fare with the gifts to his folk beloved,*

1878.   *hale to his home, and in haste return.*

1879.   *Then kissed the king of kin renowned,*

1880.   *Scyldings' chieftain, that choicest thane,*

1881.   *and fell on his neck. Fast flowed the tears*

1882.   *of the hoary-headed. Heavy with winters,*

1883.   *he had chances twain, but he clung to this,*

1884.   *that each should look on the other again.*

As Beowulf prepares to leave Heorot and return to Geatland, Hrothgar gives him treasures and proclaims peace and alliance between the Geats and the Danes. The old king, knowing that his own life is almost over, weeps as Beowulf leaves, but he hopes to see the hero again.

WHY IT'S KEY

Setting: In this passage, Hrothgar's farewell speech to Beowulf recalls the political instability of the world in which the poem is set, as well as the need for strong and continued alliances between clans such as the Geats and the Scyldings. Although Beowulf and Hrothgar come from different lineages, they both can be seen as acting for the good of others, and their actions will earn them renown and glory for centuries to come. The significance of Beowulf's victories extends beyond the fact that he has saved Heorot, or that he was God's warrior against the evil Grendel; his actions have also forged an alliance between the Geats and the Danes, sealed by Hrothgar's speech and the treasure presented to Beowulf.

Central Concept: This passage complicates the concept that monsters or demons pose the greatest threat to human survival. While the spiritual landscape depicted in the poem does separate human heroes such as Beowulf and Hrothgar from demonic monsters such as Grendel, Hrothgar's speech also reveals the impact that human feuds, battles, and invasions have had on the stability of society, both in Hrothgar's time and for the poem's later audiences: the "murderous strife, such as once they waged" (1866-7).

Author's Craft: In this passage, the poet uses Hrothgar's speech to foreshadow what will happen when Beowulf returns to the land of the Geats. As Hrothgar predicts, when the Geat King dies in a blood feud, Beowulf will "hold [his] kinsman's kingdom." (It is worth noting that earlier in this section, Hrothgar also predicts the sudden arrival of the dragon.) Just as the heroic legends of the past are retold and preserved in song, the feats of heroes such as Beowulf are foretold or predicted, as if heroic lives transcend the normal human experience of time. That heroes achieve some kind of temporal immortality through poetry and literature is worth considering, especially as students read the final section of the poem.

YOUR STUDYSYNC® TV

Discussion Prompt: Why does Hrothgar, in his farewell speech to Beowulf, praise the hero's "keen mind" instead of simply praising his physical strength or his God-given fortune, as he has earlier in the poem? How might Beowulf's accomplishments so far in the poem be seen as feats of intelligence, as well as feats of strength and courage?

Standards: RL.11-12.1, RL.11-12.4; SL.11-12.1.A, SL.11-12.1.C, SL.11-12.1.D

VOCABULARY

vouchsafe
vouch•safe *verb*
To provide or give something, as a favor or as a show of greater status
Since he had inherited several million dollars, the man chose to vouchsafe his long-time cook a piece of land.

wax
wax *verb*
To accumulate or grow in quantity
As the demand for sustainable building increased, the profit margins for her low-energy-lighting business began to wax.

odious
o•di•ous *adjective*
Extremely disgusting or unlikeable; said of a person, action, thing, or situation
He found it odious that his younger sister was constantly telling their parents when he snuck out of the house at night.

bode
bode *verb*
To indicate how a situation will turn out; to show a hint of what might happen in the future
The baseball team had three pitchers on the disabled list, which did not bode well for the team in the upcoming series.

laud
laud *verb*
To praise someone (or something), usually by speaking or writing about them in public
Before the honoree's name was announced, the CEO gave a short speech that lauded her for her years of good service to the company.

CLOSE READ

QUESTION 1: Why is the hilt of the sword that Beowulf gives to King Hrothgar such an important and honorable gift?

Sample Answer: The sword had been used to kill Grendel's mother as well as giants from older times, so it shows the power of men such as Hrothgar and Beowulf over evil or unholy monsters.

Standards: RL.11-12.1

QUESTION 2: What kind of advice does Hrothgar give to Beowulf after Beowulf returns from the battle with Grendel's mother? Use evidence from the text to support your answer.

Sample Answer: Hrothgar cautions Beowulf against forgetting that he is mortal, and taking his glories for granted: "Yet in the end it ever comes / that the frame of the body fragile yields" (1761-2). Hrothgar reminds Beowulf that even in times of triumph, disaster can come suddenly, as it did with Grendel's attacks on Heorot: "Lo, sudden the shift! To me seated secure / came grief for joy when Grendel began to harry my home" (1782-4).

Standards: RL.11-12.1

QUESTION 3: Why does Beowulf return the other sword Hrunting to Unferth, even though Unferth didn't join him in battle and the sword wasn't enough to kill Grendel's mother? Use evidence from the poem to support your answer.

Sample Answer: Beowulf seems to think that although the sword and Unferth aren't as legendary as they might be, they still have some heroic value: "he counted it keen in battle" (1819). Beowulf is generous about Unferth's status as a lesser warrior: "twas a big-hearted man" (1821).

Standards: RL.11-12.1

QUESTION 4: How does Hrothgar react when Beowulf leaves for his ship, and why does he react in this way?

Sample Answer: Hrothgar weeps—"fast flowed the tears" (1881)—when Beowulf leaves. Because Beowulf has killed Grendel and made peace between the Geats and the Danes, the king loves the warrior, but he fears that because of his own old age, they will never meet again— "Heavy with winters" (1882-3).

Standards: RL.11-12.1

LINES 1897-2468: A New Monster

KEY PASSAGE

2406.	Thus safe through struggles the son of Ecgtheow
2407.	had passed a plenty, through perils dire,
2408.	with daring deeds, till this day was come
2409.	that doomed him now with the dragon to strive.
2410.	With comrades eleven the lord of Geats
2411.	swollen in rage went seeking the dragon.
2412.	He had heard whence all the harm arose
2413.	and the killing of clansmen; that cup of price
2414.	on the lap of the lord had been laid by the finder.
2415.	In the throng was this one thirteenth man,
2416.	starter of all the strife and ill,
2417.	care-laden captive; cringing thence
2418.	forced and reluctant, he led them on
2419.	till he came in ken of that cavern-hall,
2420.	the barrow delved near billowy surges,
2421.	flood of ocean. Within 'twas full
2422.	of wire-gold and jewels; a jealous warden,
2423.	warrior trusty, the treasures held,
2424.	lurked in his lair. Not light the task
2425.	of entrance for any of earth-born men!
2426.	Sat on the headland the hero king,
2427.	spake words of hail to his hearth-companions,
2428.	gold-friend of Geats. All gloomy his soul,
2429.	wavering, death-bound. Wyrd full nigh
2430.	stood ready to greet the gray-haired man,

> 2431.   to seize his soul-hoard, sunder apart
>
> 2432.   life and body. Not long would be
>
> 2433.   the warrior's spirit enwound with flesh.

This passage comes after a long section detailing Beowulf's accomplishments as king of the Geats. Having heard that the dragon has attacked his kingdom, killed his clan, and destroyed his halls, he pursues the beast, even as he senses this battle will be his last.

WHY IT'S KEY

Central Concept: This passage shows how the same values of kin, community, and blood feud shape Beowulf's actions as king of the Geats. Although he is an old man, Beowulf becomes "swollen in rage" when the dragon attacks. Although the dragon is motivated by theft of treasure, Beowulf's quest reflects his desire to protect the community and to "avenge the killing of clansmen." Some of Beowulf's anger in this passage seems directed not only at the beast, but at the "starter of all strife and ill," the man who originally stole from the dragon. That a human would betray the safety of kin and community for personal gain offends Beowulf; this man has become more like the dragon, a "jealous warder." Earlier in the section, the poet reveals that the "thirteenth man" who stole from the dragon acted out of loneliness and isolation, having lost all his own clansmen. As in the episode with Grendel, the hero acts for his clan and community, while the monsters (and the rogue humans who provoke them) exhibit a more solitary relationship with the world. Gummere creates an interesting linguistic contrast between the material hoard of the dragon and Beowulf's "soul-hoard"; the hero's treasures are spiritual and character-based.

Character: This passage reveals an important aspect of Beowulf's heroic character, as the hero clearly sees both the greatness and the limits of his human strength. He shows the strength to lead his companions into battle, although the task will be difficult for most humans: "not light the task of entrance for any earth-born men." That said, he does so knowing that this battle will be his last, "all gloomy his soul, wavering, death-bound." The poet makes clear that Wyrd, or fate, demands the end of Beowulf's life at this point, and the hero seems to share the poet's knowledge of his doom. His acceptance that his heroic gifts are fated and therefore will run their course as fate sees fit makes Beowulf a hero in the Anglo-Saxon tradition.

Author's Craft: In a move that might seem strange to contemporary students, the poet "spoils" the ending of the poem in this passage, making it clear that the upcoming battle "doomed [Beowulf]," and that "not long would be the warrior's spirit enwound with flesh." To understand this narrative structure, one might consider that Beowulf's death would have been obvious to the poem's audience from the beginning; as a hero, his story is well-known, and a death in battle only strengthens Beowulf's legend and heroic status, in that he has the heart and the courage to take on worthy foes. This passage suggests that because such stories continue to be told and retold through poetry, heroic lives do not fully end, even as heroes face human death. His legendary deeds transform Beowulf from an ordinary human to an extraordinary one, one whose story survives despite his mortal limits. This genre of poetry resurrects ancient heroes for its audiences, connecting the past with the present. Students might be encouraged to think critically about their own experience of reading the final battle scenes, now that they know the ending in advance.

YOUR STUDYSYNC® TV

Discussion Prompt: The passage suggests that Beowulf, "all gloomy his soul," knows that the upcoming fight with the dragon will be his last. Why does he follow through with the battle, even though he knows that he is "death-bound"? Is this decision heroic? Explain your thinking. What makes Beowulf able to encourage his companions and fight bravely, even though he feels "gloomy" about the whole adventure?

Standards: RL.11-12.1, RL.11-12.4; SL.11-12.1.A, SL.11-12.1.C, SL.11-12.1.D

VOCABULARY

hale
hale *adjective*
In good health, often in reference to one who has been sick or is elderly
My grandmother plays tennis every morning, and this keeps her hale.

wile
wile *noun*
A tricky strategy or underhanded action used to deceive or manipulate someone
She claimed that washing the dishes was a fun thing to do, but her little brother was used to such wiles, and he refused to help his sister with this chore.

spurn
spurn *verb*
To turn down or reject, in a mean or despising manner
Ever since the neighbors reported Cathy for letting her dog off its leash, she decided to spurn their invitations to cookouts and parties.

burnish
bur•nish *verb*
To make something shine or glow by rubbing or buffing it
Before the company came over, they made sure to burnish the iron knocker on the front door.

implore
im•plore *verb*
To plead with someone to do something out of desperation or great importance
She implored her students to get a decent amount of sleep the night before the exam.

CLOSE READ

QUESTION 1: On returning to Hygelac's hall, Beowulf tells many stories, including the story of an upcoming marriage alliance between Hrothgar's daughter and a friend of Hrothgar's (2029-78). Does Beowulf believe that such alliances can protect people from war? Use language from the poem to support your answer.

Sample Answer: Beowulf thinks that although such alliances seem good, they might also provoke jealousy, as they force families to share ancestral wealth and status: "war hate wakens" (2055) and "be broken on both their sides oaths of the earls" (2072-3). These tensions are more powerful than "wife-love" (2074).

Standards: RL.11-12.1

QUESTION 2: Why does Beowulf give all the treasure, armor, and flags from Hrothgar to Hygelac, after telling the Geat king the story of Grendel and Grendel's mother?

Sample Answer: He gives Hygelac the treasure to show what he has accomplished, as other Geatish warriors had long doubted his prowess: "long was he spurned" (2192). He also wants to prove not only his strength but his willingness to use that strength for the good of the kingdom: "nor cruel his mood, though of sons of earth his strength was greatest" (2189-90).

Standards: RL.11-12.1

QUESTION 3: According to Beowulf, what kind of man steals from the dragon, and why does he act in such a desperate way? Use language from the poem to support and explain your answer.

Sample Answer: The man who steals from the dragon is lonely, since all of his own family have died: "my brave are gone" (2263). The man's loneliness makes him sad: "he moaned his woe, alone" (2276-7). He doesn't consider how offending the dragon might hurt other people, because he has no one.

Standards: RL.11-12.1

QUESTION 4: How does the dragon react when he finds that the cup has been stolen? What does he do in response?

Sample Answer: The dragon is angry about the theft—he is "boiling with wrath" (2313)—and he directs this rage at the entire kingdom: "war he desired" (2307). He burns down many villages and buildings, including the hall where Beowulf lives and has his throne.

Standards: RL.11-12.1

QUESTION 5: Why does Beowulf think about and review his past triumphs, as he prepares to battle the dragon not with an army but with just eleven other men? (lines 2333-99)

Sample Answer: Beowulf thinks it would bring dishonor and shame to fight the dragon with a huge army, and he seems to be reviewing his own strength in one-to-one combat with foes and monsters.

Standards: RL.11-12.1

COMPARATIVE TEXTS

Text: "Dragons" in *Mythical and Fabulous Beasts* by Jonathan D. Evans

Compare to: *Beowulf*, lines 2209-332

Connection: In his essay on dragons from *Mythical and Fabulous Beasts*, Jonathan D. Evans considers the origin of the dragon and its occurrence, for good or ill, in diverse cultures, including the Indian *naga*, Chinese *lung*, and the Greek dragon that most directly influenced the dragon in Western literature. Students will compare the dragon in *Beowulf* with one of the dragons in Evans's essay and draw conclusions about dragons' role in myth or literature.

LINES 2469-3192: Beowulf's Heroic Fate

KEY PASSAGE

3141.   . . . The dragon they cast,

3142.   the worm, o'er the wall for the wave to take,

3143.   and surges swallowed that shepherd of gems.

3144.   Then the woven gold on a wain was laden—

3145.   countless quite!—and the king was borne,

3146.   hoary hero, to Hrones-Ness.

3147.   Then fashioned for him the folk of Geats

3148.   firm on the earth a funeral-pile,

3149.   and hung it with helmets and harness of war

3150.   and breastplates bright, as the boon he asked;

3151.   and they laid amid it the mighty chieftain,

3152.   heroes mourning their master dear.

3153.   Then on the hill that hugest of balefires

3154.   the warriors wakened. Wood-smoke rose

3155.   black over blaze, and blent was the roar

3156.   of flame with weeping (the wind was still),

3157.   till the fire had broken the frame of bones,

3158.   hot at the heart. In heavy mood

3159.   their misery moaned they, their master's death.

3160.   Wailing her woe, the widow old,

3161.   her hair upbound, for Beowulf's death

3162.   sung in her sorrow, and said full oft

3163.   she dreaded the doleful days to come,

3164.   deaths enow, and doom of battle,

3165.   and shame.—The smoke by the sky was devoured.

3166.   The folk of the Weders fashioned there

3167.   on the headland a barrow broad and high,

3168.   by ocean-farers far descried:

3169.   in ten days' time their toil had raised it,

3170.   the battle-brave's beacon. Round brands of the pyre

In this passage, the Geat warriors throw the dragon into the ocean and burn Beowulf's body on a ceremonial pyre. They mourn the hero's death with great passion, and a woman fears for the wars that may occur in his absence.

WHY IT'S KEY

Setting: This passage provides a detailed and moving description of the Geatish funeral customs, in which the hero is burned on a pyre, or "funeral-pile," along with his armor and other riches. The images of the funeral fires mirror the grief of Beowulf's people: "blent was the roar of flame with weeping." The passion with which the people esteem Beowulf is mirrored in the intensity of the funeral custom: in their mourning, they are "hot at the heart." The political implications of Beowulf's death are also outlined in this passage, as the widow mourns the "doom of battle" as other warriors fight to fill the void left by such a strong and centralized leader as Beowulf. The widow's grief reminds the reader that a leader who can unite clans was rare in Beowulf's time. Earlier in the section, Wiglaf also predicts that political instability will follow Beowulf's death.

Central Concept: In this passage, the poem makes a final juxtaposition between the poem's heroes and its monsters. Beowulf is buried with grand ceremony, according to his status and wishes, and the other warriors build a lasting monument in his honor—"on the headland a barrow broad and high." In contrast, the dragon is "cast" into the water, "for the waves to take and surges swallowed." That both the Geat warriors and the poet work to make such distinctions, even after both lives have ended, suggests that medieval culture believed itself to be quite close to that more magical and monstrous world, represented by both the dragon and the ocean into which the dragon is committed.

YOUR STUDYSYNC® TV

Discussion Prompt: What practices and customs do the Geats display after Beowulf dies, and why do they honor the dead in this manner? How do these funeral customs differ from those of your own culture, and are they similar in any way? When comparing our burial practices to those seen in *Beowulf*, what does such a comparison suggest about how our world is different from Beowulf's?

Standards: RL.11-12.1, RL.11-12.2, RL.11-12.4; SL.11-12.1.A, SL.11-12.1.C, SL.11-12.1.D

VOCABULARY

resound
re·sound *verb*
To echo or reverberate; to make enough noise that the sound carries a good distance
After the soccer team scored the sudden-death goal, the screams of their fans resounded through the entire neighborhood.

steadfast
stead·fast *adjective*
Consistent or firm in loyalty or commitment to someone or something
Although she knew the three-day hike would be challenging, she proceeded along the steep trail with steadfast effort.

remnant
rem·nant *noun*
A part of something that is left behind or left over
The dog licked the remnants of his owner's dinner from the plate.

writhe
writhe *verb*
To twist or squirm bodily
After the man landed the fish, it writhed on the dock.

laggard
lag·gard *noun*
A person who doesn't complete a certain task or activity as fast as others do
Most runners had finished the 5K race, but a few laggards were still running on the course

lilt
lilt *noun*
A musical quality in somebody's speaking voice; a particular cadence or accent
Although her family hadn't lived in Mississippi for several generations, she still sometimes spoke with a Southern lilt.

sage
sage *adjective*
Something or someone that suggests timeless and lasting intelligence
Her grandmother often gave her sage advice on how to avoid bullies at school.

CLOSE READ

QUESTION 1: How and why does Beowulf choose to arm himself for the fight against the dragon?

Sample Answer: Although Beowulf fought Grendel without weapons, he fears the dragon's fire, and so decides to bring a sword.

Standards: RL.11-12.1

QUESTION 2: How do the other Geatish warriors react when Beowulf fails to kill the dragon during their first encounter, when "no victor's glory the Geats' lord boasted; his brand had failed" (2592-3), and why do they react as they do?

Sample Answer: The Geatish warriors are afraid of the dragon, and they run for the woods. One man, Wiglaf, stays to help Beowulf because he considers loyalty more important than his fear. He believes that breaking his oath to Beowulf will hurt the country and bring "shame on the law of our land" (2665-6).

Standards: RL.11-12.1

QUESTION 3: Based on his final speech, what matters to Beowulf at the end of his life? Use language from the poem to support your answer.

Sample Answer: Beowulf wants Wiglaf and others to use the dragon's treasure to enrich and protect the kingdom: "look ye well / to the needs of my land" (2809-10). Beowulf wants to be remembered by his people, so he asks Wiglaf to build a monument near the shore, "that ocean-wanderers oft may hail / Beowulf's Barrow" (2815-6).

Standards: RL.11-12.1

QUESTION 4: What will happen to the cowardly warriors who gave in to their fears and who return to find that Beowulf died and only Wiglaf stayed to help him?

Sample Answer: They will be known for their cowardice, which according to Wiglaf is a fate worse than death. They will not inherit any tokens or treasure, nor will their descendants have any heroic lineage to look up to (2890-1).

Standards: RL.11-12.1

QUESTION 5: After the other Geatish warriors learn that Beowulf has not returned alive from the fight with the dragon, why do they spend so much time discussing old blood feuds between the Swedes and the Geats? (2956-3037)

Sample Answer: The Geats fear that without Beowulf to protect their land, the Swedes will see an opportunity to settle old scores. The peace that Beowulf's renown has brought them will end, and a time of war will be coming.

Standards: RL.11-12.1

COMPARATIVE TEXTS

Text: *The Volsung Saga* (Old Norse Poem)

Compare to: *Beowulf*, lines 2397–3182

Connection: The Volsung saga is an Old Norse poem dating back to the thirteenth century C.E. It includes the story of Sigurd, renowned as a dragon-slayer. In this excerpt from the saga, which is presented here, Sigurd accompanies his foster father, Regin, in search of Regin's brother, Fafnir, who has been turned into a dragon, or "worm," as a punishment for killing his and Regin's father. Sigurd, who is armed with *his* father Sigmund's powerful sword, receives advice from the god Odin, who appears disguised as an old man. Sigurd kills the dragon, and before Fafnir dies, he warns Sigurd about his future.

Text: "Beowulf: The Monsters and the Critics"

Compare to: *Beowulf* as a whole

Connection: In 1936, J. R. R. Tolkien, author of *The Hobbit and The Lord of the Rings* and professor of Anglo-Saxon at Oxford, delivered a lecture titled "Beowulf: The Monsters and the Critics." It was the first time that an academic or a scholar had argued that *Beowulf* was not just a historical document but a masterpiece of English literature. In fact, *Beowulf* is a unique combination of history and literature and tells many stories.

WRITE TO REVISIT

IMAGINATIVE WRITING

Prompt: Beowulf's final encounter with the dragon is all action and no dialogue, different from Sigurd's encounter with Fafnir in *The Volsung Saga*. If Beowulf and his dragon had a similar give-and-take, what would their conversation be like? Using Sigurd and Fafnir's conversation as a guide, write a 300- to 500-word dialogue between Beowulf and the dragon after their battle. What would the dragon say about Beowulf's fate, about its role as the hero's foe and keeper of men's treasure, or about its long life as a dragon? What would Beowulf say to the dragon, knowing that both will die and taking a moment to look back on his life as a hero and a king? Draw on what you have learned from reading *Beowulf* and what you have learned about both heroes and dragons in this unit.

Standards: RL.11-12.2; W.11-12.3, W.11-12.4, W.11-12.5, W.11-12.9

ANALYTICAL WRITING

Prompt: Think about the many different narratives woven through *Beowulf*: (1) the rise of Christianity and the hanging on of pagan beliefs; (2) the impact of Northerners on Britain, including Viking raiders, Danish kings, and a Geatish slayer of monsters and dragons; (3) a long tradition of heroes exemplified by Theseus and Sigurd, and analyzed by Thomas Carlyle; and (4) an equally long tradition of monsters—from good dragons to a misunderstood Grendel—that are part of a new literary era. Write an essay of at least 400 words that weaves together three or more of these narratives, drawing on at least three relevant texts from this unit as well as outside research and your own ideas. Use these woven strands to express *Beowulf's* central ideas and to show that, in the story, literature and history are inseparable and even dependent on one another.

Standards: RL.11-12.2; RI.11-12.1; RH.11-12.6; W.11-12.2, W.11-12.4, W.11-12.5, W.11-12.9

Beowulf

Anglo-Saxon

translated by
Seamus Heaney
1999

INTRODUCTION

One of the earliest works of literature in English, the epic poem *Beowulf* tells the story of how Beowulf, a heroic Geat (from a land in what is now southern Sweden), saves the kingdom of the Danes from a family of brutal monsters. The monster Grendel, jealous of celebration, community, and fellowship, begins to raid Heorot, the Danish mead-hall, by night, devouring the men who serve King Hrothgar. Outraged by such evil and eager to prove his heroism, Beowulf sails from Geatland to Denmark. He kills Grendel, proving that fate (called *Wyrd* in the poem) has marked him as a great warrior and protector. Grendel's mother, avenging the death of her son, attacks the Danes at Heorot. Beowulf pursues her to her underwater lair and finally kills her with an extraordinary sword. Following his heroic achievements in Denmark, Beowulf becomes king of the Geats. After he rules for fifty years, a new challenge calls on his skill and courage: a rapacious dragon. The poem highlights important elements of early medieval society, such as clan, community, celebration of past heroes and legends, and material gifts such as rings, swords, and crowns that signalled human alliance and protection from invading forces. The monsters in the poem represent both spiritual evils and the evils that come from loneliness and isolation, from loss of clan, heritage, and family.

The author of *Beowulf* is unknown, as the poem was sung orally and then transcribed in manuscript form over a period of several centuries. The events of the poem date to the fifth century, but the only surviving manuscript copy can be dated to around 1000 C.E. Even to the poem's audiences in the ninth, tenth, and eleventh centuries, *Beowulf* would sound as it does today: a tribute to an ancient, heroic time that no longer exists, a mythic time of dragons, monsters, and legendary heroes. Although the characters of *Beowulf* live in a pagan and pre-Christian world, the poet often uses a more Christian perspective to narrate the events of the poem, showing the fusion of pagan and Christian worldviews that is essential to understanding medieval literature. The poem itself, as with the songs of other past warriors sung during the poem's feast scenes, serves to bridge the heroic past with the present by commemorating bygone times and confirming heritage. The Irish poet Seamus Heaney reinforces that bridge for 21st-century readers with a blunt, plain-spoken translation (2000) that retells this tale of medieval Scandinavia with cinematic immediacy.

As students read *Beowulf*, ask them to consider how the poem presents two sets of characters: warriors and kings (Beowulf, Hrothgar, Unferth, and Wiglaf) and monsters (Grendel, Grendel's mother, the dragon). What distinguishes the heroes from the monsters? How are they similar? Do they share any values or characteristics?

Teacher's Edition

USING THIS READING GUIDE

This reading guide presents lessons to support the teaching of the epic poem *Beowulf*. Organized by sections of grouped lines, the lessons preview key vocabulary words and include close reading questions tied to the Common Core State Standards. The lessons identify a key passage in each section that will help you guide students through an exploration of the essential conflicts, themes, and questions in *Beowulf*. This passage will also serve as the jumping-off point from which students will engage in their own StudySyncTV-style group discussion.

Each section of the reading guide also includes a list of comparative texts—provided in the *Beowulf* Full-text Unit in the StudySync Library—that go along with that section. For each comparative text, the reading guide includes important contextual notes and ideas for relating the text to *Beowulf*. The reading guide concludes with two writing prompts that enable students to revisit *Beowulf* both creatively and summatively, with reference to the comparative texts.

BEOWULF

TEXT SECTIONS

LINES 1-188: Trouble in the Danish Hall

The poem begins with an ode to the great Danish warrior-kings of the past, the ancestors of King Hrothgar. A monster named Grendel terrorizes Hrothgar's land and people for twelve years, with grisly and fatal raids on the Danish great hall Heorot.

LINES 189-661: A Hero Comes to Help the Danes

After hearing of Grendel's evil deeds, the Geatish warrior Beowulf travels from his native land to Hrothgar's kingdom and boasts that he will defeat the monster. The Danish warrior Unferth is jealous of Beowulf's claims, but King Hrothgar welcomes the hero.

LINES 662-1250: Hero Meets Monster

Although Grendel's demonic powers protect him from being wounded by human weapons, Beowulf defeats the monster by ripping off one of Grendel's arms. To celebrate Beowulf's triumph, the Danes hold feasts at Heorot, singing songs about great warriors of the past.

LINES 1251-1676: Grendel's Mother Wants Revenge

Furious about the death of her son, Grendel's mother leaves her underwater home and attacks Heorot, killing an honored Dane. Although Unferth is too afraid to fight the monster underwater, Beowulf pursues her to her lair and defeats her.

LINES 1677-1904: Gifts and Alliances

Hrothgar gives Beowulf many treasures and gifts to honor his heroic deeds. Although the two men may never see each other again, these gifts mark a new alliance between the Geats and the Danes.

LINES 1905-2509: **A New Monster**

Beowulf returns to his native Geatland as a hero, and when his lord King Hygelac is killed in a blood feud, Beowulf becomes king. After Beowulf rules wisely and justly for fifty years, a dragon begins to terrorize the Geat kingdom.

LINES 2510-3182: **Beowulf's Heroic Fate**

Beowulf fights the dragon but fails to kill him with a sword, and he suffers a chest wound. A young warrior named Wiglaf, the only Geat courageous enough to stay with Beowulf, stabs the dragon, weakening the beast and allowing Beowulf to kill it. Beowulf dies and is given a hero's funeral.

Lines 1-188: Trouble in the Danish Hall

KEY PASSAGE | Lines 144–169

This passage describes the impact of Grendel's twelve-year reign of terror over Heorot, the great mead-hall of the Danish kingdom. Although the Danish king, Hrothgar, is a descendant of the powerful and heroic Shielding lineage, he can do nothing to defeat or appease the monster, who is motivated by intense jealousy of the Danes' community. News spreads far and wide of Hrothgar's powerlessness against the scourge. There is no compensation or truce possible, as in human warfare. Grendel makes so many brutal raids against Heorot that the Danish people are afraid to gather there in celebration and fellowship. Grendel effectively rules Heorot at night, although his evil nature, as a descendant of Cain, prevents him from approaching the throne itself.

WHY IT'S KEY

Setting: This passage points out the significance of Heorot, "the glittering hall." More than just physical buildings, the great halls of the early medieval kings were sacred centers of community, where celebration always included tributes to the great heroes of the past, therefore affirming the meaning and worth of the kingdom. So much of *Beowulf* contrasts the isolated with the communal, and this passage shows that contrast clearly as Grendel, conducting his "lonely war," causes the Hall to become silent and empty. Understanding the significance of these halls in early medieval culture can help students understand why Beowulf is inspired to travel such great distances to challenge Grendel's "defiance of right." One might compare this passage to the later celebrations that occur at Heorot, after Grendel's defeat.

Alliteration: This passage establishes the poet's use of alliteration, or repeated consonant sounds at the beginning of words, a key feature of Old English poetry—"For twelve winters, seasons of woe / the lord of the Shieldings suffered under / his load of sorrow." In the original form as a poem performed or sung orally, this kind of device helped the singers remember the lines. Even in written form, the alliteration contributes to the poem's songlike quality, which connects it to the great songs of past warriors that appear throughout the text.

Central Concept: This passages provides insight into one of the poem's central question: what separates humans from the monsters that terrorize them? Here, and elsewhere in the poem, the language points to a spiritual difference between Grendel and the human characters; he is compared to a reaver, or raider, from hell; he fights not with metal weapons but with his "rabid hands"; he is "the Lord's outcast." (At many points in the poem, he is also referred to as a descendant of Cain.) While the poem has a complicated relationship to Christianity—as the characters are pagan but the poet often refers to the Christian worldview of its audience—the overall impression is that evil has a physical presence in the world, as embodied by creatures such as Grendel.

Language: Throughout *Beowulf*, Old English terms and references root the reader to important traditions of early Anglo-Saxon Europe. Translator Seamus Heaney also contributes terms from a shared Irish branch of the tree. Note *bothies* (huts outside a main building), line 140. This passage includes some of these references that may stop a reader with their unfamiliarity and setting-specific authenticity: *Shieldings* (early Danes), *lays* (medieval narrative songs), *death-price* (monetary compensation due to the family of one killed in battle), *reavers* (raiders), and *wallstead* (a walled place). Have students keep a running glossary of these time-rooted words.

YOUR STUDYSYNC® TV

Discussion Prompt: What kind of monster is Grendel, and what kind of threat does he pose to Heorot and the Danish people? If we assume that life in the early Middle Ages was more dangerous, that people were often attacked by invaders, why is Grendel such an important monster that his terror inspires an entire poem? What language or words in the passage support your ideas about the kind of monster that Hrothgar is dealing with?

Standards: RL.11-12.1, RL.11-12.4; SL.11-12.1.A, SL.11-12.1.C, SL.11-12.1.D

VOCABULARY

scourge
scourge *noun*
A creature, person, or force that causes great destruction and suffering
Sherman's army was the scourge of the deep South, leaving a path of destruction behind it.

furbished
fur•bished *past participle*
Given a fresh or renewed appearance
This year my garden is furbished with a variety of flowers of all colors.

renege
re•nege *verb*
To go back on one's word
I wouldn't renege on your promise to do the dishes if I were you.

anathema
a•nath•e•ma *noun*
An object of hatred and disgust
The presence of food in the refrigerator older than three days is anathema to my mother.

pagan
pa•gan *adjective*
Practicing a religion that differs from the major religions of the world
The missionaries considered it their duty to convert the pagan sun-worshippers to their religion.

CLOSE READ

QUESTION 1: Although the main characters of the poem are Hrothgar and Beowulf, which characters' lives are described in the poem's opening lines, and why does the poet begin with stories about these characters?

Sample Answer: The poem begins by telling the stories of great Danish kings such as Scyld, Beow, and Healfdene, who are King Hrothgar's ancestors. In the world of *Beowulf*, heroic legends and ancestors are an important part of a person's identity.

Standards: RL.11-12.1

QUESTION 2: Why does Grendel begin attacking Heorot? What makes him so hateful toward the Danish hall? Find evidence in the poem that supports your answer.

Sample Answer: Grendel hears the joyful singing and celebrating that occurs at Heorot, and his rage about his own isolation and loneliness causes him to attack; "It harrowed him / to hear the din of the loud banquet" (lines 87–8)

Standards: RL.11-12.1

QUESTION 3: Where do you see evidence in the poem of the pagan and pre-Christian religions that were an essential part of early medieval society?

Sample Answer: "ogres and elves and evil phantoms" (112), "at pagan shrines they vowed / offerings to idols" (176–7), "their heathenish hope" (179)

Standards: RL.11-12.1

QUESTION 4: Although the characters in the poem are pagan, the poem's audience in later centuries had become more Christian. Where do you see the poet appealing to or referencing these Christian beliefs?

Sample Answer: "whom the Creator had outlawed" (106), "the Almighty made him anathema" (110), "he was the Lord's outcast" (169)

Standards: RL.11-12.1

COMPARATIVE TEXTS

Text: *The Anglo-Saxon Chronicle*

Compare to: *Beowulf*, Lines 1-188

Connection: *The Anglo-Saxon Chronicle* offers a rare window on the turbulent early history of England, extending from the Roman rule of Celtic Britannia to the vying of Saxon and Anglian kingdoms within the island to the incursions of Danes from across the North Sea. Students will discuss the geography and events described in *The Anglo-Saxon Chronicle*— in particular, the conversion of pagan believers like Edwin to the new Christianity—as an introduction to the location (from Britain to Denmark and southern Sweden) and times of *Beowulf*. Students will create an entry in the model of the four excerpted chronicles describing the threat of Grendel to Heorot.

Text: *Ecclesiastical History of the English People* by Bede

Compare to: *Beowulf*, Lines 86-188

Connection: In the *Ecclesiastical History of the English People*, the English monk Bede chronicles the conversion of Edwin, king of Northumbria, from paganism to Christianity in 627 C.E., after Edwin defeats his West-Saxon foes (an event recorded in the Anglo-Saxon Chronicles StudySync entry). Edwin receives an enthusiastic thumbs-up from his high priest, Coifi, who is only too willing to destroy the pagan gods he had recently promoted. This sea change in religion is shown in the Christian values invoked in *Beowulf*, despite the pagan setting—sending, in fact, a message by depicting the conquest of pagan monsters by a "Christianized" hero.

Lines 189–661: A Hero Comes to Help the Danes

KEY PASSAGE | Lines 559–603

In this passage, Beowulf responds to the sneering of the envious Unferth, who gives an unflattering version of a famous swimming contest between Beowulf and the warrior Breca, which he believes Beowulf actually lost. Beowulf sets Unferth straight, giving a spellbinding account of the swimming competition, in which wild weather stirred one sea monster after another into attacking Beowulf, who managed to slay all nine, ridding the sea of a long-standing menace, finally coming ashore in Finland. Then Beowulf aims his scorn at Unferth, contrasting his own record of heroic combat with Unferth's empty one, enlarging his boast to raise Geats above Danes, and zeroing in on his certain victory over the Dane-hungry Grendel.

WHY IT'S KEY

Central Concept: This passage reveals an important element of the early medieval hero: the hero's boast. The great warriors achieved their status not only from heroic deeds but also from having the courage to claim what they were going to accomplish in advance. In this passage, Beowulf boasts that he will defeat Grendel, but he also criticizes Unferth for falsely boasting about his prowess while failing to protect his people from the monster. That a hero should seek out danger is shown in the story Beowulf tells about the sea-monsters; he chose to undertake the swimming test, fully aware of its perils. A hero can't rest on his achievements, which explains why Beowulf wants to fight Grendel. Students might keep this in mind later, as they consider why Beowulf, though much older and weaker, decides to fight the dragon.

Character: This passage, along with all the interactions between Beowulf and Unferth, reveals important aspects of Beowulf's character. One can see his strict adherence to the heroic codes of his day: he seeks out monsters, he battles evil forces from which ordinary humans cannot defend themselves, and he doesn't tolerate other warriors, such as Unferth, who boast but can't follow through. He seems to understand the importance not only of heroic acts but also of how others tell or sing the stories of those acts, as he takes time to set the record straight about the swimming test.

Setting: As Beowulf tells this story of his earlier underwater triumphs, the reader can see how the poem depicts the ocean, and all watery realms, as places of evil and danger, inhabited by monstrous creatures outside the control of human society and culture. Only

Copyright © BookheadEd Learning, LLC

the most heroic of humans, such as Beowulf, are capable of crossing and protecting these boundaries. This distinction between the solid land on which humans live and the supernatural realms where monsters exist will help students understand Beowulf's later encounter with Grendel's mother. Students might consider the irony of how Unferth challenges Beowulf's prowess as a swimmer in this section of the poem, as he will later prove too cowardly to fight Grendel's mother underwater.

Contextual Details (Fate): Although Beowulf tells the story of Breca and the sea monsters to protect his reputation from Unferth's challenge, he also credits his success to the power of fate, or "Wyrd" in Old English. While heroes are known for their individual courage and actions, their status also derives from more cosmic forces, such as destiny and divine will.

YOUR STUDYSYNC® TV

Discussion Prompt: Why does Beowulf talk—or "boast"—about his heroic deeds before he goes to fight Grendel? In other cultures, including our own, is boasting considered heroic? Why or why not? In what situations do we value boasting about the hard things we intend to do? Why might boasting be a difficult, challenging, or important task for a hero?

Standards: RL.11-12.1, RL.11-12.4; SL.11-12.1.A, SL.11-12.1.C, SL.11-12.1.D

VOCABULARY

canny
can•ny *adjective*
Wise and aware, especially in practical matters
It took a canny observer to figure out which doctor was an impostor.

interlopers
in•ter•lop•ers *noun*
People who enter a place or situation where they are not wanted; trespassers
The security guard confronted the three interlopers and escorted them from the party.

gumption
gump•tion *noun*
The willingness to take on a challenge with creativity and energy
Back in the locker room, the coach urged her players to show a little gumption in going after rebounds.

formidable
for•mi•da•ble *adjective*
Impressively powerful in strength, intellect, or ability
Susie was matched against a formidable opponent in the trivia contest, but she refused to be intimidated.

vied
vied *verb*
Competed with an opponent to gain an advantage or reward
The two bakers vied for the title of Royal Cookie-maker in a series of bake-offs.

undaunted
un•daunt•ed *adjective*
Not intimidated by a challenging task or a threat
"Begone, Bigbones!" the child yelled in a squeaky voice, undaunted by the giant who stood in his way.

CLOSE READ

QUESTION 1: How do the Danes react when Beowulf and his men arrive at the harbor to fight Grendel?

Sample Answer: They question the Geat hero about who he is and why he has sailed to Denmark. They're afraid of the mighty warriors who arrive in ships.

Standards: RL.11-12.1

QUESTION 2: Why does Hrothgar decide to allow Beowulf and his warriors into his kingdom?

Sample Answer: He learns of Beowulf's family heritage, and he trusts that the son of famous warriors wants to help. He knows people in Beowulf's family from an earlier time in his life.

Standards: RL.11-12.1

QUESTION 3: Does Beowulf think it possible that the monster Grendel might defeat him, or is he certain of victory? Find evidence from his conversations with Hrothgar that support your answer.

Sample Answer: Beowulf understands that Grendel might kill him. He describes what might happen in this case: "If Grendel wins, it will be a gruesome day" (442). He says that the outcome of the battle depends on fate: "Fate goes ever as fate must" (455).

Standards: RL.11-12.1

QUESTION 4: What reason does Unferth have for doubting that Beowulf will be able to save the Danes from Grendel?

Sample Answer: Unferth contends that Beowulf lost a swimming contest with another warrior, so Unferth thinks Beowulf is not as mighty a warrior as everyone else thinks.

Standards: RL.11-12.1

QUESTION 5: After Beowulf speaks, how do Hrothgar and his Queen Wealhtheow feel, and why do they feel this way? Give examples from the poem that support your answer.

Sample Answer: The Danish king and queen are happy to hear that Beowulf has the determination, heart, and courage that are needed to fight Grendel. They trust that he can take on the monster. Examples: "Then the gray-haired treasure-giver was glad" (607); "This formal boast by Beowulf the Geat / pleased the lady well"(639–40); "Never ... / have I entrusted or given control / of the Danes' hall to anyone but you." (655–7).

Standards: RL.11-12.1

COMPARATIVE TEXTS

Text: *Beowulf*, Lines 144-300 (Heaney translation)

Compare to: Lines 144-300 (Gummere translation)

Connection: Students will reread lines 144-300, from the 2000 translation by Irish poet Seamus Heaney. Heaney's translation, based on the same Anglo-Saxon text as Gummere's 1910 translation, has been described as "both direct and sophisticated, making previous versions look slightly flowery and antique by comparison." Students will draw their own conclusions from a comparison of the two translations, exploring the same themes in different modes of expression.

Text: *On Heroes* by Thomas Carlyle

Compare to: *Beowulf*, Lines 189-662

Connection: Thomas Carlyle's consideration of heroism begins with an essay on the hero as a reflection of the divine. He discourses on the wonder with which pagans, or worshippers of multiple gods and goddesses, regarded nature, a divinity especially conferred on humanity, and achieving its highest stature in hero worship. Students will apply Carlyle's ideas to the portrayal of the Anglo-Saxon hero, namely Beowulf.

Lines 663-1254: Hero Meets Monster

KEY PASSAGE | Lines 749–851

This passage sees Beowulf's defeat of Grendel through to the end, beginning with Grendel's shocked realization that he has met his match, and more, in Beowulf's steely grip. While Beowulf grapples with Grendel, the hero's men try to come to his defense with swords. The monster has enchanted himself, and cannot be cut by any man-made weapon, but Beowulf prevails bare-handed, ultimately ripping off one of Grendel's arms. Mortally wounded, Grendel flees back to his marsh lair to die.

WHY IT'S KEY

Character: Because Grendel is not human and therefore is untrained in swordfighting, Beowulf chooses to fight him hand-to-hand. Swords, as it turns out, can't harm Grendel, but the choice to fight bare-handed shows the degree to which Beowulf honors his combat enemies, even when they are monstrous. The method is also further proof of Beowulf's courage and strength.

Central Concept: This passage, as well as the preceding section that narrates Grendel's final attack on Heorot, shows in sometimes gory detail the qualities that distinguish the monster from the human world he hates so much. The depth of Grendel's anger at humans is mentioned, as is his spiritual desolation (810) and the lonely and unholy fate that awaits the monster after death (806-7). This distinction between heroes and monsters is also heightened by the fact that a close view of Grendel's death isn't even shown in the poem (817-20). Since dying in valiant battle is further proof of their courage, Anglo-Saxon poetry honors its heroes through detailed and ceremonial descriptions of their final moments, as students will see in the final section of the poem.

Contextual Details (Weapons): This passage also shows the significant role that weapons play in Anglo-Saxon warrior culture and in *Beowulf*. The iron swords, as with any forged metal items, are proof that humans are different from monsters; Beowulf notes earlier that Grendel fights without armament (683-5). The Geats attempt to kill Grendel with ancestral swords, showing how swords, like the family histories that are detailed at various points in the poem, are important markers of lineage, family, and warrior status. These physical tokens of past glory relate to one of the poem's underlying purposes: to connect the legendary and heroic past with the contemporary world of its audience.

YOUR STUDYSYNC® TV

Discussion Prompt: What lesson or lessons do you think Anglo-Saxon listeners of *Beowulf* were meant to take away? Consider the real dangers the medieval population of Britain or Scandinavia faced, and the beliefs they turned to for courage and reassurance. What was the importance of a gripping tale of a contest between a hero and a monster? How has that model changed today—or is it more similar to the Middle Ages than different?

Standards: RL.11-12.1, RL.11-12.2; SL.11-12.1.A, SL.11-12.1.C, SL.11-12.1.D

VOCABULARY

spurned
spurned *past participle*
Rejected or turned away because of a lack of interest or respect
Spurned by the judges at the county fair, Mrs. Teasdale threw her custard pie at the grand prize winner.

baleful
bale·ful *adjective*
Threatening; showing extreme dislike
My cousin shot me a baleful look after I got him in trouble.

ignominious
ig·no·min·i·ous *adjective*
Disgraceful; humiliating
The principal said that my laughing fit in study hall was ignominious.

hoard
hoard *noun*
A large collection of valuable items and meaningful possessions
My uncle kept his hoard of comic books in mint condition.

prowess
prow·ess *noun*
A special skill or ability
Rupert often bragged about his prowess in archery, but it turned out he meant arching his eyebrows.

thrall
thrall *noun*
Being controlled by, or controlling, someone
Until he got loose and came home, my pet poodle was in the thrall of a family living three blocks away.

CLOSE READ

QUESTION 1: How does Beowulf prepare for his battle with Grendel, and why does he make such preparations?

Sample Answer: He takes off his armor, since Grendel fights only with brute strength; he waits all night, awake, in Heorot, since he knows that the monster is due to attack.

Standards: RL.11-12.1

QUESTION 2: What emotions motivate Grendel during his attack on Heorot? What language from the poem supports your answer?

Sample Answer: Grendel is very angry at the Danes, or perhaps at human society in general: "Then his rage boiled over" (724). He also feels happy at the chance to kill Danes: "And his glee was demonic" (730). Then he feels terrified of Beowulf: "Every bone in his body / quailed and recoiled" (752–3).

Standards: RL.11-12.1

QUESTION 3: How do the Danes celebrate Beowulf's victory, and why do they celebrate in this way?

Sample Answer: The Danes hold a feast at Heorot, and the poet sings about Beowulf's victory and other heroic acts. They do this to honor Beowulf's deeds, and to connect him to other great heroes. They also hang Grendel's arm, or "hand-spear," from the roof, to show the strangeness of the monster and the greatness of Beowulf's accomplishment.

Standards: RL.11-12.1

QUESTION 4: What gifts does Hrothgar give to Beowulf in return for killing the monsters? Why does he give him these gifts?

Sample Answer: Hrothgar gives Beowulf treasure from his hoard, including a breastplate, a helmet, a flag, and a sword. These gifts signify Hrothgar's gratitude and love for Beowulf (he adopts Beowulf "in [his] heart as a dear son"). They will also be signs of alliance between the Geats and the Danes in future battle situations.

Standards: RL.11-12.1

QUESTION 5: What gifts does Wealhtheow (Hrothgar's queen) give to Beowulf, and what is the purpose of these gifts?

Sample Answer: Wealhtheow gives Beowulf another set of armor that was once worn by Geats but is now part of the Danish wealth. These gifts are proof of Beowulf's glory as a warrior. They are also given with the expectation that he will be kind and supportive of Hrothgar and Wealhtheow's sons in the future.

Standards: RL.11-12.1

COMPARATIVE TEXTS

Text: *Grendel* by John Gardner

Compare to: *Beowulf*, lines 711-853

Connection: The story of the fateful battle between hero and monster in *Beowulf* is told from Grendel's darkly funny first-person perspective in John Gardner's *Grendel*. Grendel observes the festivities at the opening of Heorot, Hrothgar's mead-hall, bemoaning his brutish nature and stumbling across a victim of a homicide that he gets blamed for. Students will compare this sensitive, misunderstood Grendel with the purely evil monster in *Beowulf* and then analyze the different purposes of the authors.

Text: *The Fury of the Northmen* by John Marsden

Compare to: *Beowulf*, lines 915-1231

Connection: In 793 C.E., heralded by sightings of dragons, Norse Vikings came ashore on the island of Lindisfarne in northeast England, the site of a renowned monastery. The sea-raiders plundered the abbey, killing many monks. The raid is considered the beginning of the Viking Age, characterized by many similar attacks by northern raiders on British settlements over many of the next 300 years. Students will research the relationship between Scandinavians and Britons between the 8th and 11th centuries, reflected in sources such as *Beowulf* and *The Fury of the Northmen*. Students might consider the English audience of the poem; the Scandinavian characters; and the ways in which Beowulf, Hrothgar, the Danish saga-songs sung at Heorot, and Grendel's raids on Heorot all relate to or compare with Viking history and culture.

Lines 1251-1676: Grendel's Mother Wants Revenge

KEY PASSAGE | Lines 1518–1611

In this passage, Beowulf battles Grendel's mother in her deepwater lair. Finding that Unferth's sword is ineffective, he engages her in hand-to-hand combat. She gains the advantage and tries to stab Beowulf with a knife, but his chain-mail protects him. With the outcome in doubt, divine favor rests with Beowulf: he finds an ancient sword in Grendel's mother's treasure hoard, and he kills her with it. Illumined in heavenly light, Beowulf discovers Grendel's corpse and cuts off the head as a trophy of conquest. Meanwhile, Hrothgar and his retinue, believing Beowulf dead, return to Heorot while the Geats do not give up their vigil. Before Beowulf justifies their faith and surfaces, he is left with the hilt of the ancient sword as a token of victory, the blade having melted away, in a kind of divine thaw.

WHY IT'S KEY

Character: The episode with Grendel's mother, this passage in particular, provides evidence that although the poem makes clear distinctions between monsters and heroes, the monsters are still motivated by some of the same values and social customs as the humans. A blood feud, where one avenges the death of one's kin through further violence, motivates Grendel's mother. Such blood feuds are referenced throughout the poem, especially in the stories of past heroes and kings.

Contextual Details (Weapons): This passage develops the sacred significance of weapons in the world of *Beowulf*. The sword that Beowulf finds has a mystical quality, due to its ancient, mythic pedigree. Like the poem itself, which connects mythic heroes to later English society and culture, the sword connects Beowulf to the time of the "giants." By contrast, Unferth's sword Hrunting, which was lent to Beowulf prior to the combat, cannot be used in the fight. Perhaps Hrunting is tainted by Unferth's character flaws, or maybe the power to kill an evil creature of a prior generation requires a sword even older. Either way, there is irony in Grendel's mother being killed by a weapon she herself respected as a treasure to keep and display.

Central Concept: Although the poem mentions the grace of God and fate in Beowulf's battle with Grendel, the degree to which heroes' victories and monsters' defeats are determined by overarching spiritual and, more specifically, Christian forces is clearly shown in the battle with Grendel's mother. The mystical sword appears after "Holy God / decided the victory" and was able to "redress the balance" in favor of Beowulf. Grendel's mother is likely fated to lose by virtue of her kinship connections to Cain, an ancestry of evil. Further proofs are the light that appears after her demise like "heaven's candle" and the comparison of the melted sword to the melting of ice by "the true Lord." Although *Beowulf* is too influenced by Scandinavian sagas and pre-Christian culture to be considered a formal allegory, one can see in its narrative arc a shift toward that later form of medieval literature, the allegory, in which the overarching narratives of Christianity play a central role.

Language: This section contains some archaic water-related terms, such as *mere* and *tarn* for "lake," and *welter*, meaning "the turbulent formation of waves and currents." Knowing the definitions of these words might help students better understand the journey Beowulf makes to Grendel's mother's lair.

YOUR STUDYSYNC® TV

Discussion Prompt: Why is Beowulf able to defeat Grendel's mother? Is his victory proof of his prowess as a swimmer and swordsman? Or is it owed to supernatural forces that support the rightness of his cause? Is his cause more righteous than Grendel's mother's cause? Is Grendel's mother justified in her attacks on Heorot? Explain what you think this battle proves.

Standards: RL.11-12.1, RL.11-12.2; SL.11-12.1.A, SL.11-12.1.C, SL.11-12.1.D

VOCABULARY

depredations
dep•re•da•tions *noun*
Instances of preying upon, seizing, and plundering
The depredations of these ruthless pirates have terrorized us for too long!

bulwark
bul•wark *noun*
A wall providing defense; something or someone serving to protect and reinforce
When I was sick, my grandfather was a bulwark, never leaving my bedside.

tempered
tem•pered *verb*
Made stronger and harder by going through intense experience
The warriors owed their toughness to being tempered in the fire of pain and loss.

redress
re•dress *verb*
To correct, repair, or make right
After the debate, he tried to redress his insulting remarks by giving her a box of candy.

fettle
fet•tle *noun*
Condition; physical or mental health
My brother always comes down to breakfast whistling a tune, in fine fettle.

CLOSE READ

QUESTION 1: How does Hrothgar explain Grendel's mother's attack on Heorot? Use language from the poem to support your answer.

Sample Answer: Hrothgar says Grendel's mother is getting revenge for her son's death; she's acting out a blood feud between her family and the humans at Heorot: "she has taken up the feud / because of last night, when you killed Grendel" (1333–4), "driven to avenge her kinsman's death" (1340).

Standards: RL.11-12.1

QUESTION 2: What reassurance does Beowulf have for Hrothgar concerning the danger he is about to face?

Sample Answer: Beowulf tells Hrothgar not to grieve for him because a warrior's best defense in life is avenging those he holds dear and achieving glory before he dies.

Standards: RL.11-12.1

QUESTION 3: How does Unferth participate in Beowulf's quest to fight Grendel's mother in her underwater lair?

Sample Answer: Unferth is too scared to join Beowulf in the underwater battle. He does lend Beowulf his sword, called "Hrunting," for use in the battle.

Standards: RL.11-12.1

QUESTION 4: In addition to bringing back the hilt of the mystical sword, what trophy does Beowulf bring back from Grendel's mother's underwater lair?

Sample Answer: He brings back the head of Grendel. The monster had returned home to die, but Beowulf has found the corpse and decapitated it.

Standards: RL.11-12.1

COMPARATIVE TEXTS

Text: *The Myths and Legends of Ancient Greece and Rome:* Theseus by E. M. Berens

Compare to: *Beowulf*, lines 663-1656

Connection: Centuries before *Beowulf,* ancient Greeks retold the adventures of their own mythical superhero, Theseus, whose path to glory was strewn with dead giants, exiled relatives, and Theseus's most notorious foe, the man-bull called the Minotaur. How does the Greek hero's feat of ending the Minotaur's reign of terror compare with Beowulf's ending of the twelve-year siege of Grendel and his mother?

Text: *DC Comics: Sixty Years of the World's Favorite Comic Book Heroes* by Les Daniels

Compare to: *Beowulf*, lines 663-1656

Connection: DC Comics introduced Superman and Batman in 1939, ushering a new age of the superhero into American popular culture. Immediately, competitors of DC created their own comic-book heroes, including Wonder Man, Captain Marvel, Captain America, the Human Torch, Sub-Mariner, Plastic Man, Blackhawk, and Blue Beetle. Students will draw on the similarities and differences between comic-book superheroes and the Anglo-Saxon hero to create a graphic adventure for Beowulf.

Lines 1677-1904: Gifts and Alliances

KEY PASSAGE | Lines 1813–1887

In this passage, Beowulf prepares to leave Heorot and return to Geatland. He delivers a gracious speech, promising to return with a force of thanes if Hrothgar needs help in the future. Hrothgar, deeply moved and full of affection for Beowulf, gives him treasures and proclaims peace and alliance between the Geats and the Danes. He predicts that Beowulf will someday make a great king of Geatland. He expresses his hope to see the hero again but has a foreboding that he might not live long enough to see that happen.

WHY IT'S KEY

Setting: In this passage, Hrothgar's farewell speech to Beowulf recalls the political instability of the world in which the poem is set, as well as the need for strong and continued alliances between clans such as the Geats and the Scyldings. Although Beowulf and Hrothgar come from different lineages, they both can be seen as acting for the good of others, and their actions will earn them renown and glory for centuries to come. The significance of Beowulf's victories extends beyond the fact that he has saved Heorot, or that he was God's warrior against the evil Grendel; his actions have also forged an alliance between the Geats and the Danes, sealed by Hrothgar's speech and the treasure presented to Beowulf.

Central Concept: This passage complicates the concept that monsters or demons pose the greatest threat to human survival. While the spiritual landscape depicted in the poem does separate human heroes such as Beowulf and Hrothgar from demonic monsters such as Grendel, Hrothgar's speech also reveals the impact that human feuds, battles, and invasions have had on the stability of society, both in Hrothgar's time and for the poem's later audiences: the "hatreds we have harbored in the past" (1858).

Author's Craft: In this passage, the poet uses Hrothgar's speech to foreshadow what will happen when Beowulf returns to the land of the Geats. As Hrothgar predicts, Beowulf will "undertake the lordship of [his] homeland" after the Geat king, Hygelac, dies in a blood feud. Just as the heroic legends of the past are retold and preserved in song, the feats of heroes such as Beowulf are foretold or predicted, as if their legends were already part of the national lore. Students might discuss whether heroes, though mortal beings, achieve immortality through poetry and literature.

YOUR STUDYSYNC® TV

Discussion Prompt: Saying farewell to a hero can be complicated. Discuss the mixed emotions Hrothgar feels—gratitude, a fatherly affection, and perhaps a feeling of separation anxiety: What will we Danes do without you? Remembering Unferth's envy of Beowulf's reputation, might there be some resentment on the part of Danes watching the hero part with a huge treasure hoard? Or does the godlike power of a hero make such feelings beside the point? Compare Beowulf's exit to that of other heroes, such as the boasting athlete or the lone stranger riding off into the sunset.

Standards: RL.11-12.1, RL.11-12.4; SL.11-12.1.A, SL.11-12.1.C, SL.11-12.1.D

VOCABULARY

venerable
ven•er•a•ble *adjective*
Well-respected, especially for age and wisdom
Their history teacher, a venerable figure in the school, was retiring after fifty years.

lavish
lav•ish *adjective*
Giving richly and generously
The grateful family was lavish in their praise of the boy who saved their dog.

mainstay
main•stay *noun*
A central figure on whom the welfare of many others depends
She was the mainstay of the library, working tirelessly until enough funds were raised to keep it going.

pariah
pa•ri•ah *adjective*
Outcast, shunned, unwanted
After she confessed to stealing her rival's recipe, Pauline became the pariah member of the Cooking Club.

alacrity
a•lac•ri•ty *noun*
Quick eagerness
Marjie's date moved with alacrity to open the passenger door of the car for her.

CLOSE READ

QUESTION 1: Why is the hilt of the sword that Beowulf gives to King Hrothgar such an important and honorable gift?

Sample Answer: The sword had been used to kill Grendel's mother and has the value of antiquity, dating to the time of giants, wielded by them or used to slay them; so it shows the enduring power of men over evil or unholy monsters.

Standards: RL.11-12.1

QUESTION 2: What advice does Hrothgar give to Beowulf after Beowulf returns in triumph? Use evidence from the text to support your answer.

Sample Answer: Hrothgar cautions Beowulf to learn from the example of Heremod, a "pariah king who cut himself off from his own kind" and became bloodthirsty with greed. He reminds Beowulf that the power of his youth is brief—"it fades quickly" (1762) and is soon followed by any number of reversals of fortune until "death will arrive, / dear warrior, to sweep you away" (1767-8). With this in mind, Hrothgar counsels Beowulf to avoid the traps of pride and greed, to "understand true values" (1723) and seek "eternal rewards." (1760)

Standards: RL.11-12.1

QUESTION 3: How would you describe the relationship between Beowulf and Unferth as Beowulf prepares to leave? Use evidence from the poem to support your answer.

Sample Answer: Beowulf is going out of his way to be polite toward Unferth as he returns the sword Hrunting to him. Even though it was ineffective for Beowulf in battle, he assures Unferth that the sword "was a friend in battle." (1810) The poet calls Beowulf "a considerate man" for not blaming Unferth for lending him a defective sword. (1812) There is a touch of condescension—noblesse oblige—in Beowulf's attitude toward his former heckler. He all but pats Unferth on the head.

Standards: RL.11-12.1

QUESTION 4: How does Hrothgar react when Beowulf leaves for his ship, and why does he react in this way?

Sample Answer: Hrothgar embraces Beowulf strongly and weeps as Beowulf leaves. He is deeply grateful to Beowulf for killing the two monsters and forging an alliance between the Geats and the Danes, and he is emotional because he guesses that his own old age makes it unlikely that they will meet again.

Standards: RL.11-12.1

Lines 1897-2468: A New Monster

Copyright © BookheadEd Learning, LLC

KEY PASSAGE | Lines 2391–2424

This passage comes at the end a long section detailing Beowulf's accomplishments as regent of Geatland, then, with the death of Hygelac's son and heir, as king of the Geats. After avenging the crown prince's death, Beowulf rules wisely and well for fifty years. But now Beowulf has learned that a vengeful dragon, robbed of a goblet by a Geat slave, has attacked the kingdom and destroyed his home. The hero makes ready to pursue and slay the beast, as he had with monsters in his prime, though he senses that he will not survive this final battle.

WHY IT'S KEY

Central Concept: This passage shows how the same values of kin, community, and blood feud shape Beowulf's actions as king of the Geats. Although he is an old man, Beowulf heeds the call of duty when the dragon attacks. Beowulf's duty reflects his desire to protect the community and to avenge the razing of his home. Earlier in the section, the poet reveals that the man who stole from the dragon acted out of desperation, a slave caught between flight from his master and guilt for fleeing—he steals a would-be peace-offering and causes catastrophe. Beowulf acts for his society, to repair the damage done by a man disconnected from society, unsure of who he belongs to. Ironically, the slave finds himself the thirteenth man of Beowulf's group, retracing his steps for the good of the Geats.

Character: This passage reveals an important aspect of Beowulf's heroic character, as the hero clearly sees both the greatness and the limits of his human strength. He shows the strength to lead his companions into battle, knowing that this battle will be his last. His acceptance that his heroic gifts are finite—recalling Hrothgar's warning to prepare for the inevitable waning of old age—and therefore will run their course as fate sees fit makes Beowulf a hero in the Anglo-Saxon tradition of self-sacrifice for a noble cause.

Author's Craft: The poet makes an interesting juxtaposition in this passage, contrasting two scenes in multiple ways. First, we see Beowulf, now king, scouting the dragon's lair in the "earth-vault … an underground barrow near the sea-billows / and heaving waves," reminiscent of the underwater lair of Grendel's mother, site of Beowulf's earlier triumph over a monster. Next we see "the veteran king … on the cliff-top," not buried in a treasure hoard but looking over his past and contemplating a different treasure, "his coffered soul," which he knows will soon be separated from his physical self in death. So we have a deep place versus a lofty place; an earthly, temporal treasure hoard versus a spiritual, immortal one; and a life devoted to glory in battle versus death and closure.

YOUR STUDYSYNC® TV

Discussion Prompt: This key passage presents two sides of Beowulf—the enraged king underground, having to clean up another mess; and the sad king on the cliff-top, contemplating his death. Discuss this portrait of the hero in old age, drawn into a final battle. Why not sit this one out, leave the challenge for younger heroes-in-the-making to meet? Is there something in the hero's job description that requires him to sacrifice himself? Or are the rules being written by the storyteller and the audience, the rules of mythology? How does Beowulf feel about his impending death?

Standards: RL.11-12.1, RL.11-12.4; SL.11-12.1.A, SL.11-12.1.C, SL.11-12.1.D

VOCABULARY

hale
hale *adjective*
In good health, often in reference to one who has been sick or is elderly
My grandmother plays tennis every morning, and this keeps her hale.

wiles
wiles *noun*
Cleverness in strategy, often used to deceive or manipulate someone
She claimed that washing the dishes was fun, but her little brother was used to such wiles, and he politely declined.

cache
cache *noun*
Items of the same kind gathered and hidden in a secure place
We dug up a metal box with a cache of valuable baseball cards inside.

vehement
ve•he•ment *adjective*
Forceful, passionate, driven by strong emotion
The protesters were vehement about their opposition to the candidate.

prodigiious
pro•di•gious *adjective*
Great, vast, impressive or extensive
She had a prodigious gift for languages and spoke eight fluently.

CLOSE READ

QUESTION 1: On returning to Hygelac's hall, Beowulf tells many stories, including the story of an upcoming marriage alliance between Hrothgar's daughter and a friend of Hrothgar's (2020-68). What is Beowulf's attitude toward such arrangements? Use language from the poem to support your answer.

Sample Answer: Beowulf thinks that although such alliances seem logical, they might also "stir up trouble," (2046) as they force families to share ancestral history and ancestral rancor and resentments that go with it.

Standards: RL.11-12.1

  Teacher's Edition

QUESTION 2: Why does Beowulf give all the treasure, armor, and flags from Hrothgar to Hygelac, after telling the Geat king the story of Grendel and Grendel's mother?

Sample Answer: He gives Hygelac the treasure to show what he has accomplished, as other Geatish warriors had long doubted his prowess. He also wants to prove not only his strength but his willingness to use that strength for the good of the kingdom.

Standards: RL.11-12.1

QUESTION 3: According to Beowulf, what feelings likely drove the original owner of the treasure hoard to bury it? Use language from the poem to support and explain your answer.

Sample Answer: The man who buried the treasure was probably lonely and indifferent to his possessions, since all of his own family and retinue had died and he had no one to enjoy the treasure with. (2247–2270)

Standards: RL.11-12.1

QUESTION 4: How does the dragon react when he finds that the cup has been stolen? What does he do in response?

Sample Answer: The dragon is angry about the theft and he directs this rage at the entire kingdom. He burns down many villages and buildings, including the hall where Beowulf lives and has his throne.

Standards: RL.11-12.1

QUESTION 5: How does Beowulf react after hearing about the dragon's destructive attacks? Why does he prepare to battle the dragon not with an army but with just eleven other men?

Sample Answer: At first Beowulf is cast into despair and confusion, wondering why this attack happened. Then he focuses on revenge, ordering a great shield to be made. He has too much pride to fight the dragon with a huge army, having defeated monsters so handily before, as he reviews past victories over a variety of foes. (2324–66)

Standards: RL.11-12.1

COMPARATIVE TEXTS

Text: "Dragons" in *Mythical and Fabulous Beasts* by Jonathan D. Evans

Compare to: *Beowulf*, lines 2209-332

Connection: In his essay on dragons from *Mythical and Fabulous Beasts*, Jonathan D. Evans considers the origin of the dragon and its occurrence, for good or ill, in diverse cultures, including the Indian *naga*, Chinese *lung*, and the Greek dragon that most directly influenced the dragon in Western literature. Students will compare the dragon in *Beowulf* with one of the dragons in Evans's essay and draw conclusions about dragons' role in myth or literature.

Teacher's Edition

Lines 2510-3182: Beowulf's Heroic Fate

KEY PASSAGE | Lines 3110–3182

In this passage, Wiglaf, the only thane to stand with Beowulf against the dragon, takes charge of fulfilling Beowulf's last wishes. He orders the building of a funeral pyre. He picks seven thanes to loot the dragon's hoard. The Geat warriors throw the dragon's corpse into the ocean. Then they burn Beowulf's body on the pyre. They mourn the hero's death with great passion, and a Geat woman fears for the wars that will occur in his absence. Finally, the Geats build a barrow, or ceremonial mound, where they bury Beowulf's ashes and the remaining treasure hoard as a memorial for their king whom they deem "kindest to his people and keenest to win fame." (3182)

WHY IT'S KEY

Setting: This passage provides a detailed and moving description of the Geatish funeral customs, in which the hero is burned on a pyre, or "funeral-pile," along with his armor and other riches. The images of the funeral fires reflect the grief of Beowulf's people. The passion with which the people esteem Beowulf is mirrored in the intensity of the pyre. The political implications of Beowulf's death are also outlined in this passage, as the woman (perhaps a parallel to Grendel's mother) bemoans the certainty of war as invaders try to fill the void left by the death of Beowulf. Earlier in the section, Wiglaf also predicts that political instability will follow Beowulf's death.

Central Concept: In this passage, the poem makes a final juxtaposition between heroes and monsters. Beowulf is cremated with grand ceremony, according to his status and wishes, and warriors build in his honor a barrow on a cliff (echoing the one where he pondered his death). In contrast, the dragon is summarily heaved into the waves like garbage. Yet in Beowulf's life the hero and monster are inextricably linked. The hero who earned glory from exterminating monsters is fated to die from his wounds battling a dragon. And in the poem's final words, a kind of epitaph, Beowulf is remembered as a fair-minded king to his people *and* as a fame-hungry superstar—the kind of fame that obviously comes from killing monsters. Hence this poem.

YOUR STUDYSYNC® TV

Discussion Prompt: What practices and customs do the Geats display after Beowulf dies, and what does it say about the Anglo-Saxon culture that the people honor the dead in this manner? How do these funeral customs differ from those of your own culture, and are they similar in any way? What does such a comparison suggest about how our world is different from Beowulf's?

Standards: RL.11-12.1, RL.11-12.2, RL.11-12.4; SL.11-12.1.A, SL.11-12.1.C, SL.11-12.1.D

VOCABULARY

outlandish
out·land·ish *adjective*
Bizarre, not conforming to what is expected
The clown looked completely outlandish in his oversized purple pajamas.

bane
bane *noun*
A regular source of misery
Those two bullies were the bane of my existence until I posted a video of them harassing me.

remnants
rem·nants *noun*
Smaller parts of an organized whole that are left behind or left over
The remnants of the crowd hung around the city square, reluctant to go home.

writhed
writhed *verb*
Twisted or squirmed bodily
After the man landed the fish, it writhed on the dock.

languishing
lan·guish·ing *verb*
Losing strength or vitality; wasting away
Without daily exercise and companionship, the zoo animals would be languishing, not thriving.

rebuke
re·buke *noun*
An expression of forceful disagreement or disapproval
The old woman stood up in the Town Hall meeting and delivered a stinging rebuke to both candidates.

dire
dire *adjective*
Gravely serious, requiring aid urgently
The reporter on the news said that the situation was dire for the refugees.

disconsolate
dis·con·so·late *adjective*
So unhappy as to be beyond consoling or cheering up.
When her favorite team lost she felt disconsolate for days.

CLOSE READ

QUESTION 1: How does Beowulf choose to arm himself for the fight against the dragon, and why?

Sample Answer: Although Beowulf fought Grendel without weapons, he must contend with the "molten venom" of the dragon's fire, so he arms himself in "mail-shirt and shield" and brings a sword as well.

Standards: RL.11-12.1

QUESTION 2: How do the other Geatish warriors react when Beowulf fails to kill the dragon during their first encounter, and why do they react as they do?

Sample Answer: Almost all of the Geatish warriors are afraid of the dragon, and they run for the woods. One thane, Wiglaf, stays to help Beowulf because he considers loyalty more important than his fear and knows the Geats owe an incalculable debt to Beowulf.

Standards: RL.11-12.1

QUESTION 3: What are Beowulf's final wishes expressed to Wiglaf? Use language from the poem to support your answer.

Sample Answer: Beowulf wants Wiglaf and others to use the dragon's treasure to enrich and protect the kingdom (2794–2801). Beowulf wants to be remembered by his people, so he asks that a barrow be built to his memory on a coastal headland. (2802–8) He rewards Wiglaf's steadfastness by bequeathing him his gold collar, warshirt, and gold helmet.

Standards: RL.11-12.1

QUESTION 4: What does Wiglaf predict will happen to the cowardly warriors who return to find that Beowulf died and only Wiglaf stayed to help him?

Sample Answer: Wiglaf predicts they will lose their property to enemy invaders who will be emboldened by Beowulf's death; and the warriors will have to live with a shame worse than death for their abandonment.

Standards: RL.11-12.1

QUESTION 5: Why does the messenger who delivers the news of Beowulf's death review the history of battles long past with Sweden?

Sample Answer: The messenger is making the point that without Beowulf to protect the Geats, the Swedes will see an opportunity to settle old scores. The peace that Beowulf has brought the Geats will end, and a time of war will be coming.

Standards: RL.11-12.1

COMPARATIVE TEXTS

Text: *The Volsung Saga* (Old Norse Poem)

Compare to: *Beowulf*, lines 2397–3182

Connection: The Volsung saga is an Old Norse poem dating back to the thirteenth century C.E. It includes the story of Sigurd, renowned as a dragon-slayer. In this excerpt from the saga, which is presented here, Sigurd accompanies his foster father, Regin, in search of Regin's brother, Fafnir, who has been turned into a dragon, or "worm," as a punishment for killing his and Regin's father. Sigurd, who is armed with *his* father Sigmund's powerful sword, receives advice from the god Odin, who appears disguised as an old man. Sigurd kills the dragon, and before Fafnir dies, he warns Sigurd about his future.

Text: "Beowulf: The Monsters and the Critics"

Compare to: *Beowulf* as a whole

Connection: In 1936, J. R. R. Tolkien, author of *The Hobbit* and *The Lord of the Rings* and professor of Anglo-Saxon at Oxford, delivered a lecture titled "Beowulf: The Monsters and the Critics." It was the first time that an academic or a scholar had argued that *Beowulf* was not just a historical document but a masterpiece of English literature. In fact, *Beowulf* is a unique combination of history and literature and tells many stories.

WRITE TO REVISIT

IMAGINATIVE WRITING

Prompt: Beowulf's final encounter with the dragon is all action and no dialogue, different from Sigurd's encounter with Fafnir in *The Volsung Saga*. If Beowulf and his dragon had a similar give-and-take, what would their conversation be like? Using Sigurd and Fafnir's conversation as a guide, write a 300- to 500-word dialogue between Beowulf and the dragon after their battle. What would the dragon say about Beowulf's fate, about its role as the hero's foe and keeper of men's treasure, or about its long life as a dragon? What would Beowulf say to the dragon, knowing that both will die and taking a moment to look back on his life as a hero and a king? Draw on what you have learned from reading *Beowulf* and what you have learned about both heroes and dragons in this unit.

Standards: RL.11-12.2; W.11-12.3, W.11-12.4, W.11-12.5, W.11-12.9

ANALYTICAL WRITING

Prompt: Think about the many different narratives woven through *Beowulf*: (1) the rise of Christianity and the hanging on of pagan beliefs; (2) the impact of Northerners on Britain, including Viking raiders, Danish kings, and a Geatish slayer of monsters and dragons; (3) a long tradition of heroes exemplified by Theseus and Sigurd, and analyzed by Thomas Carlyle; and (4) an equally long tradition of monsters—from good dragons to a misunderstood Grendel—that are part of a new literary era. Write an essay of at least 400 words that weaves together three or more of these narratives, drawing on at least three relevant texts from this unit as well as outside research and your own ideas. Use these woven strands to express *Beowulf's* central ideas and to show that, in the story, literature and history are inseparable and even dependent on one another.

Standards: RL.11-12.2; RI.11-12.1; RH.11-12.6; W.11-12.2, W.11-12.4, W.11-12.5, W.11-12.9